THE **Thinking Eye** THE **Seeing Brain**

W. W. NORTON AND COMPANY
NEW YORK LONDON

James T. Enns

UNIVERSITY OF BRITISH COLUMBIA

THE Thinking Eye
THE Seeing Brain

EXPLORATIONS IN VISUAL COGNITION

W. W. Norton & Company has been independent since its founding in 1923, when William Warder Norton and Mary D. Herter Norton first published lectures delivered at the People's Institute, the adult education division of New York City's Cooper Union. The Nortons soon expanded their program beyond the Institute, publishing books by celebrated academics from America and abroad. By mid-century, the two major pillars of Norton's publishing program—trade books and college texts—were firmly established. In the 1950s, the Norton family transferred control of the company to its employees, and today—with a staff of four hundred and a comparable number of trade, college, and professional titles published each year—W. W. Norton & Company stands as the largest and oldest publishing house owned wholly by its employees.

The text of this book is composed in Galliard, with the display set in Avenir.
Composition by TSI Graphics
Manufacturing by Phoenix Color—Book Technology Park

Editors: Jon Durbin and Aaron Javsicas
Project editor: Thomas Foley
Manuscript editor: Alice Vigliani
Production manager: Benjamin Reynolds
Photography editors: Neil Ryder Hoos, Stephanie Romeo, and Nathan Odell
Drawn art provided by ElectraGraphics, Inc.
Book designer: Angela Foote
Editorial assistant: Andrea Haver

Library of Congress Cataloging-in-Publication Data

Enns, James T.
    The thinking eye, the seeing brain: explorations in visual cognition/James Enns.
        p. cm.
    Includes bibliographical references and indexes.

ISBN 0-393-97721-8 (pbk.)

    1. Visual perception. I. Title.

BF241.E56 2004
152.14--dc22   2003070223

W. W. Norton & Company, Inc., 500 Fifth Avenue, New York, N.Y. 10110
www.wwnorton.com

W. W. Norton & Company Ltd., Castle House, 75/76 Wells Street,
London W1Y 3QT

1 2 3 4 5 6 7 8 9 0

For Camilla, Joanna, and Katherine.
May visual illusions always thrill you!

BRIEF CONTENTS

CONTENTS

It is an exciting time to be a vision scientist. For many in our field, the excitement comes from the unprecedented technological advances of the past decade. We have seen rapid advances in our ability to look at brain activity while a study participant is sensing, seeing, thinking, and acting. Biotechnology is quickly moving to a place where the implantation of a surrogate eye, in those with limited sight, may soon be as routine as cochlear implants have become for those with limited hearing. Computer scientists and electrical engineers have built numerous robots with impressive visual capabilities that promise (or threaten, depending on your perspective) to do our laundry and mow our lawns. It is clear that many advances in technology go hand in hand with progress in the vision sciences.

Yet my personal excitement in the vision sciences lies in making new discoveries in human vision. It is still possible in our field to discover something new on almost any given day. The joy of discovery is open not only to a vision scientist like myself, but also to students who are still new to the field. The process typically begins when we see something out of the ordinary and take care to note the actions or experiences that we have in conjunction with what we see. We then study these experiences by planning and conducting controlled experiments. These experiments sometimes require sophisticated equipment, but they often require nothing more than a personal computer or other standard office and kitchen supplies. These experiments are planned using our best understanding of how vision works. Yet more often than not they lead to new insights and questions that go well beyond what we thought we knew before.

In my view, there are three features of vision science that allow for such immediate rewards. First, this is a science in which the researchers' own visual system is both the best available tool and the subject matter of the investigation. All sciences rely on observation in one way or another, and therefore on the human senses, but only in the cognitive sciences are these primary tools also the subject matter. This recursive aspect of the science leads to a number of special research challenges, as we will see, but it also contributes to the excitement and immediacy of discovery. With every new result we know ourselves a little better!

Second, vision science is relatively young, so there is still much more to be discovered. Even students have a realistic prospect of being able to contribute, provided they adhere to the scientific practices that reduce experimenter bias and that lead to reproducible results. In contrast, many other sciences require students to spend several years reproducing laboratory demonstrations of classical results before they are able to add meaningfully to new knowledge in their field.

Third, vision science is poised to reap the benefit of some important general trends in science. One of these is the advent of multidisciplinary movements, including the *cognitive sciences* themselves (a melding of philosophy, cognitive psychology, computer science, and linguistics) and *cognitive neuroscience* (adding anatomy and physiology to the former list). These movements have not only made it 'cool' to consider private or hidden mental events as the appropriate subject matter of science, but they have made it possible. Prior to this, questions about visual consciousness, and the neural underpinnings of private thoughts and emotions, had been hiding in the closet. Behaviorist critics early in the century had declared these topics off limits. The information-processing perspective that reigned during the second half of the century acknowledged these topics but considered them superfluous to 'real' cognition. Re-reading some of the reports from those times illustrates just how difficult it is to understand vision when the experiences of the study participant are considered to be out of bounds.

The Thinking Eye, The Seeing Brain was created out of personal necessity. In 1995, I was charged with teaching an "Introduction to Cognitive Science" course at the University of British Columbia. My first instinct was to slant the material toward what I know best, which is human vision and visual attention. An added bonus of taking this route was that vision is by far the best understood of the human senses, and it often serves as a model for emerging research in the other senses. But I could not find a suitable text to use for the class, one that would serve as an outline to the vision science I wanted to impart to students of psychology, computer science, medicine, linguistics, and philosophy. *Vision* is the most mysterious, complicated, important, and intuitively compelling topic in all of the cognitive sciences. Yet I was unable to find a book that covered the necessary ground as an introduction to the brain, the mind, and the role that vision plays in constructing each of them.

In my first year of teaching the course, I realized that my favorite book on vision from when I was an undergraduate, Richard Gregory's *Eye and Brain* (1966), had not kept pace with changes to the field. I tried to convey to my students the excitement over the debates of vision researchers in the 1960s and 1970s, but they instead were drawn to the findings that vision researchers were publishing in new journals such as *Nature Neuroscience, Psychological Science,* and *Trends in Cognitive Science.* To keep pace with my students' interests, I had to start talking about what is happening in the field today.

This book is the outcome of that effort. It reflects what I have tried to teach my students in the cognitive sciences. But having the content in hand and writing a book are two different things. That's where Jon Durbin, editor at W. W. Norton & Company stepped in. I was fortunate to have him appear in my office one day when I was particularly frustrated by the amount of time I was spending assembling material for my class. What he brought to the project, in addition to unbelievable persistence and unrequited cheerfulness, was a connection with the team at Norton. Along the way I have gained a great appreciation, sometimes bordering on awe, for the work of Aaron Javsicas (Assistant Editor), Andrea Haver (Editorial Assistant), Marian Johnson (Managing Editor, College Department), Thom Foley (Project Editor), Nathan Odell and Stephanie Romeo (photo researchers), Ben Reynolds (Production Manager), and the artists at Electragraphics. Alice Vigliani (Manuscript Editor) deserves special thanks for her ability to take a sow's ear of a sentence and turn it into a silk purse.

Jon Durbin made an argument that I found particularly persuasive in deciding to take on this project. It was that instructors and students in introductory courses in the cognitive sciences, vision sciences, and sensation and perception needed a primary text that was reasonably priced. This was a compelling point because I, like many instructors, prefer to teach with both a primary textbook and a list of favorite supplemental books and readings. Having to buy several books can seriously strain a student's budget. I have tried to write this book with that consideration in mind, and Norton has met its end of the bargain (go to *www.wwnorton.com* for details). At the end of each chapter is a short list of readings that will complement the material covered, often in the form of extended treatments in secondary sources. The references in the body of the text are intended to allow researchers and students to read the original experiments in their primary sources.

The book also benefited from critical reviews by Rick Gilmore (Penn State University) and Tom Sanocki (University of South Florida, Tampa). Colleagues and students in my own department were also very helpful, even after they were subjected to readings of multiple drafts of some chapters. Vincent Di Lollo, Erin Austen, Geniva Liu, Jillian Fecteau, Alexa Roggeveen, and Shahab Ghorashi deserve special thanks in this regard. Mary Peterson (University of Arizona) graciously served as my host on a sabbatical year in 2000–2001, during which I was able to engage with her and her students on many ideas that eventually took shape in the book. I am also deeply grateful to my friends and colleagues Patrick Cavanagh (Harvard), Mel Goodale (University of Western Ontario), and Mary Peterson for reviewing the book at the galley stage. The mistakes that remain are, of course, all mine.

James Enns
Vancouver, Canada, 2004

1 WHAT IS VISION SCIENCE?

FUNDAMENTAL QUESTIONS

- How does our naive understanding of what it means to see differ from the way the brain sees?
- Why do we have vision in the first place?
- Which sciences are involved in trying to understand vision?
- How do vision scientists talk about and measure light?
- What is a visual stimulus?
- What makes the measurement of human behavior different from the measurement of physical quantities?

SEEING AND THINKING

Seeing and thinking are ideas that seem to need no special definition. They are common words in our everyday language. Our visual experiences are so immediate and so obvious that we assume they hardly require an explanation. Thinking seems to occur in an abstract medium, not limited in any obvious way by what we are seeing or have seen. As this book will show, these common understandings of vision and thought are based on inaccurate and outmoded concepts. We will find that seeing is much more dependent on a healthy brain than on an optically correct set of eyes. In fact, no amount of seeing is actually accomplished by the eyes at all. We will also learn that much of what we call thinking relies heavily on the same parts of the brain that are used when we see the world around us. These are only two examples of the kind of rethinking that we must do in order to understand what modern science tells us about human vision.

To fully appreciate the story that will unfold in this book, you will have to be open to a revolution in your own beliefs about sight and thought. This is a revolution no less mind-changing than those that took place when humans began to appreciate that the earth was not the center of the universe or that the heart muscle was not the seat of our emotions. In many ways, it is an even more unsettling revolution because it affects the very way in which we understand ourselves, our beliefs in how we are connected through vision to the external world, and our understanding of how others like us see the world. Redefining ourselves is not something most of us do willingly or easily. But I want to encourage you to stick with it because the process can also be very satisfying. For those who do, this book points toward answers to many of the deep mysteries that surround our understanding of sight and thought. Of the six sensory systems that most humans share (vision, audition, touch, taste, smell, and balance), vision is the sense that we as modern beings rely on most of all. Yet we probably spend the least amount of time thinking about it—that is, until some parts of it no longer work like they used to. Then vision becomes very important and very mysterious.

WHAT VISION IS NOT

To begin thinking about vision in a new way, it is useful to be very clear about what vision is not. We will do this by considering four widespread, but also largely mythical, beliefs about human vision: (1) the myth that seeing provides a faithful record of the world in front of us, (2) the myth that seeing occurs automatically and without any thoughtful activity on our part, (3) the myth that our eyes are responsible for our sight, and (4) the myth that we can think without using our senses. Modern vision science has shown that we must abandon these myths if we are to understand how the eye and brain really work.

The myth of seeing as a faithful record

As used in our everyday language, the word *seeing* refers to a fairly faithful process of recording light that has been reflected from surfaces. The most common metaphor for seeing in this sense is the process of photography: the eye as a camera. Just as the camera focuses light onto the flat surface of photographic film to form a faithful image of the pattern of light that existed in one instance of space and time, so the eye is believed to focus a more or less faithful image on its light-sensitive rear surface. Moreover, the eye continues to do this as long as it is open, making it more like a high-resolution video camera than a camera for taking snapshots. This is the myth of vision as a faithful record.

This myth directly conflicts with many visual illusions we can see and experience for ourselves. A strikingly good example is shown in Figure 1.1a, which looks like a spiral converging toward its center. Yet you can easily demonstrate that it is not a spiral by tracing one of the concentric circles with your finger, or perhaps even tracing one with a black pen, after you have photocopied the image, as shown in Figure 1.1b. All the "photographic" information that these are really concentric rings is lying right before your eyes. Yet you see only the spiral, even after you have demonstrated that there really are concentric rings in the figure.

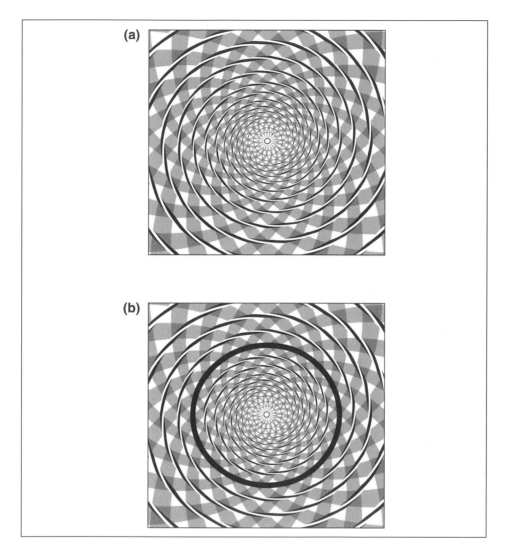

FIGURE 1.1 **(a)** The Fraser Spiral illusion is a series of concentric circles composed of black and white elements. Human vision sees these circles as a continuous spiral of connected black and white elements. **(b)** You can reveal the illusion by manually tracing one of the circles.

Illusions like the Fraser Spiral pose a problem for the myth of vision as a faithful record. In order to preserve the myth, philosophers and even some vision researchers have had to place illusions such as these into a special category. One of the most eminent visual theorists of the twentieth century, J. J. Gibson (1966), tried to do this by dismissing such illusions as highly unusual circumstances in which the eyes are fooled. He was reluctant to consider the alternative way of thinking about them—namely, that illusions reveal the normal workings of human vision. The apparent philosophical danger he was trying to avoid was the conclusion that all of vision might be an illusion. Indeed, vision scientists following in Gibson's footsteps are reluctant to venture down that slippery path, largely because they have come to trust their visual sense through experience. The information gained through sight can often be confirmed by information gained through touch and hearing, or even by physical measurements made with rulers and cameras. The word *illusion* carries too strong a connotation of deceit, or perhaps even magic, to describe something that works well most of the time.

We will see in the following chapters that these two alternatives—of vision as a faithful record and vision as an illusion—are a false dichotomy. Vision is certainly not a faithful process of recording light; it is better described as an "illusion" when considered from the perspective of only these two alternatives. Yet at the same time it is an illusion that provides us with enough information to see the important aspects of our world. In this way of thinking, illusions do not mislead.

In fact, rather than continuing to use the term *illusion* to describe vision, we will find it more helpful to think about vision as a "construction project." Just as a house or a bridge is manufactured in a series of steps—from the assembling of raw materials, to the combining of appropriate elements into a larger structure—so too we can think of vision as a project involving a series of steps or processes that lead to a product greater than the sum of the individual elements.

The construction project metaphor captures two important aspects of vision. First, it preserves the important distance between physical reality and perception that is highlighted by the term *illusion*. Vision is, after all, dependent on reflected light for providing information about distant objects. It does not provide direct contact with those objects, as the sense of touch does. Second, the construction metaphor conveys a sense of the usefulness of vision to an observer trying to understand and act upon objects in the external world. It takes the emphasis away from the connotations of deceit and magic. To accomplish the "vision project," both the eye and the brain have cooperative work to do. Indeed, we will see that a large number of brain regions work together to complete the vision project.

Figure 1.2 illustrates the usefulness of the vision project. You can see three tables in the picture. Two of the tabletops have quite similar dimensions in the world of three-dimensional objects. It is therefore not difficult to tell that Table A has a different overall shape from the other two. However, Tables A and B have identical dimensions when measured with a ruler on the page. Thus there is a conflict between similarity of shape as defined on the page and similarity of shape in the depicted world of three-dimensional objects. Yet we do not ordinarily experience this conflict. Vision opts without ambiguity for the interpretation of these drawings as objects rather than as markings on a flat surface. The view constructed and seen by the vision project relates to real objects rather than to pictured ones.

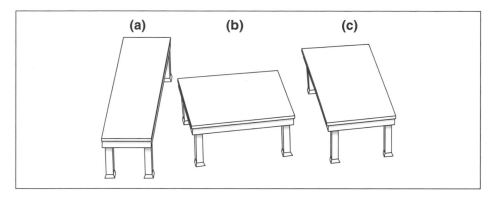

FIGURE 1.2 **(a-b)** Two tabletops with identical dimensions as measured on the page, but with very different dimensions as judged by a visual system that automatically interprets real-world shape. **(c)** This tabletop has very different dimensions on the page from those of either (a) or (b), but in reality it has a similar three-dimensional shape to (b).

This outcome of the vision project—that is, for objects that we see as having volume and shape in three dimensions—simplifies our lives enormously. Stop for a moment to consider the many forms of modern communication and entertainment that are premised on human vision working in this way. Movies, which consist of a rapidly presented series of still photographs, would be far less engaging and enjoyable if we had to keep reminding ourselves that each stationary image on the flat screen was there to help us "imagine" the moving world of solid objects. Pictures in museums, books, and magazines would have to be "read" like text rather than seen as objects. Chances are, we wouldn't bother with creating and enjoying representational art of any kind if the vision project didn't work so well. Vision as a faithful record would drain life from the visual arts.

The myth of vision as a passive process

We open our eyes and see, without any apparent effort, a world of objects rich in color, form, texture, and motion. This experience has been turned into a myth about the underlying processes by the cliché that "seeing is believing." The myth is also supported by a legal system that places the highest value on eyewitness testimony and by visual artists who claim to paint "what they see, not what they know." But is it justified? To what extent is vision a passive process, one that is therefore roughly the same for all observers in the same visual circumstances? If it is the same, why aren't the reports of well-intentioned eyewitnesses always reliable?

The Dutch artist M. C. Escher delighted in creating demonstrations that pointed to the inherently active nature of vision. One example appears in Figure 1.3a,

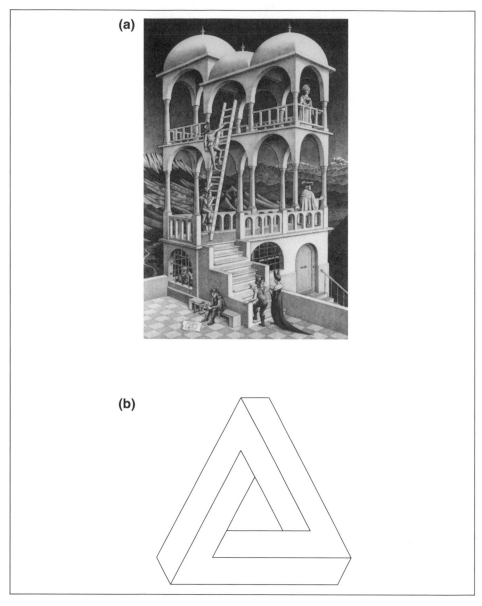

FIGURE 1.3 Pictures of impossible objects. **(a)** *Belvedere* by M. C. Escher. **(b)** An impossible triangle.

and a simplified figure making the same points appears in Figure 1.3b. Not only do these pictures give us the experience of seeing a wide-angled field of view in rich detail, but they also brilliantly point out the illusory basis of this perceptual experience. We do not, in fact, see these small pictures in very rich detail. Instead, we suffer from what some vision researchers call the *grand illusion of complete perception*. If we had the complete perception that our subjective experiences suggest we do, we would instantly recognize the building in Figure 1.3a as either a flat drawing without a hint of solidness or a horribly twisted three-dimensional wreck. Instead, we tend to see it as a solid object with generally right-angled corners, but with a few curious features. Curious indeed! Examine the building by imagining that you are walking up the same staircase as the couple on the ground floor are approaching. When you arrive at the top of the stairs, you are standing on a corner of the lower open floor. Of the four corners of the building, the one near where you are standing is also nearest to the observer (the painter). Now imagine climbing the ladder to the upper floor. At this point, even though you have made no reversals in direction, you are standing on the second floor in a part of the building that is much farther away from the observer. The depicted building violates several laws of simple solid geometry without so much as attracting your attention. Why not?

Escher's art takes advantage of an important principle that has become the serious focus of vision research only within the past thirty years: Vision is not uniformly rich in detail. There are two contributing factors. One is the small portion of the visual field in each eye that is capable of making a faithful record of the color and form detail that is potentially available to the eye. As we will discuss in Chapter 2, this region is about the size of our thumbnail held at arm's length. But this fact runs counter to our experience of a wide field of view, rich in color, shape, and other details. How could our experience be so wrong? Apparently the visual system takes for granted that our immediate world is relatively unchanging. That is, some of the objects in that world might be in motion, and we the observers might be in motion too. But this motion of a relatively small number of objects is set against a larger backdrop of general stability. There is no need to form a mental image of the scene when it is constantly available, lying before our eyes, waiting to be seen. We can simply sample from it on a need-to-see basis. The illusion is that we think the rich detail of the world is represented as such in our minds, rather than being available when we need it.

The second factor contributing to vision that is less detailed than we seem to experience involves the limits on attention we will discuss in Chapters 5 through 7. We will see there that even when visual acuity is not a factor, there are serious limits on the degree to which vision can bring multiple objects and spatial regions to our awareness. For the most part, our vision seems to be devoted to seeing only one event, object, or location at a time. While vision is engaged in seeing one of these, we do not sense that other objects have disappeared. And confirmation of this always awaits us, in that the other objects are still before our eyes when we turn our attention to them. Once again, it is easy to believe that the rich details in the world have been duplicated in the movie screen inside our heads. But that is wrong.

These two factors lead to a principle that is the other side of the coin from vision that is not rich in detail: Vision is an active process. It is active in the sense of guiding the center of the eye to various regions of a scene to make available to the brain the rich detail required for certain visual tasks. It is also active in the sense that ongoing decisions must be made (though often not consciously) as to which object or event should be at the center of visual awareness at any given moment. The eyes must be guided to look at some subset of the image, and they must look at subsets in a certain order.

These ways in which vision is active make it much easier to understand how two observers could encounter the same visual scenes and yet have highly different visual experiences. Their experiences reflect the very different ways in which their vision is active. Much of the research we will describe in this book leads to the conclusion that it is indeed difficult to see what we are not prepared to see. This is a fundamentally different perspective from the one we so often assume, in which seeing is a passive record of reflected light.

The myth of the seeing eye

Everyone knows that looking and seeing are accomplished with the eyes, whereas perception only occurs when the images recorded by the eyes are sent to the brain for analysis and interpretation. Right? This myth is demonstrably incorrect on several levels, but it persists in our popular imagination.

The main ingredients of this myth are illustrated in the criticisms sometimes leveled against the impressionist artist Claude Monet. Monet is one of the best-known painters representing a movement that tried to capture "raw sensations" on the canvas. Impressionism encouraged deliberately hurried paintings; the artists painted with a minimum of thought in order to freeze the momentary view of a scene, complete with its unique lighting, viewpoint, and composition. In the translated words of Monet, "Try to forget what objects you have before you . . . merely think, here is a little square of blue, here an oblong of pink, here a streak of yellow, and paint it just as it looks to you, the exact color and shape, until it gives your naive impression of the scene" (Vitz & Glimcher, 1984).

Monet and other impressionists had critics, but it is interesting that these critics did not question the assumption that it was possible to paint what was seen with the eyes. Instead, they castigated impressionists for painting only with their eyes, for ignoring the important contributions the mind could make to art. To this charge, defenders of Monet, including the artist Paul Cézanne, have been quoted as saying that Monet may have painted with his eye, "but Great God, what an eye!" Others have called Monet the "First eye." Again, the important point is that both sides in the debate seem untroubled by the premise that it is possible to paint only what the eyes see. They were concerned instead with the artistic merit of doing so.

To be fair to artists and their critics, the myth of the seeing eye has a long and distinguished history within the study of vision. Since the earliest days of experimental research in visual perception, the field has been divided into those who studied uninterpreted, or raw, sensations and those who preferred to study perception. Many college courses in vision are still divided along these lines.

But modern research in vision has made it increasingly difficult to sustain this division. Indeed, it has become more difficult to separate the role of the eye from that of the brain in ascribing what each does in the vision project. To begin to understand why this is so, let's try to take seriously, just for a moment, the view that seeing comes first, followed by perception or understanding.

For seeing, we will use the conventional idea of photograph-like images being laid down in neural terms within the eye. When we examine the nature of these neural images, we find them to be incomplete and highly distorted when compared with our common understanding of "photographic quality." They are incomplete because of blindspots, not only where the optic nerve leaves the eye chamber but also where large blood vessels overlay the light-sensitive receptors. The neural images also are distorted in several ways. For example, much more detail, as well as different kinds of detail, is represented at the center of any given image than in the surrounding regions. In addition, the neural processes within the eye have already begun to dramatically transform the image, so that faint edges become exaggerated and specific luminance and wavelength values are discarded in favor of the preservation of luminance and wavelength differences. I will have much more to say about this in the next few chapters.

When we examine the first stages of visual processing in the cerebral cortex, as opposed to the eye, proponents of the conventional view of seeing will find that the brain has many more of the kinds of images that were already described for the eye. They are images in the restricted sense of being topographically mapped representations of some of the information presented to the eye, but they are also very different from photographic images because of incompleteness and distortion. If seeing consists of forming these kinds of images, then we have to conclude that seeing occurs everywhere in the brain.

Where, then, does perception take place? Where are the interpretation and analysis? Once again, we find that they are everywhere. Before the neural signals triggered by light leave the eye, they undergo some very sophisticated analyses—the kinds of analyses that would undoubtedly be considered intelligent if they were performed by a machine. In fact, multiple images have been formed within the same eye, with some neurons devoted to analyzing luminance information, other neurons analyzing color information, and still others analyzing edges. One of the deep ironies of making comparisons across different biological visual systems is conveyed by the principle that some scientists express as "the dumber the animal, the smarter its retina." For example, the eyes of frogs and rabbits perform a sophisticated analysis of visual motion, an analysis that occurs in only the higher levels of the brain in monkeys and humans. Every way we try to examine it, we must conclude that interpretation and analysis are already occurring in even the earliest forms of visual processing. There is no seeing that occurs prior to perception.

The myth of imageless thought

Even though it may be impossible to separate seeing and understanding, sensation and perception, surely higher levels of cognition—such as long-term memory retrieval and problem solving—can be separated from the processes of vision. Thinking, after all, should not be dependent on vision, as many people with poor sight will attest. But this, too, is a myth that we will try to dispel.

Support for this myth is evident in most university departments of psychology, where researchers of cognition and vision, respectively, often do not read the same scientific journals. They are often also guided by entirely different theories. The underlying assumption is that the main job of systems for perception (including vision) is to record and store information about the environment and pass it on to separate systems whose job is to perform the higher-order cognitive functions of language and thought. However, research is again showing that this assumption is fundamentally wrong. Much of cognition is inherently perceptual (and often visual) and involves the same neural machinery as the senses, although sometimes the shared neural machinery operates in different ways for seeing and thinking.

Try to answer the following questions to the best of your ability: *In the house or apartment that you lived in just previous to your present residence* (it's best not to use your present residence because you may be sitting in it as you read this), *how many windows were visible to you when you approached the front door or the main entrance? What were the shapes of these windows?* If you are able to answer these questions, how do you do it? Research on long-term memory tasks reveals that answering such questions requires the formation of mental simulations that can be "seen" in ways similar to seeing the immediate world. Our brains re-create the conditions in our mind's eyes as best they can. Furthermore, these simulations rely on the same brain regions and the same neurons that would be required to see the solution if you were actually standing in front of your former residence.

What if you were asked to imagine approaching the same residence from one of two different perspectives before being posed the same questions? In one case, you imagine yourself in a helicopter looking down at your residence. In the other, you imagine yourself in a wheelchair approaching your front door. Research indicates that you would be much more likely to make downward-looking eye movements while imagining yourself in a helicopter and upward-looking eye movements while imagining yourself in a wheelchair. You would make these eye movements spontaneously, and your eyes would point toward a region of visual space unrelated to the mental problem being posed. That is because what you would be seeing would only be inside your head. You would not be anywhere near the actual location of the imagined scene when you answer this question. Yet you would act out a visual scenario all the way down to re-creating the appropriate eye movements. Acting out the unnecessary movements suggests that when you imagine an event, you use the same vision and action systems as you would if you were actually seeing the event.

What about thought that is not directed toward specific visual experiences stored in your memory but that involves a more general form of knowledge? Consider the question *Does a pony have a mane?* This question is trivially easy to answer correctly and seems to not require any vision at all. Yet if you had to answer it shortly after being posed the question *Does a horse have a mane?* you would be faster to respond correctly than if you had recently answered the question *Does a lion have a mane?* If this kind of knowledge were organized as a set of abstract nonvisual ideas or propositions, as is claimed by many standard theories of mentally stored world knowledge, then the previous experience associated with the word *mane* should benefit the question about the pony. And it should do so regardless of whether it was presented in the context of a horse or a lion. However, if you solved these problems by mentally simulating the experience of actually seeing a pony, then the visual similarity between the pony and the horse would be of greater benefit. And this is in fact what researchers have found.

As we will see in Chapter 8, traumatic damage to brain regions that disrupts vision of certain objects, such as birds, also severely disturbs brain-damaged individuals' ability to solve conceptual problems involving birds. In fact, when the brain regions that are important for the *imaginary manipulation* of objects are identified in healthy individuals, it turns out that they are the same brain regions that are critically involved in *seeing* objects. Findings such as these point to close links between thought and vision.

WHAT IS VISION FOR?

We have now reviewed what vision is not. The recurring themes of this book will be that vision is constructed (as opposed to faithful), that it is active (rather than passive), that seeing is based in the brain (rather than in the eye), and that thought is intimately linked to vision (rather than standing alone). But none of these themes tells us directly what vision is for. What is the purpose of having vision in the first place?

The answer that probably comes to mind most readily is that vision exists in order to inform us about the world around us. Other senses, of course, do this to some extent. Taste tells us about the chemical composition of water-soluble particles we place into our mouths. Smell lets us know about the molecules in the air that surrounds us. The vestibular sense and proprioception give us information about our bodies' position with respect to gravity and the relative position of our limbs. Touch uses mechanical pressure to inform us about the locations, shapes, and surface qualities of objects within our reach. Hearing lets us know about the near and distant world through the transmission and reception of sound waves.

But only vision can give us detailed information about the shape, color, position, and motion of objects and surfaces that are quite distant. Imagine trying to learn about the stars without vision. Imagine learning the layout of a new environment through only smell, touch, and hearing. Imagine trying to recognize a friend from a distance. Light can be considered a medium that has the potential to convey rich messages over distances, whereas the "media" that the rest of our senses use—such as sound waves, mechanical pressure, and airborne molecules—convey messages that are generally less precise and much more immediate to our location.

The summary answer to the question *What is vision for?* that emerges from this sort of thinking is that vision's purpose is to inform us about our world by using the medium of reflected light. Such an answer seems straightforward. But it is not complete. Vision scientists do not consider it a complete statement of purpose because from this perspective, vision would be an imperfect and in many ways a defective means of becoming informed about the world. Such a statement does not take into account the nature of the eye's lens, which is unable to simultaneously provide sharp focus for lights of all wavelengths, blindspots, and blood vessels that obscure our view of the full pattern of light entering our eye (Chapter 3), the very small portion of our retina that can form a detailed image (Chapter 4), the almost constant eye movements required to compensate for this small field of view, and the limited amount of visual information that our consciousness can hold at any given moment (Chapters 5–7).

As we saw in the previous section, if vision were faithful to the reality of the world, we would be unable—among other things—to appreciate moving pictures. Instead of experiencing events on the screen as "live action," we would see a series of still pictures flashing one after another. Moreover, we would see each still picture as being flat. That's what vision would do if it were fully achieving the goal of "informing us about our world."

This way of thinking about the purpose of human vision lacks any consideration of how our visual system developed. At this point, introducing a biological perspective is very helpful: Animals' nervous systems evolved to facilitate survival. What it means to survive, at a most basic level, is to reproduce oneself in the form of offspring. To be successful at reproduction, one must find nourishing food over an extended period, seek out shelter, and find healthy mates. Danger—in the form of lack of food or the presence of predators—must be avoided. In short, animals that have ways of sensing these aspects of the world—both life-sustaining and life-threatening—are more likely to survive than those that don't. In the case of human evolution, it is safe to assume that all our senses, including vision, have developed to promote our survival in very effective ways.

Seen from this biological perspective, the overarching goal of human vision is to aid in survival. An accurate portrayal of the world around us through vision would certainly benefit us in this regard, but it is by no means the only critical factor. Among other, equally critical, factors is the amount of time required to obtain this information. Imagine being in the territorial neighborhood of a hungry tiger. Imagine having to choose whether your visual system will provide (1) an accurate image of the tiger, or (2) the earliest possible warning of the tiger's presence. I'm confident that both you and the evolutionary process would opt in favor of the latter. Early crude information is usually preferable to highly accurate information if the accurate information comes at the expense of the precious time needed to make a decision. This would be true not only for avoiding predators but also for gathering food and recognizing acquaintances.

In addition to the emphasis on early results over accurate results, another critical factor in the design of the visual system is the layered nature of evolutionary change. If change in the visual system is needed, as may occur when a species that used to forage for food at night is pressured by a change in the environment to forage during the daytime, the design changes must build on the existing system that has been adapted for low levels of light. In this case, the new daylight vision system that evolves may have quirks in its design that are simply inherited from the previous need to see in low lighting conditions. In short, a species is not able to go back to the drawing board to create an optimal design every time a change in the environment pressures it to change its visual system. Successful adaptations must occur within the range of genetic variability and the potential mutations that preexist in the species at the time the adaptation is needed. This layered nature of evolutionary change has led some scientists to say that evolution promotes the "survival of the just barely adequate" rather than the "survival of the fittest."

All this is to say that the human visual system wasn't built from scratch. Some early animals developed light-sensitive depressions in their outer covering or skin; later variability permitted some of these animals to develop a fluid-filled depression that focused light onto the rear surface of the depression; some of these animals then developed vision that worked primarily under conditions of low light; others developed vision that worked only in bright daylight; some developed differential sensitivity to the wavelength of light; others developed eyes that could see in both dim and bright light. The important point is that what we now call human vision incorporates the legacy of many earlier, more specialized visual systems. Thus we should not regard human vision as a monolithic, all-purpose seeing device. Rather, it is an evolutionarily layered collection of systems that now coexist within the same organism.

Some of the specializations we will explore in this book are: separate systems for performing conscious perception of objects as opposed to unconscious action toward objects (Chapters 2, 9), separate systems for analyzing luminance and color (Chapter 3), separate systems for seeing in dim and bright light (Chapter 4), and separate systems for perceiving shape, color, and motion (Chapters 2–7). Box 1.1 explores an important question concerning how vision is constructed from the analyses of all these systems.

BOX 1.1

"Subjective" versus "arbitrary" perceptions

A worrisome question that students of vision often raise when they are first told to think of vision as an active construction project of the mind is whether this implies that vision is highly subjective and variable, making it impossible to study vision objectively or to find general principles. In other words, is a science of vision even possible?

In short, the answer from vision scientists is "Yes, a science of vision is still possible." Humans' need to construct a mental model in order to see an object does not imply that perception must differ arbitrarily from person to person or even from time to time in the same person. To understand this, we must carefully distinguish visual experiences that are "subjective" from those that are "arbitrary."

Look at the object pictured in Figure 1.4. What do you see? Most viewers say they see something like a "wire cube." Somewhat more than half of them say they see it as being viewed from above; the rest say they see it as being viewed from below. After examining it for a few seconds, most view- ers report seeing the cube flip from one orientation to the other. Researchers have carefully studied the tendency for these perceptions to flip back and forth, and they consistently report two findings. First, some viewers see one orientation more often than the other. Second, the proba- bility of seeing one orientation or the other at any time is random for each viewer.

Although these research results make it sound as though perception of the cube is arbitrary, we must also consider all the possible perceptions that could have been constructed but were not. Figure 1.5 shows some possible other interpretations.

Why are only the views at each end of this range of possibilities seen spon- taneously by human observers? Each of the other views, or perceptions, was—in principle—as reasonable as any of the others, given the ambiguous nature of the image. In fact, an infinite number of possible perceptions cor- respond perfectly well to every image we will ever see. What puts this severe limit on our perceptions, so that most of the time we entertain only one possibility—and in the case of ambiguous images such as the wire cube, only two possibilities?

The answer lies in the fact that humans have similar brains and similar visual environments. These similarly constructed brains and similar environments have conspired through evolution and developmental experience to make the active construction of perception very similar in different people.

This doesn't mean that different people's perceptions will always be the same when faced with the same images. Nor does it mean that different environments won't lead to different perceptions. People's different experiences, interests, and purposes ensure that the active processes of vision will lead to different visual results on many occasions. But humans do share a great deal of similarity in the assumptions they bring to the vision project. In the case of the wire cube, these include the assumptions that objects are generally convex, that straight lines in images are generally straight edges in the world of solid objects, and that junctions of three edges correspond to right-angled corners. These shared assumptions limit the ambiguity of perception in this case to only two of an infinite number of possibilities.

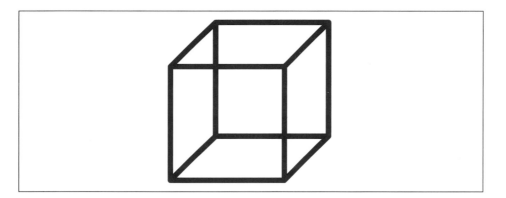

FIGURE 1.4   An ambiguous wire cube.

WHO ARE THE VISION SCIENTISTS?

As a newcomer to the science of vision, you may be curious to know more about the people who work in this field. What do they do on a daily basis? Where do they work? How are they organized professionally? The answers to these questions are fascinating for any science, but they are especially interesting for vision science because these people represent a very wide range of backgrounds and work environments. In this section you will be introduced briefly to several kinds of vision scientist. I have tried to present categories that span as wide a range as possible and overlap as little as possible. Most vision scientists have much broader interests than are indicated by the categories here.

Ophthalmologists and optometrists

Ophthalmology is a specialization within medicine that focuses on the function and diseases of the eye. Ophthalmologists are medical doctors who specialize in treating the eye, making measurements for corrective lenses, and caring for individuals who are partially blind. Training for the MD degree with a specialty in ophthalmology includes a college degree, four years of medical school, one year of a general internship, and three years of a hospital-based residency in ophthalmology with special training in the diagnosis and treatment of eye conditions.

Most ophthalmologists practice a mixture of medicine and surgery, ranging from lens prescription and standard medical treatment to delicate surgery. A typical ophthalmologist sees around 100 patients each week in addition to performing two surgical procedures. The removal of cataracts (particles that cloud the lens) is the most common surgical procedure. Other specialization categories are: diseases of the outer layers of the eye, increased pressure in the eye (glaucoma), lesions and tumors of the optic nerve and retina, examination of tissue specimens from the eye, facial reconstruction following trauma that involves the eye, retinal diseases such as macular degeneration and retinitis pigmentosa, and childhood eye conditions such as crossed eyes (strabismus) and lazy-eye (amblyopia).

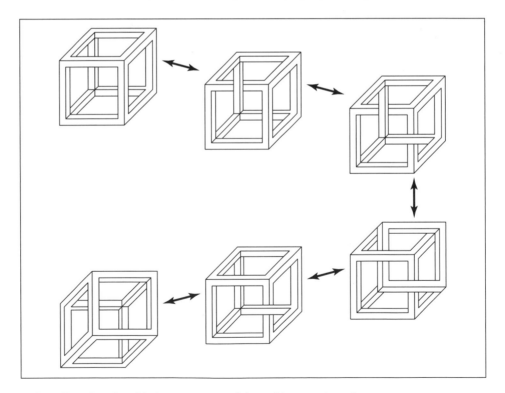

FIGURE 1.5   Possible interpretations of the ambiguous wire cube.

People are often confused about the relation between ophthalmology and optometry. The main difference is that ophthalmology is a specialty of medicine whereas optometry addresses screening for vision problems and prescribing and dispensing corrective lenses. The training for optometry is substantially shorter; a doctorate in optometry requires only four years of training following a college degree.

Research in ophthalmology and optometry is conducted largely by university professors and their staff. Within university departments of ophthalmology and optometry, graduate students train for careers in eye research. A majority of them are simultaneously training to be practitioners and will therefore receive an MD degree (medicine) or an OD degree (optometry) along with a PhD degree to acknowledge their specialized training in research. A smaller number of students are aiming solely for the PhD degree and will follow a career devoted entirely to eye research.

The largest organization in North America that promotes research in these fields is the Association for Research in Vision and Ophthalmology (ARVO). This association holds an annual meeting in Florida attended by more than 10,000 members. Approximately 45 percent of the members hold degrees in ophthalmology and 30 percent have PhDs, with the remainder including optometrists and veterinarians with an interest in vision.

The largest funding source for eye research and the promotion of eye health in the United States is the National Eye Institute, which is a branch of a larger government agency, the National Institutes of Health (NIH). Besides funding research in over 250 locations in the United States, it conducts research of its own in labs on the NIH campus in Bethesda, Maryland.

Neuroscientists, neurologists, and neuropsychologists

Neuroscience, the study of nervous systems, covers all aspects of neural function in biological organisms. Neurology is a specialty within human medicine (in the same sense as ophthalmology) devoted to the function and diseases of the brain and spinal cord. Neuropsychology is a specialty within clinical psychology focused on the care and treatment of individuals with disorders of the brain. Visual neuroscience, visual neurology, and visual neuropsychology represent subdisciplines within each of these much larger fields.

Since visual neuroscience is the most general of these three, let's consider it first. The largest professional organization for this group of scientists, the Society for Neuroscience, has around 30,000 members. Over 60 percent of them hold PhD degrees, and an additional 25 percent hold medical or optometric degrees. This society holds an annual meeting attended by 15,000 to 20,000 members.

A typical training period to become a neuroscientist involves five to six years of graduate study for the PhD degree, followed by two to four years of postdoctoral work in one or two labs to learn a variety of specialized techniques. About 50 percent of the membership works in medical schools and hospitals, another 30 percent in colleges or universities. The remaining 20 percent works about equally in industry (private pharmaceutical and medical companies) and in government laboratories.

The National Institutes of Health, National Science Foundation, Department of Health and Human Services, and Department of Defense provide research funding for neuroscience and neuropsychology in the United States. In Canada, the Institutes of Health Research and the Natural Sciences and Engineering Research Council provide funding.

Neurologists are physicians who care for patients with neurological disorders. Among the most common disorders they treat are Parkinson's disease, Alzheimer's disease, stroke, epilepsy, and multiple sclerosis. If surgical treatment is recommended, specialists trained in neurosurgery typically perform it.

Neuropsychologists have a PhD degree and specialize in the relationship between brain and behavior. They receive extensive training in the anatomy, physiology, and pathology of the nervous system. Some specialize in research, whereas others specialize in evaluating and treating people with brain disorders. Many clinical neuropsychologists work as part of a larger team in a medical setting that includes physicians, neurologists, geriatric specialists, and social workers.

Cognitive psychologists, psychophysicists, and cognitive neuroscientists

The field of experimental psychology is the study of the mind through an examination of behavior. It is about 150 years old. Over that time it has undergone many changes in methodology and theoretical orientation. For example, in its early days there was a strong movement toward using introspective reports from highly trained observers to study the contents and workings of the conscious mind. However, with the advent of a philosophical movement called *behaviorism* in the 1920s and 1930s, acceptable behavioral measurements were restricted to those that could be observed, repeated, and altered with systematic changes in experimental conditions. The post–World War II years ushered in an era in which electronic communication (the telephone and then the computer) became the main metaphor for understanding the mind. Theories once again focused on the hidden workings of the mind, but methodology no longer involved the introspective reports of the early days. Experimental research methods remained rigorously objective but now focused on *how* what was seen and experienced had an influence on observable behavior. By 1980, almost all experimental psychologists were calling themselves cognitive psychologists to reflect this regained interest in the mind.

Throughout these 150 years, two areas of vision research remained relatively unfazed by the shifts. One was psychophysics, an area identified by the German scientist Gustav Fechner in 1850 that focused on the relationships between the physical intensity of a stimulus and its perceived magnitude. This field has contributed most of the theoretical foundations for the objective measurement of behavior in the study of vision. These foundations are taught in every modern graduate program in cognitive psychology and perception.

The other field with a history of few interruptions is visual perception. Some of the behavioral methods in use today can be traced to the German scientists Hermann von Helmholtz and Ewald Herring. Both of these early researchers contributed to the study of visual illusions as windows to the inner workings of the eye and brain.

A typical period of training to become a modern cognitive psychologist, or perception researcher, is similar to that of a PhD in neuroscience. It involves around five years of graduate training in a university research lab, followed by two to four years of postdoctoral training.

Most experimental psychologists are professors who perform research and teach in a university setting. A small but increasing percentage work in industry, business, and government laboratories. Industrial research often has a strong emphasis on human factors (ergonomics) and other applications of behavioral research to interactions between human beings and machines. Business-oriented research often emphasizes marketing and communication. Funding for university research in the United States comes from the National Science Foundation, the National Institutes of Health, and the Department of Defense. Funding in Canada comes from the Institutes of Health Research and the Natural Sciences and Engineering Research Council.

Several professional organizations in North America promote research in visual psychophysics and cognition. Among the largest are the Psychonomic Society, with 2,500 members, and the Vision Sciences Society, with 1,000 members.

The most recent trend among vision researchers with a background in experimental psychology involves conducting experiments that not only measure behavior but also produce brain scans (images of a subject's brain in action while performing a task). This research is often in search of the "neural correlates" of perception, action, and consciousness. Its proponents are actively multidisciplinary and call themselves cognitive neuroscientists to reflect this diversity. There is now a professional society, as well as a journal that goes by the name *Cognitive Neuroscience*.

Computer scientists and engineers

A number of research areas within computer science and engineering are closely allied to the visual sciences. They have all emerged within the past thirty years, being children of the computer revolution. Perhaps because they are very technology intensive they have developed simultaneously in university and industrial settings.

The effort to build machines that can see and act without direct human intervention has been called by various names, including *artificial intelligence, biological cybernetics, robotics,* and *machine vision*. The theoretical approach underlying these efforts is called *computational vision* to emphasize that behind any machine of this kind is the idea (sometimes still only a hope) that the functions of vision can be replicated by properly chosen computations. Scientists in this area have had some success in building machines that can solve specific visual problems, such as picking up and manipulating parts on an assembly line. A more general visual system that can learn new objects and recognize old ones for manipulation has been much more elusive and still remains out of reach.

A rapidly growing related area is human-computer interaction. Here, the main idea is to use research in human vision and visual cognition to improve the two-way communication between humans and machines. One example of a wildly successful innovation of this kind is the ubiquitous mouse-based graphical interface used by Microsoft Windows. It is based on an earlier concept used on the Macintosh, which in turn was based on work at the Palo Alto Research Center (a subsidiary of Xerox Corporation), which in turn can be traced to earlier research at Stanford University and the Massachusetts Institute of Technology.

The problem of effective scientific visualization is a growing one for many sciences. It is often difficult to analyze, or even visualize, modern datasets because of their extremely large size: They usually contain millions of data points and hundreds of highly interrelated variables. Scientific visualization is a specialization within the larger field of computer graphics that tries to manage this problem by combining the strengths of the computer and of human vision while avoiding the weaknesses of each. For example, human vision is very efficient at detecting patterns and structure, provided that the visual properties used to convey these patterns match its strengths. Computer programs are well suited for exploring large datasets without the biases acquired from recent human experiences or faulty human memory. Research in this area therefore has significant potential to improve the way that scientists in many fields explore their data.

A final specialization within computer science that bears mention, because it is closely related to the vision sciences, is known by several names, including *neural nets, parallel distributed processing,* and *connectionism.* Here, the goal is to simulate the workings of the brain by joining a large network of units inside a computer. The "units" in the computer are thought to be analogous to the neurons in the brain. These units are usually segregated into at least three categories: input units for receiving information, output units for action, and "hidden" units in between. One of the most appealing features of these brain simulations is their ability to learn from experience without human supervision. Scientists in industry are excited about this development because it suggests the real possibility of commercial products that will adapt themselves to their users. (Imagine a washing machine that remembers and anticipates the settings you use for cleaning different types of clothing.) But scientists doing basic research are equally excited because this development promises the possibility of understanding how learning such as language acquisition and visual object recognition take place.

MEASUREMENT IN VISION SCIENCE

This book is intended for readers who do not have a great deal of technical or engineering background. As such, I have tried to keep the calculations and mathematical concepts to a minimum. At the same time, vision depends on light and its influence on behavior, and both light and behavior have some precisely defined and measurable characteristics. Also, one of the purposes of this book is to convince you that further study (perhaps even a career) in vision science is worthwhile. A few equations and some concepts of measurement are indispensable in getting a start in this field. If you are reading this book solely for your own enjoyment, you can probably skim the next section—or even skip it—without jeopardizing your understanding of the remaining chapters. If you are reading it because you are interested in a career in one of the vision sciences, please pay careful attention to it.

Light

You may find it ironic that something as fundamental to our universe as light can be defined only in relative rather than in absolute terms. What humans call *light* cannot be defined without reference to the human experience. The full electromagnetic spectrum, of which light is a small portion, does have a completely objective definition. It includes the kind of energy present in gamma and X-rays at one end and in radio waves at the other. These are arranged according to wavelength, which is a measure of the physical distance between peaks (and valleys) of energy. X-rays have extremely short wavelengths (smaller than a few billionths of a meter), and radio waves have very long wavelengths (many thousands of meters). Human vision is sensitive to only a tiny portion of energy in this entire range, which is measured in technical units known as *nanometers* (nm). One nm is one billionth of a meter, and the sensitivity of the human eye extends from approximately 360 nm to 780 nm. This range of energy is what we refer to as light. Thus the very definition of light is anthropomorphic, or human centered. If we had different visual systems—ones that were sensitive to the infrared portion of the spectrum, as some other animals' visual systems are—our definition of light would be different. But humans define light as that portion of the electromagnetic spectrum to which we are sensitive. If this discussion sounds a little circular, rest assured that it is. (But it is our own visual system we are trying to understand, after all. Why shouldn't we be able to define the terms?)

There are four primary aspects of light that influence the response of our visual system. One aspect is wavelength. Although the physical differences between wavelengths may be too tiny for us to appreciate, we can easily understand their consequences because they produce uniquely different color experiences. In nature, the full range of wavelengths is evident in the rainbow. A glass prism can display wavelengths in the lab. If you want to produce the same effect at home, try spraying water lightly out of your garden hose in sunlight with your back to the sun. In each case, reddish colors will lie toward the upper portion of the rainbow, yellow and green colors will lie near the center, and blue-tinged colors will appear toward the bottom. This ordering corresponds to the degree to which light rays are bent (refracted) as they pass through a medium that is denser than air—for example, a glass prism or water. From now on, we will refer to the wavelength of light by using the nm units. Some rough rules of thumb are that 480 nm corresponds to a widely agreed upon "blue," 540 nm corresponds to a universally acceptable "green," 565 nm to "yellow," and 590 nm to a "primary red." A more extended discussion of the relation between wavelength and color appearance will appear in Chapter 3.

A second aspect of light is intensity, or amount. One thing that complicates the understanding of light—something that even physicists have not yet managed to work out satisfactorily—is that light is at the same time both particle and wave. When light is characterized as a wave, certain of its properties are easier to understand; when it is characterized as particles, or small packets of energy, other properties are easier to express. The intensity of light is best understood in the particle sense. When a greater number of particles (photons) are emitted or reflected, we can say there is more light; when fewer photons are emitted, there is less light.

It is convenient for the vision scientist that there are devices to measure precisely the number of photons landing in some portion of space over some period of time. These measuring devices are *photometers*. They make it possible to measure the intensity of light at a number of different points in the photons' journey, from an artificial light source (e.g., lamp, computer screen), to a reflecting surface in the environment (e.g., wall, screen), to the receiving surfaces of the eye (i.e., cornea, retina). The light intensity measure that is most relevant to the functioning of the eye is the *photon catch,* or the number of photons that actually make contact with the light-sensitive receptors in the eye.

We will not often need precise measurements of light intensity for the purposes of this book, but when we do we will use the unit scientists call the *candela*. The candela has a faintly romantic definition, being the amount of light emitted from a solitary standard candle shining directly onto a surface that is one square meter in area, at a distance of one meter. Calibrated with respect to a household light bulb, it corresponds to a bulb $\frac{1}{1000}$ of a watt with a peak wavelength of 555 nm.

One aspect of light intensity that will be important in some discussions is the distinction between light shining onto a surface and light being reflected from that surface into the eye. The words vision scientists use to make this distinction are *brightness* (referring to the intensity of the source of light) and *lightness* (referring to the degree to which a surface reflects light). The distinction is easy to make, as when we think of being in either a dark or a light room (brightness) and viewing either a dark or a light piece of paper (lightness). However, the distinction poses a fundamental problem to our visual system at work in the everyday world. Under normal circumstances, the photon catch for a given region of the visual field depends on a combination of source intensity (brightness) and surface reflectance (lightness). One of the jobs of vision is to determine the combination of brightness and lightness that generates the total photon catch at the eye. For example, are we looking at a black piece of paper illuminated by a bright light, or at a white piece of paper under dim lighting conditions? Both pieces of paper may be reflecting similar amounts of light to our eyes. In fact, the black piece of paper in the bright light may be reflecting more light. This is only a glimpse into the complicated problems being solved every time we open our eyes. For a more complete discussion of this issue, you will have to wait until Chapter 3.

I have already mentioned a third important aspect of light without being completely explicit: space. When photons rain onto a reflecting surface and bounce toward our eyes, we must define any measurement of the intensity of that light with respect to a spatial region or area. As previously mentioned, when defining a candela we take area into account. We also define units of brightness and lightness with respect to a spatial area of some size. Even the pupil—the hole that permits light to enter the eye—changes size according to the overall brightness of the environment.

The standard units for measuring space in the visual domain are degrees of visual angle, or arc. An *arc* is a segment of a circle, which in its entirety covers 360 degrees. Degrees of arc are appropriate units because they express the extent of the retinal surface that is receiving light from a given region in space. This is illustrated in Figure 1.6. The eye is approximately circular, with a lens at the front that focuses light on the rear inner surface (the retina). As a result, the angle formed by imaginary lines (rays) extending from the lens to the object is the same as the angle formed by rays extending from the lens to the retina. This is the *visual angle*, and it can be calculated easily if one knows the size of the object (S in the formula) and the distance from the eye to the object (D in the formula). The formula is also shown in Figure 1.6. Don't worry too much about the fact that it contains a term called the *inverse tangent*. This is a button press or two on most electronic calculators.

To make distinctions involving spatial areas that are less than 1 degree of visual angle, you can divide degrees into smaller units known as *minutes of arc*. There are 60 minutes of arc within 1 degree.

Expressing the size of something in terms of the retinal extent of the light pattern (in other words, the retinal size) turns out to be very convenient because it takes into account both the size of the object and its distance from the eye. The unit that limits the eye's sensitivity to spatial variation is the retinal size, not the object's size or the viewing distance. Notice that you can see very distant objects, such as stars, if their light is sufficiently intense or their size is sufficiently large, as

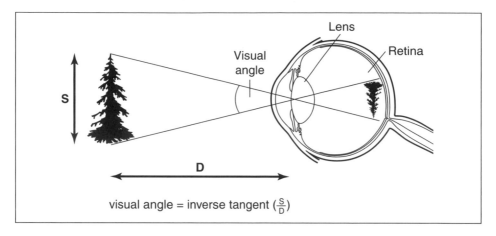

FIGURE 1.6   The size of an object can be expressed in units relevant to the eye by measuring the angle between imaginary rays of light extending from the eye to the object. The units for measuring visual sizes and distances are degrees of visual angle. The formula is given below. It is important to measure the size of the object (S) and the viewing distance (D) in the same units—whether inches, centimeters, or some other unit.

when increased through magnification. You can even see very small objects, such as grains of sand, if their retinal size is sufficiently large, either through close proximity or through magnification. The spatial measure of visual angle in degrees is therefore an efficient way of summarizing size with respect to the light-receptive surface of the eye.

The fourth aspect of light that influences the response of our visual system is time. Our discussion of light so far has implied a constant flow of photons from some region of the visual field into the eye. However, natural viewing conditions are very different from this: Our eyes are almost constantly in motion, or have just completed a move, or are about to move. The amount of time that light shines onto a particular part of our eye from any surface depends on how long the eye is stationary between movements. It also depends on how frequently we blink and to what extent the objects in our visual field are in motion or become occluded by other objects.

There are several ways in which time is important for vision. If we ask how long photons must flow onto a single retinal receptor to generate a response, the answer is "surprisingly little time." Under optimal conditions, a photon coming into contact with a retinal receptor can produce a cascade of action potentials throughout the visual system. Thus the unit of time required for photon contact is too small to enter meaningfully into any calculations. However, if we ask how long it takes the visual system to communicate this event to the brain, time becomes of greater practical concern. At the level of a single cell (a neuron) that conveys information about light, a single cycle of neural activity in response to incoming signals (the action potential) takes between 1 and 10 milliseconds. One millisecond, which is abbreviated as ms, is one one-thousandth of a second. This means that the maximum time needed to convey information from one neuron to another is on the order of 10 ms. When we consider the number of neural cycles, or steps, of this kind between the retina and the cerebral cortex, there are four steps, or about 40 ms, of elapsed time. When we measure the minimum possible time for a visual signal to be translated into a motor action such as an eye or limb movement, the shortest time is just under 200 ms. That is the same as one-fifth of a second.

Another way to understand the role of time in vision is to ask how much time must elapse between volleys of light for the visual system to signal their separation. Here the answer depends on the kind of visual neurons that we examine. Neurons measured right inside the eye, called *ganglion cells,* can respond in time with a pulsating light that turns on and off up to 300 times a second. That is a repetition of the cycle that consists of a 1.5 ms "on" period followed by a 1.5 ms "off" period. At the level of visual neurons in the cerebral cortex, sensitivity to changes over time is much reduced. Here, neurons are able to track a pulsating light only up to 50 or 60 cycles per second. That's a repeating pattern of 8 ms "on" followed by 8 ms "off." It's interesting to note that the individual frames of a modern movie change every 30 ms or so (33 cycles per second), and we are blissfully unaware of the individual stationary frames.

Every visual system, including the human eye, is designed to trade light intensity for time. Thus in a fundamental sense, the eye is unable to distinguish whether its total photon catch consists of (1) a large number of photons presented over a brief period, or (2) the same number of photons presented over a long period. The same equation applies to space. At some unit of analysis, the eye cannot distinguish whether the number of photons it has detected were concentrated in a small region of the retina or were distributed over a large region. These fundamental uncertainties are called the *time constants* and *space constants* of the eye, respectively.

There are actually two time constants of the human eye because of the two types of receptors: cones for vision under bright illumination, and rods for vision under dim light. For cones, the time constant is around 100 ms, meaning that 1,000 photons could be presented in a very brief period (say, 1,000 photons within a 1 ms period) or over a long period (such as 200 photons in each of five 20 ms periods) for the same visual effect. The cones influenced by the two periods would be unable to tell the difference. For rods, the time constant is closer to 400 ms, meaning that they catch photons over a much longer period in order to detect very low levels of light.

The space constants of the human eye are limited by the size of and interaction among cones and rods. Near the center of the eye, where cones are most densely packed and physically smallest, the space constant is about 10 minutes of arc. This means that the total photon catch can be distributed in any way over a circular region about one-sixth of a degree of visual angle and the eye will not be able to distinguish a difference in its shape. In the periphery of the visual field, the space constant is larger and increases proportionately in distance from the center of the eye, as we will see in Chapter 4.

The visual stimulus

What is the immediate cause of the visual experience? What is the stimulus for a visually guided action? Is it the activity of neurons in a region of the brain that supports conscious visual awareness or action? Is it the pattern of activity in the neurons of the eye generated by the incoming light? Is it the pattern of light that entered the eye? Is it the objects and surfaces that reflected light in the direction of the eye? Is it perhaps even the perceived relevance of these objects and surfaces for the observer? The answer to all these questions is "yes!" But answering "yes" complicates matters for the vision researcher who wants to establish systematic relations between a stimulus and a human action or experience. The stimulus has many potential definitions and therefore many possible measurements.

Vision researchers can reduce this problem's complexity by focusing on different aspects of the stimulus for different kinds of research. A neuroscientist studying the physiology of a class of neurons needs to consider only the neural input to that class of cell. Whether that input originated as light reflected from surfaces in the external world or as a stimulus generated by an electrode makes little difference. The "system" being studied is a particular class of neurons. In a similarly narrow fashion, a retinal physiologist may be interested only in the relationship between photons that make contact with a class of cones and the neural signal that those cones generate.

A psychophysicist, however, will likely take a broader approach, systematically varying the three-dimensional or depicted objects shown to the observer under carefully controlled lighting conditions in order to see which differences among objects or pictures can be discriminated in experience. A cognitive neuroscientist may do something similar with the stimuli but be interested in the response of a specific brain region, more than in the observer's experience as reported by actions or words.

In the face of this diversity, we will often return to the distinction between the world of three-dimensional objects and surfaces (called *the scene*) and the projection of light reflecting from these objects into the eye (called *the image*). This distinction is fundamental because a scene has three dimensions in space (left-right, up-down, and front-back), whereas an image has only two (left-right, up-down). Front-back gets lost in the translation from objects to image—in the sense that it is no longer represented topographically in the same way that horizontal and vertical dimensions are. The length of time and amount of mental work required to recover the missing third dimension, and the extent to which it can ever be fully recovered, are topics of great importance. They will be discussed in Chapters 5 to 7.

The distinction between scene and image is also central to the question of whether the observer is responding to the physical properties of the objects or to the physical properties of light reflected from those objects. This is not a matter of splitting semantic hairs or playing with word meanings. It is of critical importance to understanding the vision project. Consider the option that the observer is responding to objects' physical properties. If this is the basis of vision, then how can the observer infer those properties from the pattern of light? For example, a common situation involves viewing a red apple under lighting conditions heavily biased toward the yellow portion of the wavelength spectrum. How can the observer's eye and brain, which are presented with light that is more yellow than red, deduce the true color properties of the apple's surface (its intrinsic redness, if you will)? This is the problem of color constancy we will consider in Chapter 3. We will examine similar problems of shape and size constancy in Chapter 5.

However, considering the alternative option—that the observer is responding to light reflected from objects—does not lead to any easier solutions. Under this option, we have to explain how the observer can experience and act consistently in response to different patterns of light coming from the same object. For example, the pattern of light coming from your friend's face in profile and at a distance is different from the pattern of light coming from her face seen head-on and nearby. Yet your friend still looks the same and certainly much different from a stranger seen head-on and nearby, even when the pattern of light coming from his face is similar to that coming from your friend's. Vision scientists call this the *problem of object invariance*. How could the visual system be designed to generalize appropriately on the basis of some aspects of the light while ignoring other aspects that vary just as much but are irrelevant? In the area of object recognition, this is the problem of being able to form consistent categories of objects that represent vast differences in image size, viewing angle, object orientation, color, and lighting (Chapter 5). We will see that researchers in some fields are divided on this issue. When we encounter it, we will need to remind ourselves that the debate is about whether the stimulus for vision is better thought of as the world of scenes (three-dimensional objects) or of images (two-dimensional patterns of light).

Human behavior

How can you be certain that some aspect of a visual stimulus has made an impression on an observer? How do you know that an observer can reliably tell the difference between two stimuli? If humans were faithful recorders of light, there would be no need to ask these questions. Light presented to the eye would be light recorded by the brain. Differences in light would be differences in vision.

But vision does not work in this way. To answer these questions, you will have to become a psychophysicist. Psychophysicists measure the influence of a stimulus by monitoring responses that consistently correspond to the light pattern being presented. This means (1) looking for reactions that occur whenever a certain visual stimulus is presented, and (2) looking to see that the same reactions do not occur whenever that stimulus is not presented.

Perhaps the simplest relationship to explore is the one between the presence of a stimulus and its detection by an observer. How much of the stimulus must be presented before the observer can detect its presence? How much luminance is required? How much time must pass? How large must the stimulus be? Where on the retinal surface must it land? These are all questions of detection, and they can be measured with a variety of methods. Each method links, in a unique way, the probability of detection by the observer with changes in the intensity of the stimulus. Figure 1.7 shows this relationship, which is called the *psychophysical function*. When a stimulus is too weak, the observer can only guess whether a stimulus is present. When it is too strong, the observer will detect it every time. Halfway between these two points is the *threshold*. In many of the chapters that follow, a *threshold measure* will be given in describing the performance of observers viewing displays. When such a measure is given, you should remind yourself that the threshold is really only a convenient summary of the relationship between the intensity of the stimulus and the observers' ability to detect it.

A more complex question is whether the observer can tell the difference between stimuli. This is the question of *discrimination*. It can be determined either by measuring response accuracy in a situation where observers make errors (confusing one stimulus for another) or by measuring response time in a situation where observers rarely make errors but one decision takes longer than the other. However, subtle issues complicate the accurate measurement of both response accuracy and response time, and we should consider them briefly.

One issue concerns the wide variety of ways in which observers may choose to respond when they really cannot see anything at all. If you are being tested in an experiment and you fail to discriminate any difference among stimuli on a given trial, how would you respond? One way would be to always guess "no difference" when you really hadn't seen any difference. Psychophysicists call this a *conservative* response strategy. Another way would be to simply guess by choosing one of the two possible responses at random. Psychophysicists call this an *unbiased* response strategy. Finally, another way would be to always guess "a difference" when you really hadn't seen any difference. Psychophysicists call this a *liberal* response strategy.

The important thing to note is that even though these three response strategies produce very different results in an experiment, they all still point to the fact that the observer has been unable to detect any difference in the stimulus. For this reason, psychophysicists use experimental designs that ensure they will be able to sep-

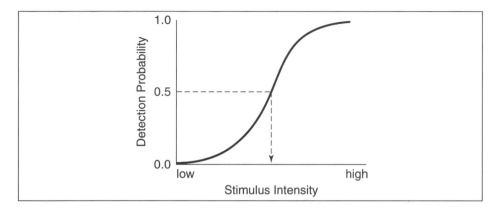

FIGURE 1.7   A psychophysical function expressing the observed relationship between the probability of visual detection and the intensity of a stimulus. It is common to use the midway point between the chance level of guessing and perfect performance as the experimentally defined threshold of the observer.

arate an observer's response tendencies from his or her true ability to discriminate differences among the stimuli.

For instance, they may include an equal number of "difference" and "no difference" trials in an experiment so that they can determine the guessing strategy of the observer. An observer with an unbiased strategy will respond "no difference" on no more than one-half of the trials in which he or she sees no difference, whereas an observer following a conservative strategy will respond "no difference" on most of them and an observer following a liberal strategy will respond "no difference" only rarely. Note too that the best performance that is theoretically possible for an observer using any of these strategies, but who is otherwise insensitive to the stimulus differences, is 50 percent. This is because the unbiased strategy would lead, by chance, to 50 percent correct on the "difference" trials and 50 percent correct on the "no difference" trials. The conservative strategy would lead to 100 percent correct on "no difference" trials and 0 percent correct on "difference" trials, and together these would average 50 percent correct overall. The conservative strategy would lead to 0 percent correct on "no difference" trials and 100 percent correct on "difference" trials, again for 50 percent correct overall. Even a mixture of strategies in this experiment, where the stimulus difference is undetectable, would lead to no better than 50 percent correct. For this reason, 50 percent correct is considered the chance guessing level in an experiment involving only two alternatives, 33 percent correct is the chance guessing level when there are three equally likely alternatives, and so on.

When observers make mistakes in discrimination, there are two ways in which they can go wrong. One involves the sensitivity of the visual system. When an observer confuses two stimuli, it may be because both stimuli activated identical or similar neurons in the eye and brain. In that case, the stimuli are similar in neural effect and also in terms of the conscious experience they evoke, even though other measurements may show the stimuli to be physically different. When two stimuli produce greater differences in neural activity and associated perceptual experience, the probability of an observer making a differential response to the two stimuli increases.

The second way in which observers can make mistakes involves tendencies to respond that lie outside any neural pattern generated by the visual stimulus. Such tendencies, called *response biases,* can influence accuracy in a number of ways. For example, consider a baseball umpire trying to determine whether a base runner is "out" or "safe" at base. An obvious source of perceptual error arises when the time difference between the base player's tagging "out" and the runner's foot contacting the base is imperceptible. However, another source of error is any bias the umpire may have to respond "safe" or "out" when he is uncertain. This bias need not be prejudicial in the sense that he favors one team. It may be an application of a well-rehearsed rule (such as "any tie goes to the runner"), or it may be unconscious (such as lingering doubts over a previous call in a similar situation). In any event, it is important for psychophysicists to distinguish sources of errors that emerge from bias over those that arise from limits in sensitivity. To do this, they have developed sophisticated tools of statistical analysis.

Measurement of how long it takes the visual system to respond to a stimulus is complicated by the relationship between time and accuracy that we all know well from our experience in taking tests. We can usually perform more accurately on a question if we are given more time. If we have to respond quickly, the likelihood of making an error increases. Figure 1.8 illustrates the general nature of this relationship. Imagine an experimental situation in which vision researchers are testing an observer's performance in response to a stimulus that involves a visual difference between two objects or events. When the researchers compare the observer's performance only in terms of response time, there is always uncertainty over whether the observer traded accuracy for time in deciding how to respond. To prevent such uncertainty, vision researchers always report response accuracy in addition to response time in characterizing performance. Any report of a more rapid response to a visual difference must be accompanied by fewer errors in response in order to justify the conclusion that the observer discriminated the visual difference more rapidly than some other difference.

ARE YOU READY?

You are now prepared for an exploration of human vision. The story about to unfold is that vision is much more than the "videotape process" that most people imagine it to be. Instead of merely capturing the moving, colored image of light

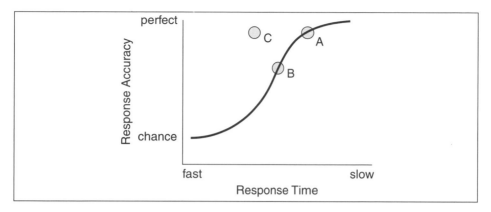

FIGURE 1.8 The relationship between response accuracy and response time. Response accuracy is limited at its lower end by the probability of guessing correctly by chance. Response time is limited by the time required for a visual stimulus to influence an action after the observer reaches a decision. Response accuracy can be increased only at the expense of more processing time in reaching a decision; alternatively, response time can be decreased only at the expense of a likely larger number of errors. Performance in condition A is actually equal to that in condition B. Condition A appears to be more accurate, but at the cost of taking longer to respond. Condition B appears faster, but at the cost of lower accuracy. Only condition C has better performance than A or B. It could not possibly represent performance that could be related to conditions A or B by a tradeoff in speed for accuracy.

that meets the eye, the human visual system does some wonderfully useful and intelligent things. These analyses begin in the eye and involve almost the entire brain in one way or another. They are much more useful to us than a videotaped record could ever be. Are you ready?

FURTHER READING

Barsalou, L. W. (1999). Perceptual symbol systems. *Behavioral and Brain Sciences, 22,* 577–609.

Coren, S., Ward, L. M., & Enns, J. T. (2004). *Sensation & perception* (6th ed.). New York: Wiley.

Dawkins, R. (1986). *The blind watchmaker.* New York: Norton.

Locher, J. L. (Ed.). (2000). *The world of M. C. Escher.* New York: Abradale Press.

Spivey, M., & Geng, J. (2001). Oculomotor mechanisms activated by imagery and memory: Eye movements to absent objects. *Psychological Research, 65,* 235–241.

Zeki, S. (1999). *Inner vision: An exploration of art and the brain.* Oxford, England: Oxford University Press.

2 EYE AND BRAIN

FUNDAMENTAL QUESTIONS

- How do scientists study the biological equipment used for vision?
- How are personal experiences important to the vision scientist?
- Why do we experience the world rather than the activity of neurons in our brains?
- What do migraine headaches tell us about vision?
- How is visual information routed through the brain?
- Why does seeing depend as much on the brain as on the eyes?
- How does a stroke impair vision differently, depending on where in the brain it occurs?

Now that we have reviewed some of the ways in which vision is different from a high-quality video recording and have gone over some important background to the vision sciences, it is time to turn our attention to our own visual systems. What biological equipment do we use in making sense of the patterns of light that fall onto our eyes?

Throughout this book we will consider the biological equipment that humans bring to the vision project. Each chapter will give us unique insights into this equipment and how it works. In this chapter I will not try to introduce all of this material at once. Rather, I will present the physiology of the eye and brain on a "need to know" basis. I begin by sketching the outlines in broad terms. In later chapters I will rely on this outline as we consider certain topics in greater depth.

It is important to remind students of vision science that many of the topics considered in this book do not yet have explanations that can be firmly grounded in physiology. Often it is not even clear what aspects of physiology are relevant to a given perceptual experience or visual influence on behavior. With this sober but fair warning, let's explore a little of the anatomy and physiology that are relevant to vision.

TOOLS OF THE TRADE, REVERSE ENGINEERS, AND EMPTY BOXES

The first question we must answer is *How do we know?* What are the ways in which researchers have achieved their present understanding of how the human eye and brain work? What are the ways in which researchers can probe the structure and workings of the human brain? As it turns out, the twentieth century experienced an explosion in new technology that led to new ways of understanding the brain. Figure 2.1 (see color appendix) shows a fast-forward, schematic overview of technological developments in brain research over the twentieth century.

In the nineteenth and early twentieth centuries, state-of-the-art brain research was essentially record keeping. Doctors would see patients who were suffering from various behavioral symptoms, and they would make careful notes of these problems. Sometimes, rough areas of brain damage would be known because of the nature of the trauma, so doctors would attempt to link these brain areas with consequences in a patient's behavior. In a few cases, following the death of a patient, careful dissections of brain tissue revealed the exact site of damage that doctors could only guess at while the patient was alive.

One of the most famous cases was that of Phineas Gage, a railroad construction foreman who suffered a horrible accident in 1848. An accidental discharge of explosives sent an iron bar through his skull, over 1 inch in diameter and over 3 feet long. The most remarkable aspect of this accident, as noted by the local newspaper, the *Free Soil Union,* was that the accident left him the next day in "full possession of his reason and free from pain." Careful reconstruction of the accident, through medical records from that time and Gage's own skull donated to medical research upon his death, indicated damage to much of the left frontal region of his brain. This had caused significant change in his personality but little or no change in his perceptual or cognitive capacity. It was clear even at that time, then, that some brain regions are more important for vision than others. The left frontal lobe is apparently not one of them.

By the middle of the twentieth century, the development of equipment to record small amounts of electrical activity had made it possible to "eavesdrop" on the behavior of single cells in the brains of animals—such as cats and monkeys—that are close biological relatives to humans. Such equipment is still the main tool of neuroscientists studying animal brains; it involves *electrophysiological recording.* In human patients undergoing surgery for various brain disorders, similar techniques can sometimes be employed, along with direct brain stimulation using tiny electrodes.

As early as the 1940s, the Canadian neurosurgeon Wilder Penfield had begun to directly stimulate patients' cortical surfaces in preparation for surgery. He found that the actions, sensations, and experiences evoked by applying small amounts of electricity to the brain were systematically organized on the brain's surface. Penfield used these functional maps to guide his scalpel so as to excise a tumor or prevent the spread of epileptic activity while minimizing the extent of damage in surrounding areas.

More recently, some of the electrical recording techniques developed with monkeys have been applied successfully to patients undergoing treatment for epilepsy. Part of this treatment involves the temporary placement of electrodes directly into the brain. While the surgical procedure proceeds, it is possible to measure the responses of a small number of neurons to pictures of faces, objects, and naturalistic scenes. One of the remarkable findings of this research is certain neurons respond to these images in a very similar way, regardless of whether the images are actually presented to the eyes or only recalled into the mind's eye from memory.

By the 1960s and 1970s, methods such as *computer-assisted tomography* (CAT scans) were emerging to assist in the study of the brain's structure in live, healthy individuals. Observations of brains at work also became possible around the same time with the advent of *positron emission tomography* (PET scans) and *event-related potential* (ERP) recordings.

PET scans follow a radioactive tracer through the bloodstream of the brain, and they are usually performed only when a patient requires a brain scan for diagnosing a possible medical condition. In contrast, ERP involves recording the average neural activity that can be detected through the scalp; the patient has nothing injected into the bloodstream and is not subjected to any electrical current. Scientists therefore refer to the ERP method as "noninvasive." The basis of the signal is a small electrical difference in the brain that occurs when one region is more active than another. *Magno-encephalography* (MEG) is an even more sensitive and noninvasive measurement of brain activity recorded through the scalp. This technique is based on the magnetic field differences caused by brain activity rather than differences in the brain's electrical potential.

In the 1990s, brain images based on *magnetic resonance imaging* (MRI) were able to give scientists clear "photographic" images of the bends, folds, and valleys of an individual's cortical tissue. A related tool that was built on this foundation, *functional magnetic resonance imaging* (fMRI), gives researchers detailed images of brain activity based on changes in blood flow, which are in turn caused by changes in mental activity. This procedure produces images with spatial accuracy to the resolution of a few millimeters. These images can be taken from experiment volunteers who engage in a wide variety of perceptual and cognitive tasks while lying inside the powerful magnet. Although the magnet's enclosure is noisy and confining, fMRI is entirely noninvasive.

Finally, in the last five years of the twentieth century, *transcranial magnetic stimulation* (TMS) became established as a way to mimic a short-lived, reversible, and spatially focused lesion in an experiment volunteer engaged in a wide variety of perceptual and cognitive tasks. The equipment delivers a very brief but powerful magnetic discharge that briefly disrupts normal neural processing in a specific region of the brain. It is therefore electrically invasive, although almost all studies of its safety to date indicate that it produces no long-lasting effects. Combined with recording tools such as ERP or MEG, the TMS technique has given researchers the ability to stimulate the brain while noninvasively recording both the electrical-magnetic effects of the magnetic jolt and the consequences to perception and cognition.

Despite the importance of each of these technological developments, you may be surprised to learn that one of the most important tools for studying the human brain has always been, and still is, the researcher's own visual experiences—that is, visual experiences that are carefully planned, systematically recorded, and analyzed with the help of critical thought and statistical reasoning. In fact, these are scientific experiments in which the main data derive from the report of a participant who has experienced and responded to a carefully designed visual display. Among vision scientists this is known as a *behavioral experiment* because the measured response is an objectively observable behavior, whether it be a verbal report, an action made by the limbs, or an eye movement or a blink.

Philosophers of the mind sometimes refer to the information obtained from these kinds of experiments as *first-person data* to emphasize that they are suspicious of information based solely on the private reserve of conscious experience. They are especially suspicious if it is someone else's experience. Because consciousness is inherently subjective, these philosophers sometimes doubt that an objective science based on "experiences" is possible.

In contrast to this position, many psychologists think of these experiments as their "bread and butter" and refer to them as *psychophysical tests*. They are less suspicious than the philosophers because they are concerned only with the measured similarities among the reports of different observers. Whether the subjective experiences associated with those reports actually differ among individuals does not cause psychologists to lose much sleep. The important point for them is that the reports can be recorded objectively and repeated by different researchers to establish reliability. Neuroscientists—researchers whose tools bring them in closest contact with the brain—also rely heavily on these kinds of data. Psychophysical and behavioral studies often provide the inspiration that drives neuroscientists to direct their electrical recording devices and brain scanners to specific areas of the visual system in search for the "neural correlate" of the perceptual experience in which they are interested.

Fortunately for the student of vision, behavioral research is the kind of activity we all can participate in, even when we don't have access to expensive technology, unusual neurological patients, or colonies of research animals. It is the activity that first prompted many researchers who are now well established in the field to begin thinking about how vision works. It is the kind of activity I am going to encourage you to undertake as you read this book.

TOOLS OF THE TRADE

The kind of thinking described above makes use of current knowledge about the structure of eye and brain but is not limited to it. There is precedence for this. One of the great success stories in the study of vision began long before scientists were able to analyze the tissue of the eye with sophisticated molecular techniques and to examine the structure of the eye with high-resolution microscopes. It began in 1807 when a twenty-two-year-old British physician, Thomas Young, proposed to the British Fellows of the Royal Society that the human eye contained three distinctly different types of light receptors. In Chapter 3 we will find out that he was correct and that definitive proof of his ideas came more than 150 years after he proposed this theory.

Young proposed the idea on the basis of his attempts to organize the results of color matching experiments, which merely involved carefully recorded reports of the experiences of observers who had been shown pairs of colors on a white background. To be sure, Young tried to make his theory consistent with the current limited knowledge about the structure of the eye. But he did not limit himself to existing knowledge of eye and brain structures. In fact, his genius lay in his willingness to propose and test theories about the inner parts and workings of structures that were impossible to see. Today scientists call this the *empty box approach* to theory development. By no means peculiar to the study of vision, it is an approach used in all sciences. The "empty box" refers to the inner workings of a structure that cannot be observed directly. In fact, empty boxes are as important to theory development in astronomy and genetics as they are to theories in psychology and economics. They push our understanding of what we are studying well ahead of what we can already see. They enable us to know what we are looking at when we finally see it.

It may be tempting to think that the speculative, empty box approach to studying visual physiology is a thing of the past, perhaps relevant one hundred years ago when little was known about anatomy at the necessary level of detail, but certainly not relevant now when many sophisticated technologies are available. This statement could not be farther from the truth. All the sophisticated genetic, molecular, chemical, electrophysiological, and imaging techniques of today do not by themselves provide an understanding of how the visual system works. Consider trying to understand the workings of the modern car by taking it apart, making fine slices through its most important parts, and pouring chemicals on them to study the effects. Each procedure might generate useful information, but it would shed light on how the car works only when correlated with other information *and* with the functioning of the car. What role would each part play in the actions that the car performs? How would the structure of a given part relate to what the car does? Where would the chemicals have to be poured to make a difference when the car is driven?

Cognitive scientists call this sort of analytical thinking *reverse engineering*. The term has been borrowed from industrial spies' work in figuring out how a competing company's product works. For instance, in the 1960s a radio engineer might buy the latest transistor radio put out by the competition, take it to the lab, disassemble it, and try to figure out what innovation enabled it to get better reception or to be manufactured at a lower cost. For someone studying vision in humans today, reverse engineering involves testing hypotheses about the visual system in much the same way that Young did. Modern-day researchers may engage in this sort of detective work solely to better understand how the brain works (if they are neuroscientists) or to re-create the phenomenon in a machine (if they are engineers of artificial intelligence). In any event, someone other than the original designer can understand the workings of a device such as the eye, the brain, or a radio. This is accomplished most efficiently by testing proposals about what the parts (the "empty boxes") might be and how they might work together.

What has changed most since the days of Thomas Young is not our ability to engage in systematic, scientific thinking. As far as anyone can tell, that aspect of our brain hasn't changed in two hundred or even two thousand years. What has changed most dramatically is the arsenal of tools at our disposal for assisting in the reverse engineering project of the human brain. Genetic analysis enables us to understand something about the way the visual system develops. Electrophysiological techniques permit careful analysis of the behavior of a single neuron. Brain imaging offers detailed snapshots of the structure of the resting or the deceased brain, provides clear pictures of the sites of brain damage in stroke patients, and increasingly enables us to see brain activity in a healthy, awake, and thoughtful individual. Brain stimulation—either directly during surgery or at a distance through TMS-induced changes in the magnetic fields of the brain—is enabling us to observe the consequences of simulated and temporary brain damage.

The following pages will present information gained from each of these new technologies. Let's try to keep in mind, however, that our most important tool is still our own brain—the very brain whose visual functioning we are trying to understand. The new technologies and gadgets are just that: tools to help us think. Some philosophers have argued that this recursive process, of the brain trying to understand itself, places a limit on how much we will ever be able to know. Only time will tell if their argument is correct. In the meantime, we can take comfort in the large strides in understanding that were made during the twentieth century. The importance of these strides will not be diminished even if it turns out someday that recursion really does impose a ceiling on our self-understanding. So far, it seems, we have not even begun to approach this ceiling.

LESSONS OF THE MIGRAINE AURA

Do you, or someone you know, suffer from migraine headaches? The causes of this painful and often debilitating condition are not well understood. Some scientists think it occurs when too little blood flows to a specific region of the brain. Without enough blood, there is insufficient oxygen going to some neurons, causing them to be active in chaotic ways. Other scientists, while acknowledging these changes in blood flow, do not think a disruption in blood flow is the primary cause. Instead, they think migraines result from a disruption in the normal balance of neurotransmitters—the chemicals involved in neural communication—in the brain. This disruption in the chemical signaling system is therefore thought to lie behind both the decreased blood flow and the associated effects on brain function.

People who suffer from migraines will be interested in the true causes of the condition. Proper treatment awaits this understanding. However, for our purpose in this chapter, it doesn't matter too much what the causes are. What matters most is that the condition known as the classical migraine provides a useful window to some of the design features of the human visual system. Of course, we can understand these features better through our own experiences if we are migraine sufferers, but it is also possible to understand them vicariously if we are fortunate to have never had a migraine headache ourselves.

The classic migraine headache has up to three phases. The first, or prodromal, phase consists of subtle changes in experience—including but not necessarily limited to visual experience—that often turn out to be harbingers of the full-blown attack. Among these signs are changes in mood, irritating brightness from ordinary lights, halos appearing around streetlights, unexplained yawning, and sometimes even craving for chocolate. If there is an effective drug treatment for the subsequent acute attack that works for you as a migraine sufferer, this is the time to take it.

The second phase, which occurs in 15 to 20 percent of cases, consists of the aura. It can last from several minutes to an hour before the third phase sets in, the full-blown headache. The aura is the phase of most interest to us because it involves neural disruptions in the brain regions that are specialized for vision. The most common aura experiences are visual, frequently involving a light show. These might be flashes of light in parts of the visual field or a blindspot in a certain region of the field, encircled by jagged, shimmering bars of light. An illustration of these effects is shown in Figure 2.2. Of course, if you consistently experience these troubling but painless symptoms immediately prior to the prolonged, painful agony of a long-lasting migraine headache, they may not hold much scientific interest for you. But as I will try to explain, because migraine auras result from disrupted neural activity in predictable places in the brain, they are extremely useful in helping us understand the design of the visual system.

It is interesting that a small percentage of people who experience auras never experience the headache itself. For some reason, the aura simply subsides. The medical world refers to this as a *migraine equivalent,* although if you are a migraine sufferer you might beg to differ. I must also point out that the same symptoms may occur, without leading to a headache, in people suffering from a

FIGURE 2.2   An illustration of what the migraine aura looks like and how it may change over a 15- to 20-minute period.

transient ischemic attack, or TIA. There is a wide range of causes for these attacks, some of them quite serious, and if you experience anything like them you should consult your physician.

Neural activity cannot be experienced

One of the most important lessons of the migraine aura is that the electrical activity of neurons associated with perception is not experienced as neural activity. Instead, it is experienced as something "out there": as a flash of light, as a set of oriented bars that move around the field of vision as the eyes move, or as a gray patch that blocks the view of anything underneath it. Visual perception, when performed by the human brain, seems to be always offering experiences of objects and events "out there" in the world. When a migraine sufferer has an aura, he does not experience it as a series of events inside his own head, even though it surely is. It is never experienced as an event at the back of the head, where the neural activity actually resides. Instead, the fragmented colored bars, gray patches, and starbursts have particular shapes, arrangements, and locations that can be seen in the visual field in front of the viewer.

This lesson is not confined to the migraine aura. When you lie back against the grass on a warm day and stare at the blue sky, those spots that you sometimes see traveling slowly across the sky are not really in the sky, even though they may appear to be. Everyone who has had this experience soon learns that the spots' origin can be deduced by making a few eye movements and watching the results: The spots drift along with the eye movements, usually lagging behind a step and rarely appearing at the center of the gaze. Any attempt to focus on a spot results in a frustrating game of tag that the eye can never win. This link between the movements of the eye and the spot's location, coupled with the drifting motion of the spot, soon leads everyone to the right conclusion: The spots are actually inside the fluid of the eye. The technical term for these spots is *floaters,* given to them because of their appearance and because they are small bits of eye tissue that have become detached in the normal course of tissue replacement. Yet despite this knowledge, the next time you experience floaters they will still seem to be "out there" in the sky. Vision, it turns out, is always "about" the world outside of the brain that is doing the seeing.

Seeing does not require the eyes

Another lesson of the migraine aura is that we can actually see without using our eyes. The changes in vision experienced during the migraine aura are not generated by signals coming to the brain from the eyes. The changes are generated entirely from within the brain. We can understand this lesson by paying attention to certain common experiences. For instance, if you think about how you experience dreams, you will realize that dreaming is also an instance in which the brain performs the functions of seeing without sensory input from the eyes. But many people, including some researchers, think of dreaming as being quite different from the ordinary processes of perception. They regard the conscious states associated with sleeping and being awake as so different that "seeing" in the two cases cannot be fairly compared.

The migraine aura helps out in this regard by demonstrating that the experience of sight generated from within the brain can be every bit as vivid and real as the experience of sight that accompanies our open eyes during normal vision. The changes in vision that migraine sufferers experience may be a little odd, since they are out of step with other visual events experienced at the same time through the sufferers' eyes, but as far as their experience is concerned, the changes in vision are just as real as the visual objects seen in the world around them. To deny the existence of those changes in vision, or visual events, in the migraine sufferers' experience is preposterous; it involves the distasteful argument that they could not possibly be experienced because they do not exist in the external world.

This lesson is worth emphasizing now because we will encounter it often in our study of vision. The normal brain is quite accomplished at seeing, even in the absence of direct stimulation from the eye. This occurs, for instance, when part of an object is projected onto the many blood vessels that lie in front of the light-sensitive regions of our eyes. It occurs when part of an object's image falls on the blindspot in each eye. It occurs when we experience a complete object even though only parts of it are visible behind a nearer, occluding object. In each case, it is much easier for the brain to generate internal perceptions than to faithfully record what is on the retina. These internal perceptions are usually consistent with those suggested by the eyes on the basis of other regions of the visual field that are actually being stimulated.

Our brains' flexibility in basing vision on information either from the eyes or from internally generated events means that our subjective experience is often an unreliable guide to the origins of our perceptions. As a result, we will have to find subtle ways of demonstrating their existence. For now, you may want to look at Box 2.1 and Figure 2.3 to explore some of the ways in which the brain sees things in a region of the retina that has no sensitivity to light.

We will encounter this lesson of the "seeing brain" again, later in this chapter, when we discuss the pathological condition called Charles Bonnet syndrome. People with this condition, like migraine sufferers, experience simultaneous and incongruous events that are inspired in some part by the eyes and in some part by the brain. In the most vivid descriptions of the syndrome, patients report seeing cartoon movies played out upon a screen in the region of their visual field where they have a blindspot as the result of eye or brain damage. It is one of the most compelling examples of perception involving the interplay of input from the eye and experiences generated by the brain. Although we may be tempted to dismiss such experiences as mere hallucinations, we will eventually understand that the ability to hallucinate in this way is an essential aspect of the brain's ability to see anything at all.

Visual mapping in the eye and brain

The third lesson of the migraine aura brings us to a discussion of other details of the human visual system. Many migraine sufferers are surprised to learn that their personal visual experiences can be linked directly to neural activity in particular locations in their brain. This information might be disconcerting because of our belief that we are highly individual, self-willed, and unique human beings. How dare someone else claim to understand our hallucinatory experience, never mind being able to predict its neural location with precision?

The diagram in Figure 2.4a illustrates the concepts that are needed to understand this lesson. It is a diagram of some visual anatomy that we all share. Imagine staring straight ahead at an object, using both eyes. The center of gaze for each eye is aimed at a spot on the object that will form the imaginary reference point for the rest of this discussion. The object can first be sectored into four quadrants (using only your imagination, of course). It is important to label these quadrants because we are going to want to keep track of them as we discuss various parts of the brain

BOX 2.1

Seeing your own blindspot and filling it in

Background

Each of your eyes has a region at the back and slightly toward the nose that is completely insensitive to light. This region, called the *optic disc,* is the one place in the eye where all the nerves that register light and all the blood vessels that nourish the inner eye come together to make an orderly exit out of the fluid-filled rear chamber. Its location is shown in Figure 2.3a below.

You don't spontaneously notice this hole in your visual field because the blindspot corresponds to a different portion of the visual field in each eye. Thus the two eyes working together cover the entire visual field. To experience the blindspot, you must shut one eye and arrange to have a visual stimulus fall on the region of the visual field that corresponds to your blindspot.

Instructions

Close your right eye, and fix your gaze on the small black dot at the center of Figure 2.3b on the next page. Hold the book about 6 inches from your

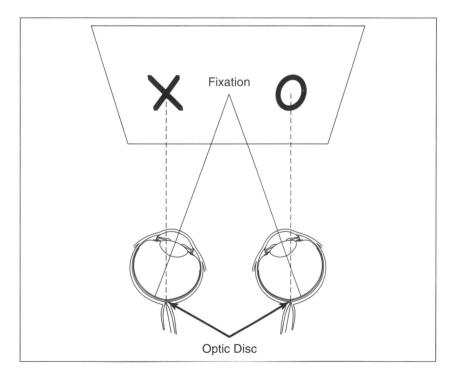

FIGURE 2.3   **(a)** Location of the optic disc.

FIGURE 2.3   (b) Blindspot exercise 1: X and O.

face. Move the book slowly toward your face and then away, always keeping your left eye fixed on the black dot. When the X falls on your blindspot,
it will disappear from your sight and you will have found the blindspot in
your left eye. You can find the blindspot in your right eye by closing your
left eye and repeating the procedure until the O disappears from view.

Now close one of your eyes and move your gaze to the black dot below
(Figure 2.3c), holding the book at the same distance that you used to locate
the blindspot in the previous exercise. What do you see when the gap in
one of the bars falls onto your blindspot?

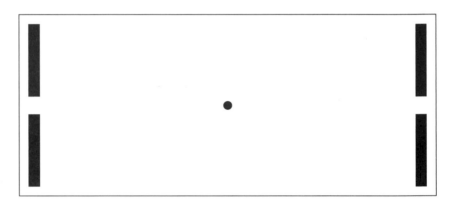

FIGURE 2.3   (c) Blindspot exercise 2: bars.

Repeat the procedure for Figure 2.3d below, using your left eye (your right
eye must be closed). Hold the book so that the white disc at the center of
the middle donut falls on your blindspot. What do you see?

FIGURE 2.3   (d) Blindspot exercise 3: donuts.

> **Analysis**
>
> Most observers do not report seeing the gap in the bars or the hole in the center donut. Instead, they report that the bars seem to be continuous through the blindspot region and that a solid disc appears among the donuts. Both perceptions are evidence that the brain can generate experiences that correspond to a location in space, even in the absence of direct sensory input from that region of space.

that are responsive to the light reflected from the object. We could label the visual field quadrants as upper-left, upper-right, lower-left, and lower-right, for instance, but I suggest using the simpler labels of visual quadrants, 1, 2, 3, and 4, as shown in Figure 2.4.

Light travels in a straight line from all points in the visual field and passes through the small transparent opening at the front of the eye called the *pupil*. Because the eyes are filled with transparent fluid and are roughly spherical, those light rays can reach the back of each eye, where the light comes into contact with light-sensitive neurons, called *receptors*, that are arrayed over the entire inner surface of the eye. This array is called the *retina*. Note that for each eye the image in visual quadrant 1 is projected onto a quadrant of the retina that is located opposite with respect to both up-down and left-right. The retinal quadrants are labeled a, b, c, and d in Figure 2.4a, so we can note that visual quadrant 1 maps onto retinal quadrant d, visual quadrant 2 maps onto retinal quadrant c, and so on. The end result is that the entire visual field is projected onto the retina in a point-to-point fashion, with the image flipped upside down and mirror-reversed.

Each retinal receptor is connected to several other types of neurons inside the eye, which we will discuss in greater detail in later chapters, but for now we can note that the entire image is transported through neural signals from the eye to several sites in the brain. In each site a point-to-point mapping of the original image is preserved, although we will also see that these maps get segmented into discrete regions at some points and distorted by a stretching transformation at others. The phrase used for point-to-point correspondence is *topographic mapping*.

The long extensions of the neurons (called *axons*) that exit the eye form a tight bundle (called the *optic nerve*) that is similar to a densely packed modern communications cable that holds many individual fibers. Even though these more than one million fibers are tightly packed, they still maintain their organization such that when they eventually arrive at the brain, the topographic mapping of the image that was present in the retina is preserved. En route to the brain, however, one-half of the fibers take a detour. This is shown in Figure 2.4b at a location called the *optic chiasma*. Here those fibers representing the left half of each retina are sent to a brain region on the left side of the head, and the fibers representing the right half of each retina are sent to a region on the right. As a net result of this

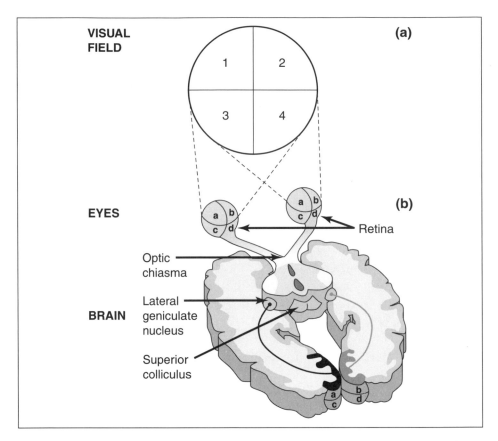

FIGURE 2.4 How the visual field maps onto the eye and brain. **(a)** Visual fields are left-right reversed and upside down on the human retina. **(b)** At the optic chiasma (where nerves from the two eyes come together), left visual field information is separated from right visual field information in the brain.

division, not only is the original image still upside down and mirror-reversed, but the left half of the visual field is represented in a part of the brain that is not even directly connected to the part of the brain representing the right half of the visual field. Figure 2.4b also points to two structures of the midbrain through which the neural signals pass on their way to the cortex: the lateral geniculate nucleus and the superior colliculus.

The most important location in the *cortex* (the convoluted gray matter on the surface of the brain) to which these signals are sent is a region at the very back of the brain called the *primary visual area,* or *area V1* for short. It is shown in Figure 2.5 in two different ways, first as an imaginary separation between the two cortical hemispheres (A) and second as an imaginary inflation of

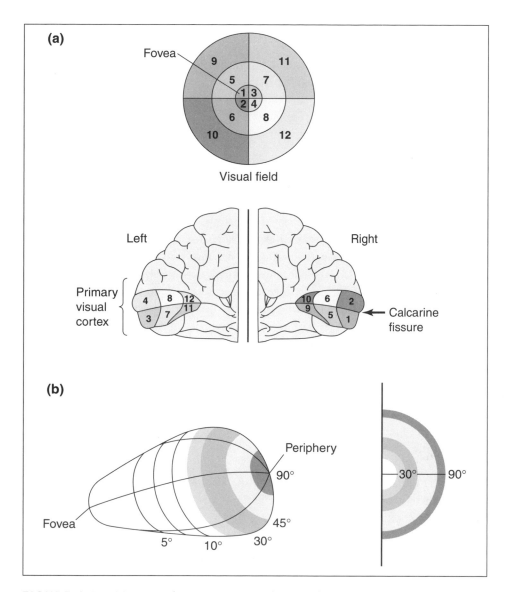

FIGURE 2.5 (a) A cortical area V1 preserves the visual field mapping of the eye such that spatial information is both left-right reversed and upside down. The numbers in the visual field areas correspond to the same numerical locations on the cortical surface. (b) The left visual field is mapped onto the cortical tissue of area V1 on the right side after an imaginary smoothing and inflating of the cortex to show the entire surface. Note how much more cortical tissue is devoted to the center of the visual field than to the periphery. The cortical region devoted to the central five degrees of the visual field is disproportionately represented.

the cortical surface for one hemisphere (B). Area V1 preserves the mapping seen in the retina such that points of light from the left visual field are represented by neurons in the right side of V1 and points from the right visual field are represented on the left side of V1. In addition, all the points from the lower visual field are represented by neurons in the upper portion of V1 and points from the upper visual field are represented in the lower portion of V1. An anatomical landmark on the cortex, the *calcarine fissure,* separates these upper and lower field representations.

If we think of the cortical surface of V1 as representing a map of the visual field, the map is centered at the point on the cortical surface that is closest to the back of the skull. Points on the cortical surface lying closer to the front of the head correspond to points in the visual field that are correspondingly farther away from the center of gaze. But in addition to being an upside-down and mirror-reversed map, it is distorted in another important way. The amount of cortical tissue devoted to each part of the visual field gets increasingly smaller as we move from the center of gaze (corresponding to the farthest rear portion of V1) to the visual periphery (corresponding to the most forward regions of V1). What this means in functional terms is that the neurons representing the central part of the eye are able to register and analyze much finer details than the neurons devoted to the outer reaches of peripheral vision. This relationship between visual acuity and retinal location is known as the *cortical magnification factor,* and its effects can be seen in Figure 2.6 (see color appendix).

Now that we have reviewed the main pathway taken by visual information from the eye to the brain, it is time to return to the story that prompted our diversion into anatomy. Recall that people experiencing an aura just prior to a migraine often have a blindspot (technically called a *scotoma*) surrounded by flashing or shimmering bars. These visual events have specific locations in the visual field. For instance, the scotoma may occur to the left and a little down from any object that is currently the object of fixation. This indicates that the disturbance includes a region of area V1 on the right side and above the calcarine fissure. The migraine sufferer can confirm that the blindspot has an origin in the brain, and not in the eye, by alternately shutting each eye while staring at the same location. The scotoma, and any accompanying shimmering, will occupy the same visual field location in each eye.

The precise region of the cortical disruption can now be established by carefully mapping out the extent of the blindspot in the visual field. For instance, someone with an aura can be given a large sheet of graph paper to examine and asked to indicate with a pencil which region of the graph paper appears to be blank when the eyes lock onto a central fixation marker. A fairly precise map of the cortical disturbance can be determined by measuring the location and size of this region and then using a little geometry to convert these units to degrees of visual angle, as described in Chapter 1. In the office of an ophthalmologist, an even more precise map can be obtained by having the patient report when he or she sees lights turn on inside a large hemispherical viewing screen. Those lights that the patient cannot detect correspond to the location of the cortical disturbance.

UP AND DOWN THE CORTICAL HIERARCHY

There are over 100 million neurons in the human cortex that respond when the eyes open to a visual scene. These neurons are distributed over large portions of the entire brain, with most estimates saying that more than one-half of the brain regions that researchers have probed in humans' closest biological relative, the monkey, are responsive to visual input. Figure 2.7 (see color appendix) shows the locations of the most intensively studied regions.

Each one of the millions of neurons can be described in principle by (1) its particular window on the visual field, and (2) a preference for certain visual properties within that window. The technical term for the preferences of each neuron is *receptive field*. The reason I say a neuron's receptive field can be described "in principle" is that there are far too many neurons in any given brain to exhaustively record each one's preferences. Figure 2.8 illustrates the procedure for mapping the receptive field of an individual neuron.

The anatomical hierarchy

There are two important ways in which we can determine how the many visually sensitive regions of the brain work together to accomplish vision. The first way is to establish the general flow of information from one brain region to the next by examining the anatomical connections. (The second way, by understanding the temporal hierarchy, is discussed in the next section.) The connection between individual neurons is technically called a *synapse,* but I will simply refer to each connection as a *step.* Regions separated by only a single step are more closely related; those separated by two or more steps are more distantly related. By examining between-area connections, researchers can draw flow diagrams of visual information in the cortex, such as Figure 2.9 (see color appendix) shows.

Neural signals from the eyes come into contact with cortical area V1 after passing through a lower brain structure known as the *lateral geniculate nucleus,* as we saw in Figure 2.4. Thus the main staging area for visual analysis in the cortex, area V1, is two steps away from the eye. From area V1, visual information is broadcast to a large number of regions, but these can be grouped into two general streams, as shown in Figure 2.10.

The *dorsal stream*—so called because it involves brain regions that lie on what anatomists think of as the "back" of the brain—consists of topographic maps of the visual field in which individual neurons are sensitive to visual information

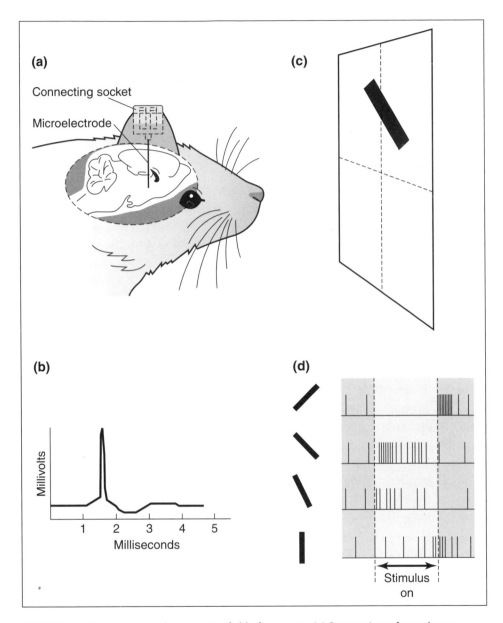

FIGURE 2.8   Mapping the receptive field of a neuron. **(a)** Surgery is performed on an animal to insert a tiny glass tube filled with saltwater, called a *microelectrode,* into the body or axon of a neuron in a region believed to be visually sensitive. **(b)** The continuous changes in electrical activity are displayed on a viewing screen in which voltage (millivolts) is shown over time (milliseconds). **(c)** Visual stimuli (in this case, bars) are presented to the animal in an attempt to elicit a change in the electrical activity of the neuron. **(d)** The response of an orientation-selective visual neuron to four different bars. The differences in response while the bars are presented (over a few seconds) indicate that the cell is tuned to a left-leaning vertical bar.

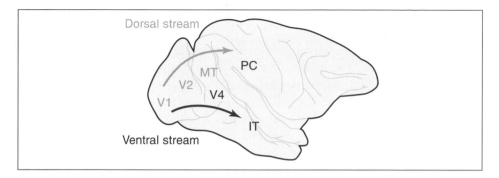

FIGURE 2.10 Locations of the dorsal and ventral visual streams in the cerebral cortex in the monkey.

about movement, spatial location, and actions that might be taken in response to the information, such as eye, limb, and body movements. The *ventral stream*—a term that refers to regions lying along the "belly" of the brain—consists of additional topographic maps that are sensitive to objects' shape, color, texture, meaning, and use.

An important pattern underlies the sensitivity of neurons in each successive step of information flow in these two streams. When researchers examine single neurons in these maps by using sophisticated techniques of electrical recording and brain imaging, two trends become apparent. First, neurons at each step are progressively more sophisticated in the kinds of visual attributes to which they respond. For example, whereas ganglion neurons in the eye respond to small spots of light in highly specific visual field locations, neurons in area V1 respond most vigorously to edges and bars of particular orientations, and neurons even higher in the ventral stream hierarchy respond most vigorously to particular objects such as faces, buildings, and cars.

Second, and equally important, neurons at each step respond to their preferred stimulus over progressively larger regions of the visual field. So whereas neurons in area V1 usually respond to edges within a window of the visual field that is a small fraction of a degree of visual angle, neurons in the temporal cortex usually respond to their preferred stimulus over a window that may be as large as one-quarter to one-half of the entire visual field.

These two trends—of increasing sophistication of response and increasing size of the receptive field with each step—are often called the *hierarchy of visual processing*. This phrase is appropriate because it captures the idea that larger and more complex perceptions are built from smaller and simpler elements of sensation in the brain. However, it is important to remember that this initial hierarchy of vision is only part of the story. If visual processing were complete with this forward sweep of processing—"up the hierarchy," so to speak—our visual systems would be severely handicapped.

One of the problems would involve not knowing precisely where a detected object was located in our visual field. The confusion would occur because the neurons that encode the interesting properties of the object have large receptive field windows, so at that level the detected object could be anywhere within a large region. Another problem would involve not being able to take our expectations into account about where to look for information and what we are likely to see there; our perceptions would be dictated entirely by the new information coming up the hierarchy from the eyes without any regard for the knowledge stored in higher-level regions of the brain. A final problem would involve not being able to coordinate our perceptions of objects with the actions we intend to perform on them because the neurons in the dorsal visual stream, which are specialized for determining *where* things are, would not be in communication with neurons in the ventral stream, which are specialized for determining *what* things are.

For these reasons, we must also consider the other way of determining how the visually sensitive regions of the brain work together. This is evident when we draw a diagram of visual information flow based on the time at which information presented to the eyes reaches various cortical regions. Figure 2.11 (see color appendix) presents such a diagram.

The temporal hierarchy

Recordings made from single neurons, measuring the time it takes for signals to reach various regions in the monkey cortex, indicate that neurons in the middle temporal area, or MT (part of the dorsal stream), and the frontal eye fields, or FEF (an area in the frontal lobes), receive signals at about the same times as neurons in area V1. The fastest recorded signals come in at about 40 milliseconds, which means that each step from the eye to the brain has taken about 10 milliseconds. The chapters that follow will explore in greater detail the two steps within the eye (receptor to bipolar cells to ganglion cells) and the two steps from the eye to area V1 (ganglion cells to lateral geniculate nucleus to V1). This turns out to be about as fast as neurons can be expected to pass information, physiologically speaking, since it takes about 10 milliseconds for a neuron to fire again immediately after it has been active.

What is surprising about this news, from the perspective of the cortical anatomical connections, is that two cortical areas considerably farther along in the anatomical hierarchy than area V1 are activated just as early as it is. The explanation is that there is more than one neurological road to the visual brain. In addition to the ganglion cells that send signals to the lateral geniculate nucleus (see Figure 2.4b), other ganglion cells send signals to another lower brain structure called the *superior colliculus*. In fact, there are two such structures, one on each side of the brain, not too far from the lateral geniculate nucleus, and these structures are themselves connected to one another with additional neurons. The superior colliculi are of considerable interest in their own right, and I will discuss them in greater detail in later chapters. For now, it is important to know that they send signals to areas MT and FEF and are critically important in the control of eye movements. A fair way to summarize this information is to say that at the earliest possible time, physiologically speaking, different brain regions are simultaneously receiving signals with regard to *where* new information is and, in a rudimentary sense, also receiving information about *what* that information is.

A second factor leading to differences between the visual hierarchies derived from studies of anatomy and those derived from studies of the time at which regions are active is the existence of two different kinds of ganglion cells in the retina: large, or *magno,* neurons; and small, or *parvo,* neurons. The distinction is preserved through the lateral geniculate nucleus and in area V1, where the two cell types occupy different layers. I will say more about the two cell types later, but for now I will note that the magno cells conduct signals much more quickly than the parvo cells. Thus brain regions that are fed primarily by magno neurons—which include the superior colliculus, most regions in the cortical dorsal stream, and some regions in the frontal lobe—receive their information well before regions fed primarily by parvo neurons. In fact, certain layers in area V1 are fed almost exclusively by magno neurons, so those layers receive input well before other layers that receive primarily parvo neural input.

On the basis of such considerations, vision scientists hypothesize that certain regions of the brain consistently receive updated information from the eyes more rapidly than other regions of the brain. We can identify the dorsal stream with more rapid updating and the ventral stream with slower updating. However, after about 100 milliseconds (that is, one-tenth of a second), all visually sensitive regions of the brain have been updated.

But visual processing by no means ends with this first forward sweep of information up the hierarchy, which we can call *feedforward processing.* Two other important kinds of connections must be identified. *Horizontal processing* refers to neurons communicating with one another at the same level in the hierarchy or even within the same anatomical region, such as the horizontal and amacrine cells in the retina that we will discuss in Chapter 4. *Feedback processing* refers to neural connections from regions higher in the anatomical hierarchy flowing down to lower regions.

Dynamic receptive fields

The important role of horizontal and feedback processing is evident when researchers examine the behavior of a neuron's receptive field over time. One very important feature of an individual neuron's behavior is that it continues to be active even after no new information is received from lower regions in the hierarchy. Box 2.2 will enable you to experience the effects of this continued activity.

For example, in the first 100 milliseconds of recording from a single neuron in area V1, the neuron will respond only to very simple visual properties, such as an edge at a particular orientation, and only when that property is in a small exclusive region of the visual field. This is called the *classical receptive field* of the neuron, or cRF. However, shortly after 100 milliseconds, the same neuron will begin to respond to visual properties that are well outside that same region and to much more complex visual properties. This behavior reflects the action of horizontal and feedback processes arriving at the same neuron. The neuron can now be said to possess a dynamical receptive field, in that the neuron's behavior varies depending on the time and the immediate spatial context.

An important feature of neurons that continue to be active after they have stopped receiving new information from lower brain regions is that they do more than act as simple pattern detectors. Although they may be doing nothing more than this on the first forward sweep of processing, in later stages of processing they may contribute to analyses of entirely different visual properties. For example, neurons in area V1 have been shown to respond to simple straight edges in the first 100 milliseconds and then to respond to the presence of a surface whose edges lie far outside the classical receptive field of those neurons.

Some neurons in the ventral stream seem to act as simple face detectors in the first 100 milliseconds and later respond selectively, depending on whether the face has a specific emotional expression or corresponds to a particular individual. In the parietal area, which is part of the dorsal stream, similar dynamic changes occur in the receptive fields of individual neurons. Early responses are typically based on highly specific stimuli occurring in certain visual field locations, whereas later responses are selective for perceptual and motor decisions made with respect to those stimuli. Figure 2.12 illustrates a dynamic receptive field for several neurons in area V1.

Recent research has begun to explore the origin of the later influences on the receptive field. Research with monkeys involves rapidly cooling certain brain regions to render them temporarily inactive while researchers study the behavior of neurons in a lower region. In research with humans, this can be done with transcranial magnetic stimulation (TMS). The procedure generates a short-lived, highly localized, and powerful change in the magnetic field close to the scalp. It briefly creates chaos in the neural activity in the region of the cortex closest to the magnet. When TMS stimulation is applied to area V1 simultaneously with the presentation of a visual stimulus, perception of the stimulus can be severely disrupted. This is not surprising because the TMS signal wreaks havoc with the normal neural processes required to create a perception. More telling, a TMS signal presented 100 to 200 milliseconds after the stimulus also disrupts perception. The timing of the latter effect suggests

BOX 2.2

Experiencing the effects of visible persistence

Here are three enjoyable ways to experience the effects of neurons that continue to be active after a stimulus has been turned off.

Inexpensive animation

Do you recall drawing simple moving cartoons when you were a child? Perhaps an adult you knew then would try to amuse you by making two similar drawings, placing the drawings on top of one another, rolling up the top page around a pencil, and then simulating repetitive motion in the pictures by rolling the pencil back and forth. You can achieve a similar effect by flipping smoothly through the pages of a notebook with your thumb. Make a drawing on each page that is identical to the previous drawing, with the exception that the location of the object or object part that you want to see in motion differs from one page to the next. Flipping through a series of these drawings at the right speed can create a vivid illusion of motion. Cartoonists and movie makers call this *animation.*

The rubber pencil

Hold a standard pencil between your thumb and first finger near the eraser so that it lies horizontally with respect to your eyes. Begin by waving the pencil up and down slowly, using only motion in your elbow. Now loosen your grip on the pencil, without letting it go, but continue to wave the pencil slowly. What does the pencil look like while it is waving in this way?

How many fingers?

Hold up one finger and wave it back and forth quickly in front of your face. As you wave it back and forth, ask yourself how many fingers there appear to be. Now hold up two fingers and wave them in the same way. Do the same for three fingers. Is your ability to see the actual number of fingers being held up becoming more difficult? Try this test on a friend or two who are willing to open their eyes only after you have place your hand in motion in front of their eyes. Can you fool them?

Analysis

Each illusion depends on *visible persistence,* the perceptual experience associated with neural activity that continues after a stimulus has moved on the retina or disappeared from view. In some instances this continued activity is an annoyance, as when we try to discriminate the detailed shape of an object in motion. At other times it aids perception, as when we can see motion from a series of still pictures. The feedback processes in the brain use visible persistence to sustain and even alter the perception of an object after it has moved or disappeared, helping to generate a smoothly continuous visual experience.

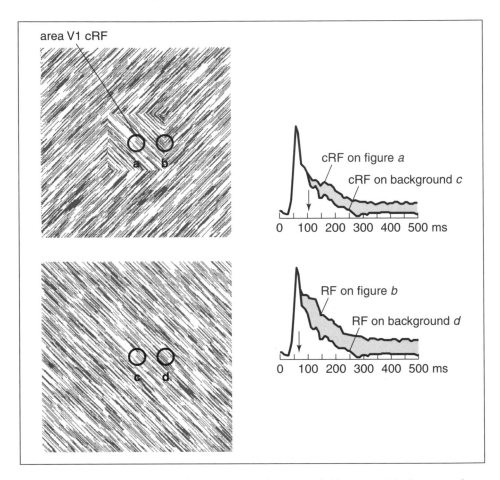

FIGURE 2.12   An example of a dynamic visual receptive field in action. The locations of two classically defined receptive fields (cRF) for neurons in area V1 are shown superimposed on two textured surfaces. Locations *a* and *b* are on a surface that includes a "figure" (the small square surface defined by a difference in texture orientation). Locations *c* and *d* are on a surface that contains only "background" texture. The average activity of area V1 neurons appears in the two panels on the right. Following the onset of the texture, neurons for each of the four receptive fields become active within 50 milliseconds. Even though locations a and c have physically identical information (texture elements slanting toward the left), by 80 to 115 milliseconds the locations on the texture-defined surface (*a,b*) are more active than the ones on the background (*c,d*).

that perceptual awareness cannot be based on the feedforward sweep of activity alone; rather, it requires some degree of feedback processing.

In almost every chapter that follows in this book, we will return to the important role played by horizontal and feedback processing in perception. For now, the most important lesson is that visual processing in the brain is always a two-way street. What we see is almost always based on a combination of signals: those generated by the external patterns of light on the retina, and those generated by processes internal to the brain.

VISION WITHOUT SOME PARTS OF THE BRAIN

Some of the most important clues about the roles of specific brain regions in vision come from the "natural experiments" that occur when people suffer brain damage. These are often tragic and life-changing events for the people afflicted, but they constitute valuable evidence for vision researchers. In fact, the careful study and documentation of brain-damaged individuals beginning almost 150 years ago enabled researchers to determine that the loss of function in certain brain regions was much more detrimental to vision than similar loss in other regions. They also learned that the nature of the visual impairment varied according to the location of the brain injury. Ironically, the introduction of new technology—namely, high-velocity bullets in the Russo-Japanese War and World War I—made it possible to document the links between discrete lesions in the brain and the visual impairments that resulted.

In this section we will consider several case studies of individuals with damage in visually sensitive brain areas in order to illustrate the importance of various brain regions to vision. As presented here, each case study describes a composite fictional character, but they are all based on case reports in the neuropsychological literature. As you read, it is important to remind yourself that with only one exception (Charles Bonnet syndrome), none of the individuals described had the slightest impairment in the function of his or her eyes. The blindness described in each case was entirely based in the brain. For this reason, some of their conditions have been labeled *psychic blindness, cortical blindness,* or *visual agnosia.* Despite the continued appeal of these terms to some people, I will avoid these labels because they do not describe the more detailed links that we now know to exist between the region of damage and the particular kind of vision that is lost or spared.

Blindsight

Dan had surgery in his early thirties to remove a large tangled mass of enlarged blood vessels in his right primary visual cortex. This mass of tissue had caused excruciating headaches when he was a teenager. The headaches were often foreshadowed by a visual experience similar to a migraine aura, including an oval "gray" blindspot on the left side of his visual field that was surrounded by flashing lights. The headaches themselves would begin with a bout of vomiting and could last for up to two days. By the time Dan was in his twenties, he was having one or two episodes every month. He also had a permanent scotoma, a region in his lower left visual field that was completely insensitive to small flashes of light.

Dan's surgery was considered a success because it relieved him of the awful headaches. However, it had involved removing most of his cortical area V1 on his right side. The predictable consequence was that Dan had no experience of any visual events that occurred to the left of where his eyes were fixating at any given moment. This is illustrated in Figure 2.13. In order to see an object on that side, Dan had to look to the extreme left side of the object so that its image would be projected onto his preserved right visual field. But even this was a compromise because most of the object had to be viewed in the near periphery of his visual field, where his acuity was not as sharp. Fixating at the center of the object caused the left half of it to disappear once again.

Dan's case was especially useful as a natural experiment because it enabled researchers to compare within the same individual both a fully functioning area V1 (in the left hemisphere) and an almost entirely excised area V1 (in the right hemisphere). Cases like Dan's are exceptionally useful for behavioral scientists because comparisons within the same individual eliminate one of the most troubling complications of research, namely, uncontrolled differences among individuals. Dan's performance on standard tests of visual function, such as detecting small spots of light flashed unpredictably in his visual field, revealed that he was indeed blind for all practical purposes in his entire left visual field.

However, Dan's inability to report the presence of light flashes on the left side did not mean that he had lost all visual function in that field. One of the first clues that some function remained came from an examination of his eye movements in response to the flashes. Even though Dan reported seeing nothing, his eyes explored the regions in which the flashes occurred to a degree that was well above the lucky guesses he might be making with his eyes. When researchers asked Dan to point with his finger to the locations of the flashes, he laughed because it seemed like a bizarre and somewhat cruel request. How could he point to something he could not see? Nonetheless, Dan's pointing accuracy was almost as good in his "blind" left visual field as it was in his sighted right visual field.

The researchers then began asking Dan to make guesses about the identity, orientation, and texture of simple shapes. Although on any given trial he was unable to say whether anything was appearing in his left visual field, his guessing accuracy was well above the chance level of 50 percent when he had to choose between only two alternatives. For example, he guessed correctly that an X rather than an O was appearing, even though he did not always guess correctly that something was actually appearing. When Dan learned of his excellent performance on this forced-choice task, he was astonished. Such a high level of accuracy did not coincide with his perceptual experience.

Both the impaired vision and the spared function associated with selective removal of Dan's cortical area V1 reveal important aspects of this region's role in vision. The lack of visual experience that accompanies removal of area V1 suggests,

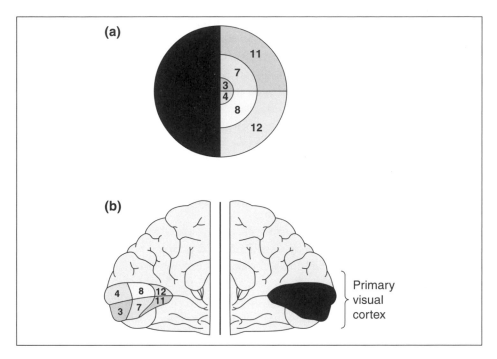

FIGURE 2.13 **(a)** An illustration of the regions of the visual field in which Dan is "blind," as far as his visual experiences are concerned. **(b)** The region of Dan's visual cortex (area V1) that was removed by surgical means to eliminate his debilitating headaches. The number in the visual field areas correspond to the same numbered locations on the cortical surface.

first, that not all parts of the brain are equally involved in conscious perception. For some reason, even though brain regions other than area V1 are receiving signals from the eyes (both from the spared left area V1 and from the collicular pathway from the eyes), they alone are not capable of providing Dan with a visual experience.

Indeed, because of cases such as Dan's, some researchers have been tempted to attribute awareness to the activity of the neurons in this brain region. But this interpretation is likely shortsighted because it considers only the feedforward sweep of visual processing in the brain. An alternative interpretation is that the lack of conscious experience can be attributed to the interruption of normal feedback processing. When a healthy brain is functioning normally, higher cortical areas can be in close and continuous contact with area V1. The surgical removal or lesioning of area V1 breaks this loop. Cortical regions beyond area V1 in the anatomical hierarchy will still be fed by signals from the superior colliculus and the lateral geniculate nucleus to cortical visual regions. Yet these cortical regions will no longer be able to set up ongoing feedback circuits (technically called *recurrent loops*) with a deactivated area V1.

The sparing of some visual function in the absence of a functioning area V1 is the reason for labeling Dan's condition as *blindsight*. The visual functions that are spared inform the question of how well other regions can perform on their own when area V1 has been taken out of the system. The very well preserved system for the control of visually guided action, seen in Dan's systematic eye and arm movements, indicates that the visual control of action is not entirely dependent on area V1. This reflects the importance of the "other" path of vision from the eye to the brain—the one that goes from the superior colliculus to the visual maps of the dorsal stream and the frontal cortical regions that support vision for action. Research with animals, in which lesions of restricted size can be made precisely, indicate that the removal of area V1 has little effect on dorsal stream processing but greatly impairs ventral stream processing.

One of the frustrating aspects of the selectively spared visual function in blindsight is that it doesn't appear to be of much use to people like Dan in their everyday world. It would be gratifying to help Dan and others like him to get in touch with their spared, even if unconscious, visual functions. This might enable them to interact with objects—such as picking up a fork on the left side of their plate—even though they would not consciously see those objects. Unfortunately, so far this seems not to be possible, at least for the performance of intentional actions. However, it is possible that the preserved function is important in the largely unconscious processes involved in walking and avoiding obstacles. Much more research needs to be done in this area.

What does the condition of blindsight imply for the visual functioning of an intact, healthy brain? One interesting possibility is that it might provide an explanation for some of the mysterious experiences we all have from time to time. For example, you may have felt that you were being watched while engrossed in some other activity. When you examined your larger visual field, perhaps by moving your gaze to the likely location, sure enough, someone was staring at you. The condition of blindsight suggests that it is indeed possible for some regions of the visual brain to process visual input without making it available to the conscious processes. A more mundane and more practical implication is that the processes of blindsight are at work every time we move rapidly and appropriately without even "thinking about it." Consider this the next time you drive a car or play a sport requiring rapid coordination of eye and limb.

Neglect and extinction

Naomi was nearly eighty years of age and living in a nursing home when she suffered a stroke caused by a clot in one of the arteries to her brain. Naomi never lost consciousness during this event and in fact was unaware that anything unusual had happened until her friends noticed some odd behavior. Naomi seemed to have difficulty finding objects on her left side. For instance, she would use the utensils on the right side of her plate when eating, but she wouldn't touch those on the left side. Often she would complain that her portions of food were very small and that she was still hungry after a meal, even though she had only eaten the food on the right side of her plate. Visitors who approached from her left side would go unnoticed, whereas visitors who approached from the right would be greeted warmly.

When a neuropsychologist evaluated Naomi, he noted first that she was well educated and very articulate. She told him she had worked as a university librarian for many years prior to retirement. When the neuropsychologist asked whether she would consent to a few simple pencil and paper tests, she warmly agreed. First he asked her to copy some simple line drawings of shapes and common objects. Naomi's drawings were faithful reproductions of the right side of each object, but the left side of her drawings were severely shrunken in horizontal extent or omitted entirely. When the neuropsychologist asked Naomi to place a pencil mark through each line on a page containing many randomly oriented line segments, she began by ticking off the lines closest to the right edge. When she had marked about half of the lines, working her way from right to left, she handed the page back to the neuropsychologist, a little annoyed that he had given her such simple tasks. Throughout the testing session Naomi and the neuropsychologist had a lively discussion on topics ranging from current events to life in a university setting. As far as the neuropsychologist was concerned, Naomi showed no signs of senility.

Neglect of one-half of visual space, also called *unilateral* or *hemispatial neglect,* such as Naomi demonstrates, is a common neurological impairment. For reasons we will explore, it is often the outcome of brain damage to the temporal-parietal junction of the brain on one side (see Figure 2.14), especially when the damage occurs in the right hemisphere. The severity of the condition can vary widely, with some individuals showing neglect of objects to one side only occasionally and only when they are stressed. More severely affected individuals not only ignore one side of the objects they encounter but also ignore one whole side of their own bodies. They may shave or apply makeup to only one-half of their face and may bump into doorways, tables, and wheelchairs that they encounter on one side. In the condition's most extreme form, some individuals even deny ownership of parts of their bodies on the neglected side. In fact, they regard the presence of "someone else's" arm or leg in the bed with them as an annoyance. This occurs most often for neglect of the left side of the body, since right parietal lobe damage is the most common trigger for the condition.

A different form of neglect is sometimes labeled *extinction*. It reveals itself when affected individuals are asked to report on objects that are presented concurrently in each visual field. For example, if the neuropsychologist holds her arms outstretched and wiggles a finger in the individual's visual periphery, he will see it. That is, the wiggling finger will be detected in both the visual field projecting to the damaged parietal region and the visual field projecting to the healthy parietal region. Yet when the neuropsychologist wiggles one finger on each hand at the

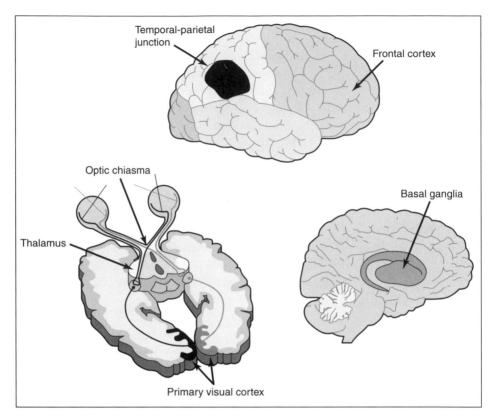

FIGURE 2.14   The typical site of a lesion for an individual with left side neglect is in the right hemisphere—specifically, the temporal-parietal junction, shown in black. Other brain regions associated with neglect are the frontal cortex, the thalamus, and the basal ganglia. In healthy individuals these brain regions constitute a large part of the network involved in the guidance of spatial attention.

same time so that both visual fields are stimulated, the individual will report seeing only one finger, failing to see the wiggling finger on the side opposite to the site of the parietal lobe damage.

One of the most interesting features of neglect and extinction—and one that makes them quite different from blindsight—is that the affected individuals are largely unaware of their condition. Naomi does not experience a world like Dan's in which only half of it can be seen because of a visual impairment. Rather, Naomi is certain that the world is no larger than the one she can see. From the point of view of the neuropsychologist, Naomi no longer experiences all the visual space around her. The side of the world she "neglects" has for all intents and purposes ceased to exist.

The lesioned sites in the parietal cortex most commonly associated with neglect cluster around the darkened region shown in Figure 2.14. It is interesting that lesions centered just a few centimeters from this site in the upward direction do not cause complete neglect but are associated with related disorders, such as extinction and problems with visually guided reaching. However, sites that are far away from the parietal cortex have also been associated with neglect, as shown in Figure 2.14. This suggests that the deficits of attention seen in neglect are probably governed by a distributed network of brain regions.

How do the parietal lobe functions that are damaged in patients with neglect operate in the healthy brain? The brain regions that are involved appear to be critically important in what some researchers refer to as the "disengage" operation of attention. You may never have considered the possibility that every time your attention shifts from one part of a scene to another, your brain must undertake the effortful task of terminating the processing of the first part of the scene. Attending first to one object and then to another seems effortless for a healthy brain. But researchers can measure this process in several ways.

One way involves studying the behavior of an immature nervous system. When a human infant is around one month of age, he often exhibits a strange behavior that can cause both himself and his caretaker considerable worry. His eyes become locked onto a particularly strong vertical contour, such as the edge of a window frame or a stripe in some paneling. Even though the caretaker may rock the baby's head gently from side to side or the baby may move his own head, his eyes will not unlock their gaze from the vertical contour. At one month of age, this failure to disengage may be so complete that when left alone the baby stares at the same contour for many minutes. Most babies find this distressing and begin crying, a behavior that actually helps them unlock their gaze from the contour because it makes them close their eyes—or at least move their heads sufficiently so that the contour inadvertently moves outside the visual field. This tendency to be captured by strong contours is associated with the immature status of a baby's nervous system. In this context it is interesting to note that one of the least mature regions of the cortex at birth, and therefore one of the regions that undergoes the most development after birth, is the parietal lobe.

Another way to determine the importance of parietal lobe functioning in everyday shifts of attention involves taking brain scans of study participants in the lab performing a simple visual detection task. The task is illustrated in Figure 2.15. When participants make a button press to indicate the onset of a target shape, the speed of their response depends on whether they have already been attending to the box in which the target disc appears or whether they must first switch their attention to the location of the target disc. Brain images in the form of event-related potential (ERP) recordings and positron emission tomography (PET) scans indicate selective neural activity in the parietal lobes during this task, on the side opposite to the location of the target. These measurements confirm that switches in attention to the target location depend on neural activity in the parietal lobes.

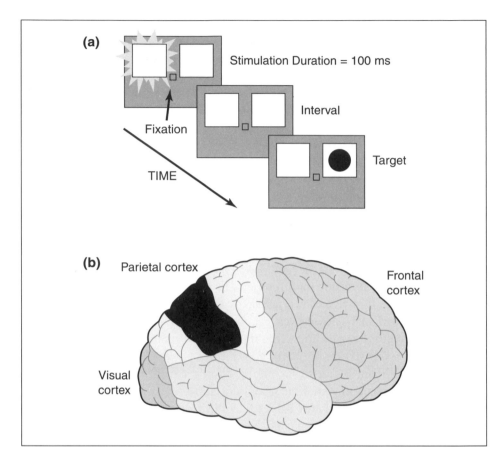

FIGURE 2.15   **(a)** The sequence of video screens in an experiment measuring participants' ability to rapidly switch attention from one object to another in a display. **(b)** The region of the cortex that is selectively active during the performance of a task requiring switches in spatial attention.

As in people with blindsight, it is important to ask whether individuals with neglect process the information on their neglected side at an unconscious level. Remember that in a pure case of neglect caused by a discrete lesion to the inferior posterior parietal cortex, as Figure 2.14 illustrates, other parts of the visual brain continue to operate as they did before the damage. Thus there is a fully functioning area V1, the maps in the ventral stream are intact, and the other pathway from the eye to the brain is operating—with the exception of its inputs to this region of the parietal cortex.

One group of researchers addressed this issue by having individuals with neglect report on the contents of their visual images (Bisiach & Luzzatti, 1978). They were asked to describe a famous piazza in Milan, Italy, that they all knew well. The critical part of the study was that they first had to imagine themselves standing at one end of the piazza and to report what they remembered about the scene. Consistent with their condition of right parietal damage, the study participants failed to report buildings and features of the piazza that would have been on their left side in the imagined scene. However, when the participants had to imagine themselves at the other end of the piazza before reporting their images, they failed to mention the buildings they had reported earlier and now described the buildings they had neglected earlier. This suggests that (1) the brain records the information that is neglected at some level, but that (2) the brain damage makes conscious access of that information very difficult.

There is also more direct evidence of unconscious processing of the neglected information. One group of researchers showed an individual with neglect a picture of a pair of identical houses vertically aligned along the center of gaze (Marshall & Halligan, 1988). The study participant correctly reported that the houses looked the same. However, the researchers had drawn flames on the left side of one of the houses, making it look as though the house was on fire. Because the participant had right parietal damage, she gave no verbal indication of seeing the flames. Yet when the researchers asked which house she would rather live in, she repeatedly chose the house without the flames. The researchers concluded that some part of her visual processes knew about the fire and could help to influence her active choice, but that those processes could no longer inform those parts of her brain that gave rise to conscious visual experiences. Other studies have shown repeatedly that actions can be influenced by stimuli presented in the neglected visual field, even though the participant is unable to orient his or her eyes and head toward those stimuli or to report their existence.

Balint syndrome

Robert, an elderly person like Naomi, suffered a stroke that damaged his parietal lobe. However, in Robert's case the damage occurred in both hemispheres of the brain and was more widespread, including some regions of the occipital cortex that bordered the parietal lobe. After the stroke, Robert needed nursing home care because he was no longer able to reliably reach out and grasp objects in his immediate environment. This made it impossible for him to accomplish dressing, daily hygiene, and meal preparation on his own. To compound this serious impairment in visually guided actions, Robert no longer showed interest in the events going on around him, sometimes sitting for extended periods staring at a single common object such as a desk lamp or a shoe on the floor.

A neuropsychologist who visited Robert noted that he seemed unable to change his fixation from an object once his gaze was locked onto it (similar to the one-month-old infant we discussed earlier). Also, like the cases of hemispatial neglect we discussed, Robert ignored many of the visual events around him except for the one object that had captured his gaze. But he was also different from the neglect cases in that he could fix his gaze on these single objects in either visual field. Yet at the same time he ignored all the other objects in each visual field. This exclusive and prolonged attention to single objects in the visual field is the hallmark of Balint syndrome.

Another profound impairment that Robert suffered was a general disorientation in terms of objects in his immediate visual field and the locations of other rooms in the nursing home. For instance, Robert had a great deal of difficulty finding his way to the dining room on his own, and he could not recognize photographs of locations that were very familiar to him prior to the stroke. When he was tested formally, by being asked to report the color and identity of two large letters on a computer screen, he often combined the color of one letter with the name of the other. In fact, he was often unable to indicate which letter was on the right as opposed to the left side of the screen. It is interesting that these are the kinds of errors healthy normal individuals make when their attention is overloaded or misdirected at the time a brief display is presented. We will discuss this more in later chapters, but for now you can get a sense of the difficulty involved in the accurate binding of visual features by following the exercises in Box 2.3.

Tests of unconscious visual processing in individuals with Balint syndrome reveal that they, too, process much more of the visual world than they are aware. For instance, participants in one study were shown color squares, one at a time on the screen, and asked to report the color of each in turn. Since this task involves a single object on the screen at a time, they were able to do it accurately. However, without telling the participants, the experimenters included some trials in which there was a second square in a different color from the central one. Although the participants were unaware that a second square had been presented, the time it took them to name the color of the central square was longer than on trials on which the second, unseen square was the same color. Similar effects have been reported when study participants with Balint syndrome are asked to name pictures of objects. In this case, participants are sometimes able to report the identity of two objects, but only if they are closely related in meaning.

People with Balint syndrome provide a window on the issue of whether it is possible to perceive more than one object at a time. Robert clearly cannot. Is perception in healthy individuals free of these limits, enabling them to attend to several objects at a time, or are healthy individuals simply more efficient at rapidly switching attention among objects in the visual field? We will discuss these questions further in Chapter 5.

Cerebral achromatopsia

Michael suffered an unexpected stroke when he was in his thirties. The stroke left him with a variety of long-lasting visual impairments, including very poor peripheral vision in his upper visual field and trouble recognizing some of his friends on

BOX 2.3
_____

Searching for feature combinations

Instructions

Each of the boxes in Figure 2.16 (see color appendix) contains a large number of items: pairs of colored bars in (a), and "chicken part" combinations in (b). In a typical visual search task, conducted to study the binding of visual features and object parts into the perception of whole objects, study participants are first shown the target search image and then asked to find this object in the large display as rapidly as they can. For the two search displays below, the target images are shown at the top of each display. The target is a "vertical green bar on top" in (a) and a "whole chicken" in (b). Find the target in each of the search displays now. How difficult was it to find them?

Analysis

When this experiment is conducted in the laboratory, search time is measured with millisecond accuracy and the main factor that is varied is the number of potential target items to be inspected. The result for complex combinations such as these is that search time increases by 50 to 100 milliseconds for each additional item placed into the display. Thus even though participants know precisely what they are looking for, the target does not leap immediately into their awareness as soon as it appears on their retina. They must inspect each item briefly and in turn until they find the target. This research finding indicates that the perception of objects does not occur spontaneously and in parallel all over the visual field. Object perception requires the effortful mental biding together of relevant parts and features, even when all the parts and features lie before our eyes.

Pssst . . .

Were you aware that there were actually two targets in each display? If you didn't see both of them the first time, look again. Your failure to see both targets the first time means you didn't mentally bind together all the features and parts of each object.

the basis of vision alone. It is interesting to note that as soon as these friends would speak, he had no trouble identifying them on the basis of their voices. He was also frustrated that the names and uses of common objects would sometimes elude him. But the change in vision that bothered him most was that the world no longer appeared to be in color! He said it looked pale and washed out, as though he were seeing it through an old black-and-white television.

Clinical testing confirmed these reports. When Michael was asked to arrange a series of color chips that were carefully balanced in brightness, he could do no better than a random arrangement. In contrast to this poor performance on colored chips, he had no trouble arranging a similar series of chips that differed only in lightness, or gray level. He also had no trouble correctly answering questions about the colors of common objects, such as *What color is a banana?* Thus his problem was not one of finding the correct meanings or labels for color terms.

A neuropsychologist labeled Michael's condition *cerebral achromatopsia* and delivered the disappointing news that there was little chance his color vision would return. This prognosis was based on a long history of recorded cases of color blindness in the absence of any apparent retinal damage going back over one hundred years. In fact, these early reports are remarkable in how closely they resemble modern cases, even though at the time there was no ability to image the brain and tests of color vision were less refined. Some cases included individuals with achromatopsia in only half of the visual field (hemiachromatopsia). One case involved an accomplished artist who was able to produce rich renderings of the difference in appearance for the two sides of his visual field.

Brain scans revealed the site of Michael's stroke to be a fairly circumscribed area, in both hemispheres, that included the region shown in Figure 2.17b. Because this was the site of the stroke damage, neuropsychologists were not surprised that Michael's color impairment was accompanied by both an upper visual field scotoma and difficulty with face and object recognition. They had read reports of this constellation of impairments before and knew that the cortical region important in color vision was adjacent to both the area of V1 that maps the peripheral region of the upper visual field and the region that is important in face and object recognition.

In comparison to cases of "unexplained" color blindness reported in neurological journals fifty to one hundred years ago, modern diagnoses of achromatopsia benefit from clinical testing that can confirm conclusively that the condition is not caused by damage to the eye. When these individuals are tested for their ability to detect lights of various wavelengths, their responses follow the sensitivity of a normal eye containing three healthy cone types. That is, the threshold sensitivity peaks at three distinct places along the wavelength continuum, corresponding to the maximum sensitivity of the eye to these wavelengths. Yet despite this behavioral evidence of the response of a normal eye to light of different wavelengths, these individuals can say nothing about the color of the lights to which they are responding.

As with other impairments of vision caused by cortical damage, individuals with achromatopsia process more information about color than they are aware. We have already seen that their eyes process more color information than the brain can make available to consciousness, but there is also evidence that other parts of the brain are processing the color information. For example, in one study, participants with achromatopsia were able to see the motion of a striped pattern consisting of

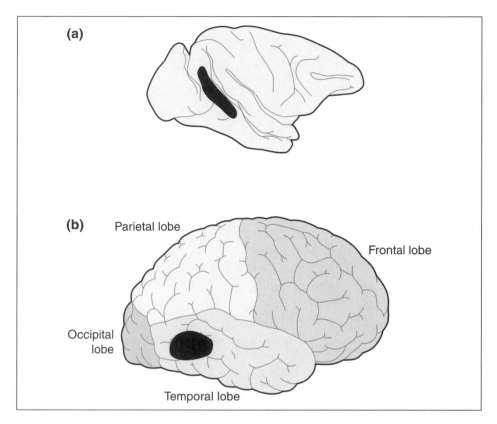

FIGURE 2.17   Region of the brain that when damaged tends to result in impaired color experiences in **(a)** monkey cortex and **(b)** similar area in human cortex.

differences in color. That is, even though they were unable to report seeing any color differences in the moving patterns, they were still able to discriminate the direction of motion in the patterns—even though the motion signal consisted of a difference in color, not luminance. This result indicates, at a minimum, that the color differences are being analyzed by some parts of the brain and that the signal is being sent to the centers responsible for the processing of motion. What clearly is not occurring in achromatopsia, however, is the neural processing required to support the experience of color.

Motion blindness

Linda had a stroke when she was in her forties that damaged cortical tissue in both of her cerebral hemispheres near the junction of the occipital, temporal, and parietal lobes. These regions are shown in Figure 2.18. There appeared to be no damage to the tissue in area V1. Neuropsychological testing revealed mild impairments

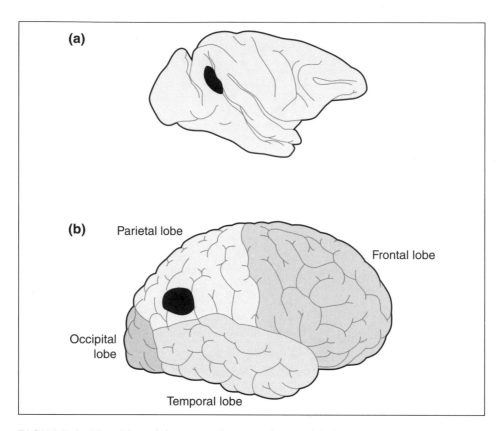

FIGURE 2.18   Bilateral damage to the tissue shown in black in **(a)** monkeys and **(b)** humans can render an individual blind to motion even though it spares other aspects of visual perception, including form and color perception.

in performing arithmetic calculations and in finding words for some common objects, but by far the most serious impairment was an almost complete inability to see objects in motion. As Linda described it, she now experienced a great deal of difficulty pouring a cup of coffee because the liquid appeared to be frozen in place, like a glacier. From one moment to the next, the cup seemed to flip from being empty to overflowing. Linda also described a difficulty in comprehending everyday conversation because the speaker's mouth seemed to be like a series of frozen snapshots. Crossing the street had become very dangerous because Linda was no longer able to distinguish cars that were moving from those that were standing still.

Tests of Linda's other visual functions showed normal color and depth perception, along with normal object and word recognition. Tests of motion perception in the modalities of touch (e.g., feeling a pencil move along her arm) and audition (e.g., judging the proximity of a car by listening to the change in sound) also revealed normal functions. Careful psychophysical tests of motion perception in all three dimensions showed that Linda was still able to discriminate the direction of motion in some simple displays, especially when the speeds were slow, but the most remarkable aspect of her case was the highly selective nature of her impairment for visual motion perception. This form of motion blindness is entirely cortical in origin and is sometimes called *akinetopsia*.

When the brain regions that are thought to be homologous to the one that was damaged in Linda's case are experimentally lesioned in monkeys, similar syndromes are induced. This region is called *middle temporal,* or MT, in monkeys. The neurons in this region are specialized for combining the motion signals from many smaller motion-sensitive receptive fields in area V1 in order to perform such visual functions as object motion perception, three-dimensional shape perception through motion, and the analysis of optic flow.

Charles Bonnet syndrome

James, a man in his fifties, had been experiencing a gradual loss of vision because of retinitis pigmentosa, a degenerative disease of the eye. This inherited disease causes the rod receptors in the eyes to die slowly, leading initially to night blindness and later, as the disease advances, to diminished peripheral vision. It is thought that the lack of normal input from the diseased rod receptors leads to the general decline over time in peripheral visual functioning.

As if this condition weren't enough for James to bear, imagine his fright one day when he began to see tiny people in storybook costumes acting out what appeared to be plays in his living room. His first thought was that he was becoming delusional, and because of this he was reluctant to discuss the experience with his doctor. He wondered whether some of his medicine was the cause or whether he might even have a more serious illness such as Alzheimer's disease. But the hallucinations continued, sometimes for several minutes at a time, so he finally mustered enough courage to ask his ophthalmologist what they might be.

The ophthalmologist told James that these sorts of hallucinations were not uncommon in people suffering from severe problems with sight. He also reassured James with the news that the very fact that James understood the difference between the people in the hallucination and the real objects in his visual world was a sign that the hallucinations were a byproduct of his advancing eye disease and not the harbinger of an unrelated senility disorder. In the case of hallucinations associated with mental illness, individuals have trouble telling the difference between their fantasies and reality. They often come up with tortured explanations for the things they are seeing that leave the hallucination and the reality hopelessly intertwined.

James learned later that his hallucinations indicated Charles Bonnet syndrome. This name gives credit to a Swiss philosopher of the 1700s who first documented these kinds of hallucinations in his grandfather, who had been partially blinded by cataracts. Since that time many cases have been recorded. The diagnostic criteria now include the presence of complex hallucinations along with clear insight regarding which aspects of one's experience are derived from the hallucination as opposed to the eyes. Another important aspect of the diagnosis is that the affected individuals do not suffer from hallucinations in any of their other senses.

Once people with Charles Bonnet syndrome understand that their hallucinations are not a sign of mental illness, they rarely find them upsetting. In fact, some find them quite enjoyable, since it is a little like being able to watch a "picture-in-picture" version of a dream while being fully awake. Sitting quietly alone in a familiar environment, especially under low lighting conditions, seems to be optimal for eliciting the hallucinations. A change in body position or lighting can be enough to make the pictures disappear.

Charles Bonnet syndrome gives us an insight into the workings of a fully functioning visual system, at least at the level of the brain, that is handicapped by a set of eyes that are no longer being informed by the external world in the way they once were. The existence of hallucinations is evidence that the feedback processes of the brain are capable of generating their own visual experiences, ones that seem every bit as vivid as the experiences that begin in the eyes. Just like visual experiences induced by the migraine aura or by floaters in the eyes, the internally generated perceptions can be easily distinguished from the perceptions derived from the external world in that they do not change consistently along with changes in the visual world. Rather, they enjoy an existence that is free from the constraints of ordinary sensory input. It is interesting that many people with Charles Bonnet syndrome report that the hallucinations stop spontaneously a year or so after they began. Perhaps it is the failure on the part of the brain to resolve the incongruity that leads to the abandonment of this short-lived experiment in self-generated perceptions.

IS IT ENOUGH?

If this is your first encounter with trying to understand your own brain, you may be reeling from trying to put together all the different stories you have read in this chapter. Is all this information really needed to understand how we see? However, if you have previously read other books about the relations between brain and behavior, you may be protesting that this chapter provides hardly enough background in neuroscience to launch into the study of how the eye and brain do their job in vision. Much more detail is needed.

Both reactions are justified. I share both of them myself. In fact, the field of vision science is caught on the horns of this dilemma. For instance, the longstanding tradition in psychophysics is to try to understand as much as possible by examining only the relations between physical stimuli and the resulting experiences in the study participant. In contrast to this functional approach is the emphasis placed on the structures of the eye and brain by practitioners of ophthalmology, neuropsychology, and neuroscience. Because this book attempts to bridge the two approaches to the study of vision, at least by way of introduction, the tension is going to be with us in every chapter.

You, the reader, will be encouraged to think about visual experiences and functions in every chapter, at the same time that you will be asked to consider the equipment that is available for performing these functions. If straddling this fence means that neither the "pure" psychophysicist nor the "pure" neuroscientist is entirely satisfied, so be it. For my part, I am going to emphasize the benefits of having even a little knowledge of what is traditionally viewed as the domain of the "other camp." More often than not, it seems that progress in vision science has occurred when scientists have peeked over the fences of their traditional disciplines into the domains of other, related ones.

FURTHER READING

Cavanagh, P., Hénaff, M-A., Michel, F., Landis, T., Troscianko, T., & Intriligator, J. (1998). Complete sparing of high-contrast color input to motion perception in cortical color blindness. *Nature Neuroscience, 1,* 242–247.

Farah, M. J. (2000). *The cognitive neuroscience of vision.* Malden, MA.: Blackwell.

Friedman-Hill, S. R., Robertson, L. C., & Treisman, A. (1995). Parietal contributions to visual feature binding: Evidence from a patient with bilateral lesions. *Science, 269,* 853–855.

Heywood, C. A., Wilson, B., & Cowey, A. (1987). A case study of cortical colour "blindness" with relatively intact achromatic discrimination. *Journal of Neurological and Neurosurgical Psychiatry, 50,* 22–29.

Kreiman, G., Koch, C., & Fried, I. (2000). Imagery neurons in the human brain. *Nature, 408,* 357–361.

Lamme, V. A. F. (2000). Neural mechanisms of visual awareness; a linking proposition. *Brain and Mind, 1,* 385–406.

Lamme, V. A. F., & Roelfsema, P. R. (2000). The distinct modes of vision offered by feedforward and recurrent processing. *Trends in Neuroscience, 23,* 571–579.

Meadows, J. C. (1974). Disturbed perception of colours associated with localized cerebral lesions. *Brain, 97,* 615–632.

Pomerantz, J. R. (1983). The rubber pencil illusion. *Perception & Psychophysics, 33,* 365–368.

Posner, M. I., & Raichle, M. E. (1994). *Images of mind.* New York: Scientific American Library.

Ramachandran, V. A. (1992, June). Compensation of the blind spot. *Scientific American.*

Ramachandran, V. S., & Blakeslee, S. (1998). *Phantoms in the brain: Probing the mysteries of the human mind.* New York: William Morrow.

Rizzo, M., Nawrot, M., & Zihl, J. (1995). Motion and shape perception in cerebral akinetopsia. *Brain, 118,* 1105–1127.

Sacks, O. (1992). *Migraine.* Berkeley: University of California Press.

Teunisse, R. J., Cruysberg, J. R., Hoefnagels, W. H., Verbeek, A. L., & Zitman, F. G. (1996, March 23). Visual hallucinations in psychologically normal people: Charles Bonnet's syndrome. *Lancet, 347,* 794–797.

Tootell, R. B. H., Hadjikhani, N. K., Mendola, J. D., Marrett, S., & Anders, M. D. (1998, May). From retinotopy to recognition: fMRI in human visual cortex. *Trends in Cognitive Sciences, 2,* 174–183.

Weiskrantz, L., Warrington, E. K., Sanders, M. D., & Marshall, J. (1974). Visual capacity in the hemianopic field following a restricted occipital ablation. *Brain, 97,* 709–728.

Zeki, S. (1990). A century of cerebral achromatopsia. *Brain, 113,* 1721–1777.

Zeki, S. (1993). *A vision of the brain.* Oxford, England: Blackwell Science.

3 COLOR

FUNDAMENTAL QUESTIONS

- In what way is "color" different in the world, in the eye, and in the brain?
- An object seems to change color under different colored lights; an object appears to be the same color under different colored lights: Which is the real illusion?
- How are colors organized differently at various places in our visual system?
- Why do all humans not see the same colors?
- When does the color of an object help us to recognize it?

WHY DOES THE SKY LOOK BLUE?

Why the sky looks blue is a question that puzzles children in many cultures as well as world-renowned scientists including physicists, physiologists, and psychologists. It is an excellent question to begin our discussion of color because a complete answer will introduce us to important background in three essential areas: the physics of light, the physiology of human vision, and the psychology of color experience.

Let's begin in the way we might in a typical high school science class. In that context, the question would probably be *Why is the sky blue?* Whether you think this is the same question as the one we began with depends on your view of vision. If you think human vision is a faithful and passive process of recording the physical conditions around us by using reflected light, then these questions are indeed the same. This is, after all, the common understanding of vision. If, however, you appreciate that human vision is an elaborate construction project undertaken to help individuals accomplish the subtasks of biological survival, then these are not the same questions at all. In fact, the blueness of the sky might be something that resides only in the sight and mind of an individual with a visual system similar to your own. The physical attributes of the sky—that is, the material properties that elicit the color blue in your experience—might in fact turn out to be completely described and understood without ever appealing to the color blue at all.

But rather than introducing too much complexity all at once, let's return to our high school science explanation of the sky's color. In that answer we could begin by noting some important physical characteristics of light. We could note that light is a form of electromagnetic energy and, as such, can vary in wavelength. As we learned in Chapter 1, human eyes are sensitive to this energy only over wavelengths ranging from about 360 to 780 nanometers (nm). We could also note that the behavior of light particles (photons) coming into contact with other particles in the air is predictable from the wavelength measurement of light. We could then examine some of the physical properties of the sky—that is, the air in the earth's atmosphere. We would find that air particles scatter and reflect short wavelength light to a greater extent than medium or long wavelength light. The longer wavelengths tend to pass by the air molecules with much less interference. This information would bring our answer to the point at which physics intersects with physiology: Short wavelength light is scattered by air particles to a greater extent than light of other wavelengths. But how do our eyes and brain derive "blue" from this phenomenon?

The high school answer at this point usually omits all discussion of physiology and appeals to a correlation that most humans can observe: Different wavelengths of light result in predictably different color experiences. As Isaac Newton demonstrated a few hundred years ago in Cambridge, England, light from the sun can be broken down into its wavelength components by using a prism. Newton used a prism made of glass; the same correlation can be seen in the natural prisms of water droplets in rainbows. Light passing through a medium that is denser than air (in this case, water droplets) is bent by an amount that is related to its wavelength. Short wavelength light bends the most, medium wavelength light bends less, and long wavelength light bends the least. When the light emerges from the prism, you see distinct bands of color with reds and oranges at the top, yellows and greens in the middle, and blues and violets toward the bottom. This is the evidence that links short wavelength light with the color blue, long wavelength light with the color red, and the intermediate wavelengths with the colors in between.

Newton's prism experiments provide a link between physics and our own experience that is consistent with what I have just said about the color of the sky. In terms of viewing both the rainbow and the sky, the color blue is associated with short wavelength light. Thus it is tempting to conclude that the sky looks blue because the air scatters more short wavelength light than light of other wavelengths. In general, we might even be tempted to conclude that our eyes and brain translate the physical property of light wavelengths into the experience of color. Red apples reflect a preponderance of long wavelength light to the eyes. Grass reflects mostly medium wavelength light. End of story, or is it?

Color vision is fascinating precisely because this answer to *Why is the sky blue?* is incomplete. For brevity, I will continue to call this the answer from high school science. It is incomplete not only because it bypasses all the physiological steps between the physical stimulus (short wavelength light) and the experience (blue); filling in those steps wouldn't be too hard if the mapping of wavelength to color experience were this straightforward. But it is also incomplete because the mapping among light, visual processing, and color experience is not simple at all. In the sections that follow, we will repeatedly encounter violations of a direct mapping between wavelength and color. These violations are the best clues to the construction project that we call color vision.

Color constancy: Superficial light and enduring surfaces

Examine the picture in Figure 3.1 carefully. It is a picture of a cylinder resting on a checkerboard surface. Light seems to be shining down from the upper left of the scene, as indicated by the shading on the cylinder and the shadow cast by the cylinder onto the checkerboard surface. Now here is the trick question: *How many different shades of gray do you see on the checkerboard surface?*

A hasty answer might be there are only two shades: a lighter gray and a darker gray. This answer would be correct if the question were *How many different colored paints were used in the actual construction of the checkerboard surface?* Clearly only two. But the question was *How many different shades of gray do you see?* In response to this hint, many people notice the effect of the shadow on the appearance of the checkerboard and acknowledge that there are really four different shades: a light gray and a dark gray in the nonshadowed regions, and a slightly darker light gray and a darker dark gray in the shadowed region. A really astute observer might even point to the shading at the edge of the shadow (technically called its *penumbra*) and claim to see more than four shades, but that's an unnecessary detail in order to understand the point I'm after.

The trick on your eye and brain is that there are really only *three* shades on the checkerboard surface: a light gray, a medium gray, and a dark gray. To help you understand this, although you probably still will not be able to see it, I have taken the three shades used for the checkerboard patches and placed them below the picture. I took the light gray from the nonshadowed light regions, the medium gray from the nonshadowed dark regions *and* from the shadowed light regions, and the dark gray from the dark gray patches in shadow. The illusion is that the light gray patch inside the shadow is precisely the same shade (as measured at your eye) as the dark gray patch outside the shadow. Yet they seem unquestionably different in appearance.

This illusion is an example of a color construction our visual system undertakes every time it evaluates color in the everyday world. The construction is that of *color constancy,* which is the ability to ignore the color of the ambient light in order to zero in on the true color of a surface. The picture in Figure 3.1 illustrates that

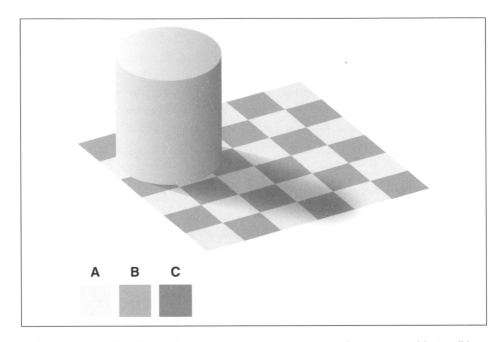

FIGURE 3.1   The illusion of color constancy is very strong, making it impossible to tell by visual inspection that the light gray patch within the shadow is the identical shade *in the picture* as the dark gray patch outside the shadow. The same shades in blocks below the picture help you see the shading differences outside of the three-dimensional interpretation. A is the shade of the light gray patches outside the shadow, B is the shade of the light gray patches inside the shadow and the dark gray patches outside the shadow, and C is the shade of the dark gray patches inside the shadow.

this is not a trivial issue. Indeed, the light entering our eye from any particular place in a scene is always a combination of surface color *and* lighting conditions.

To better understand this situation, we need to know a few things about the "true," or intrinsic, color of surfaces and the effect of lighting conditions on color. Just as the sky can be characterized by its material properties with respect to light (i.e., it consists of small particles that scatter short wavelength light more than light of other wavelengths), the surface of any object can be characterized by its light-interacting properties. (Sometimes the actual physical measurements of surface materials are very tricky in themselves, but I will leave that problem to the physicists.) For understanding color vision, it is important to know that some surfaces absorb most wavelengths of light and reflect only a small range of wavelengths, giving them a distinctive hue such as red or green. Other surfaces reflect the entire spectrum of wavelengths about equally and so appear to be white or gray. When vision scientists talk about the *intrinsic color* of a surface, they are describing how that surface responds to light over the entire spectrum of wavelengths.

But lighting conditions also contribute to color vision. The primary natural source of light in our world—the sun—emits *broadband* light; that is, all the visible wavelengths are represented more or less equally. Artificial sources of light, however, are much more biased, ranging from the yellow-tinged hues of household light bulbs made of tungsten, to the blue-tinged hues of fluorescent light bulbs and television screens, to the candy-colored spotlights on a performance stage. In addition to the color of the light source, lighting conditions include such features as shadows (which always reduce the brightness of the colors) and colored filters (which range from sunglasses to clouds, smoke, tree leaves, and water).

The complicated visual problem for which color constancy is the solution is *object invariance*. It is often critical to the well-being of humans and other animals to know when they are seeing the same surface—or at least the same colored surface. If color is going to be the basis for object recognition and categorization, it is important to know the object by its intrinsic color. We will want to recognize the object by its color when it is in direct sunlight, in shade, or inside the house. It is less important to know when the lighting and viewing conditions are similar for an object viewed at two different times. In fact, for the purposes of optimal color vision in the everyday world, it would be of great benefit if the influence of lighting conditions could be removed from the evaluation of surface color. But this is no easy feat. It requires a lot of intelligent guesswork. Fortunately, our visual systems are specialized to make exactly those kinds of guesses.

Figure 3.2 illustrates the factors that make color constancy a difficult problem. The graphs profile the wavelength composition of light at three different places. The first shows the wavelengths of light at the source, which is biased toward the short wavelength end of the spectrum. If we saw this light shining in an otherwise black room, we would call it "blue." The second graph profiles wavelengths at the surface onto which the light is shining. This profile is a description of the light-reflecting characteristics of the surface. It should be read as a summary of how the surface would appear if we saw it in white (broadband) light. It is a description of the *intrinsic* color of a surface. The third graph profiles wavelengths at the eye. Here the effects of the light source profile and the surface reflectance profiles are combined. The problem of achieving color constancy involves finding some way to subtract, or remove, the contributions of the light source in order to see the intrinsic color of the surface.

Demonstrations such as those shown in Figure 3.1 and described in Box 3.1 below are proof that human vision can "remove" the influence of the lighting conditions on color vision—at least under some circumstances. In fact, in these demonstrations our vision does such a good job of discounting the lighting conditions that it is impossible to see the wavelength properties of the light that reaches our eyes. We see instead something much closer to the reflectance profile of a surface. This is a remarkable achievement, especially in terms of the myth of vision as

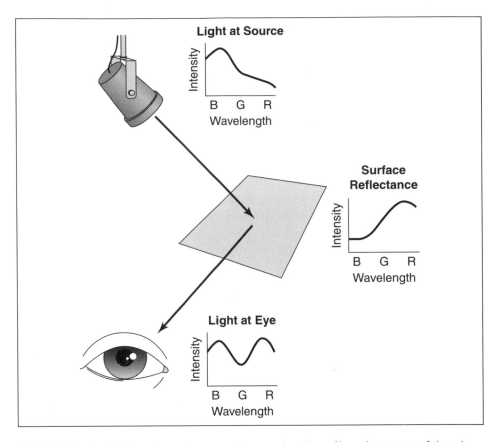

FIGURE 3.2   Each small graph represents a *wavelength profile:* a description of the relative amount of light (y-axis) for each of the wavelengths in the visible spectrum (x-axis). The
wavelength profile for the light source that is shown indicates that it has a blue (B) tinge. The
wavelength profile for the reflecting surface indicates that the intrinsic color of the surface is
toward the red (R) end of the spectrum. The wavelength profile for the light at the eye shows
that the other profiles have been mixed by the time the light reaches the eye.

a faithful process that we discussed in Chapter 1. If color vision were indeed faithful to the physics of light, it would allow us to see that the dark patch outside the
shadow in Figure 3.1 and the light patch inside the shadow are in fact the same
shade. Instead, color vision in this case is faithful to an intelligent guess about the
intrinsic color (i.e., shade) of the checkerboard surface. The physics of the light at
the eye turns out to be superficial as far as the eye and brain are concerned,
whereas the physics of the surface material is the enduring property that should be
recorded by the brain.

Like any other aspect of the vision project, color constancy sometimes fails to operate effectively. Many people experience this, along with some dismay, when they
return from a shopping trip and look at an article of clothing they purchased. The

BOX 3.1

Color constancy revealed with overhead transparencies

Materials

The materials list for this demonstration is more elaborate than usual, but it creates a very compelling effect so I encourage you to try it. The list includes (a) access to a color photocopier that can be used to copy a color image, and (b) a transparency that can be used with (c) an overhead projector. In addition, you will need (d) scraps of multicolored paper that can be cut into rectangles of various sizes, (e) a piece of thick paper of any color that can cover the entire viewing surface of the overhead projector, and (f) several sheets of blue-tinged transparency (e.g., cellophane) that can act as colored filters.

Begin by constructing a montage of many differently colored rectangles that touch and overlap one another. If you are familiar with the work of the Dutch painter Piet Mondrian, you will know what I am after here. If you are not familiar with Mondrian, don't worry. These are very simple displays to construct, although yours may not be as aesthetically pleasing and balanced as his works. Make your "mondrian" large enough to cover the entire viewing surface of the overhead projector you plan to use. In the center of this display, include a square patch of white paper. This will be your target stimulus.

Use a color photocopier to copy your mondrian onto a transparency for viewing by overhead projector. Cut a hole in the piece of thick paper to match the size and location of the white square in your mondrian. This will be the reduction screen for viewing the white square in isolation.

Instructions

The demonstration is most effective when conducted in five steps.

Step 1 Begin with the projector turned off. Place the mondrian transparency on the projector and overlay it with two blue transparencies. Make sure the edges of the mondrian are covered so that no stray light will shine onto the white screen. Turn off all the lights in the room and then turn on the overhead projector. What is the color of the central square patch on the screen?

Step 2 Slowly remove the uppermost blue transparency by sliding it off the mondrian, stopping when one of its edges is in the middle of the central square. What are the colors on each side of this edge?

Step 3 Remove the second blue transparency in the same way, stopping again when one of its edges straddles the central square. What are the two colors on each side of this edge?

Step 4 With no colored overlays remaining, place the reduction screen over the transparency so that only the central square is visible. What is the color of the square?

Step 5 Place a colored overlay over the central square, but still viewed through the reduction screen. What is the color of the square?

Analysis

Record the reported colors for the central square in each of the five steps, using a table like this. Evidence for color constancy consists of the reported color being "white" in Steps 1 and 2.

STEP	VIEWING CONDITION	COLOR AT EYE	REPORTED COLOR?
1	mondrian with two blue overlays	blue	
2	mondrian with one blue overlay	light blue	
3	mondrian alone	white	
4	reduction screen alone	white	
5	reduction screen with blue overlay	light blue	

color they now see does not match their memory of the color they saw in the store. These failures of color constancy are as important as its successes in helping scientists to understand how the color vision project operates. Both results are important clues to the operation of color vision. Moreover, in this context it is difficult to know whether the success of color constancy is an "illusion," as we referred to in Figure 3.1, where the correct color of the light at the eye could not be seen. Perhaps it would be better to reserve the word *illusion* for failures of color constancy, as in our disappointment when we reexamine the clothes we bought on our shopping spree. Use of the word *illusion* for either case hinges on the goals we set for the visual system. If the goal is to see the wavelength composition of light, then the success of color constancy is the illusion. If the goal is to see the similarity and differences between the surfaces of objects, then only the failure of color constancy is an illusion.

WHAT DOES THE VISUAL SYSTEM DO WITH WAVELENGTH?

Color constancy is only one of many factors that violate a direct mapping between wavelength and color experience. It is a violation that serves us well in that it helps us respond in similar ways to objects and surfaces with the same physical properties even when we view them under very different lighting conditions. To understand other factors that violate the direct mapping between physics and experience, we must first become familiar with the ways in which our visual equipment responds to light that varies in wavelength. We will begin with the eye and then consider color processing in the brain. Along the way, we will have to remind ourselves that obtaining accurate wavelength recordings is not the principal objective of human color vision. More important goals are (1) discriminating among objects that have different intrinsic colors, and (2) generalizing across surfaces that have similar intrinsic colors.

Color in the eye

In Chapter 2 we met the brilliant physician Thomas Young, who speculated—almost 150 years before it could be proven by direct observation—that the human eye contained light receptors that were maximally sensitive to three different wavelengths spread out along the visible spectrum. He proposed three versions of the same structure in the eye, each sensitive to a different region of the spectrum. The receptors he speculated about are now known to be *cones,* one of the two types of pigment-laden neurons that lie at the interface between physics (light of different wavelengths) and physiology (our experience of color categories). The other type of receptor, *rods,* are all equally sensitive to wavelength and are active only under dim levels of light. We will discuss them further in Chapter 4.

We now know a great deal more about cones than that there are three types: long wavelength sensitive (L-cones), medium wavelength sensitive (M-cones), and short wavelength sensitive (S-cones). Microscopic studies of their responsiveness to light have demonstrated that although their peak sensitivity lies at different regions along the spectrum, each type responds to light over a broad range of wavelengths. Figure 3.3 (see color appendix) illustrates both of these features.

As you can see in Figure 3.3, the sensitivity ranges of the three cone types do not cover the wavelength spectrum in a uniform way. Whereas the peak sensitivities of M- and L-cones are 30 nm apart, the peak sensitivity of S-cones is more than 100 nm distant. In addition, S-cones are both weaker in overall response and less frequent in occurrence. They account for only 5 to 10 percent of all cones in the retina. Thus if an object is presented in uniquely short wavelength light to the eye, its edges will not be represented as sharply as objects presented in medium and long wavelength light. S-cones are also not as uniform in distribution, occurring much more frequently in the visual periphery than in the center of the eye. In fact, in the fovea—the center of the retina, where the greatest concentration of cones occurs—there are no S-cones at all, making human vision there essentially blind to small blue spots. Inequalities such as these make the mapping between the physics of light and the experience of color rather complex from the very outset of color processing.

The arrangement of three types of cones with overlapping ranges of sensitivity has important consequences for the way the eye processes wavelength information. One profound result is that the information carried by any given cone is ambiguous with respect to wavelength and intensity. For example, consider an activity level for a cone that, when measured in some arbitrary unit, is equal to 10. These 10 units of overall activity could have been generated by a weak light (say, of power level 2) near the peak wavelength sensitivity for that cone (multiplying the effect by 5). But they could just as easily have been generated by a strong light (say, level 5) farther away from the peak wavelength sensitivity (multiplying the effect by 2). A single cone would be blind to these differences. Thus in order to achieve sensitivity to different wavelengths, the output from at least two cones must be compared. Some processing, and therefore neural wiring, is involved.

Studies comparing the cones of different species, as well as studies of the genetic basis of cone pigments in humans, indicate that the earliest form of color vision in mammals was based on a two-cone system. One constituent was the S-cone, with a peak sensitivity similar to that of modern humans. The other was an L-cone with a peak sensitivity lying somewhere between that of the modern M- and L-cones in humans. This two-cone system is an almost universal feature of the retina of mammals. For instance, cats and dogs have only two cone types and thus a reduced range of color vision in comparison with the majority of humans, who have three cone types.

A later development in the evolution of primates was the separation of the generic L-cone into two varieties: and M- and an L-cone. The modern genetic similarity between M- and L-cones is evident in their DNA sequences, which are identical over 96 percent of the strand. It is also evident in their location. Genes for producing the pigments that distinguish the M- and L-cones are adjacent to each other on the X chromosome, one of the two chromosomes that determine an individual's sex. This can occasionally lead to genetic mix-ups between the instructions for building the two cone types. As a result, some humans have only two cone types: S- and M-cones, or S- and L-cones. (These individuals are said to be colorblind.) In contrast, genes for producing the pigment in S-cones are located a long distance away on a chromosome that is shared by males and females alike. The likelihood of genetic variations among individuals for this cone type is very small.

It is important to recognize how much color sensitivity can be achieved by a system with only two types of cones spanning the visible spectrum. Figure 3.4 (see color appendix) shows a two-cone system similar to that of dogs, cats, and "colorblind" humans. A comparison of signals between the two cone types could specify most of the wavelengths lying between blue and red. However, certain ambiguities would remain, especially if light from a mixture of two or more wavelengths fell on the cones. Consider the consequences of a light formed from the mixture of 530 nm and 375 nm. These are shown as solid lines in Figure 3.4a. Assuming the two wavelengths were of equal intensity in the mixture, it would result in 0.70 units of activity in L-cones and 0.40 units of activity in S-cones. Thus a rudimentary form of color vision could be based on a comparison of the two activity levels in L- and S-cones. A ratio of 0.70 to 0.40, or 1.75, could be a signal to correspond to the color mixture that was presented. However, there is a problem: The same ratio could result from presenting these cones with a different mixture of light— say, 460 nm and 600 nm (dashed lines in Figure 3.4a). This light mixture, although based on different wavelength constituents, would result in precisely the same ratio in activity in the two types of cones. That is, L-cones would be active at a level of 0.70 units and S-cones at a level of 0.40 units. Two physically different stimuli would be indistinguishable to this system.

Lest you think I am going through these arithmetic exercises to make an argument "in principle," let me assure you that human color vision is beset with exactly these kinds of ambiguities. Except for the 8 percent of males or the less than 0.5 percent of females with only two types of cones, the ambiguities are not as bad as this example implies. The chief benefit of having three cone types instead of two is the ability to match any light consisting of a single wavelength (a so-called "pure" or "spectral" color) with a mixture of lights. Someone with three distinct cone types would require a mixture of three wavelengths, in different amounts, to successfully match a target color. Someone with only two cone types would require only two wavelengths to create an acceptable color match. This would cause greater color ambiguity, and therefore broader color categories, for a person with the common form of colorblindness called *dichromacy* (literally, two-colored vision).

The standard tool an ophthalmologist uses to detect dichromacy in an individual is the *anomaloscope*. The individual looks through a viewing tube to see a round field divided in half. A spectral color is presented on one-half of the viewing field that looks "yellow" (589 nm). On the other half, light from a spectral color that looks "red" (671 nm) can be combined with a spectral color that looks "green" (546 nm). The individual can adjust the intensity (the amount) of the red and green lights. His or her task is to increase or decrease their intensity until the two halves of the viewing field are identical.

Color mixtures that are not distinguishable from spectral colors or from other color mixtures are called *metamers*. In the task described above, the ways in which the anomaloscope settings for metamers differ from those for color-normal observers indicate the particular type of dichromacy the observer may have. For instance, dichromats (i.e., people who have dichromacy) missing the L-cone find metamers with abnormally high levels of green in the mix to be acceptable matches, whereas dichromats missing the M-cone find metamers with abnormally high levels of red to be acceptable matches. Box 3.2 will guide you through the generation of some color metamers of your own using a desktop computer with a color screen.

BOX 3.2

Creating metamers using a desktop computer

Materials

You will need a desktop computer with a color monitor that has an application installed such as Microsoft Word, Microsoft Powerpoint, Adobe Illustrator, or Adobe Photoshop. Each application will enable you to choose some "custom colors" for rendering fonts, shapes, or backgrounds. Consult the Help command if you don't know where to select the "custom color" option. You will also need a few sheets of colored paper, preferably with bright colors that are mixtures of the primaries such as yellow, orange, purple, and pink.

Instructions

Once you have selected "custom colors," you will find several options for something called a "color picker." These include such names as HLS Picker, CMYK Picker, and RGB Picker. For this demonstration, select the RGB Picker, which refers to a color selection scheme based on the three primary colors red (R), green (G), and blue (B). Each color is associated with a sliding scale that can range from 0 to 100 percent. The colors that result from any combination of values on these three scales will appear in a box called NEW.

Begin by sliding all three scales down to 0 percent. The NEW box should now be black, since you have requested no contribution from any of the three primary colors. Next, slide each of the scales to 100 percent, one at a time, to confirm that the R scale really produces red colors, the G scale produces green, and the B scale produces blue. Slide all three scales to 100 percent to confirm that an equal amount of all three colors produces white.

Now place your yellow sheet of paper beside the NEW box and try to find a RGB combination that matches the paper color exactly. Since there is no Y scale for yellow, you will have to find the matching yellow by creating the appropriate mixture of R and G. If this seems confusing at first, begin by sliding the R scale close to 100 percent. Then start adding more and more G until the NEW box begins to look yellow. Once you are close to matching the color of the yellow paper, you may find it necessary to decrease the overall amount of R in the mix to find the exact match. Sometimes you will even need to add a little B to make the match as perfect as possible.

Now do the same color mixing to find the best match for the colors of the other papers you prepared.

Analysis

The computer monitor consists of three different color phosphors at each of the many small points on the screen. That is, if you were to magnify the screen, you would find three distinctly different color points at each screen location, or picture cell (called *pixels*). When you select the B scale in the

RGB Picker, you selectively activate the electrons coming into contact with blue phosphor in those pixels. Thus at the microscopic level only three primary colors can be presented on the screen. The thousands of different colors that can be created on the screen all result form different combinations of these three primaries. Therefore, when you found a color match for your yellow sheet of paper, you were finding a metamer for yellow based on the appropriate mixture of red and green light.

Cones are just the beginning of color vision in the eye. They are really nothing more than *transducers,* the first line of neurons that can convert light energy into an electrical signal that can be transmitted throughout the nervous system. Figure 3.5 is a schematic diagram showing the relations among the five main types of neurons in the eye that process signals concerning wavelength.

Cone receptors, bipolar cells, and ganglion cells form the first three main layers in the beginning of the feedforward visual hierarchy. That is, there are generally fewer bipolar cells than cone receptors, and generally fewer ganglion cells than bipolar cells. The one exception is at the fovea, where cone receptors, bipolar cells, and ganglion cells stand in a 1 to 1 relationship with each other.

In addition to this feedforward stream of processing in the retina, extremely important lateral lines of communication are carried out by the horizontal and amacrine cells. For instance, horizontal cells are important in modulating the responses of all the bipolar cells within their reach in accordance with the overall level of illumination. One way to characterize their function is to say that they measure the overall level of light within their local neighborhood of influence and then subtract it from the signal sent by the bipolar cells to the ganglion cells. The "intelligent" process of color constancy thus begins, in a fundamental sense, at the second layer of processing in the eye.

Amacrine cells also contribute to the organization of neural signals at the level of ganglion cells. Much work remains to be done in understanding this layer of neurons, since at last count there were over twenty-nine different kinds of amacrine cells in the human eye. But what researchers already know is quite remarkable. For instance, one class of amacrine cells behaves in a similar way to the horizontal cells in adjusting the response of the ganglion cells in accordance with the overall level of light entering their receptive fields. Another class responds to signals from the rod receptors, which we will discuss in greater detail in Chapter 4. Still another class is involved in a feedback circuit with bipolar cells, which seems to cause a cluster of ganglion cells to *depolarize* or fire, in synchrony. It is possible that such correlated volleys of firing signal unity among a group of ganglion cells that otherwise would not have overlapping receptive fields. That is, these ganglion cells can behave as one even though they

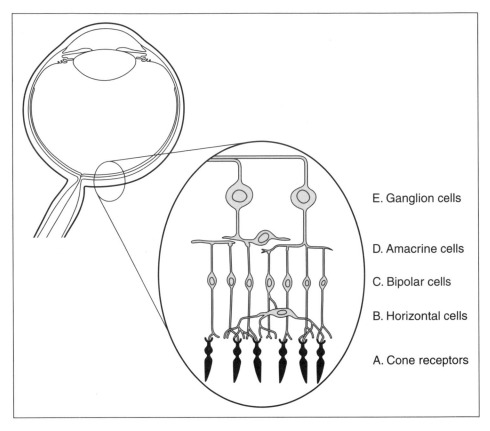

FIGURE 3.5   A schematic diagram of the five major types of neurons in the eye concerned with color vision: (a) cone receptors, (b) horizontal cells, (c) bipolar cells, (d) amacrine cells, and (e) ganglion cells.

each respond directly to only a small portion of a larger visual pattern. When we encounter this kind of neural lock-step behavior again in later chapters, we will refer to it as *binding*.

The ganglion cells are the last step in neural processes within the eye, and as we saw in Chapter 2, they send their information to the brain via long axons. Because of the relative ease with which they can be accessed for study, this layer of cells in the eye has received more study than any other. As a result, researchers know quite a lot about the receptive field organization of ganglion cells, both in humans and in many other species.

As far as color processing is concerned, there are two important classes of ganglion cell. One class is responsive only to input from bipolar cells that have been triggered by S-cones. As shown in Figure 3.6, some of these ganglion cells are excited by short wavelength light and inhibited by medium and long wave-

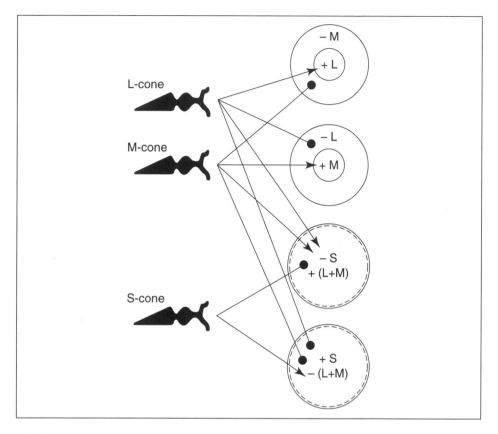

FIGURE 3.6 The receptive field organization of color-sensitive ganglion cells in the human eye. Arrows form the cones represent a signal to increase (+) neuronal firing. Dots from cones represent a signal to decrease (–) neuronal firing. L – M opponent ganglion cells are spatially more selective than S – (LM) ganglion cells, as shown by their smaller excitatory centers. This means we are able to detect red and green color edges with greater spatial resolution than blue and yellow color edges.

length light. It is convenient to think of medium and long wavelength light in this context as "anti-blue" or yellow. Other ganglion cells of this type are inhibited by short wavelength light and excited by medium and long wavelength (yellow) light.

Consistent with the relative scarcity of S-cones in the eye, the receptive fields of these ganglion cells are not spatially very selective. That is, they respond to blue and yellow light over their entire receptive field in much the same way.

The receptive fields of the other class of ganglion cells shown in Figure 3.6 involve contrasts between medium and long wavelength light and also are much more spatially selective. That is, if they have a center that is excitatory for long wavelength light, then the surround of the receptive field is inhibitory for medium wavelength light. Conversely, if the center is excitatory for medium wavelength light, then the surround of the receptive field is inhibitory for long wavelength light.

It is easy to understand why the receptive fields of these cells are called *color-opponent* or *color-antagonistic*. Colors that we think of as complementary have opposite effects on these cells. A cell that is excited by blue light will be inhibited by yellow light, and vice versa. A cell that is excited when shown a red light at the center of its receptive field will be inhibited when shown a green light in the same place. Notice how this changes the basic scheme for coding colors. When we examined the cones, there appeared to be only three primary colors corresponding to three cone types: S-cones (blue sensitive), M-cones (green sensitive), and L-cones (red sensitive). Now, only two layers of cells into the processing hierarchy, at the level of ganglion cells color seems to be arranged according to four primary colors (blue, yellow, red, and green), with these four colors being further organized into two pairs of oppositional colors (blue versus yellow, and red versus green). The answer to the age-old question of how many primary colors there really are seems to hinge on which class of cells we pose this question to in the eye. The cones will answer "three"; the ganglion cells will answer "four."

Color in the brain

Ganglion cell axons that originate in the eye terminate in two different and important structures deep within the brain, as shown in Figure 3.7. These structures are part of the evolutionarily "older" parts of the brain; we share them with many other animals that have similar visual systems.

For our present discussion of color vision, we can conveniently ignore one of these pathways, namely, the one going to the *superior colliculus* (SC). Many visual functions benefit from this pathway, but for now we will only note that it is relatively blind to color differences. The other structure that receives input from the ganglion cells is the *lateral geniculate nucleus* (LGN). Ganglion axons from the eye terminate in six distinct layers of this structure. However, color-opponent ganglion cells terminate in only the top four cell layers. Once again, we see that color is channeled selectively among all the regions of the eye and brain that are sensitive to light.

This pattern of specialization continues into the visual cortex. Of all the cells in area V1, only a relatively small number retain the color-opponency seen in the ganglion cells. The rest of the cells respond broadly to a wide range of wavelengths. Cells that are color opponent in this way are also clumped together in the cortical tissue as small islands that neuroscientists call *blobs*. This descriptive term caught on after these islands of color-sensitive tissue were discovered, somewhat accidentally, through the use of a new cell-staining technique. The dark blob-like regions in area V1, which formed in response to the stain, turned out to be the home of cells with color-opponent receptive fields.

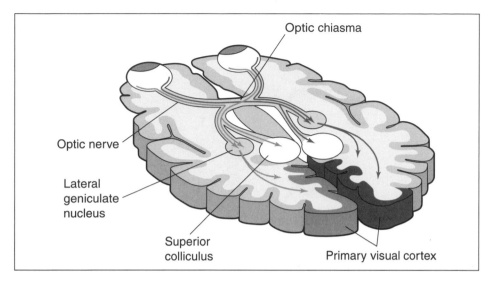

Optic chiasma

Optic nerve

Lateral
geniculate
nucleus

Superior
colliculus

Primary visual cortex

FIGURE 3.7   Location of the lateral geniculate nucleus and the superior colliculus shown inside an imaginary horizontal slab of the brain.

When the various cell layers of these blobs were probed systematically, a new form of color-opponency was discovered among cells in area V1. Figure 3.8 illustrates this type of receptive field. Its overall function can be summarized as that of a color-opponent difference detector. To illustrate what this means, let's consider some example ideal stimulus patterns for the cell labeled a in Figure 3.8. We'll begin with a small red spot, surrounded by gray, that is positioned perfectly on the center of the cell's receptive field. Red in the center excites this cell, so its activity will increase. Note that gray in the surround of this receptive field is neutral, adding neither excitation nor inhibition to the total activity level of the cell.

Now let's compare the same cell's response to a green donut with a gray center that lands perfectly on the cell's receptive field. Green in the surround also excites this cell, so its activity will increase. Gray in the center is neutral, adding neither excitation nor inhibition. So, in effect, we have encountered a color-sensitive neuron that is unable to distinguish between a red spot and a green donut centered in the same locations. Both stimuli will activate the cell equally. What does it mean to find cells for which red spots are *metamers* for green donuts? The answer is that in both cases the cell does a very good job of signaling the presence of a red-green border. A small red dot on a gray background represents a red-green border—at least in the sense that a difference has been detected along the continuum from red to green. In the same sense, a gray dot on a green background also represents a red-green border. Gray is certainly more red than green when evaluated in this way. Here, then, at the level of cortical neurons, we find single cells that respond

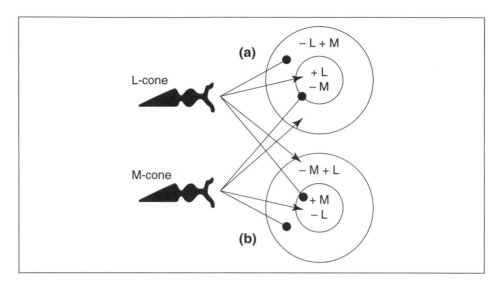

FIGURE 3.8   Double-opponent receptive fields of color-sensitive neurons in layer 4 of area V1. **(a)** Cells with this kind of receptive field respond vigorously (+) when the center of the field is stimulated with red light (L-cone) but also actively decrease (−) their response if the same center region is stimulated with green light (M-cone). A reversed response pattern occurs when the surround is stimulated; red light will decrease (−) the firing rate and green light will increase it (+). **(b)** Cells with this kind of receptive field respond well to green light (M-cone) in the center and red light (L-cone) in the surround.

only to the relative difference along some color dimension. This is exactly the kind of cell that would be blind to changes in lighting while continuing to signal the presence of a red-green border of a certain magnitude. Single cortical cells can achieve color constancy!

When we investigate visually sensitive regions of the cortex in the visual hierarchy beyond area V1, we again find much specialization. Cells in certain regions of the cortex such as the parietal lobes are largely color-blind. That is, they respond differentially to the intensity of light in their receptive fields, but they show only crude sensitivity to differences in the wavelength of light. However, one region in which brain damage is consistently linked to impairments of color vision is a small area in front of area V1. As shown in Figure 2.17 of Chapter 2, it is referred to as *area V4* in the cortical tissue of monkeys and as the *cortical color center* in humans. Selective damage to this region can cause a loss of color experience—as was the case for Michael, whom we met in Chapter 2.

But is the cortical color center in humans also involved in the achievement of color constancy? Some researchers think it is because of the way certain people behave after suffering brain damage to the cortical color center that is more extensive than brain damage to area V1. One way in which such a pattern of brain damage occurs is through extended periods of *anoxia,* or lack of oxygen. If a person survives the trauma that causes the anoxia, other visual regions in his or her brain neighboring area V1 usually suffer the most extensive damage. This is because area V1 is one of the most richly vascularized regions in the brain, consistent with its generally higher levels of metabolic activity. Even within area V1, there is evidence that the blob regions are more richly vascularized than the interblob regions. The high levels of vascularization—implying greater access to oxygenated blood flow—spare some aspects of color vision when the brain suffers prolonged anoxia.

One patient, whom we will call Peter, survived a period of anoxia following an electrocution accident. He suffered both cardiac and respiratory arrest in the accident and was in a coma for many weeks. He was able to begin communicating verbally again after four months of recovery and began to walk again after six months. He was also left profoundly blind: He did not even show the simple eye movement reactions to visual movement that sometimes accompany cortical blindness. He was incapable of recognizing common objects and could not guide himself visually. Yet despite all these visual impairments, he was still able to name various colors with a very high level of accuracy. Moreover, he reported that he was not guessing at the colors, as we might assume from some cases of blindsight. He claimed to see colors such as "red" and "blue" in the same way he had before, although now he was unable to make out the shapes that those colors denoted. He was even able to correctly report less frequently named colors such as "turquoise" and "fuchsia."

This pattern of spared vision suggests that a form of color vision can be preserved when almost every other visual function has been damaged. But what kind of color vision is it? And which brain regions are included in such a color vision system? To answer these questions, a team of researchers (Zeki, Aglioti, McKeefry, & Berlucchi, 1999) gave Peter a color-naming test using displays similar to those described in the demonstration of color constancy in Box 3.1. They asked Peter to name a large square color patch that reflected a variety of colors to his eye. The critical factor in the experiment was the presence or absence of a mondrian-like surround for the target color patch. Without the surround, Peter's color names were similar to those of healthy observers. The wavelengths that reached his eye triggered the usual color names. With the surround, the healthy control observers gave responses that were color constant. That is, the names they chose were consistent with a discounting of the lighting conditions. But this was not the case for Peter's reported colors. He continued to report colors consistent with the wavelengths reaching his eyes rather than with the underlying surface colors.

The same team of researchers then examined functional magnetic resonance imaging (fMRI) brain scans of both Peter and healthy observers when they were viewing colorful displays. Whereas the healthy observers showed brain activation in both the cortical color center and area V1, Peter showed brain activity only in cortical area V1. Studies such as these suggest that the cortical color region contributes in some way to the normal operation of color constancy. Moreover, the fact that Peter had color experiences suggests that the cortical color center is not required to support the experience of seeing a color.

THE HUMAN RESPONSE TO COLOR

How many colors are there?

Now that we are equipped with this summary of the physiology of color vision, we can tackle many of the seemingly confusing aspects of color vision. For example, why do we get such a variety of answers when we ask how many different colors can be seen?

The answer from high school science might be that an infinite number of color experiences are possible. If we begin with the ideas that the eye is sensitive to wavelengths from 380 nm to 760 nm and that changes in wavelength vary smoothly over this range, then indeed the range of possible color experiences would be as broad as our ability to discriminate wavelength differences. If we build on these elementary color sensations (which so far we have assumed correspond only to differences in "pure" or spectral colors) by considering color mixtures, then the number of possible color mixtures seems almost infinite. But herein lies a problem. We have learned that not all color mixtures look different. In fact, a large class of color mixtures can create just one metamer, or the same color experience. Moreover, some color mixture result in color experiences that cannot even be placed onto the wavelength spectrum. Some purples, for example, result from the mixture of long and short wavelength light; these colors never appear in the rainbow or light bent in some other prism. How can we begin to enumerate all these different color experiences?

Color names

Some color researchers examine our use of language to denote color categories. In the everyday language of English-speakers in North America, eleven basic color terms occur: *red, green, blue, yellow, black, white, gray, orange, purple, brown,* and *pink*. These terms are said to be "basic" because they involve a single word (not a combined term such as *blue-green*), they refer exclusively to color (not to other surface properties such as *silver* or *gold*), they can apply to a wide range of objects (not primarily to only one, like *blonde* for hair), and they occur very frequently in everyday language use (not low frequency words used by specialists, like *puce* or *mauve*).

A similar analysis of twenty other languages revealed only five more terms. One was a word for *light-blue* (similar to the way we use *pink* for *light-red* in English). The remaining four were individual words that lump together color categories that are given separate words in English. The English equivalent terms for these words were *warm* (*red* and *yellow*), *cool* (*blue* or *green*), *light-warm* (*white, red,* or *yellow*), and *dark-cool* (*black, blue* or *green*). When researchers further examined the relations among these terms, it became clear that they have a hierarchical arrangement, as shown in Figure 3.9. When a language has primarily only two color terms in everyday usage, the two terms correspond to *light-warm* and *dark-cool*. When a language has three terms, the *light-warm* category is expanded to include *white* and *warm*. With six terms, *warm* is subdivided further into *red* and *yellow*, and *dark-cool* is subdivided into *black* and *cool*.

This degree of regularity in color categories used across the twenty-one languages and cultures suggests that color terms emerge from the way the eye and brain respond to light of different wavelengths. It runs counter to the idea that color categories are arbitrary and determined primarily by the importance of color in a society. This point of view is sometimes expressed in the story that the Inuit (sometimes referred to as Eskimo) have twenty-two or more naming categories for shades of white, presumably because snow is of such great importance to their way of life. But this view is not consistent with the regularity seen across languages in the way different colors are indexed. Instead, the hierarchical arrangement of color terms suggests that language and culture primarily influence the number of terms used. Finer or coarser gradations of color may be included within a single color word, but the relations among these terms can still all be traced to fundamental divisions among *dark, cool, light,* and *warm*.

The color categories that emerge when only six terms are used are interesting in terms of the way ganglion cells in the eye respond differentially to wavelength. Remember that at this level of processing the cells' receptive fields are arranged as opponent processes, with blue and yellow being in opposition and red and green being in opposition. If we consider that other ganglion cells (see Chapter 4) are not as sensitive to specific wavelengths but nevertheless respond to the total amount of light (or darkness) within their receptive fields, then the six basic color terms can be grouped into three sets of oppositional pairs: *red-green, blue-yellow,* and *black-white*.

Color spaces

Another approach to organizing the experience of color involves asking study participants to indicate how similar two colors are to one another. This approach does not require the participants to name a color or to indicate anything about its category membership directly. They simply indicate, by giving a number from 1 to 7, or by *rank ordering* the pairs, how similar the two colors in each pair are to one another.

When this procedure includes a range of spectral colors at about an equal level of brightness, the relations between the paired colors demonstrate something amazing. The relative similarity between paired colors can be modeled as a two-

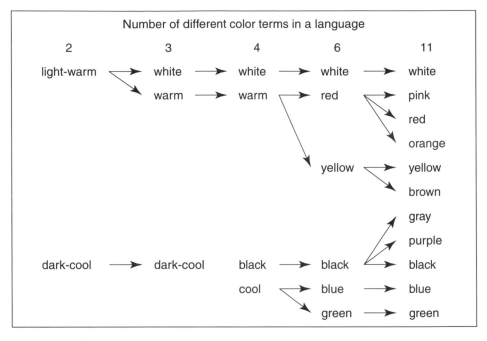

FIGURE 3.9   The hierarchical arrangement of color terms in natural languages. Every language tends to use a subset of all possible "basic" color concepts. However, the specific categories that are used can be predicted from this hierarchical diagram.

dimensional map wherein distance corresponds directly to similarity between colors. Figure 3.10 shows such a map.

One surprising feature of the map is that the range of spectral colors forms an incomplete circle. It is called the *color circle* or *color wheel*. The circle does not seem to fit with the high school science understanding of colors. Wavelengths, remember, represent a one-dimensional physical continuum. If the eye and brain map this continuum directly onto color experience, then experience should be one-dimensional as well. But color experience is two-dimensional; we can see this by acknowledging that a two-dimensional map is required to express the visual similarity among all spectral colors. Where did the extra dimension come from?

Looking at colors that are farthest away from each other in the map gives an important clue. Colors that appear to us as red and green are on opposite sides of the color circle. Moreover, if we draw a line perpendicular to the red-green dimension, we find that yellow and blue form two opposite ends of another dimension. The color wheel appears to have four spokes pointing to the very colors that are involved in the coding of color at the ganglion cell level. Thus the physiology of the eye has a direct consequence on our experience of color.

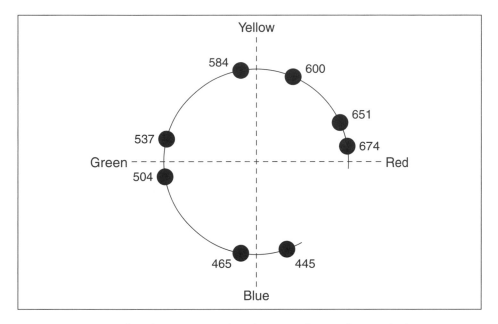

FIGURE 3.10 When the average similarity between all pairs of spectral colors is expressed as distance on a map, then the sampled colors lie on a *color circle*. The gap between blue and red occurs because there are no spectral colors between dark blue and red. Certain color mixtures can be found to fill out the circle; they correspond to purple. The numbers in this figure represent wavelength in nanometers.

Where are color mixtures on this map? We can understand color mixtures if we repeat the color similarity experiment described earlier in this section but this time also include nonspectral colors such as *gray, purple, pink,* and *orange*. Remember that the colors shown to participants in this experiment are still all roughly equated for brightness. The map that now results from the similarity ratings among all possible pairs of colors looks like the one shown in Figure 3.11.

Look first at where gray appears on the map. It lies at the center, equal in distance from all the spectral colors. Find pink next. It lies about halfway between red and gray. This suggests that the color circle is really a *color disc;* that is, color mixtures are represented on this map as the regions between spectral colors. If you imagine the line of mixed colors that run from red to green, they will move from red to pink to gray to a "washed out" green to a full green. In fact, any line drawn through the center of the wheel will run through the color-neutral gray point. The radial distance of any color from the center of the disc therefore represents color *saturation*, which reflects the extent to which a color is "pure," or spectral, in composition. By this definition, gray represents all spectral colors equally.

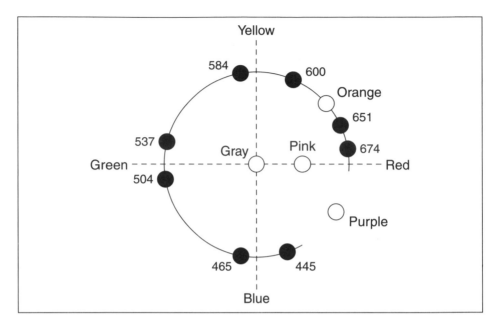

FIGURE 3.11   Another map showing the similarity relations between colors expressed as distances. The map now includes gray, purple, pink, and orange. If all the intermediate colors are filled in on this map, it becomes a *color disc*. The numbers in this figure represent wavelength in nanometers.

Now locate orange and purple on the map. As you might expect, orange lies on the edge of the color disc between red and yellow. Purple lies between red and blue. Thus the color disc captures several important aspects of the color experience. First, differences in *hue* (color categories that correspond to differences in wavelength) are distinct in our experience from differences in *saturation* (the purity of a color mixture). Second, oppositional or complementary colors are those whose mixture leads to gray rather than to a new hue.

How do variations in brightness, including black and white, factor into this kind of map? Recall that brightness was controlled artificially in the construction of the color disc by roughly equating the colors for brightness before having study participants rate their similarity. Figure 3.12 shows the solution for adding brightness; now the color disc becomes a *color spindle* or *color solid*. As brightness levels increase, the color disc becomes progressively smaller until only white remains. At the other end, as brightness levels decrease, the color disc degenerates into blackness.

As the color spindle in Figure 3.12 illustrates, the relations among colors can be expressed as a three-dimensional model—at least as far as most humans are concerned. This means that variations in the two physical dimensions of light intensity

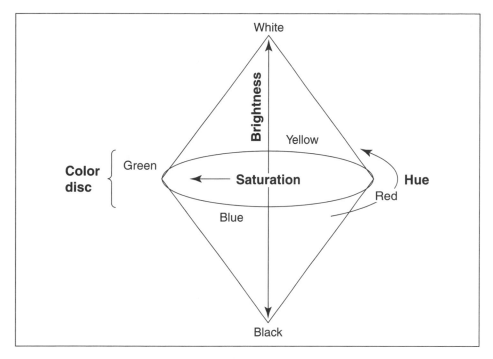

FIGURE 3.12 The color spindle. By adding variation in brightness to the colors in the color disc, we can create a three-dimensional map of colors. As colors become brighter, they also appear to be less saturated and therefore more similar to one another. At the extreme, all the colors appear white. As the colors become less bright, a similar thing happens until all colors appear to be black.

(number of photons) and wavelength (distance between recurring waves of energy) are represented in the eye and brain by the three dimensions of hue, saturation, and brightness. For this reason, the color spindle is often called the *hue-saturation-brightness*, or *HSB*, color space.

But there are other ways to represent the same information. One is especially important in modern life because it is the color space used in televisions and computer screens. It is a reduced version of the complete color solid for human vision, since television screens are capable of producing only some of the colors to which humans are sensitive. Thus it is often called a *color gamut* (rather than a color solid), referring to the colors that are actually realized on the screen rather than all colors that could potentially be seen by the human eye.

A helpful way of understanding the relation between the color gamut of a television screen and the human color spindle is to imagine a transformation of the spindle. As with all three-dimensional solid objects, the color spindle continues to have three dimensions even when viewed from a different perspective or tilted to

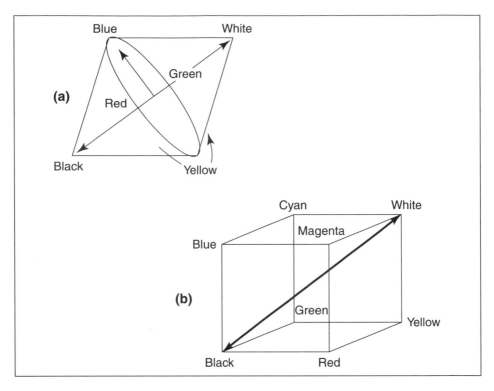

FIGURE 3.13 (a) The color spindle has been tilted so that it rests on its *dark yellow* side. (b) The spindle has been squashed and pinched a little so that its round sides become flat; now it is a three-dimensional color gamut cube in which the primary dimensions are red, green, and blue. This is known as the *RGB* color space.

one side. Tilting the color solid and viewing it as shown in Figure 3.13 leads to an important insight into the color gamut of a television screen. In Figure 3.13a, the color solid is resting so that the *dark yellow* side of the bottom cone forms the contact point with the surface. Now imagine that the spindle is squashed and pinched a little so that its round sides become flat. With a little imagination, you can compress the spindle into a three-dimensional object that looks more like a cube, as in Figure 3.13b.

When the color spindle is represented as a color gamut cube, the lower front corner of the cube on the left can be considered the origin, or the complete absence of color. Movement along the front plane away from the origin leads to increasing amounts of red; movement away from the front plane leads to increasing amounts of green; movement up from the corner results in increasing amounts of blue. Running through the center of the cube, from lower left to upper right, is the gamut of neutral colors ranging from black through gray to white. At the remaining corners of the cube lie the simple mixtures of the pairs of primary colors, with red and green leading to yellow, green and blue leading to cyan, and blue and red leading to magenta. The demonstration in Box 3.3 will help you understand the arrangement of colors with the gamut of your desktop computer screen.

The color space that vision researchers use most often with humans is similar to both the HSB and RGB color spaces. It is known as the *CIE* color space, after the scientific governing body that established it as an international standard in 1931 (Commission Internationale de l'Eclairage). It is shown in Figure 3.14 (see color appendix).

The primary goal in developing this space as the standard for vision research was to enable researchers to specify all visible colors by using as few symbols as possible. It was known that only two dimensions were required to represent all the different hues and that a third dimension was required to represent the intensity of the light. Therefore, x and y in the map specify the hue and z indicates the intensity, or the brightness of the color. Z is not shown in Figure 3.14 because it is intended to show only one intensity value for each hue.

Another goal was to represent all visible colors. It was known that if primary colors were limited to spectral colors, then not all the visible colors would be represented in the space. For example, as Box 3.3 demonstrated, some visible yellows cannot be achieved by using only one spectral red and one spectral green. For this reason, it was decided that three *imaginary* super-hues would serve as the primary colors: blue, red, and green. These values are not visible colors; they lie outside the color space as the imaginary points of a triangle and are arranged so that the coordinates of each hue in the space always equal 1.0. Thus once one knows the relative amount of x (red) and y (green) in a color mixture, the amount of blue in the mix is the remainder that makes these coordinates add up to 1.0. Gray, for instance, is represented by the coordinates x = 0.33 and y = 0.33, with the implicit acknowledgment that the amount of blue is also 0.33.

The horseshoe shape of the CIE space results from another constraint that the designers wanted to satisfy. They wanted to be sure that any mixture involving two lights would lie along the path of a straight line connecting the two colors in the mixture. Thus all the purples, which are mixtures involving the shortest and longest wavelengths visible to humans, had to lie along the straight line connecting these two wavelength points.

Before closing this discussion of color spaces, it is important to return to the question we asked at the outset of this section: *How many colors are there?* When we approach this question from an emphasis on physics, we get a very different answer from when we begin with the experience of color. Emphasis on physics leads to consideration of the numeric explosion that occurs when we imagine combining all possible visible wavelengths. Emphasis on the experience of color, however, leads to the perspective that all colors can be organized around three dimensions: hue, saturation, and brightness.

BOX 3.3

Exploring the color gamut of a desktop computer

Materials

For this demonstration you will need the same desktop computer, color monitor, and application with a "custom color" picker that you used in Box 3.2. Having done that exercise, you should be familiar with using the RGB Picker to select various amounts of each of the three primary colors and with checking the result of any color mixture in the NEW box.

Instructions

Try to find all eight corners of the color cube shown in Figure 3.13b. Black, white, and the three primaries of red, green, and blue form five of the corners. The three remaining corners are cyan (blue-green), magenta (red-blue), and yellow (green-red).

Analysis

Try to answer the following questions to test your understanding of color spaces so far. Answers are provided at the bottom of the box, but do your best to answer on your own before checking them.

1. Where in the color cube is the following color mixture located: 50 percent red, 50 percent green, and 50 percent blue?
2. Why are mixtures of any two primaries always brighter than the component primary colors in the mixture?
3. Cyan "looks like" a mixture of blue and green, and magenta "looks like" a mixture of red and blue. But yellow "looks like" a distinct primary color in its own right, not a mixture of red and green. Why?

Answers

1. This mixture defines "middle gray" and is therefore in the exact center of the cube.
2. The intensity of light from one primary has been added to the intensity of light from the second primary. The mixture must therefore be more intense (brighter) than the components.
3. Your answer must appeal to the way the visual system is built. As you can see, there is nothing in the physics that makes yellow "special." Color-sensitive cells in the human visual system, from the ganglion cell level in the eye and beyond, treat "yellow" as the combination of red and green and as the opposite of blue. In other words, the visual system from that point on treats yellow as a primary in the same way as the primaries red, green, and blue.

If we focus on the physiological steps in between the physics and the experience, we find explanations for the nature of some of the dimensions. For example, a two-dimensional model of hue and saturation can be related directly to the relative activity between two classes of ganglion cells in the eye: cells with red-green opponent-receptive fields and cells with blue-yellow opponent-receptive fields. An increase in the activity of the red-excitatory cells, for instance, will move us toward the experience of a color that is relatively more red; relative quiet in both classes of cells will cause us to experience colors in the center of the space; simultaneous increases in red-excitatory and blue-excitatory cells will produce the experience of purple.

Color mixing

Our discussion of color spaces has already introduced us to some peculiar results when we mix colors on a computer screen. For instance, combining all three color primaries of red, green, and blue produces a white screen. Combining only red and green results in yellow. This seems at odds with everything we learned in kindergarten about mixing crayons and paints. Why are computer screens so out of step with our intuitions?

The answer lies in a fundamental difference between the physics of mixing light of different wavelengths and the physics of mixing different pigments. A computer screen mixes light on its way to our eyes; a paint store mixes pigments that, when applied to a wall, will reflect the wavelengths in various degrees to our eyes.

Let's consider the more familiar case first. When paints or other pigments are combined, it is called *subtractive color mixing*. To understand these results, we have to remind ourselves that *pigments* are essentially surfaces that influence how much light—and which wavelengths—are reflected, or bounced away, when they come in contact with light. The particles of a "blue sky" scatter short wavelength light; the pigments in deep red paint absorb most wavelengths of light but reflect long wavelength light. We can summarize the pigment composition of a surface by using the diagrams shown in Figure 3.15 (see color appendix). The length of the arrows reflected away from each surface indicates the degree to which light of various wavelengths is reflected from each surface to the eye.

Two important consequences of mixing paints are evident, for example, when we mix a rich red paint and a rich blue paint. First, as Figure 3.15 demonstrates, each time we add paint to the mix, less overall light can be reflected from the resulting surface. Adding pigments can only *reduce* the total amount of reflected light. This is why each paint company begins the construction of any given color with a base color that is essentially the brightest possible white. Any pigments added to the base white to achieve a particular target hue will reduce the overall brightness of the mixture.

Second, the color that results from the mix is predictable from the physics of the situation. If a pigment that reflects only long wavelength light is combined with a pigment that reflects only short wavelength light, then the color mixture must reflect both long and short wavelength light, although each in some reduced amount. A mix of red and blue paint will therefore result in a magenta or purplish color that is darker than the original red or blue.

In the everyday world, predicting the outcomes of paint mixtures is more difficult than this because of the difficulty of finding wavelength-pure pigments. Any given pigment may reflect primarily one range of wavelengths, but a careful examination of the surface's reflectance profile will reveal that it consists of a complicated function with several peaks at various locations along the wavelength spectrum. This is why each paint company has its own formulas for achieving color mixtures from its own primary pigments.

Mixing colors on the computer screen differs dramatically from mixing paint because on the computer we are directly combining light sources of different wavelength composition. The process is called *additive color mixing*. To explain the results, we must understand the physiology of human color vision as well as the differences in visual physiology between any two observers.

In additive color mixing the more light that is combined, the more intense—or bright—is the overall result. Color mixtures can begin with very small amounts of light that look dark gray regardless of wavelength and end with very intense levels of light that appear to be white, again regardless of wavelength. In between are the various colors represented in the color spindle (Figure 3.12). You may want to review the exercises in Box 3.3 if these concepts are still not becoming familiar.

The observation that only three primary hues are required to generate all the visible colors is what Thomas Young took as a starting point in his lecture to the British Royal Academy of Science in 1822, when he proposed that human color vision is based on three receptors that are differentially sensitive to wavelength. This fact is also the basis for the diagnosis of differences in color vision among humans, to which we will now turn.

COLOR STRANGERS AMONG US

Getting by without the third cone: Dichromats

Because there are three different wavelength-sensitive receptors in the typical human eye, it is reasonable to assume that there are at least three different ways in which color vision can "go wrong" in development. Someone could be missing the L-cone system, the M-cone system, or the S-cone system. Indeed, someone could be missing two or even all three of these cone types, which is a possibility we will consider in Chapter 4 when we examine human vision without a functioning cone system of any kind. For now, let's consider color vision with only one pair of the three cone types intact. These individuals can be referred to as *dichromats* (literally "two-colors"), in contrast to the majority of *trichromats* ("three-colors") in the human population.

As I have mentioned, color vision problems involving a missing M- or L-cone are much more prevalent than those involving the S-cone system. The main reason is the similarity in genetic structure for these two cone types. The genes specifying their development are in close proximity on the same chromosome (the sex-specific X), and their genetic sequences are highly similar. Only seven changes in the sequence of amino acids are required to switch the instructions for making the M- into the L-cone photopigment. Thus small variations in development can result in mix-ups in the genes for these two cone classes. Such mix-ups do not result in fewer cones in the eye overall; rather, they result in the "replacement" of one class (for example, L-cones) with those of the related class (M-cones).

The most frequent genetic mix-ups result in individuals who have only S- and M-cones. These individuals are called *protanopes* to indicate that they lack the cones that are sensitive to the "first" color, red. (Red is called the "first" color arbitrarily. Scientists had to start counting somewhere.) Individuals with only S- and L-cones are called *deuteranopes,* indicating that they lack the M-cone system. Finally, *tritanopes* are those extremely rare individuals who lack the S-cone system. In fact, tritanopia occurs so rarely as a result of a genetic mix-up that an intensive search in England in the 1950s led to the discovery of only seventeen in a population of more than thirty million. Milder forms of tritanopia are more prevalent as the result of exposure to chemical toxins, traumatic injury to the eye, and the hormonal cycles of women. These factors all have a greater impact on the less prevalent S-cones than on the more prevalent M- and L-cones.

What are the consequences of being a dichromat of the protanope or deuteranope variety? Perhaps the most important thing to bear in mind is that dichromacy refers only to the composition of the first layer of neurons in the eye. The rest of the color vision system, from ganglion cells to cortical organization, seems to be "wired" in exactly the same way in dichromats and trichromats. Also, the S-cone input is intact. So the question becomes, *What are the consequences of a color vision system that is unable to distinguish medium wavelength light from long wavelength light?*

I mentioned earlier that dichromats have a greater range of tolerance in finding acceptable metamers (color matches) for colors that differ in medium and long wavelength composition. If you know someone who is a dichromat, you should be able to see this by having them do the exercises in Box 3.2. A dichromat should find a much wider range of mixtures of primary red and primary green to be acceptable matches to a yellow sheet of paper. Specifically, protanopes should be tolerant of a much wider range of red in the mix, and deuteranopes should be tolerant of a much wider range of green in the mix, since these are the wavelengths to which they are not as sensitive.

Another consequence of dichromacy concerns the color disc (Figure 3.11). If you ask dichromats to rate the similarity among pairs of colors, you will find that colors that differ on the red-green dimension of the two-dimensional color disc will be rated as much more similar than the same color pairs when rated by trichromats. That is, dichromats will judge reds and greens that are approximately equal in brightness to be quite similar. They will also rate as highly similar colors such as blue and purple, which differ only by the relative amount of red in the mix, and colors such as yellow and lime, which differ only by the relative amount of green in the mix. This has the net effect of "squashing" the color disc along the red-green axis in the dichromats' experience. The color disc that trichromats experience becomes a "color oval" for dichromats.

Adding a fourth cone: Tetrachromatic superwomen

Color researchers have noted for many years that when they compare the color judgments of women and men, women as a group are often able to make finer color discriminations than men. Within a group of women, some often show evidence of a richer color experience than other women or men. The traditional way of interpreting this finding is to assume that different patterns of socialization and experience for some women are responsible for these effects. However, some very exciting research conducted over the past ten years is now enabling scientists to understand this difference in color vision as the expression of a genetically based difference in the structure of these women's retinas (Jameson, Highnote, & Wasserman, 2001; Neitz, Carroll, & Neitz, 2001).

To understand this research, we have to remember that dichromacy involving the M- and L-cone systems is a genetically inherited trait. Moreover, it follows a pattern of *sex-linked inheritance:* It is passed from one generation to the next on the X chromosome. Humans typically have two sex chromosomes, with females having a pair of X's and males having an X and a Y. This is why males are much more likely to be dichromats. If there is any defect in a male's genes for these cones, he will be colorblind; if there is a defect in the same genes in a female, the second copy of the genes on the other X chromosome will prevent her from being a dichromat. Yet she will still be a "carrier" of dichromacy, meaning that she can receive the dichromacy gene on one X chromosome from her father and pass it on to her children without her own vision being affected. She will then have a 50 percent chance of having a dichromatic son. If her husband is trichromatic, her daughters will likely also be trichromats, but they also will have a 50 percent chance of being carriers for dichromacy. If a woman's father is a dichromat, she will certainly be a carrier of dichromacy because the X chromosome she received from her father was the same X chromosome that made him a dichromat.

The recent genetic research shows that women who are carriers for dichromacy are most likely to have the genetic makeup to develop four different cone types. The technical term for this individual is *tetrachromat*. One of the cone types of a tetrachromat is, of course, the S-cone that is not involved in red-green dichromacy. The other three cones are variations on the M- and L-cone systems that are specified at neighboring gene sites on the X chromosome. The proximity of these gene sites leads to what geneticists call an "unstable arrangement." It allows for genes from the M- and L-cone sites to misalign during cell development and to intermix in the gene sequences. The chimeric genes (meaning "of diverse origin") formed from such intermixing produce cone types that are intermediate in wavelength sensitivity between the standard M- and L-cones. These genes are free to express themselves in the same way that atypical genes on an X chromosome in a male are free to be expressed. There is no partner gene on the other chromosome pair to block their development and expression.

Two of the three M- and L-cone types of a tetrachromat would likely be very similar to the standard M- and L-cone types that have peak wavelength sensitivity near 530 nm and 560 nm. These would be specified by the "normal" genes on the X chromosome that the women received from one of their parents. The third cone type would likely fall somewhere in between, as shown in Figure 3.16 (see color appendix). It would be specified by the genes on the "atypical" X chromosome that the women received from their colorblind fathers or their "carrier" mothers, or from one that formed as a chimeric gene in development.

As of the writing of this book, it is not clear whether this genetic potential has actually been expressed in four distinct cone types. Making such a determination will not be possible for some time because it will involve a postmortem molecular analysis of the eye of one of these women. The research is so new that such an opportunity has not arisen. However, it is possible at this point to test the color vision of women who have been identified through genetic analyses as being candidates for tetrachromacy. A comparison of their results with those from women and men who have the genetic makeup for trichromacy should indicate whether these cone types actually exist. But there are several complications to this seemingly straightforward logic.

First, it is not clear what the proper vision test for tetrachromacy should be. The color matching procedures, which have been the standard of color vision screening for many years, are inadequate because they work on the assumption that no one will require more than three primary colors to match any given spectral color. Yet tetrachromats should require four primary colors to create optimal metamers.

Second, the peak sensitivity of the fourth cone would lie between and very near that of the standard M- and L-cones. It is not clear what consequence such a small difference in sensitivity between cone inputs might have on color vision. The standard M- and L-cones have sensitivity differences that are only 30 nm apart. Tetrachromats might have a fourth cone type that, at best, is different from these by only 15 nm. Would such small differences in sensitivity make a difference to color appearance?

Third, no one knows how the presence of a fourth cone type would influence color processing in the rest of the visual system. Would there be a fourth opponent process at the ganglion cell level in the eye? (It would be an opponent process in addition to the blue-yellow, red-green, and black-white processes that we already know exist.) If so, what contrast would be added?

In one of the most thorough studies so far (Jameson, Highnote, & Wasserman, 2001), a total of 38 women and 26 men performed several color vision tasks and also underwent a molecular genetic analysis. The vision test that yielded the strongest differences in perception was one in which participants had to indicate how many distinct color boundaries they could see in a full rainbow spectrum of colors, ranging smoothly from 380 nm to 780 nm. In addition, they had to indicate the location of each color boundary along the spectrum. Figure 3.17 (see color appendix) shows a sample spectrum of this kind.

The genetic analysis identified 23 women with the genetic potential for tetrachromacy, 15 women and 22 men with the genetic sequences for trichromacy, and 4 men with the genetic sequence for dichromacy. On average, the tetrachromats indicated 10 discrete color bands visible in the "rainbow" stimulus and the trichromats indicated an average of 7.5, and this result did not vary between men and women. Finally, the dichromats indicated an average of 5.6 distinct bands of color. It is clear that the participants' genetic makeup had a direct influence on the number of distinct colors that they saw. Also, we must remember that this was a relatively weak test of tetrachromacy in that the 23 women identified were genetic carriers for four cone types. Had the study been able to isolate those women who actually expressed this genetic information in four distinct cone types, these differences might have been even greater.

Thomas Young's idea about color vision, informed by careful observation of human experience, had to wait over 150 years before it was confirmed by direct observation of the human retina. As he had predicted, it turned out that typical human color vision really is based on a system that begins with three distinct types of retinal receptors. Today, in much the same way, scientists are waiting patiently to find out whether the genetic and behavioral differences in some individuals are really based on a fourth type of retinal cone. It is unlikely that this answer will be as long in coming as it was for Thomas Young's idea.

As the new research shows, these are truly exciting times in which to be studying vision. In the area of color vision alone, scientists ranging from physicists to molecular geneticists to neuroscientists to experimental psychologists and even some philosophers are all working on the same problem. Each field is bringing new and sophisticated tools to the workbench. Each has a unique perspective on how physiology transforms the physics of light into the human experience of color.

LEARNING ABOUT COLOR THROUGH PLAY

Playing with color and with color illusions lends itself very well to an improved understanding of the human vision project. There are several reasons for this, including that (1) the physics of the wavelength properties of light are so well understood, (2) so much is already known about the physiology of color vision, and (3) color results in such immediate and compelling conscious experiences. No matter how many times I examine the gray patches in Figure 3.1, the lighter patch in the shadow still looks lighter to me than the darker patch outside the shadow. These "illusions" give me direct insight into processes behind my own color experience, since I can confirm with a photometer (light meter)—or by using a computer screen—that physical quantities of light do not always correspond with my experience of the light.

Illusions involving color are as old as the study of color vision itself. We have already encountered some of them, including the notion of metamers and color constancy. In this final section I want to introduce a selected set of color illusions—illusions that are not only fun but also helpful in introducing topics we will consider in later chapters.

Illusions of color contrast and averaging

One of the oldest illusions is that of *color contrast*. It is evident in a wide variety of circumstances and is important in the design of artificial spaces. The main idea is that some colors work in pairs of opposites, such that blue is opposed to yellow and red is opposed to green. This opposition is evident when two members of a pair of colors are placed side by side. Each member of the pair seems stronger or more vibrant as a result.

Color contrast is also evident when one member of the pair is absent. For instance, a neutral gray patch placed in close proximity to a blue will take on a tinge of yellow. The same gray patch placed next to a yellow will adopt a bluish tinge. If you stare at a patch of blue long enough to form an *afterimage* (meaning that when you then look at a blank white wall or piece of paper, you see the same form), the form will appear in a less saturated version of yellow. Staring at a yellow patch for 20 to 30 seconds will allow you to see a blue afterimage of the same shape. Figure 3.18 (see color appendix) contains some patterns that will enable you to experience the effects of color contrast.

It is not possible to predict these color contrast effects on the basis of the physics of light because none of the wavelengths "oppose" each other in any way. It is also not possible to explain the contrast effects by examining the function of the cones. In fact, for many years, before evidence for the three types of cones had been observed directly, some color vision scientists argued that Thomas Young's trichromatic theory must be wrong because color opposites played no special role in it. We now know that trichromacy theory is not "wrong." It is absolutely correct as a description of the cone receptors. However, it is incomplete as a comprehensive theory of color vision. We can now understand the color contrast effects in terms of the opponent and double-opponent receptive field organization of cells farther along in the processing hierarchy. Human color experience seems dominated by these processes, not by the initial registration of wavelength in terms of three different cone types.

Another illusion that has been known for a very long time is that of *color averaging*. In fact, we indirectly referred to it earlier when we noted that a computer screen consists of tiny phosphors of red, green, and blue at each screen location (pixel) that are activated by different amounts to form the impressions of all the colors. The color mixing occurs because the spatial resolution of the eye is not fine enough to resolve these differences. Some pointillist painters, such as Georges Seurat and Paul Signac, employed the same concept. These artists tried to create colors in the viewer's mind by using small dots of paint in close proximity to one another. The displays in Figure 3.19 (see color appendix) will help you consider color averaging in a few different ways.

All these examples of color averaging demonstrate that the visual system's spatial resolution for hue differences is not nearly as fine as its spatial resolution for differences in brightness. That is, edges demarcated by differences in luminance are registered with much greater precision in the eye and brain than edges demarcated only by differences in hue.

Neon color illusions

Figure 3.20 (see color appendix) shows some patterns in which the color seems to extend well beyond the actual borders in which the colors have been drawn. Take a close look at the blue semi-transparent disc that seems to be overlaid on the black star shape. There is actually no disc in the picture. The lines near the center of the black star have simply been colored blue; likewise, the yellow disk and the blue and yellow rings. The only color in these displays lies within the boundaries of the edges that would otherwise be black.

Yet these displays create a perception that has a number of interesting features. First, the colored surface appears to be a transparent veil and therefore seems to lie closer to the viewer than the black star shape. Second, the black lines of the star shape appear to be continuous behind the transparent colored surfaces. In a sense, we know that the lines are "black" underneath the color even though there is no black stimulus there. This is another example of the mechanisms of color constancy at work. Third, the regions between the lines of the star appear to be colored even though they are every bit as white as the background elsewhere in the display. The color of the lines seems to bleed into the surrounding white region. Fourth, the color that is seen appears to "glow" in comparison to the same colors presented as shapes in isolation.

The glow of color in these displays has led researchers to call them *neon color illusions*. However, the importance of neon colors as a window to the workings of the visual system lies less in their "glow" than in their insights into the way that color and form are combined in vision. To help understand where the glow comes from, take a look at the all-white disc and ring also shown in Figure 3.20.

These regions appear to be brighter than the surrounding background even though there is no color in the displays other than black and white. Whatever the processes are that create this illusion of increased brightness for the disc and the ring, they are likely the same ones that are responsible for the glow of color in the neon displays.

More important than the glow is the fact that the color "bleeds" to fill the shape (disc or ring) that is seen by the visual system. It is important to note that this color spreading effect is very different from the simple *color averaging* that occurs when pairs of small color patches are placed close beside each other, as in Figure 3.19 (color averaging). It is different in two ways. First, the resulting illusory color is not a simple averaging of the component colors. Rather, it is the same color as the single inducing color, albeit in a form of transparency. Second, the most important difference is that the color illusion obeys some rules of perception regarding spatial patterns. That is, the color does not bleed outside of the edges of the shapes in all directions, even though from the perspective of simple color averaging it should. The processes of shape perception restrict this bleeding in systematic ways.

The watercolor illusion

Figure 3.21a (see color appendix) shows an illusion of color that can be used to great effect if, for some reason, you want to maximize the appearance of color with a minimum of ink. Which regions of this pattern are colored? It seems beyond question that the "orange" regions are a different color from the "white" regions in this pattern. But look more closely. The pattern consists of two thin lines, one purple and one orange. The surface on which the two lines have been drawn is white. A color meter pointed in the regions between lines would record identical values on both sides of the lines. Yet there is a white region (between the purple lines) and an orange region (between the orange lines) in our experience of the pattern. The rule for generating this compelling color illusion—known as the *watercolor illusion*—seems to be as simple as "when a dark and a lighter line are drawn side by side on a white background, the color of a region enclosed by the lighter line will appear tinted in the same color, whereas a region enclosed by the darker line will appear to be a cold white."

An illusion like this leads immediately to such questions as *For which colors does this illusion work? Do the lines have to be solid color? Does this illusion influence the natural assignment of part of the pattern as "figure" and the other as "ground?"* You can answer all these questions after a few hours of doodling with some felt-tipped markers and a few sheets of paper, or after similar doodling with a computer graphics program.

Eventually, our answers should guide us to the deeper question of *What does this illusion imply for the design of our visual system?* One of the answers to this question offered by researchers who study this illusion (Pinna, Brelstaff, & Spillmann, 2001) is that it points to simple heuristics (a technical term for "rules of thumb") involving color that human vision uses to assign regions of a scene to the foreground as opposed to the background. If so, then one heuristic seems to be that sharp contrasts in luminance should be taken as evidence favoring the boundary of a surface. This assigns all the white-dark edges to outer boundaries of potential surfaces. A second heuristic is that the entire surface interior to a bounding edge is the same color. This would assign the region between the lighter lines as uniform in hue.

As a test of this concept, researchers prepared a pattern with pairs of vertical lines, as shown in Figure 3.21b. When the lines were all the same color, study participants tended to see those that were closer together as belonging together. This made the pattern appear to be a series of narrow regions (demarcated by the two closer lines) separated by wider regions (demarcated by the pairs of lines separated by a greater distance). When researchers prepared the same pattern with bicolored lines, as shown in Figure 3.21c, participants saw the region between the lighter colors as the figure, making the more widely separated lines the edges of the "figure" seen against a "background" of narrow regions. Thus color relations are involved in determining the visual organization in these patterns.

DO WE KNOW THEM BY THEIR COLOR?

Does color help us recognize objects and scenes? Although this probably seems like a simple question—and one with an obvious answer—it has generated a surprising amount of controversy among vision researchers. We will consider the larger question of object recognition in Chapter 5, but for now we will weigh the evidence on both sides of the question. Does the color of an object contribute to the ease or accuracy of object recognition?

The argument that color is not essential to object recognition appeals to neuroscience researchers showing that an object's color is processed by specialized neural pathways and brain regions that are distinct from the pathways and regions devoted to the analysis of object shape and identity. Also, at the crude level of "natural experiments" that occur following brain damage, we saw that object recognition could be largely preserved in the face of the complete loss of the experience of different hues. You might recall the condition of cerebral achromatopsia we encountered in the individual called Michael in Chapter 2. In the present chapter we encountered the flipside of this condition in Peter, who retained the experience of color following traumatic brain injury but lost all ability to see the shape and locations of individual objects. These kinds of evidence indicate that color is not absolutely essential for object recognition.

But we can still ask whether color helps. That is, does color play an important role in our brain's recording of the features of an object for later recall? Is color central to the way in which we see and remember objects, or is it something like "wrapping paper" in that it must be removed from an object every time it is encountered by the brain and then thrown on again once an object is retrieved from memory? This question has been studied by James Tanaka and other researchers (Tanaka, Weiskopf, & Williams, 2001), who presented study participants with pictures of objects for rapid naming but varied whether the objects and scenes were rendered in typical colors, atypical colors, or brightness-equated levels of gray. Figure 3.22 (see color appendix) presents examples of displays such as these.

These studies show that color makes an important difference to the recognition of only some scenes and objects. Specifically, color matters for the recognition of objects in which color is highly diagnostic of the objects' identity. Thus, for example, a lemon and a lime are very similar in shape but importantly different in color. In a picture, color may be the only clue to their difference. Other natural surfaces such as the sky, trees, sand, and water also have diagnostic colors. When these objects and surfaces are rendered only in levels of gray or in atypical colors, naming speed suffers. However, there are many other objects, such as hammers, cars, and shopping malls, for which color is not very diagnostic. For these objects and scenes, color has no measurable influence on naming speed.

WHAT IS COLOR FOR?

As we will see many times in this book, the workings of human vision are tuned to correspond to the environment in which that visual system operates. Some of the tuning has occurred through evolution; some tuning occurs with experience during the lifetime of the individual; and some tuning occurs on a moment-by-moment basis, depending on our immediate goals. In trying to understand how vision works, however, we must be reminded again about what human vision is *not*. It is not an all-purpose system for the faithful recording of light that reaches the eye.

This point has been made very forcefully in our study of color vision. Human color vision begins with an analysis of the wavelength and intensity of light and ends up being an analysis of the light-reflecting properties of solid surfaces. Along the way, much of the specific information regarding wavelength and intensity is abandoned in favor of information about the relative differences in the color of objects. We will see this theme played out time and again in our upcoming discussions of visual edges, objects, time, and space. In every case, the registration of light that occurs in regard to these visual attributes serves the more important goals of knowing where objects are in our environment, what they are, and what their significance is to us.

FURTHER READING

Adelson, E. H. (2000). Lightness perception and lightness illusions. In M. Gazzaniga (Ed.), *The new cognitive neurosciences,* 2nd ed. (pp. 339–351). Cambridge, MA: MIT Press.

Berlin, B., & Kay, P. (1969). *Basic color terms.* Berkeley: University of California Press.

Boynton, R. M., & Gordon, J. (1965). Bezold-Brucke hue shift measured by color-naming technique. *Journal of the Optical Society of America, 55,* 78–86.

Dacey, D. M. (1996, January). Circuitry for color coding in the primate retina. *Proceedings of the National Academy of Science, 93,* 582–588.

Kay, P., & McDaniel, C. K. (1978). The linguistic significance of the meanings of basic color terms. *Language, 54,* 610–646.

Masland, R. H. (2001, September). The fundamental plan of the retina. *Nature Neuroscience, 4,* 877–886.

Roorda, A., & Williams, D. R. (1999). The arrangement of the three cone classes in the living human eye. *Nature, 397,* 520–522.

Shepard, R. N. (1962). The analysis of proximities: Multidimensional scaling with an unknown distance function. I & II. *Psychometrika, 27,* 125–246.

4 EDGES

FUNDAMENTAL QUESTIONS

- In what way is the edge the foundation of human vision?
- How is visual acuity related to edge perception?
- How do the eye, the lower brain, and the cortex analyze edges?
- In what way is our perception of any edge an illusion?
- What makes a good line drawing?
- Why can we sometimes identify an object in a cartoon more quickly than the same object in a color photograph?
- What is special about the edges of silhouettes and shadows?

THE IMPOSSIBILITY OF READING BY MOONLIGHT

I once made a bet with a friend who, like me, enjoys spending time in the mountains. We had just completed the ascent of Mount Forbidden in the Pacific Northwest and had returned to our tent for the night. A full moon had greatly assisted our successful descent of the peak. The high mountain air, in combination with the snow on the ground and the absence of artificial lights, had ensured plenty of light to permit safe passage down 2,000 feet of granite and an icy glacier even though the sun had set long ago. We counted our blessings a second time when we realized we had not packed our headlamps for the daytrip but had foolishly left them at the tent site earlier that morning. The full moon had really saved our long day.

What prompted the bet was my friend's offhand remark that the moon was shining so brightly we should be able to read our guidebook. I acknowledged the romanticism of the idea but also seized on the opportunity to make a bet that I knew I couldn't lose. This wager was not based on any personal experience of mine (I had never actually tried to read by the light of the moon); it was based on my understanding of the way our visual system works under dim light conditions.

In this chapter we will consider how the visual system analyzes the edges that it detects in all views of the world. In covering this material, we will encounter the numerous findings that allowed me to win my bet about reading in the moonlight. Reading the printed word places severe demands on our visual system's ability to analyze edges, as it involves making very fine distinctions among letters. After all, letters differ from one another only by the location and arrangement of a small set of short line segments.

We will begin by examining the physical characteristics of edges so that we can better understand the patterns of light that the eye and brain work with in making conclusions regarding edges in the external world. We will then examine the structures of the eye and the parts of the brain that analyze, exaggerate, ignore, and sometimes even hallucinate edges. Later in the chapter we will examine human behavior with regard to edges. As in many areas of vision science, researchers know more about the behavior of the system as a whole than about its component parts. As our understanding of edge perception becomes more sophisticated, we can ask increasingly sophisticated questions about the way in which the neurons of the visual system interact in their analysis of edges. Finally, we will examine the extent to which vision can be based solely on edges.

WHAT IS AN EDGE?

As we noted in Chapter 1, four fundamental aspects of light are important to vision: *intensity*, *wavelength*, and the distribution of light over *space* and *time*. This chapter focuses on *luminance edges*, which are technically defined as changes in light intensity across space. A visual system that is sensitive to spatial changes in intensity has the basic equipment necessary to perceive spatial structure. By *spatial structure* I mean the shapes, locations, and orientations of objects and surfaces in space. We will examine the perception of those higher-order concepts in Chapter 5 when we consider object perception. But before we do that, we need to examine what is involved in perceiving the edges that make up a shape in the first place.

I must note at the outset that a luminance edge—that is, an edge created by a change in light intensity over space—is only one of many types of edge. Although luminance edges are the main focus of this chapter, let's consider other kinds of edges that occur in our natural environment, some of which are illustrated in Figure 4.1 (see color appendix). For instance, wavelength differences can define an edge for a color-sensitive visual system, even in the absence of associated changes in light intensity. These edges are defined solely by the hue dimension of color, as discussed in Chapter 3.

Edges based on changes in luminance and hue are often called *first-order edges* because they involve two fundamental aspects of light; intensity and wavelength. But a variety of *second-order edges* are also possible, as Figure 4.1 illustrates. Texture edges involve changes in the spatial arrangements of texture elements, motion edges involve changes in the dominant direction of motion of image elements, and depth edges involve changes in the distance of surfaces from the eye. In images obtained from scenes of the natural world, the same edge in the scene often corresponds to many or all of these properties.

The luminance profile

Luminance edges have two important features that determine their ability to activate the light-sensitive receptors and neurons in the visual system. This is shown in Figure 4.2. One feature is the rate of change over space, with the visual system generally responding more vigorously to abrupt changes than to gradual changes. The other feature is the magnitude of the change, or the difference in intensity on each side of the edge. Vision scientists often refer to the rate of change as *spatial frequency* and quantify it for any given image by measuring the number of times the reflected light changes in intensity from dark to light within a given unit of space (usually one degree of visual angle). The magnitude of the change is quantified in a measure called *contrast*: the difference in intensity across the edge, divided by the sum of the intensities on each side of the edge. The reason for dividing the difference by this sum is to make the contrast measure relative to the total amount of light reflected from the image.

One of the tools vision scientists use to quantify the number and kinds of edges in an image is *Fourier analysis*. This is a mathematical process by which any image, no matter how complex, can be analyzed as a set of simple sinusoidal (sine wave) patterns of changes in light intensity. When the patterns change along only one dimension, they are called *gratings*. Figure 4.3 presents examples of grating of various spatial

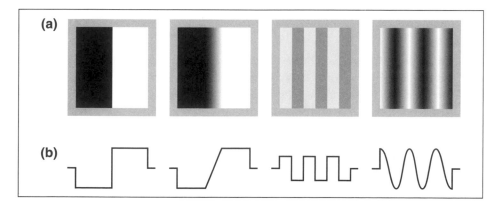

FIGURE 4.2 (a) Several kinds of edges found in visual images. (b) The luminance profile of these edges that would be obtained by sweeping a photometer (a device measuring light intensity) across them from left to right.

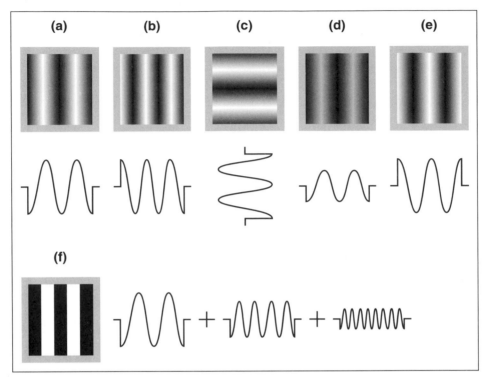

FIGURE 4.3 One-dimensional patterns, called *gratings* by vision scientists, that differ from (a) the standard grating in (b) spatial frequency, (c) orientation, (d) contrast, and (e) phase. The luminance profile associated with each grating is also shown. The gratings in the upper row are all simple gratings: a single sinusoidal modulation underlies each pattern. The grating in the last panel (f) is a complex grating: its luminance profile can be decomposed by Fourier analysis into a set of simpler sinusoidal patterns.

frequencies and contrasts, along with their associated luminance profiles. Each grating can be described completely by only four measurements: spatial frequency (the number of times it completes a dark-light cycle with one degree of visual angle), orientation (relative to the vertical), contrast (the magnitude of the greatest light-dark difference), and phase (the position of the grating relative to some reference point).

In addition to being a mathematically efficient way to describe the spatial distribution of light in an image, Fourier analysis provides researchers with graphically meaningful methods to characterize the way a visual system treats an image. For instance, your own visual acuity (your ability to resolve spatial detail on the basis of differences in luminance) can be described completely by measuring the detection threshold (the smallest difference that can be detected reliably) for gratings of different spatial frequency and contrast. You can summarize your own visual acuity by following the instructions in Box 4.1 and looking at Figure 4.4. The image there increases in spatial frequency as you move right across the figure and decreases in contrast as you move upward in the figure.

The important thing to understand about this figure is that for any horizontal line drawn across the image, the contrast for each of the stripes is exactly the same. You will have to take my word for this, as your own eyes will not allow you to see it for yourself! If you insist on proof, you could use a spot photometer to make measurements of the reflected light all the way across the image. These measurements would show that the same high level of light is recorded every time the lightest gray is encountered and the same low level of light is recorded every time the darkest gray is encountered. Yet when someone with a healthy visual system and optically normal (or corrected) lenses looks at this image, he or she sees black stripes extending to different heights, depending on whether the stripes are thick, intermediate, or thin. As you can see for yourself, the stripes just to the left of the center of the image seem to extend the farthest distance up the page. This is an indication that your visual system is more sensitive to contrast at intermediate spatial frequencies than at lower or higher frequencies. Most estimates of the optimal frequency for contrast detection by the human eye are between 4 and 6 cycles per degree of visual angle.

Spatial frequency

Figure 4.5 illustrates the different kind of information that low and high spatial frequencies convey. Some of these faces are easier to recognize than others. Even if you don't know some of these famous people, it is easy to see that more of a person's face is visible in some pictures than in others. Researchers have found that very little information is needed for humans to recognize that a visual image contains a face as opposed to another object or body part. Furthermore, it is easier to make this judgment on the basis of small amounts of low-spatial frequency information than on small amounts of high-spatial frequency information. However, for discriminating among different faces such as those of your same-sex friends, you also require high-spatial frequency information. In general, face recognition is most accurate for faces in which an optimal middle range of spatial frequencies has been preserved.

It is very interesting that the so-called "optimal range" of spatial frequencies for face recognition cannot be defined with respect to the absolute size of the image. That is, the relevant unit for the spatial frequency calculation is not cycles per degree of visual angle but, rather, cycles per object. Estimates of these optimal frequencies cluster around 8 to 13 cycles per face width (Liu, Collin, Rainville, & Chaudhuri, 2000; Nasanen, 1999; Peli, Lee, Trempe, & Buzney, 1994). The existence of this form of object constancy on what is essentially a visual acuity task indicates the extent to which even the seemingly earliest and lowest-level visual

BOX 4.1

Seeing your own contrast sensitivity function

Materials

You will need a clear plastic transparency, an erasable marker, and Figure 4.4. You should prop the book up so that the image can be viewed from various distances. Alternatively, a friend may be able to hold the book for you. The transparency and the marker can be the kinds used with overhead projectors. Overlay the transparency on the image, and mark the outline of the image on the transparency with the marker.

Instructions

First, view this figure at arm's length, overlaid with the transparency, and mark several locations on the image with a dot where you can no longer make out any difference between light and dark stripes. If you connect these dots, you should have a rough boundary separating visible and invisible stripes. Now view the same image from a distance of 10 to 15 feet, and have your friend mark the boundary of visibility on the transparency. Finally, make a record of the boundary of visibility after you have spent about 10 minutes in a dark room and then have viewed this image under very dim illumination.

Analysis

How do the three boundaries of visibility differ? First, compare the boundary for near and far viewing conditions under standard daylight or room illumination. It is likely that the biggest differences are evident on the right side of the image, since when you moved away from the figure the high spatial frequency on that side of the pattern became even higher. Your eye could no longer resolve the detailed pattern. Second, compare the boundary under standard daylight and dark adapted conditions. In addition to being less sensitive to high spatial frequency, you are now probably also less sensitive to the very lowest spatial frequencies on the left side of the image.

analyses (in this case, the analysis of edges) are influenced by the later and higher-level analyses that they serve (in this case, the recognition of a familiar face). Research has shown that this finding is not restricted to face recognition but holds for many objects (Gold, Bennett, & Sekuler, 1999).

WHAT DOES THE VISUAL SYSTEM DO WITH EDGES?

All biological visual systems have been designed to respond in a special way to change, and our own visual system is no exception. If we are placed in an environ-

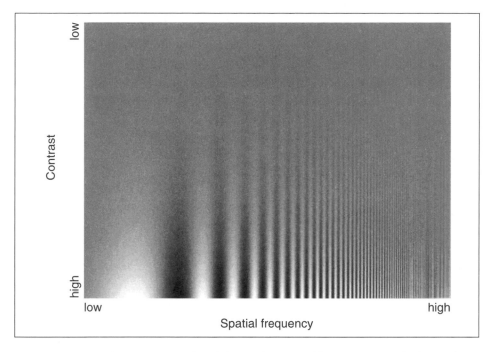

FIGURE 4.4　　This image varies from left to right in spatial frequency (low to high) and from bottom to top in contrast (high to low). The point in the image where you no longer are able to resolve differences between darker and lighter bars is your threshold of sensitivity to edges of a given spatial frequency.

ment in which visual change is eliminated, an experience called *visual blankout* occurs. As suggested by the name, instead of the persistent experience of the visual input that is actually present, the visual system behaves as though it is receiving no input at all. Box 4.2 gives you ideas for several ways in which to experience the condition of blankout for yourself.

Rods and cones

One of the recurring themes in this book is that human vision is able to act as a general-purpose system because it interleaves specialized subsystems into the same anatomical structures. This applies to our discussion of edges in that there are two different kinds of light-sensitive receptors at the back of the large chamber in the eye. One kind of receptor, *cones*, responds to generally high levels of lighting, whereas the other kind, *rods*, is active only under generally low levels of light. These names correspond approximately to gross differences in the shapes of the receptors, with cones being conical and rods being more uniformly thick when

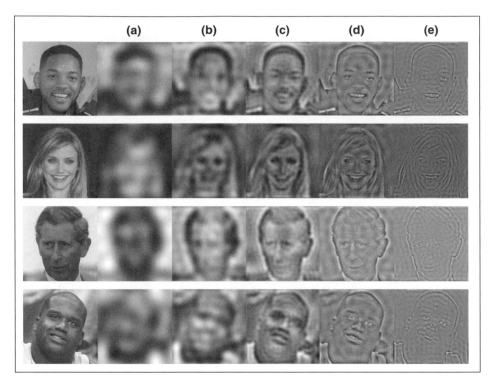

FIGURE 4.5   Which of these faces is easiest to recognize? These are images of four celebrities that have been band-pass filtered, which mean that some of the low and high spatial frequency content of the original image has been removed. For the celebrity in each horizontal panel, all but a narrow band of spatial frequencies have been preserved. This band is two octaves wide and is centered at 2 cycles per face (**a**), 4 cycles per face (**b**), 8 cycles per face (**c**), 16 cycles per face (**d**), and 32 cycles per face (**e**).

viewed under a microscope. Almost everyone remembers learning in grade school that the cones are used for color vision and that rod vision is only possible in shades of gray.

However, contrary to popular knowledge about the eye, cones are not primarily specialized for color vision and rods are not best at distinguishing among levels of gray. Rather, cones are specialized for registering light under typical daylight and roomlight conditions, whereas rods are specialized for registering light under very low light conditions—the kind we might encounter on a moonlit night. This is not to say that cones and rods are equally color sensitive or that rods cannot be used to distinguish light grays from dark grays. They clearly have different abilities to signal certain properties of an image. But that is not their fundamental difference.

What makes cones and rods fundamentally different is that they generally are not active at the same time. For example, for the conditions under which you are

BOX 4.2

Vision without edges

Simulated blankout

A simple and inexpensive way to experience visual blankout is to cut a yellow or green ping-pong ball in half and to place one half over each eye. (Be careful to file or sand off any rough edge before you place the halves over your eye sockets.) You may want to hold them in place underneath a pair of glasses. Have a friend help you, since once your eyes are covered you will not be able to see any forms, although you will be able to distinguish broad differences in light and dark illumination within the room. How long does it take before the light looks gray and is no longer colored?

Stabilized images

An inexpensive way to experience what vision is like once edges have become stabilized on the retina is to stare at the black dot in the center of the gray circle on the left-hand side of Figure 4.6a below. Cover or shut one eye so that you are using only one eye in this exercise. Because the edges of this disc are gradual, your involuntary eye movements while staring at the black dot are not large enough for your eye to register the corresponding differences in the retinal position of this edge. As you continue to stare at the dot, the gray disc will appear to get smaller. If you keep your eyes very still, it may even disappear. Performing the same exercise with the gray disc on the right-hand side will not cause it to disappear. Instead, the disc may appear to become uniformly gray because the dashed gray ring has edges that are too abrupt to be stabilized through voluntary fixation. This condition allows a perceptual filling-in process to occur.

FIGURE 4.6 **(a)** Stabilized images: Shutting one eye and fixing the gaze of your open eye on the black dot on the left will make the gray disc fade away. While fixing your gaze on the black dot will cause the gray disc to fill the region contained by the dotted line.

Filling in

Examine the checkerboard region below, in Figure 4.6b, noting the gray cross on the left and the gray square on the right. Shut your right eye and stare at the gray cross on the left side with your left eye for 30 seconds or longer. The reason for using your left eye is to ensure that the gray square does not fall on your blindspot. The point of this exercise is to make the gray square disappear even though it continues to stimulate the retina in your left eye. After staring at the gray cross for a few seconds, most people report that the gray square disappears from view. However, instead of there being a hole where the gray square used to appear, the region appears to be filled with the same checkerboard pattern as in the surround. Rather than reporting the absence of any seen edges at local regions of stabilized images, the visual system is more likely to create the illusion that the edges that still can be seen are continuous through the region of a stabilized image.

FIGURE 4.6   **(b)** Filling in: Shutting your right eye and fixing the gaze of your left eye on the gray cross will make the gray square fade away.

likely reading this book (typical indoor room light), only your cones are active in response to the letters and words. Your rods are resting, since at these high levels of light they have become chemically bleached or depleted and are therefore incapable of responding to spatial patterns until they have been replenished. If you were to take this book outside on an evening with a full moon, your cones would no longer be activated by the dim light reflected from the pages. Only your rods would be active. Both your rods and cones may be active during a short period at twilight or during other conditions of medium lighting. The technical terms relating to cone-vision and rod-vision are *photopic* (literally, relating to light vision) and *scotopic* (literally, relating to dark vision), respectively.

This difference in specialty between cones and rods constitutes the main reason why it is impossible to read normal text by moonlight. In order to be an effective visual system under dim light conditions, the design of rods and the neural circuits to which they are connected emphasizes a light-catching function rather than one specialized for spatial or temporal pattern perception. But, you may ask, why do these two visual functions—light catching and pattern perception—naturally compete with one another? To understand this tradeoff it is helpful to consider the differences in the light-responsiveness of cones and rods, as well as differences in the path neural signals take from rods and cones as they travel from the eye to the brain.

The chemical and structural composition of rods is such that they signal the presence of light more slowly than cones do. The benefit of the rods' slower response is that a larger number of photons can contribute to the magnitude of the response than if the response were faster. The trade-off is that the sluggish rod system does not record as faithfully any changes in light levels over time. This has a direct effect on the speed of our actions in response to visual events at night. Whether we are driving a car or hitting a tennis ball under dim illumination, our ability to respond is slow.

There is also a direct consequence of the sluggish rod response for reading in moonlight. For example, the small eye movements that normally occur when we try to fixate on a single location on the page, called *optokinetic tremor*, now have a tendency to blur the edges. This occurs because the image falling on any small patch of retina will have changed, as a result of the eye movement, before the rods have finished signaling their response from the original position. Thus all the edges are rendered less sharply than they would have been if viewed by receptors with a more rapid response rate.

More important than the sluggish response of the rod receptors is the neural circuitry in the eye associated with the rods. Rod-vision differs from cone-vision in that it involves specialized circuits. Some circuits involve neurons that are shared with the cone system, but others involve specialized neurons that are devoted solely to signals from rods. To understand this, look at the five main layers of neurons in the eye shown in Figures 4.7 and 4.8. In general, both rods and cones synapse onto bipolar cells, which in turn synapse onto ganglion cells. The long axons of the ganglion cells form the optic nerve bundle that leaves each eye through the optic disc (see the discussion of the blindspot in Chapter 2). But, in addition to these feedforward connections, there are neurons that communicate laterally, called *horizontal* and *amacrine* cells. One type of amacrine neurons, known as AII amacrine cells, are special in that they are connected only to rods. Their response to light is delayed by 65 to 70 milliseconds when compared to cone responses seen in ganglion cells or horizontal cells.

The feedforward connections for rods and cones also differ in two important ways, as shown in Figure 4.8. First, there is greater spatial convergence for rods; many more rods send signals to the same ganglion cells than do cones. This has the beneficial effect of allowing each ganglion cell to be activated by a larger number of photons at any point in time, but it also means that spatial detail is lost.

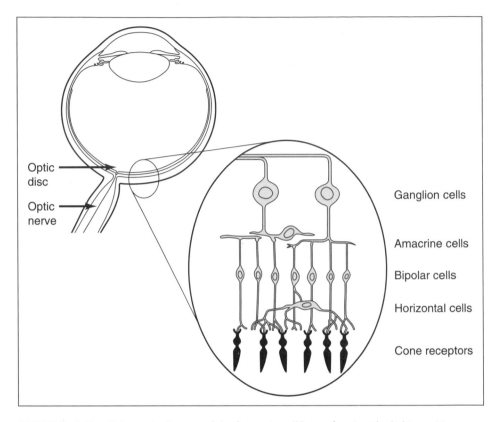

FIGURE 4.7   Schematic diagram of the five main cell layers forming the light-sensitive portion of the retina, shown in exploded view for a small portion of the eye.

Differences in intensity over space will be detected only over larger regions. Second, cone signals are involved in both excitatory and inhibitory connections on their way to the ganglion cells, whereas rod signals are primarily excitatory. This has very important consequences, as we will discuss next.

Although individual ganglion cell axons ultimately transmit signals that originate in both cones and rods (though usually at different times because of the differential sensitivity of the two receptors to the overall level of light), the two types of signals undertake quite different journeys en route to the ganglion cells. Cones make direct connections to both bipolar cells and horizontal cells. In addition, the horizontal cells synapse with bipolar cells. The critical part of this circuit for cones is that whatever the sign (excitatory +, inhibitory −) of the direct connection—and there are an equal number of excitatory and inhibitory connections of this sort—the indirect connections to the same bipolar cell through the horizontal cells are opposite in sign. This has the effect of trans-

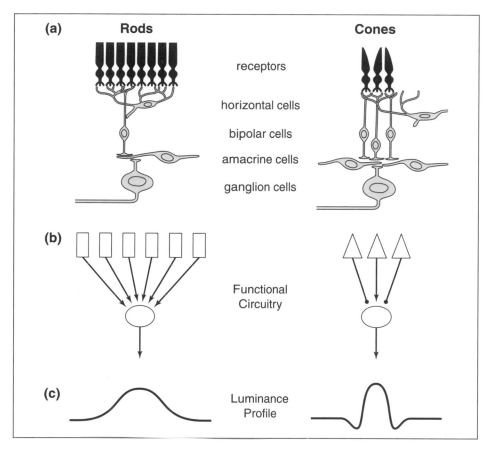

FIGURE 4.8 Retinal cell circuitry for rods and cones. **(a)** The upper panel shows the relations among various cell types in the circuits. **(b)** The middle panel is a schematic diagram illustrating the main features of each circuit. Arrows represent a signal to increase neuronal firing. Dots represent a signal to decrease neuronal firing. The axons of the ganglion cells together form the optic nerve. **(c)** The bottom panel illustrates the effects of each type of circuitry on the luminance profiles of a small spot of light shone onto the central receptor for rods and cones.

forming the original luminance profile of the image entering the eye into a representation in which the edges are exaggerated. This can be seen schematically in Figure 4.8c.

To understand the implications of these differences in wiring for cones and rods, suppose that a single spot of light were presented to each. If it were presented to the cones, only one of the bipolar cells would respond, corresponding to the location of the spot. In fact, the inhibitory connections from this cell to neighboring horizontal cells would ensure that the signal was very clear in comparison to the signal from surrounding cells. However, if a similar spot of light were presented only to the rods, it would cause many bipolar cells to increase their activity. This combined activity would ensure that the weak signal made it to the brain, but it would also promote uncertainty about the exact location of the spot of light. Thus the inhibiting connections of horizontal cells associated with cones helps to ensure detailed form perception under well-lit conditions, whereas the convergence of many rods on a single ganglion cell helps to ensure sensitivity to light under low lighting conditions.

A final important difference between rods and cones is that they are concentrated in different locations on the retina. The part of your retina centered on the visual location that you are currently examining, called the *fovea*, contains many cones but no rods. The surrounding near periphery of the retina, however, is rich in rods but has relatively few cones. An apparent consequence of the smaller number of cones in the periphery is evident in form, color, and motion perception, as described in Box 4.3 and Figure 4.9. A consequence of the distribution of rods is apparent when you view stars at night. You may have noticed that in order to see a dim star as clearly as possible, it is necessary to look slightly to one side of the star or the other. This ensures that the maximum possible number of rods—which are most densely packed a few degrees of visual angle away from your fovea—are activated by the light from the dim star.

Ganglion cells

There are more than one million ganglion cells in each eye that transmit signals to the brain. They collect signals from bipolar and amacrine cells and send them to various parts of the brain. However, ganglion cells do much more than simply pass on the information they receive. They transform that information in a variety of complex ways.

In order to understand the behavior of ganglion cells in any detail—and for that matter, all other visually sensitive cells in the eye and brain—we must explore the concept of the *receptive field*. This is simply the technical term for a neuron's preferred window on the world. Consider the ganglion cells shown schematically in Figure 4.8: one for the circuit corresponding to cones, the other for the circuit corresponding to rods. The ganglion cell in the cone diagram will be activated most strongly by a small spot of light. If this spot becomes any smaller, the ganglion cell will fire less vigorously because fewer photons will reach the cones to which it is connected. If the spot moves or becomes larger, the ganglion cell will be less active because the light will begin to encroach on the cones that inhibit this ganglion cell through their connections via the horizontal cells. Thus we can describe the receptive field of this ganglion cell as having a center-surround organization. The cell's preferred window on the world is a small circular region of a specific size at a particular place on the retina. Figure 4.10 (see color appendix) shows several types of receptive fields for ganglion cells.

BOX 4.3

Measuring the useful field of view

Instructions

Look directly ahead with your right eye closed. How wide is your field of vision? Although it often appears as though our visual field extends from almost 180 degrees to the left to the visible edge of our nose, the amount of useful information in that field of view is quite small. In the three exercises that follow, you will be able to estimate your useful field of view for the visual attributes of form, color, and motion.

Letter resolution

Gaze at one of the black dots below, in Figure 4.9a, with a single eye open. Without moving your eye, name the letters that you can read on the left and on the right of the black dot. Now move your gaze to another black dot and repeat the exercise. How many letters can you read on average when they form words? How many can you read on average when they occur randomly?

There is a • clear advantage

in trying to • identify letters

that form • familiar words.

ahfgytedjklm • qscvfrgthjmklo

huriekoklnhgds • mnbvcdfxzsy

poiunhgtredsw • jkiohygfdcxzasd

FIGURE 4.9a   Useful field of view for letters.

Color resolution

Now fix your gaze at one of the black dots in Figure 4.9b (see color appendix) with a single eye open. Again, without moving your eye, name as many colors as you can see in each row. How many colors can you name on average for the small color patches? How many can you name for the larger patches?

Motion resolution

For this exercise you will need the help of a friend. While you are staring straight ahead at a fixed point on the wall, have your friend move a hand very slowly into your field of view from the rear. Her hand should be five feet or so from your head, off to one side. Ask your friend to randomly raise one, two, or three fingers before moving her hand slowly into your visual field. Record the average location at which you can make this judgment, and use it for the second half of this exercise.

Now repeat the exercise, but instead of having her hand slowly move into your visual field, have your friend place her hand at the same location while your eyes are closed. She should again choose randomly to raise one, two, or three fingers on each attempt. When your friend is ready, she can give you the signal to open your eyes and fixate again on the fixed point. Is there a difference in your detection accuracy for fingers on the moving hand as opposed to the stationary hand?

Analysis

There is a systematic decrease in cone concentration, ganglion cell concentration, and cortical tissue for every unit of distance measured away from the fovea. The useful field of view reflects these decreases. Detailed form vision and color vision, which both depend on parvo ganglion cells (Chapter 2), fall off most rapidly with retinal eccentricity (distance from the fovea). The accurate perception of objects in motion does not degrade as drastically, in part because motion is signaled by magno ganglion cells (Chapter 2), which are more plentiful than parvo cells in the visual periphery.

The division of ganglion cells on the basis of physical size is a distinction associated with numerous important functional differences. These cells' names are based on the Latin terms for "small" and "large," *parvo* and *magno*, respectively. Table 4.1 lists some of their associated characteristics. These functional differences indicate that parvo ganglion cells carry much of the detail with regard to form and color, whereas magno ganglion cells carry more precise information with regard to time and contrast. In other words, parvo cells respond best to images with high contrast and many sharp edges; magno cells respond best to shapes with little contrast covering larger areas with smoother edges.

Parvo and magno ganglion cells are also unequal in their interactions with rods and cones. In particular, rods seem to be connected only to magno ganglion cells, the same ones that convey signals from the medium (green) and long (red) wavelength cones under brighter conditions. As indicated in Table 4.1, when magno cells are activated by rods they have larger receptive fields that are not organized in a center-surround fashion. Even when the same ganglion cell is measured, first under photopic and then under scotopic conditions, the size of the receptive field is found to be larger and the responses more sustained under scotopic conditions. This finding means that the intervening circuitry between receptors and ganglion cells is different under bright and dim lighting conditions. Recent research has shown that the photopic circuitry can be reinstated in the dark-adapted eye by administering certain drugs that apparently block the effects of the AII amacrine cells connected only to rods (Mills & Massey, 1999).

TABLE 4.1

Characteristics of Parvo and Magno Ganglion Cells

CHARACTERISTIC	PARVO	MAGNO
Receptive field organization	Center-surround	Center surround, some center only
Receptive field size	Small (~4 min. arc)	Large (~8–40 min. arc)
Contrast sensitivity	Low	High
Color sensitivity	High, SML wavelengths	Low, wavelength differences only
Spatial acuity	High	Low
Conduction speed	Slow (~2 meters/sec)	Fast (~4 meters/sec)
Retinal distribution	Most dense in fovea	Most dense in periphery and upper retina

Cones, however, are richly connected to both parvo and magno ganglion cells. But this relationship is not uniform across the retina. Because cones are most heavily concentrated at the center of the retina, falling off sharply with distance from the fovea, and magno ganglion cells are most numerous in the retinal periphery, there are several consequences for photopic vision. Most important is a rapid decline in spatial and color sensitivity with increasing distance from the fovea. Nonetheless, there appears to be some beneficial side effects for sensitivity to other visual properties: for instance, an increased sensitivity to small contrast differences and temporal flicker in the periphery largely because of the greater relative concentration of magno cells.

Another important division of ganglion cells, which cuts across the parvo-magno distinction, concerns whether the receptive field is excitatory or inhibitory at its center. In general, an excitatory cell—called an *on-center ganglion*—will respond to increases in light intensity with respect to the local surround, whereas an inhibitory cell—or *off-center ganglion*—will respond to decreases in light intensity with respect to the local surround. These two types of ganglion cells apparently occupy separate but interacting arrays within the eye. This relationship is evident when the activity from two or more ganglion cells is recorded in response to the same stimulus. Neighboring on-center cells and neighboring off-center cells will mutually excite one another, such that their combined activity is greater than if either cell is activated selectively. On- and off-center cells that are neighbors, however, will mutually inhibit one another, contributing to the differentiation of edges.

On-center cells can also be selectively turned off by administering the appropriate drug to the retina. This renders the eye sensitive to the onset of dark shapes (since these are defined by edges involving a temporary decrease in light) but blind to the onset of light shapes. At some point in the brain, signals from these two lattices are combined, because it is possible to see single shapes defined by a combination of light and dark edges. However, where and how these signals are combined is not well understood.

Lower brain structures

Ganglion cell axons that originate in the retinal layers of the eye terminate in two different and important structures deep within the brain, as shown in Figure 4.11. These structures are part of the evolutionarily "older" parts of the brain; we share them with many other animals that have similar visual systems.

The first structure, the *lateral geniculate nucleus* (LGN), is a part of the thalamus, a structure that receives input in the form of feedback from all other sensory regions of the cortex. Thus the thalamus can act as a gatekeeper, allowing only those cortical circuits that are currently of interest to the organism as a whole to remain active, while the other circuits' activity is suppressed—or, to use the neuroscientist's language, inhibited.

Because there are a pair of lateral geniculate nuclei, one on each side of the brain, positioned behind the optic chiasma, each member of the pair receives retinal input from the opposite visual field of each eye. Thus the LGN on the left side receives input from the right half of each retina. In addition to this separation of ganglion cell axons based on retinal field locations, the ganglion axons terminate in six distinct layers of the LGN. The upper four layers consist of parvo cell input, with alternating layers receiving input from each eye. The lower two layers are composed exclusively of magno cell input, one for each eye.

When neurons in the LGN of cats and monkeys are examined with single-cell recording techniques, the receptive fields of these cells display the same center-surround organization as ganglion cells within the retina. The distinctive functions of parvo and magno cells are also evident in these cells. The parvo cells have relatively small receptive fields and are responsive to differences in color, small changes

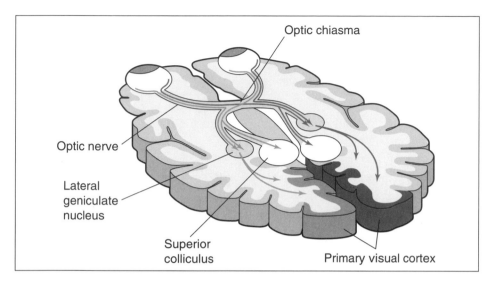

FIGURE 4.11   Location of the lateral geniculate nucleus and the superior colliculus, shown inside an imaginary slab of the brain.

in orientation, and slowly moving objects. The magno cells have larger receptive fields and are responsive to subtle differences in luminance (light versus dark) and are very sensitive to movement.

There is a rapidly growing interest in understanding the way that feedforward and feedback neural signals interact in the LGN. One reason is that it is easier to study these interactions in a lower brain structure outside the cortex as opposed to within the cortex, where the two types of signals are more intertwined. Another reason is that the LGN is the first place in the brain where feedback signals from regions higher in the anatomical processing hierarchy come in contact with signals originating from the eye.

One remarkable finding is that the cortical feedback serves to organize the activity in the LGN cells. Cortical input to the LGN seems to impose its pattern on LGN neural activity, enabling these neurons to behave in much more sophisticated ways than they could on their own. An example of this from the laboratory of Adam Sillito is shown in Figure 4.12, which schematically illustrates the feedforward and feedback connections to cells in the LGN (Sillito, Jones, Gerstein, & West, 1994). A visual stimulus that is a slowly moving luminance edge would not be recognized as such in this region of the visual system on the basis of feedforward input alone because the receptive fields of individual LGN neurons are roughly circular and therefore do not distinguish between a moving spot and a large moving edge of light. However, the neurons that respond to the moving edge in cortical area V1 send return signals to the LGN that are in topographical

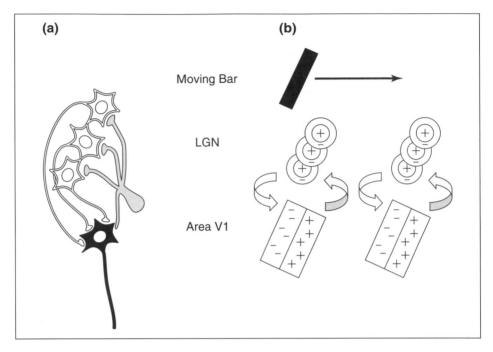

FIGURE 4.12 **(a)** A schematic neuronal circuit involving feedforward connections from cells in the LGN (white in the diagram) to area V1 (black in the diagram) and feedback from area V1 back to the LGN. **(b)** An oriented moving bar presented to the receptive fields of LGN cells would stimulate both feedforward (white arrows) and feedback (gray arrows) processes in this circuit.

correspondence. These returning signals boost the signal strength of neurons in the neighborhood of an individual LGN neuron, causing them to be more sensitive to signals in agreement with the orientation and path of motion of the moving visual edge. Taken as a whole, a feedback loop such as this acts to lock, or focus, a population of neurons onto the immediate visual stimulus.

The other lower brain structure that receives retinal ganglion cell input is the *superior colliculus* (SC), also shown in Figure 4.11. There are a pair of these colliculi (a Latin term for "bumps"), one on each side of the brain, and they receive most of their input from the magno ganglion cell axons. As a result, SC neurons receive their input quickly and respond most sensitively to changes in luminance over time (flicker) and space (motion). Neurons in the upper three layers of the SC are arranged in an orderly topographical manner, with the front portion representing the central retina and the back portion representing the retinal periphery. Because this structure also lies behind the optic chiasm, each colliculus represents information only from the half of each retina that is on the opposite side.

The deeper layer of SC neurons consists of topographical maps for hearing and touch. This makes this structure an ideal junction-box for interactions among vision, hearing, and the tactile senses. When the neurons feeding forward from the SC are examined in conjunction with the neurons feeding back to the SC from cortical regions, this functional role is confirmed. SC neurons project directly to neurons in cortical area V5 (also called the *middle temporal cortex*, or MT), the parietal cortex, and the frontal eye fields (FEF). You may recall from Chapter 2 that these are prominent regions in the dorsal visual stream. It is interesting that there appear to be no direct feedforward connections from the SC to cortical area V1. Because there are direct connections from the SC to the higher-order cortical regions for vision, they can be updated quickly when new information is obtained from a region of space regardless of whether that information comes from the eyes, the ears, or the surface of the skin. Therefore, researchers consider the SC to be a key brain structure in preparing us to orient quickly with our eyes, head, and body to the source of new information from any of these three senses.

Important feedback connections arrive at the SC from visual area V1, from the other dorsal stream regions we have mentioned, and—most interesting—from motor neurons. This means that the structure is constantly being updated, not only by new sensory information but also by information regarding signals to the eyes, body, and hands. You can see, then, why damage to one or both of the superior colliculi (as can occur in a syndrome such as progressive supranuclear palsy, or PSP) causes individuals a great deal of difficulty in making coordinated eye and body movements.

Visual cortex

It is in the convoluted gray matter of the brain, what neuroscientists refer to as the *cortex*, that we first encounter receptive fields of individual neurons that are selective for specifically oriented edges. The story of how this discovery occurred in 1958 is fascinating in its own right. At the time, two young neuroscientists, David Hubel and Torsten Wiesel, were making pioneering recordings of the activity of single cells in the visual cortex of the cat. They were building on the earlier work of other neuroscientists who had discovered the spot-like receptive fields of cells in the retina and the lateral geniculate nucleus.

At the time, their apparatus for presenting visual stimuli to the cat consisted of 1-by 2-inch glass slides on which they glued black dots of various diameters. These slides would be inserted into a projection device so that the images of the dots could be moved around the cat's visual field. Their goal was to see whether the moving black dots could evoke neural activity in any cell from which they were recording. This goal seemed reasonable because other neuroscientists had obtained a similar result when they explored the receptive fields of cells in the ganglion layer of the eye and in the lateral geniculate nucleus. Surely this information was passed on to cells in the cortex.

After about five hours of frustration in which the only recorded activity was the occasional spontaneous burst of firing that a visual neuron makes at rest, Hubel and Wiesel found an area of the cat's visual field in which they were able to elicit a response. However, the stimulus triggering the response was not the black dot. Instead, it was the faint edge of the glass slide moving across the visual field. When the glass slide tilted by 20 degrees to one side or the other, the neuron remained silent. Also, when the edge of the slide moved across this area of the visual field in the opposite direction, the neuron was silent. Only when the edge of the slide moved through the area in a specific orientation *and* in a specific direction did the neuron become very active. We now know that Hubel and Wiesel had encountered their first complex visual neuron, a type of neuron that seems to represent 75 percent of the neurons in area V1 that have ever been tested. In 1981 these two scientists received the Nobel Prize in Medicine for this and related discoveries.

Area V1 has turned out to be a richly complex region of the cortex. One way to think about it that will help you understand this complexity is as a three-dimensional object shaped something like an open book. Imagine flattening out the cortical surface of area V1 so that it is oriented in the same way as a book held open at the middle, with the inner part of the spine lying horizontally with respect to you. Treat this spine crease as though it is the calcarine fissure separating the topographic map of the lower visual field (in the upper portion of the book) from the map of upper visual field (in the lower portion of the book). At the center of the book is the representation of the fovea; moving from there to any edge takes you through the intermediate visual field locations between the fovea and the extreme periphery.

You can think of the pages of the book as different layers of neuronal types. Initially, six distinct layers of cells were identified in area V1 by using chemical staining techniques, and they were labeled layers 1 to 6. But some of these layers, in particular layer 4, have been found to consist of several additional sublayers. To cope with this new information without changing the conventional names, researchers now label these layers as 4A, 4B, 4C-alpha, and 4C-beta. As with other regions of the visual cortex, the middle layers (4C-alpha and 4C-beta, in this case) receive input from axons that originate lower in the anatomical hierarchy. Neurons in the upper, or superficial, layers send axons to other cortical regions higher up in the hierarchy, whereas returning axons from these higher regions terminate in the lower, or deep, layers. Given this rich multilayered structure, it is not surprising that sophisticated visual analyses can take place in area V1.

One of the aspects of visual perception that makes it such a rich sense is that it enables us to see the spatial structure of an object and even to recognize it—if it is a familiar object—regardless of where its image falls on our retina. This implies that area V1 has the ability to represent the spatial structure of an object anywhere it is mapped on its surface. (Note that we are ignoring the cortical magnification factor, which limits how richly fine details can be represented in the outer reaches of the visual field.)

The ability to process edges in roughly the same way anywhere in the visual field seems to occur because area V1 contains a latticework of modules that all perform the same analysis for their window on the world. These modules, called *hypercolumns* by visual neuroscientists, are approximately 0.5 to 1 mm square and 2 mm deep. In keeping with our earlier analogy of the entire cortical area V1 being a book lying open along its spine, imagine this book now being segmented into many small cubes. As a recording electrode penetrates any one of these cubes, we would find neurons at each layer that are responsive to edges of the same orientation. But as we imagine moving the electrode to one side or the other of the cube, two other aspects of cortical organization would become apparent: (1) Movement of the electrode in one direction across the top of the cube would reveal neurons that are sensitive to edges of different orientation, changing in steps of approximately 15-degree differences, and (2) movement of the electrode in the other direction along the top of the cube (at right angles to the previous direction) would reveal alternating bands of neurons. In each band, the neurons would be stimulated more strongly when their preferred edge was seen by one eye rather than by the other. The overall picture, then, is of area V1 being capable of faithfully recording the presence of edges anywhere in the visual field.

Much research in the visual neurosciences over the past forty years has been devoted to classifying the features of edges to which neurons in area V1 are sensitive. Here I will point to only three classes of edge-sensitive cells. These three classes have proven to be the most stable over time, according to new research findings, and they illustrate nicely the range of edge analysis that neurons in this area are capable of, based on feedforward processing from the lateral geniculate nucleus and on horizontal connections along neighboring neurons within this region.

The class of neurons with the simplest response to an edge is appropriately called the *simple cell*; Figure 4.13 shows its receptive fields and probable circuitry. These cells' receptive fields can be thought of as elongated or stretched center-surround receptive fields. That is, they may have a central region that is excitatory for a bar of light oriented in a specific direction, along with two flanking regions that are inhibitory for bars of light oriented in the same way. Alternatively, the receptive field of a simple cell may have only two elongated and oriented regions, each in mutual opposition to the other.

A second class of neuron, and one that occurs more frequently than the simple cell, is the *complex cell*. Figure 4.14 illustrates its receptive field and probable circuitry. It is more complex in that it will respond to an edge of its preferred orientation regardless of where within the visual field the edge appears.

The third class of neuron is the *end-stopped cell*. Not only does it respond to an edge of a particular orientation in its receptive field, but it does so only when the

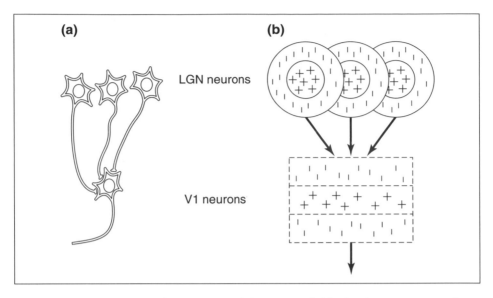

FIGURE 4.13   Simple-cell **(a)** circuitry and **(b)** receptive fields. Circular center-surround receptive fields of LGN neurons feed-forward into elongated orientation-sensitive receptive fields of area V1 neurons.

edge is of a specific length. As Figure 4.15 shows, the cell fires most vigorously when a bar of a particular length moves into the receptive field; longer bars have an inhibitory effect on the overall response. It is interesting to note that this inhibition is specific to the preferred orientation of the central region of the receptive field. If the flanking region of the receptive field is stimulated with an edge oriented differently from the edge that triggers the cell in the center region, the cell will continue to respond vigorously. This suggests that the underlying circuitry is laterally inhibitory in the same way that ganglion cells and color-opponent cells mutually inhibit their neighbors (Chapter 3). What is new in the lateral inhibition at this level of the visual system is that the receptive field properties that are inhibitory are more complex than either simple circular regions of luminance or wavelength. Here, edges that are alike in orientation and direction of motion are organized in mutually inhibitory ways.

A final point to consider in our understanding of how edges are processed in area V1 is that many of the neural signals that enter this region do not come directly from the eyes through the LGN. Many more signals also arrive as feedback from the higher-order visual areas. Thus the receptive fields can be organized in ways that would not be possible if the only signals were feedforward or horizontal.

Neuroscientists who study these feedback connections have found that cells in area V1 can be triggered by information that is distant from the classical receptive field as studied by Hubel and Wiesel. This susceptibility enables the cells to re-

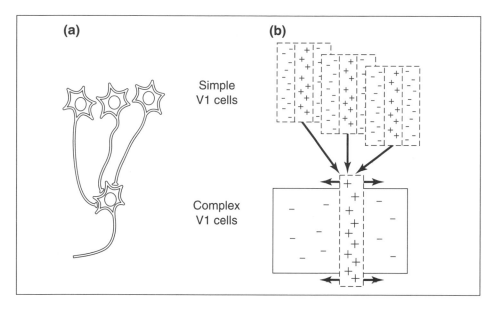

FIGURE 4.14   Complex-cell **(a)** circuitry and **(b)** receptive fields among area V1 neurons. These cells are sensitive to the appropriately oriented bar anywhere within their receptive field.

spond in the same way to direct stimulation and implied stimulation. Figure 4.16 presents an example. In that study (Fiorani, Rosa, Gattass, & Rocha-Miranda, 1992), researchers first mapped the classical receptive field of a cell in the usual way by finding the right combination of visual field location and preferred orienta-tion of edge. They then placed a stationary occluding square over the same region that was more than five times larger than the classical receptive field; this ensured that any activity in the cell could not be triggered by stimuli in its receptive field as conventionally defined. The researchers next tested the cell by sweeping an edge over the occluded receptive field that was longer than the occluding square. In re-sponse, the cell produced a burst of activity just as though it had been stimulated directly. However, cells stimulated in this indirect way tend to fire at a time that is slightly delayed relative to direct stimulation, consistent with their input arriving from feedback connections to visual regions farther along in the processing hierar-chy rather than from direct connections from the LGN.

THE HUMAN RESPONSE TO EDGES

Congenital achromatopsia: Chronic reading by moonlight

One way to understand the importance of edges is to imagine what vision would be like if edge perception was dramatically impaired. As we saw at the outset of this chapter, we do not need to rely solely on our imagination to do this. We can

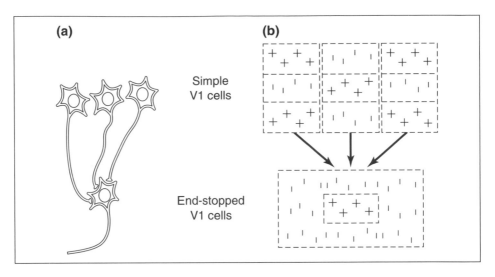

FIGURE 4.15   End stopped cell **(a)** circuitry and **(b)** receptive fields among area V1 neurons. These cells are sensitive to a bar of a specific length and orientation.

experience it for ourselves by trying to read a book or a newspaper in the moonlight. Under dim lighting we can see the effects of removing many of the edge-processing mechanisms that normally influence our vision. Shapes no longer have sharp edges, color is not an additional clue to shape, any motion of an object blurs its edges further because of increased visible persistence, and objects appear brightest not when we look right at them but rather when we view them just to one side or the other of our fovea.

Unfortunately, a condition called *congenital achromatopsia* makes the sensation of reading under moonlight a permanent condition for those who have it. This form of achromatopsia should not be confused with the cerebral achromatopsia we discussed in Chapter 2. Rather than relating to impaired color vision arising from cortical damage, congenital achromatopsia involves the underdevelopment or absence of cone receptors in the eye. It stems from a rare genetic variation that affects about 1 in every 33,000 people in North America. In some islands of the South Pacific there are small pockets of islanders for whom this condition is much more frequent, with many families having several children who are achromats. The name *achromatopsia* refers to the absence of color vision in individuals with only rod receptors, but the absence of color experience is actually a minor complication for these individuals.

By far the most limiting feature of congenital achromatopsia is the almost entire absence of vision in conditions of daylight or typical indoor lighting. Rod receptors quickly become bleached of their chemical pigment under these conditions and then fail to respond to spatial differences in light until they have

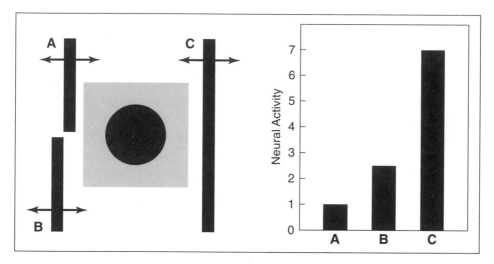

FIGURE 4.16 Stimulating a neuron with edges that are outside the classical receptive field. The black disc represents the receptive field of an area V1 simple cell as determined using the procedures established by Hubel and Wiesel. The gray square represents a stimulus that prevents the receptive field from being stimulated directly. The black bars labeled A, B, and C represent three conditions of visual stimulation outside the receptive field of the cell. The graph records the average activity (number of spikes per second) of the neuron for each stimulation condition. The cell is especially active in condition C, which is when two collinear bars move together on each side of the receptive field.

had an opportunity to recover. This requires spending 10 to 20 minutes in the dark. To preserve some rudimentary vision in normal daytime lighting, achromats often wear dark wraparound sunglasses, heavily tinted contact lenses, or sunglasses with opaque side shields to reduce the amount of light entering their eyes. Also—no surprise—two favorite times of day for achromats are early morning and dusk, when the sun is rising or setting. During these times their eyes are at their best in representing edges under lighting conditions that are neither too dim nor too bright.

Individuals with congenital achromatopsia face a unique challenge in the modern world of trying to decipher printed language, attempting to use their scotopic visual system to perform the detailed form perception that other people accomplish with their photopic system. Congenital achromatopes cope in various ways; for example, they use binoculars to follow a teacher's writing on the blackboard and use controlled low levels of light to read large-print text. In order to be effective, these aids must reduce the overall amount of light reaching the eye while also increasing the size of the features to be resolved. The range of acceptable conditions is not very large. Decreasing the light too much will make the edges indistinct even for the rods; increasing the size of the text through magnification will reduce the amount of text that can be seen at a glance, severely limiting the speed at which one can read.

An additional complication of congenital achromatopsia is a tendency for the eyes to move rapidly back and forth as though they are on a constant search. In fact, they are. The eyes are programmed from birth to reflexively lock onto contours, and when they are unable to find any they continue to rove in search of them. These involuntary eye movements, called *nystagmus*, do little to hinder congenital achromats' vision. They are, however, disturbing for other people—those with a normal set of cones—to watch. This reaction occurs because we tend to read a great deal into the eye movement patterns of those with whom we come into social contact. The nystagmus of congenital achromatopsia alters our perception of these cues.

Hermann grid: Edge enhancement at work

The photopic, or cone-based, system in the eye does not merely record edges as faithfully as it can. As described earlier in this chapter, this system actually exaggerates any edges that it encounters. This exaggeration is accomplished through the circuitry of lateral inhibition found for ganglion cells described in Figure 4.8.

The consequences of this circuitry are evident in the regular lattice of squares shown in Figure 4.17a. Notice that when you glance across the figure, gray smudges seem to appear at most of the intersections. However, one of the frustrations of actually counting the gray smudges is that they disappear as soon as you look directly at them. They seem to appear only at intersections that are not directly in your gaze.

Figure 4.17b shows what is going on at the level of ganglion cell receptive fields. Cells with receptive fields that are center-excitatory and aligned with an intersection are stimulated less vigorously than similar cells with receptive fields aligned on the spaces between squares. Less active cells signal to the rest of the brain that less light is present in a given region than in regions where the same kinds of cells are more active.

Why do the gray smudges disappear every time we try to look directly at them? The answer to this riddle lies in the way that visual acuity diminishes as we move away from the fovea. The decrease in visual acuity corresponds to ganglion cells with larger receptive fields. So regardless of the size of the receptive field that is ideal for us to see the edges clearly at the center of gaze, they are smaller than the receptive fields that create the appearance of gray smudges away from the fovea. You can confirm this by viewing the figure as closely as possible; the gray smudges near the center of gaze become less distinct. Viewing the same figure from a greater distance increases the visibility of the smudges at the center.

Viewing the same figure under very low light conditions, after your eyes have adapted to the darkened state, can give you insights into the different circuitry un-

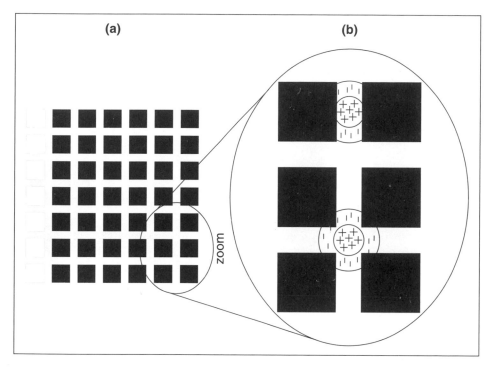

FIGURE 4.17 **(a)** The Hermann grid: a regular lattice of dark squares separated by rows and columns of white. **(b)** An illustration of the responses of two center-surround ganglion cells, one centered on a white intersection in the grid and the other centered on a white column. The total response of each cell can be determined by summing its pluses and minuses. Both cells receive equal stimulation at their centers. However, the receptive field that is centered on the intersection has more of its inhibitory surround stimulated by light, leading to more inhibition and a smaller overall response for that cell.

derlying the analysis of edges by the scotopic, or rod-based, system. You can do this by going into a windowless room and adjusting the extent to which light enters the room through the door frame. Keep lowering the light levels gradually for at least 10 minutes. When the light level is such that you can barely make out the dark squares against the white background, two things will become apparent. First, the dark smudges will no longer be a feature of the intersections in the white lattice-work. This is because the edge-enhancing lateral inhibitory circuits of the photopic system are not activated at this low level of light. Second, the white grid of rows and columns will now be shimmering instead of appearing to be stationary, as they really are. This is because your eyes can no longer lock onto the sharp edges that they see in better light. As a consequence, your eyes begin to rove in much the same way as the eyes of a congenital achromat in an endless search for the sharp edge. This produces the illusion of shimmer and motion in the white grid lines.

Connecting the dots: Edge interactions

We can study the way that edges interact in our perception by creating textured displays of short line segments, as Figure 4.18 shows. The two figures contain the same number of short line segments arranged to form a circular configuration. It is easy to see the circle in Figure 4.18a. The same circle in Figure 4.18b is invisible. The only difference is that the line segments in Figure 4.18a are aligned to lie as closely as possible on the circumference of the imaginary circle. The line segments in Figure 4.18b, although being centered on exactly the same points, are oriented at right angles to the circumference. You will be able to confirm they are there by inspecting each line segment and noting its relation to the next one on the circle. However, you will probably find it impossible to see more than four or five of them at a time as lying on a portion of the curve.

The visibility of the circle in Figure 4.18a points to the cooperative mechanisms that exist in the visual system to join neighboring edges of similar orientation. Researchers can study these cooperative mechanisms by using electrophysiological techniques in animals and behavioral and imaging techniques in humans. The same circle's invisibility in Figure 4.17b points to competitive mechanisms that keep neighboring edges of different orientation separate from one another.

Subjective edges: Seeing edges that aren't there

Take a look at the shapes in Figure 4.19a. If you had to describe all the shapes in the figure, you would undoubtedly report that a square is present among other round and oval shapes. In fact, it is highly likely that you would report a square shape lying in front of the oval and circular shapes. Not only does the square shape seem to be in front of the other shapes, but it appears to be brighter than the surrounding paper. Many people even report seeing faint edges at the place where the square shape makes contact with the background.

If you were to sweep a photometer over these faint edges, you would find that they do not exist on the page. An even simpler way to prove this to yourself is to block your view of the partially hidden round and oval shapes by using extra pieces of paper. Yet you undoubtedly see edges and a surface corresponding to a square shape. What is going on?

Edges such as those in Figure 4.19a are called *subjective edges* (sometimes also *virtual edges* and *illusory edges*). They are excellent examples of the way in which the visual system strives to find a plausible interpretation of ambiguous visual input. Not only does your visual system offer such an interpretation, but it goes so far as to create the perception of edges that don't actually exist. Notice that this imaginative creation of subjective edges does not occur every time you see a complete shape based on partial sensory information. For example, even though you tend to see the black shapes as oval or circular, you do not see any faint edges that

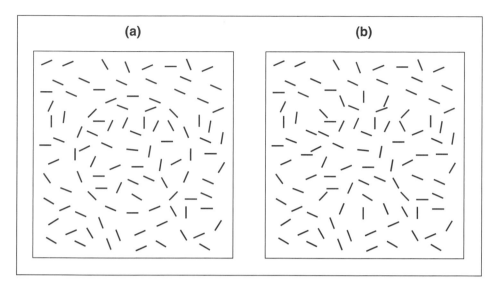

FIGURE 4.18   A circle defined by **(a)** discontinuous line segments, and **(b)** the same number of line segments oriented at 90 degrees to the circumference of the circle in (a).

correspond to the locations where you think these missing edges should be. Yet the edges corresponding to the square are unmistakable. Why the difference?

The reason seems to relate to what's visually plausible. Without any apparent effort on our part, the visual system labels edges as belonging to a surface on one side of the edge or the other. It seems to use several rules in coming up with these labels, but one of the most important is that the side of an edge that is convex—meaning it bulges out—is likely to be a surface that is nearer to the viewer. At least this is true if there is no other information about relative depth, motion, or familiarity to indicate what the true edge assignment should be. By the rule of convexity, then, the round edges in Figure 4.19a are assigned to surfaces that are apparently nearer than the white page on which they are drawn. However, the straight edges of the black shapes pose a new problem for the labeling scheme. Do they belong to the black shapes, implying that the black shapes have indentations? Or do they belong to yet another surface that lies in front of the black shapes? The convexity bias is consistent with the experience of a nearer white surface. Also consistent is the fact that the straight edges of the black shapes are aligned. The visual system is designed to take such converging evidence very seriously. Indeed, it takes the evidence so seriously that it generates a consistent perceptual experience all the way down to the level of perceived edges. In such experiences, all edges of nearby surfaces should be plainly visible, whereas edges of surfaces hidden from view should not be visible. What an imagination!

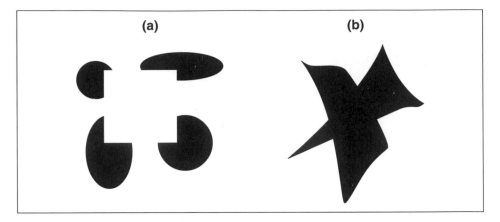

FIGURE 4.19   (a) Square is defined by subjective edges. **(b)** Two shapes that evoke the perception of different edges where they overlap, depending on which shape is seen as nearer to the viewer.

For further evidence of this flexible ability to assign edges as being visible or invisible, depending on what the larger interpretation requires, take a look at Figure 4.19b. This is an *ambiguous*, or *bistable*, figure: At times it appears as though the triangular shape is in front, and at other times it appears as though the other shape is in front. Note what happens to the edges of the shape that is seen as nearer. These edges seem to be faintly visible, whereas those for the shape behind it are not. And when the apparent ordering of shapes is reversed, so are the subjective edges that are faintly visible. Perception of these edges is indeed in the eye of the beholder.

Edges influence brightness perception

We saw in Chapter 3 that the perception of surface brightness does not depend only on the number of photons reaching the eye—that is, on the physical intensity of the surface region in the image. Surface brightness also depends on the surrounding context, such as the amount of light being reflected from nearby surfaces and the interpretation of edges. Figure 4.20 presents two simple examples.

Figure 4.21 presents examples of more complex influences of edges on apparent brightness. Here, either of two surfaces can seem transparent, as in the upper figure; only one surface can seem transparent, as in the middle figure; or sometimes neither surface can seem transparent, as in the lower figure. The relative transparency depends on the relations among the edges at the X-junction that is created when two or more surfaces meet. Briefly, if all the edges move in the same direction of luminance as one sweeps from left to right or from top to bottom (as in Figure 4.21a), then the perception of two transparent surfaces occurs. If there is

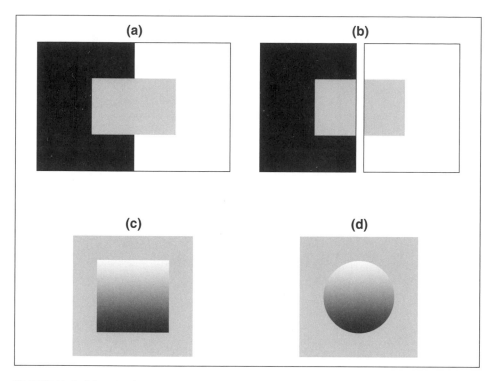

FIGURE 4.20 Brightness perception depends on the presence of edges. **(a)** The central gray square appears uniform in brightness. **(b)** When the two halves of the figure are separated by a small gap, the same gray region appears to be a different shade on each side of the figure. **(c)** The rectangular shape is shaded uniformly from white to black, going from top to bottom in the figure. **(d)** The same uniform shading gradient appears to be a convex spherical shape when surrounded with a circular edge.

one reversal in the direction of luminance in either the horizontal or the vertical direction (as in Figure 4.21b), then only the surface seen as nearer appears to be transparent. Finally, if there are reversals in the luminance change for both directions (as in Figure 4.21c), no transparency appears. Instead, the two rectangles simply appear to be adjacent to one another, along with a square of a lighter color either intervening between the two surfaces or lying on top of one of them.

PERCEPTION BY EDGES ALONE

Are line drawings enough?

Around 1960, two perception researchers performed a daring experiment with one of their own children (Hochberg & Brooks, 1962). Virginia Brooks had recently given birth, and along with her husband, Julian Hochberg, she decided to

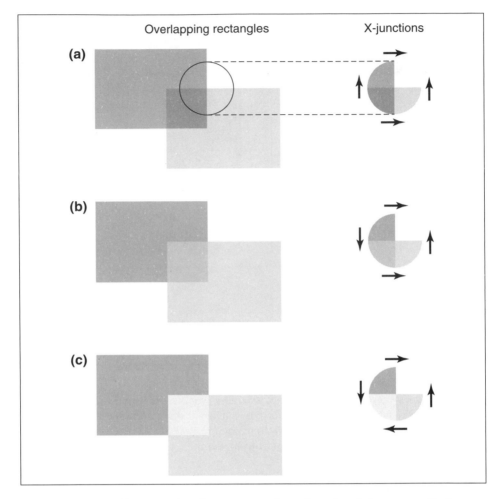

FIGURE 4.21   The perception of transparency depends on the relations among the four edges that come together in an X-junction. The X-junction for each overlapping pair of rectangles is shown in isolation on the right, and the arrows surrounding the isolated junction indicate the direction of change in luminance at the edge. The arrow points to the lighter side of each edge.

raise their son for approximately the first two years of his life with no exposure to pictorial material of any kind. These researchers wanted to see whether a young child would subsequently be able to identify objects on the basis of a pictorial representation alone. To be confident that the child was actually correctly identifying the depicted objects, they would have to wait until he had a working vocabulary that included the names of the pictured objects they wanted to test.

The experiment was heroic because it meant that the television was never on in the child's presence, nor were there any magazines, books, or product wrappers.

On occasional rides in the car, the boy's older sister had the task of shielding his eyes from road signs and billboards. The most important feature of the strict regimen was that the boy did not hear others naming or referring to objects in pictures. By the time he was nineteen months of age this regimen was becoming too difficult, so the researchers stopped the experiment. Fortunately, the child's vocabulary was sufficiently developed to permit much of the testing that the researchers intended. Confronted with a large variety of pictures, both in content and in drawing style, the child proved remarkably adept at naming pictured objects. As expected, he also showed no difficulty at naming objects depicted only as line drawings. The conclusion they offered was that no special learning is required to recognize objects based only on a pictorial representation of their edges.

This feat is doubly remarkable because line drawings don't come equipped with labels indicating which side of a line represents a surface and which side of a line is the background. Recognizing an object pictured as a set of different colored or textured shapes is one thing, since the edges can be assigned to surfaces on the basis of common color and brightness. However, recognizing a drawing consisting only of lines indicates that implied surfaces are correctly assigned to the various regions of the drawing. Hochberg and Brooks's experiment suggests that the interpretation of a line as an edge—along with the rules of edge assignment we discussed in the previous section—occurs sufficiently early in our visual systems to be used to recognize line drawings of familiar objects by the time we can name those objects.

Art and the cartoon advantage

If you have ever tried your own hand at creating a line drawing of yourself or one of your friends, you probably appreciate what a remarkable form of representation it is. What is it about a line drawing of a human face or other complex objects that makes it so difficult for a non-artist to render? At the same time, we have to ask why a properly constructed line drawing is such an accurate and speedy way to convey information from one visual system to another. This is the paradox of object perception via edges.

One of the difficulties of creating acceptable line drawings becomes apparent when we try to specify some of the rules involved in turning three-dimensional objects into line drawings that our visual system finds acceptable. Because a line drawing is essentially a static representation of a scene—and at one moment in time, at that—a reasonable way to begin is to imagine a photograph of a scene. This approach freezes the picture in space and in time from the perspective of the viewer. But which parts of the photograph should be represented by lines?

The exercise in Box 4.4 will give you some important insights into the edges that are perceptually important in an image. In this exercise you will draw a picture by representing the important edges in a scene with lines. Although you will only use lines in the drawing—you will not explicitly represent color, texture, shading,

BOX 4.4

Using a window to create a line drawing

Materials and setting

You will need a clear plastic transparency, some tape, and an erasable marker. The transparency and the marker can be the kinds used with overhead projectors. Now, find a window through which you can view a scene. Ideally, the view will contain three or four objects of different sizes and distances from you. Tape the transparency to the window in such a position that you can sit or stand comfortably in front of the window while tracing lines to represent the edges in the scene you think are important.

Instructions

It is very important in making your drawing that your head always be at a fixed place with respect to the window and that you view the scene with only one eye. This will ensure only one image of the view. Don't try to be artistic in making your drawing; just mechanically trace the outlines and edges that you think are important for someone else to recognize the objects in the scene. When you have finished, place a white piece of paper behind the transparency and make a photocopy of your drawing. Then you can erase the transparency and try another drawing.

Analysis

Examine your line drawing away from the location of the scene. How faithful a record is it of your memory of the scene? Which objects are missing? Are you surprised to see anything in the drawing that you didn't pay much attention to in the actual scene? Compare the drawn sizes and shapes of the objects. How do they correspond to the differences in the actual shapes and sizes of the objects in the scene? Finally, examine the edges that you chose to represent as lines. What rough percentage of the lines corresponds to edges of objects? to changes in surface color? to changes in texture? to shading and shadows? Are you able to recognize some objects even though not all the surface edges are represented?

and surface information—you should have no trouble creating a drawing in which others can identify three-dimensional objects and surfaces. However, equally important, you will choose only some of the edges in the scene to represent as lines.

Figure 4.22 shows the folly of trying to represent all the edges in a scene with lines. Doing this produces terrible errors. Many of the lines in the picture do not correspond to edges in the depicted scene. Many correspond to changes in lighting that derive from shading and shadows. Others correspond to changes in color

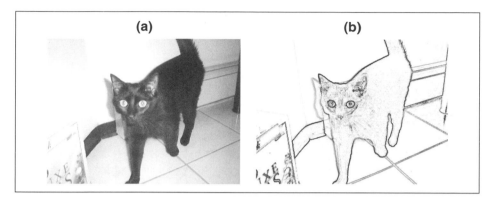

FIGURE 4.22 (a) An original photograph. (b) The same photograph in which each edge that meets a set of "edge criteria" has been replaced with a line segment. The criteria consist of measurements made on contrast changes in the picture. Both the spatial window over which these changes are measured and the magnitude of change to achieve threshold could be varied, but the general result would remain the same. Many of the lines in the picture do not correspond to edges in the depicted scene, and many edges in the depicted scene are not represented by lines.

on the same surfaces. Worse, many of the edges in the depicted scene that a human observer knows to be there are not represented by any lines at all. Clearly, in order to make an acceptable line drawing, one should primarily preserve lines that correspond to edges of surfaces in the scene. The rest should be erased. One should certainly include edges that are known to exist at places where surfaces meet in the depicted objects, even if they don't meet the criteria of the rules for rendering luminance changes as lines. Those lines need to be added.

What is needed, in short, to create acceptable line drawings of real-world scenes is a visual system that can perform object recognition. This was the advantage you had for the exercise in Box 4.4 over the edge-finding computer program whose work appears in Figure 4.22. But having only this object recognition is not enough, as indicated by the dismal failure of most non-artists to render a recognizable drawing of a complex object such as a face. Additional training is required—in most cases, a great deal of training. This training consists, among other things, of systematically learning to ignore many of the perceptual experiences that are evoked every time we view a scene. These are the experiences that enable us to see a three-dimensional object rather than a flat representation of the edges in that object. The exercise of Box 4.5 and Figure 4.23 illustrate how hard it is to ignore these experiences. In short, our natural strong tendency to draw what we think are the relations among edges in the image, based on our perceptual experience with three-dimensional solid objects, prevents us from being able to easily draw the relations among edges as they are presented to our eye.

When an artist or a cartoonist does a line drawing well, it conveys the important relations among edges in an object. It is uncluttered by all the other edges that

BOX 4.5

Drawing with the upside-down part of your brain

Materials

Two sheets of paper, a pencil, and an eraser.

Instructions

Keep this book upright at all times while you are making line drawings of the following two photos. Begin by sketching the upside-down baby's face in photo a of Figure 4.23, showing only the outline shape of the head, the eyes, the nose, and the mouth. Your drawing should also be upside down with respect to your piece of paper. Don't worry about the fact that you have no artistic experience. You don't need any for this exercise. Simply do your best to faithfully record the spatial relations between the outline shape of the head and the lines corresponding to the main facial features. Remember to label this drawing as a.

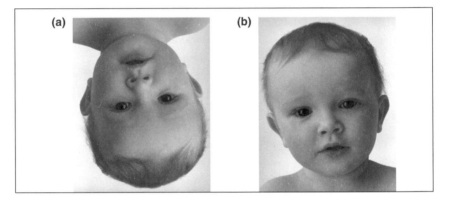

FIGURE 4.23   The upside-down part of your brain: drawing exercise.

After you have made a drawing of the face in photo a, do the same for photo b. This time, both the photo and your drawing will be upright. Don't forget to label the drawing as b.

Analysis

Now place your two drawings side by side, both in an upright orientation so that you can compare them directly. You may also turn the book over so that you can see the two photos are identical.

Which do you think is the more accurate drawing? In which drawing did you best preserve the spatial relations among facial features—such as the relative distance between the eyes, the eyes and the nose, and so on? Which drawing has the most faithful rendering of the outline shape of the baby's head? In order to answer some of these questions, it may help to compare both your drawings and the photo when they are upside down.

may have been in the visual image but were unimportant to its identification. It also renders those edges in relation to one another in a way that mimics the relations among edges in a photograph. Good portrait cartoonists go a step farther and exaggerate those facial features that distinguish a famous face from other faces.

All the features of the well-done line drawing work together to permit a viewer to process this visual information in record time. There is, in fact, a long line of research in visual perception called the *cartoon advantage*, referring generally to line drawings, and the *caricature advantage*, referring specifically to face recognition. If we measure the time required to identify an object or a person in a picture, we can do it more quickly for some line drawings than for corresponding color photographs of the same objects or people. Sometimes less information is better. In this case, line drawings really can be considered the superhighway to visual recognition and object identification.

Silhouettes and shadows

Skilled artists can use the very minimum of edges and lines to convey a great deal of information and to evoke a full range of moods in viewers. Are some edges better rendered than others in the construction of a line drawing? Visual artists and vision researchers seem to agree that the faithful rendering of at least some segments of an object's silhouette is very important to successful object recognition. The silhouette is simply the outer edges of an object viewed from a fixed vantage point. These are the edges cast by the shadow of an object when the light source is either in exactly the same location as the viewer (e.g., looking east at sunset) or on the exact opposite side of the object from the viewer (e.g., looking west at sunset).

Vision researchers have noted that newborn infants begin their visual exploration of an object primarily through the systematic study of its outer edges. Researchers have also noted that adult human viewers can rapidly identify many objects solely on the basis of silhouettes and are sometimes oblivious to the internal details of a well-known shape, as shown in Figure 4.24. The fact that many people "recognize" the famous person on the left in Figure 4.24b is significant in this regard, since that person's actual face is absent in the photo. All that remains in the digitally altered photo are his hair and shoulders, which comprise most of the silhouette edges. The facial details belong entirely to the well-known person on the right.

Several renowned artists, including Picasso and Matisse, made studies of art that involved the rendering of primarily silhouette edges. Figure 4.25 presents a few famous examples. Note that whereas Picasso's shadowed figures are whole object silhouettes, Matisse's figure is a silhouette comprised of "parts" delineated by edges. We will discuss the relation between parts and wholes in object perception, as well as the role of shadows in perception, in greater detail in Chapter 5.

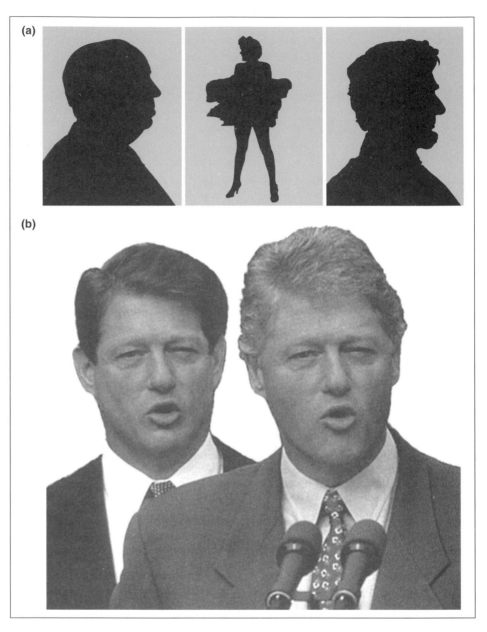

FIGURE 4.24 **(a)** Many famous people are easily recognized solely on the basis of their silhouettes. **(b)** Some people are even "recognized" despite the fact that incorrect facial details appear in the regions of the face interior to the silhouettes. This photo has been digitally altered replacing the facial interior of Al Gore with a copy of Bill Clinton's face. Nonetheless, about 75 percent of viewers identify Al Gore in this photo.

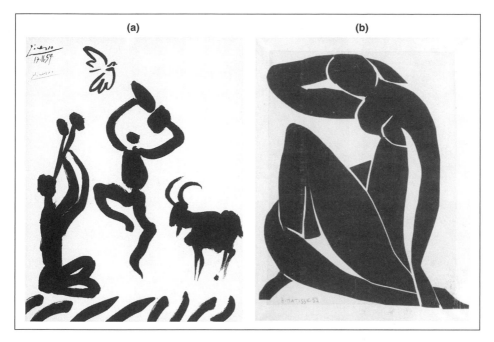

FIGURE 4.25 Objects depicted primarily through silhouettes. **(a)** Musicien, Danseur, Chevre et Oiseau, 1959, by Pablo Picasso. **(b)** One of the *Blue Nudes* by Henri Matisse.

Next to the outline or silhouette edges of an object, the most important edges to render in a line drawing are those that occur at sharp changes in surface orientation within the object. The effects of rendering only those edges are evident in a class of pictures known as *Mooney faces*, as shown in Figure 4.26 (Mooney, 1957). These are pictures of faces that began as photographs but in which almost all the details concerning changes in luminance have been removed. Cartoonists and digital artists call this process *thresholding* the image: All the luminance values in the image below some cutoff point are converted to black, and all the luminance values above some cutoff point are converted to white. The viewer's visual system interprets the white regions as reflecting more light and the black regions as reflecting less. It also assumes that light is shining from above. When this assumption is violated, as it is for the upside-down pictures in Figure 4.26, the viewer has difficulty seeing the images as faces.

But there is more to a good Mooney face than thresholding and light direction. Simply performing the thresholding procedure on any photograph of a face does not guarantee a recognizable result. The best results are obtained when the original photograph is taken with strong overhead lighting from either the left or the right of the camera. This has the effect of placing much of one-half of the face in

FIGURE 4.26   Examples of
Mooney faces in both upright and in-
verted orientations.

shadow, which removes some important information. However, the real benefit of
the lighting arrangement is that it highlights surface changes on the front of the
face—in particular, the forehead, nose, lips, and chin. It essentially produces a
profile of the face from an oblique or foreshortened perspective. Once again, we
see that the important edges to represent in an image are those that correspond to
changes in surface orientation.

WHERE ARE WE NOW?

If you have been reading the chapters in this book in order, it is time to mark a
rite of passage. We have now considered the building blocks of vision from several
perspectives. We examined some of our dearly held but incorrect beliefs about vision in Chapter 1 before meeting the vision scientists and some of their methods.
We also considered in some detail the biological equipment available for accom-
plishing the vision project (Chapters 2, 3, and 4). We surveyed the visual world in
terms of the most elementary units that the visual system is sensitive to: wavelength, intensity (Chapter 3), and the spatial distribution of light (Chapter 4).
But knowing all this, we are still a long way from understanding vision. It is time
to turn our attention to the higher-order objects and events that pervade our

conscious experiences and guide our actions. I'm talking about visual objects such as chairs and people (Chapter 5), about the role of attention in the selection of objects for vision (Chapter 6), about our perception of the space around us (Chapter 7), and about our perception of images that exist entirely within our minds (Chapter 8). In the following chapters, we will leave behind our discussion of the building blocks and raw material of vision in order to see what the vision project looks like from the perspective of these end-products.

FURTHER READING

Graham, N. V. S. (1989). *Vision pattern analyzers*. New York: Oxford University Press.

Hubel, D. H. (1988). *Eye, brain, and vision*. New York: Scientific American Library.

Rodieck, R. W. (1998). *The first steps in seeing*. Sunderland, MA: Sinauer.

Sacks, Oliver. (1997). *The island of the colorblind*. New York: Knopf.

Wurtz, R. H. (1996). Vision for the control of movement. *Investigative Ophthalmology & Visual Science, 37*, 2131–2145.

5 OBJECTS

FUNDAMENTAL QUESTIONS

- How much can we see when we first glance at a scene?

- How much of a picture can we remember?

- What is a visual object?

- What do we assume to be true about the three-dimensional world even though it may not be justified?

- How do we recognize an object the first time we see it?

- How long-lasting is our picture memory? What aspects of picture memory last the longest?

Not too many years ago, researchers studying the role of eye movements in vision stumbled across a remarkable finding that shook the foundations of vision research at the time and is still responsible for much controversy. The finding is so interesting because it surprises the average reader just as much as it did the original researchers. It is simply that when we look at a scene, we see very little of it in any detail. How can this be? In what sense is vision not the rich, detailed experience we seem to have every time we open our eyes? Through the demonstrations and discussion that follow, you will begin to understand what this means. But first, a little background.

The researchers who made this finding knew that during the inspection of a typical everyday scene, humans make an eye movement on average three to four times a second. A typical eye movement sequence consists of a period of 250 to 300 milliseconds during which the eyes are relatively stationary in their gaze, followed by a 10- to 15-millisecond period during which the eyes jump quickly from one location to another. The stationary phase is called the *fixation*; the jump is called a *saccade*, a term borrowed from French that literally means "jerk." A series of fixations is required to view most scenes because of the narrow region of the entire visual field that can be seen with high resolution during any fixation (Chapter 2). Several fixation-saccade sequences occur spontaneously every second we are viewing a scene, and they increase in number if we are looking for something specific in the scene. Figure 5.1 (see color appendix) shows a typical sequence of fixations (circles) and saccades (arrows) for the inspection of a photograph.

The researchers also knew that most of the information acquired from a scene is gained during the fixation. Very little information is gained during the saccade, in part because it occurs so rapidly but also because the visual system shuts down temporarily while the saccade is occurring. The shutting-down feature is called *saccadic suppression.* Its neural basis is not well understood, but its functional effects are clear. Without saccadic suppression, the rapid motion of the image across the retina during a saccade would produce a blurred or smeared view of the scene.

The question of interest was how a sequence of fixations is "knit together" to provide us with the rich experience of being able to see a whole scene at once. The researchers knew this couldn't occur without eye movements, and they knew there were gaps in the acquisition of information because of saccadic suppression. Just how does vision work so that we can see the whole visual field at once? One way of thinking about this that seemed obvious to the researchers was that with each fixation more information was being added to something like a picture in the brain. This would have to involve some form of memory, so that old information could be maintained at the same time that new information was being added. It would also have to align new and old information in space. Without such an alignment operation, perception would become a jumbled montage of snapshots—something that would look more like a work by Picasso than a single photograph. The researchers began to call the picture-like memory they were interested in *transaccadic memory.*

The researchers' approach to studying transaccadic memory involved making subtle changes to an image while study participants observed it on a computer screen. The level of detail for which observers detected changes could be taken as direct evidence of how rich this form of visual memory actually is. To make things more exciting, the researchers had recently perfected the technology to monitor an observer's eye position and to make the subtle pictorial changes only during the very brief time that the observer was making a saccade. That is, the scene would change while the observer's eyes were moving from one fixation locale to the next. By studying the image changes that observers could and could not detect under these conditions, the researchers hoped to map out the kind of information that was being stored in transaccadic memory.

RICH VISUAL EXPERIENCES AND POOR VISUAL REPORTS

The researchers began by making small changes to the computer pictures during saccades, such as increasing the size of a window on the wall of a building or making a small displacement in the position of the entire scene. Almost no observers detected these changes. In fact, when the researchers tested themselves with the equipment, they found it difficult to detect the changes even when they knew where to look and when the changes would occur. This experience indicated to them that transaccadic memory did not hold much information about the details in the scene. They next tested more qualitative changes to the pictures, such as deleting a large object during a saccade and introducing a large new object to the picture. Observers were still unable to detect many of these changes. After some time the researchers became very bold, making such changes as rearranging the hats on two men in a street scene that were clearly the center of interest in the picture. The hats were very different and took up a sizeable portion of the screen. Still, a majority of observers were unable to report that anything had changed. Where was the transaccadic memory that should have been able to detect these scene changes?

In one sense, these experiments were disappointing because they offered little evidence of any transaccadic memory that might support our experience of a wide-angled visual field. Certainly, there was no evidence of a "photographic" short-term memory that the researchers had set out to study. However, their experiments turned out to be revolutionary in setting a new direction in the research. If nothing else, these findings indicated that some of the researchers' basic assumptions were wrong. Vision must be far less photographic than subjective experience suggests it to be. Perhaps, as we have seen in discussing other topics, vision involves the construction of a mental model of the external world, not a detailed registration of the images that arise from such objects.

The researchers who moved the study of transaccadic memory forward from this initial "failure" took their clues from the conditions that sometimes led to successful change detection. For instance, pictorial change detection was always more accurate (1) when observers knew where to look, and (2) when the change occurred to objects of interest to the observers at any given moment. For instance, a change to an object that was about to be the target of a fixation was much more likely to be detected than one made to an object that had recently been fixated. Also, when the same changes occurred during a fixation rather than during a saccade, they were almost always detected because the change in luminance and color at the site of the change seemed to draw attention to itself. This suggested to the researchers that the critical variable in change detection had nothing to do with eye movements at all. Instead, they reasoned, the contents of transaccadic memory might be linked to the contents of an observer's momentary awareness. That is, what an observer might be "knitting together" when viewing a scene might depend on both (1) his or her goals and expectations in viewing the scene, and (2) the momentary changes in awareness caused by the attention-grabbing properties of details in the scene itself.

This change in emphasis on what transaccadic memory was required a rethinking of how to examine its contents. The former view—of the piecemeal construction of a mental photograph—could be tested by briefly presenting a view of a scene and then probing its contents in various ways. In contrast, the new view—of a dynamic representation that depended on an interaction between the state of an observer's visual system and a scene—required methods of testing that would enable the internal mental states of the observer to come into play.

Change blindness in the lab

In one of the first studies emphasizing the dynamic nature of transaccadic memory, observers were shown pairs of pictures such as those in Figure 5.2 (see color appendix). Take a minute to inspect each pair of pictures. Can you see the difference? If not, begin comparing the pictures until you detect the difference. What did you need to do to find the difference? Notice that once you have found it, seeing it is very easy. It actually involves a large change to the image, and some parts of your visual system are responding to these different aspects of the pictures even when you don't notice them.

In experiments conducted by Ron Rensink and his colleagues (Rensink, O'Regan, & Clark, 1997), the two frames were never shown at the same time. Instead, one picture filled the screen for a brief time (around 250 ms), and then the other filled the screen for the same amount of time, separated by a brief blank interval (80 ms or more). The two images cycled on and off until the observer could correctly identify the part of the picture that was changing between frames. Cycling the pictures in this way meant that no eye movements were required to detect the differences. That is, regardless of where the eyes are fixated, the changing object was stimulating the same retinal location. If the observer had any trouble detecting the difference between images, it could not be blamed on a failure to align information from glances taken at different locations in space.

One of the factors in these experiments was whether the objects undergoing the change were at the center of the observers' awareness. This was determined crudely, but effectively, by having some observers who did not participate in the change detection experiment rate the objects in the picture for how "central" or "marginal" they were to the meaning of the scene. As expected, given the new dynamic interpretation of transaccadic memory, observers took much less time to detect a change when it involved an object of central interest rather than marginal interest. In later studies, researchers examined pictorial "interest" by having experts view scenes in which changes occurred to objects that were very familiar to them. For instance, computer experts were better able to detect pictorial changes to office scenes involving different computers, whereas recently trained experts in coffee mug design were better able to detect pictorial changes involving coffee mugs.

Other researchers soon began to take these concepts out of the lab to see whether transaccadic memory would be just as dynamic when it involved vision in a social situation. In the most famous of these studies, the so-called "door study" of

Dan Simons and Dan Levin (Simons & Levin, 1998), an experimental stooge (a confederate of the experimenters) walked up to an unsuspecting person on a college campus and asked for help in interpreting the directions on a campus map. After the stooge asked some questions about the directions and made eye contact with the unwitting participant, two other experimental stooges came by carrying a large door. These stooges interrupted the social exchange of the two people discussing the map, rudely inserting themselves between the two as they passed by with the door. At this point, the original stooge moved along with the door while one of the new stooges remained with the same map to continue the conversation. To everyone's surprise, most of the unwitting direction-givers failed to detect the change in stooges asking for help with the directions. This *change blindness* persisted even though a structural and detailed interview followed the social exchange portion of the experiment in an effort to extract any memory of the change in stooges.

Just as the laboratory studies previously mentioned, change blindness in real-world settings is sensitive to observers' internal states. For instance, when the stooge asking for help with directions was a college student of similar social standing to the student giving directions, many more subjects detected the change than when the stooge was a construction worker dressed in a hardhat and work clothes. This occurred despite the researchers making sure that visual differences between the two individuals in each case (e.g., different colored shirts and different body build) were as equal as possible.

Once you begin to think of vision in this way, you will have no trouble recognizing these dynamics at work all around you. Just think back to the last time you had a close call in traffic. A majority of traffic accidents have a large component of what experts call the "looked but didn't see" effect. The information about the impending collision was on your retina all along; you simply didn't expect to find it there. The growing body of research on change blindness shows that failures in detecting change can be induced by any number of visual interruptions, including eye movements, simple eye blinks, a change in viewpoint as in a movie cut or following a shoulder check in traffic, a temporary occlusion of the changing object, and small splashes or "mudsplats" that occur to the picture while you are viewing it. Box 5.1 gives instructions on a simple card trick that you can try on your friends, following the principles of transaccadic memory as outlined in this research.

The illusion of detail

Even when vision involves the inspection of a single image, meaning that there is no possibility for a change to occur between successive fixations or views, it is still possible to have the experience of seeing detail in an image that is not actually present. Visual artists and computer graphics experts are well aware of this and often use it to their advantage to evoke the illusion of detail. A few dabs of the

BOX 5.1

A simple card trick

Try this trick on yourself first by looking at the six face cards in Figure 5.3 (see color appendix). First, cover Figure 5.4 with a piece of paper. Then look at all the cards in Figure 5.3, but select only one to remember. Make sure you don't tell anyone which card you have chosen. Now, look at Figure 5.4 (see color appendix). The secret card you selected has disappeared! How does this trick work?

Materials

A standard deck of playing cards. Remove from the full deck a random set of six face cards and another random set of five face cards. These eleven cards are the only ones you need for the trick. Keep the set of six separate from the set of five.

Instructions

Announce to your audience that you have recently discovered you have the power to read minds. They may find this a little difficult to believe, so reinforce your claim by telling them you recently received a little training in the dark art of mind reading in a book you read. You can also mention that the author has a special interest in mental powers that do not depend on the standard senses of seeing and hearing.

Show your audience the six face cards, as in Figure 5.3, and ask each person to carefully look at each card before choosing one to be the secret card. Warn them not to tell anyone else which card they have chosen, or your power to read minds will be weakened.

When each audience member has his or her card firmly and privately in mind, remove the six cards and say, with the flourish of a stage performer, "I will now use my special powers to remove your chosen card from the set." Then return the second set of five cards for viewing by the audience.

Be warned that many will not believe you have actually read their minds. Instead, they will think you have somehow attracted the attention of all audience members to the same card in the original set. That would be a good trick too, if you could do it.

Analysis

This trick fools people for two simple reasons, both of which are key to a general understanding of change blindness. First, human viewers generally assume that the world is stable. Objects do not mysteriously appear and disappear. Second, viewers do not detect changes in objects to which they have not attended. The cards that they viewed but did not select for memory registered only at the crude categorical level of "face card." The specific combinations of face (jack, queen, etc.) and suit (hearts, spades, etc.) were not individually coded and in fact cannot be coded rapidly for six objects that are so similar.

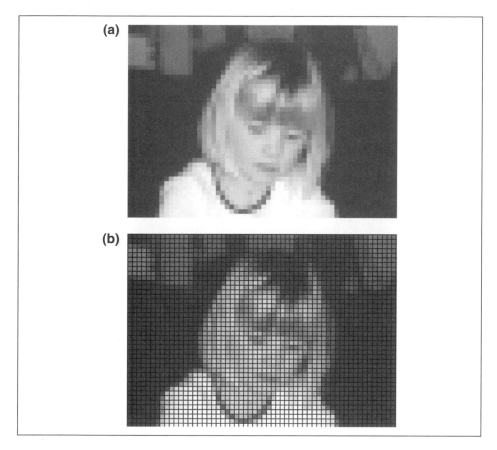

FIGURE 5.5   Which picture includes more detail of the girl?

paintbrush using well-selected colors and locations can leave the viewer with the impression that more detail has been painted than a careful examination supports. Painters of the Enlightenment period, rendering people in pose, often used this technique in painting their subjects' costumes. This presumably enabled the painters to spend more important time and resources on the careful rendering of the skin—especially the subjects' faces and hands, which viewers would inspect the closest.

Figure 5.5 offers a good example of an illusion of detail. Look at the two pictures, one showing the face of a girl behind a fine screen and the other showing the same picture in "blocky" form, and ask the question *Which picture includes more detail of the girl?* Most viewers reply that the picture of the girl in Figure 5.5b looks "less jagged" or "less blocky" and therefore contains a finer-grained degree of shading. Any "blockiness" in this picture can be attributed to the screen that separates us from the picture of the girl. In fact, the two images are identical, with the exception that each block in Figure 5.5a has been outlined with a black line in Figure 5.5b. The black lines can be interpreted as a fine screen, but otherwise nothing has altered each of the original blocks in the picture. Yet it appears that when interpreting the picture with the screen, the visual system assumes that the luminance differences among neighboring blocks blend into one another. The assumption is false in this case, leading to the illusion. No similar "external" interpretation can apply to the abrupt changes in luminance in Figure 5.5a, so this picture looks just as blocky as it really is.

HOW MUCH CAN WE SEE AT A GLANCE?

The examples we have just discussed point to the fact that vision is less like a mental photograph than it is like a built-to-order construction project, designed to accomplish specific tasks and goals. But the examples are also limited in what they can tell us about the details of how this dynamic process works. For that we have to go back into the lab. In the section that follows, we will consider a variety of laboratory tasks that reveal important limits on what we can see at any moment and on the kind of information we can retain over the short interruptions that occur with saccades, blinks, and changes in the viewpoint of a scene.

Bridging the gap: Short-term memory

Figure 5.6 shows a pair of images that are identical except that one shape is different in the two pictures. A square in one image is at the same location as a triangle in the other. These two images are presented in rapid alternation so that they appear to flicker on the screen. One of the advantages of using this flicker method to study transaccadic memory is that it permits careful control over the amount of information that study participants, or observers, must retain from display to display in order to detect a difference. For instance, the total number of items that observers must monitor for a change can be varied systematically. So, too, can the length of time for which each frame is displayed.

Experiments indicate a sharp upper limit on the number of items, or shapes, that can be monitored for change. And this limit is surprisingly small for most healthy observers. It is around four. There appear to be some individual differences in the upper limit, with some highly skilled and practiced observers being able to monitor up to seven items successfully. But individual differences also occur in the other direction, such that in some studies healthy senior citizens can monitor only one or two items at a time. For now, we will use the number four as a useful average since it agrees with estimates of the capacity of short-term visual memory based on other tasks.

One task involves a simplified version of the cycling displays in which only two frames appear, as in Figure 5.7. We can call the first frame the *sample* display and

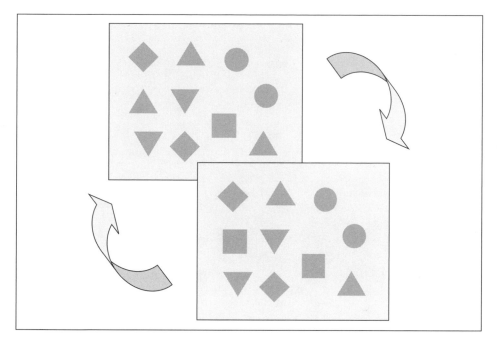

FIGURE 5.6   Pairs of images used in the flicker method for studying change blindness. When the number of shapes that observers must monitor for change is four or less, detection times are rapid and similar. But when the number exceeds four, the time needed to detect a change increases sharply with each additional shape.

the second one the *test* display. The observer's task is to indicate whether he or she detects a change in one of the items from sample to test display.

Studies measuring change detection in such sample and test displays point to an upper limit of four items for most individuals. In studies by Steven Luck and colleagues (Vogel & Luck, 1997; Vogel, Woodman, & Luck, 2001), the researchers took a great deal of care to ensure that a pure form of visual memory is required to perform the task. For instance, they used items that observers could not readily label verbally so as to remember the individual items. If color patches were the target items, then each color would appear in both the sample and the test displays. Also, the researchers minimized verbal rehearsal as a beneficial strategy by having observers engage in other verbal tasks simultaneously with the visual memory task.

These studies indicate that memory over short intervals such as 100 ms is restricted to about four items. One of the most interesting secondary findings is that the limit of four holds regardless of whether (1) each item consists of a single property, such as color, or (2) each item is a bundle of features including color, orientation, length, and texture. Thus the limit of four refers to collections of

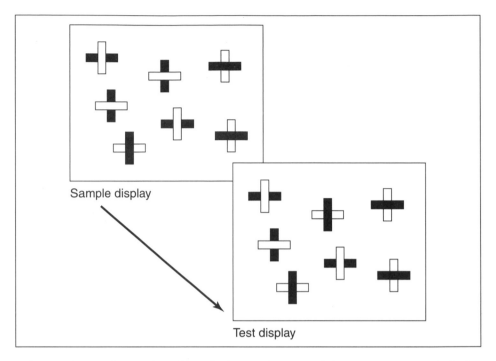

FIGURE 5.7   The sample and test displays used in a typical short-term memory task. Each cluster contains a combination of features including color, orientation, and depth ordering. Performance is sharply limited by a memory capacity for about four items in these displays.

visual features at four distinct locations in space, not simply to four different pieces of information.

Counting sheep: How many?

Look at the displays in Figure 5.8, and count the black bars in A as quickly as you can. Now count the vertical bars in B. Finally, count the vertical *and* black bars in C. This counting task, technically called *visual enumeration*, involves keeping a record of the total number of items of a given kind in a display.

Two qualitatively different patterns of results occur in studies of visual enumeration. When observers try to enumerate either a small number of items presented by themselves in a display or a small number of items distributed among other items that differ by a simple visual feature such as color (e.g., black) or orientation (e.g., vertical), then the time to do the task varies little with each increase in item number. This rapid enumeration process, called *subitizing*, underscores the feeling that counting is not necessary for these displays. The number simply pops into mind.

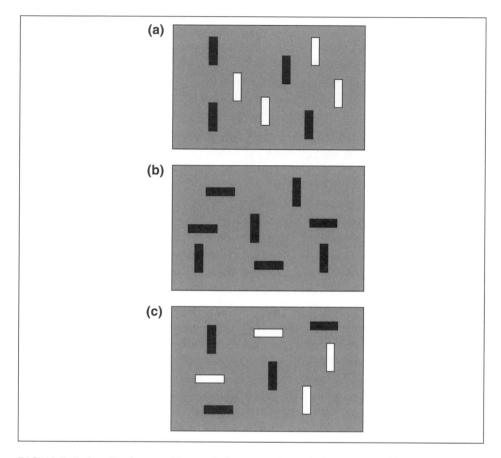

FIGURE 5.8 Displays used in a typical enumeration task. **(a)** How many black bars are there? **(b)** How many vertical bars are there? **(c)** How many black and vertical bars are there?

When observers try to enumerate more than four items or a small number of items distributed among other items that differ in feature combinations (e.g., they are either black or vertical but not both), then task time and errors increase sharply with each additional item to be enumerated. This slower enumeration process, called *counting*, feels like the mental arithmetic operations involved in keeping a running total of a set of events.

As in the studies of short-term visual memory, we again encounter the number four as a limit on performance. Apparently, the conscious processes of vision are able to "keep their fingers" on only four objects at a time. If more than four objects are involved, then some time-consuming and error-prone mental processes are engaged to bridge the gap between the information reaching the eye and the information accessible to visual awareness.

Keeping tabs: Tracking objects in motion

Another task in which performance is limited by a number factor involves tracking objects in motion. Imagine that you have to do the task shown in Figure 5.9. At the beginning, all the dots are identical and stationary on the screen. Suddenly, a few of them blink a few times. This is your cue to track these dots in an upcoming movie sequence. All dots in the display then begin to move randomly for 10 to 15 seconds. When any given dot reaches the edge of the screen it changes direction, like a billiard ball hitting the edge of a pool table. At the end of the movie, all the dots stop and one of them flashes several times. Your task is to indicate whether this dot was part of the original set.

If you can answer this question correctly, it means that you were somehow able to keep track of the target dots over the period that all the dots moved randomly in the screen. You can accomplish this tracking only by keeping a mental "finger" on each dot. But how many dots can our mental fingers track at a time? No surprise, the answer is four. It is clear that all the dots form a part of our general visual experience, but only a small subset of up to four dots can be treated as individuals in this visual task.

Studies on the nature of the memory involved in the tracking task indicate that it is a crude form of space-time memory. Every few moments, it updates the position of each targeted item and retains very little information regarding the item's identity. For instance, if the dots differ in color and then become the same color just before the probe screen appears, accuracy for reporting the color of the target dot is very low. Accuracy is also low for reporting changes in the identity of the target dots that occur during the movie sequence. The only thing this form of memory is good at is keeping track of the spatial positions of up to four moving target items.

The magical number one

Demonstrations of change blindness and short-term visual memory limits are valuable because they illustrate the large gap between the way vision appears to function and the way it actually works. On a daily basis, we are fooled about the extent to which we constantly make eye movements and the extent to which these eye movements contribute to the illusion that a whole scene is simultaneously in view. Some scientists refer to this phenomenon as the *grand illusion of complete perception* to make the point that it is the most pervasive and fundamental of all the visual illusions that have been discovered so far. The illusion is adaptively supported by our habitation of a world that is more or less stable. For instance, my hypothesis that there is a detailed, colored object in my peripheral field of view is usually confirmed by making a quick glance in that direction. Detailed vision occurs "just in time." When something in my field of view actually moves or changes in ap-

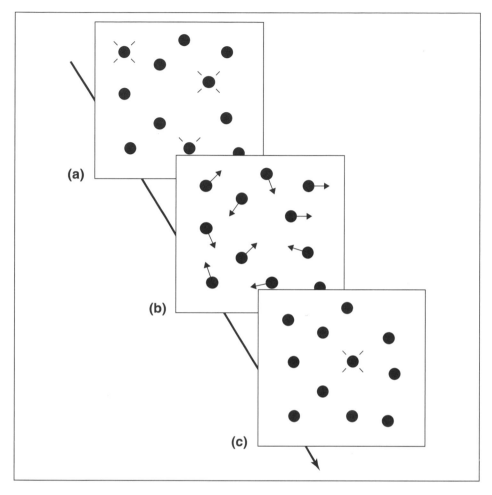

FIGURE 5.9 Displays in an object-tracking experiment. **(a)** A subset of dots flashes at the outset of a movie sequence, indicating which dots are to be monitored. **(b)** During the movie, all the dots move randomly inside the viewing area. **(c)** At the conclusion of the movie when all the dots stop, one dot flashes again. The viewer must indicate whether it was one of the dots that flashed originally.

pearance, a local change in brightness and color alerts me to examine in greater detail the visual field at the location of the change.

It is only artificial circumstances of unannounced scene changes made during eye movements—or of alternating displays, or of cuts in video sequences—that point to the severe limitations on our ability to maintain a continuous mental record of what we see. Even these artificial "experiments" are increasingly relevant in our modern, technological world. It is a world in which humans operate vehicles on land and in the air at speeds that far exceed the limits of the neural connections between sight and action. It is increasingly a world in which the tools we use often provide a sense of reality that is one step removed from the physical world. Consider the tasks of monitoring a security video channel, operating a flight simulator, or performing surgery or space exploration at a distance. In these virtual worlds, where we cannot assume the stability of the visual world with the same certainty as the real world, the principles of change blindness and grand illusion of complete perception become even more critical.

As we have seen, research on the limits of vision at a glance converges on the number four. This small number of objects is certainly far fewer than we think we remember when we look at an everyday scene. But a closer examination of the kinds of visual tasks we can perform on this handful of objects seen in a glance suggests the situation is even more dire. In terms of having a high-fidelity visual representation of something we see—the kind we usually assume when glancing at our friend's face or recognizing our car in a parking lot—the limits of attention are often reduced to a single object.

An especially striking example of being able to attend to only one object at a time occurs when we create a pair of images such as those shown in Figure 5.6, but this time we ensure that each shape changes identity from frame to frame, with the exception of one shape. Figure 5.10 provides an example of such a display sequence. The time it takes to determine whether a pair of alternating images has a shape that *stays the same* increases with each additional display shape, even when there are fewer than four. This comes as a surprise to most people, including most vision scientists. Even though we can monitor change in up to four shapes at a time (Figure 5.6), monitoring for constancy in object identity reduces our effective visual window to a single object (Figure 5.10).

A similar thing happens when we are asked to report on more than one of the shapes we were monitoring in a short-term visual memory task (Figure 5.6). If we subsequently have to report the color and orientation of only one shape, our accuracy on both reports is nearly perfect. This result might suggest that we have rich and detailed memory of up to four shapes or objects at a time. However, if the task changes slightly, still requiring reports on only two visual properties—but this time on the color of one object and the orientation of a second—then our accuracy is significantly reduced on both reports. Accurate reporting of multiple visual properties is only possible for a single object seen in a glance.

This principle holds equally for visual enumeration and object-tracking tasks. If enumeration depends on the proper linking of two or more visual properties (e.g., color and orientation), or if successful object tracking depends on accurate monitoring of any identity changes, then the number of objects that can be seen in a glance is reduced to one. The general rule seems to be that any visual report requiring us to divide our attention among the details of two or more objects leads to a dramatic drop in accuracy. Thus some researchers propose that the "magical

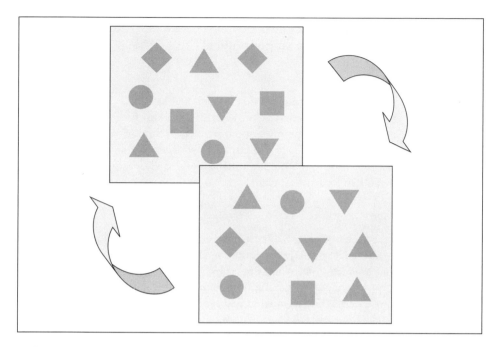

FIGURE 5.10 Pairs of images used in the flicker method for studying change blindness. In this case, the identity of every shape but one changes from one frame to the next. Can you spot the one shape that remains the same?

number" in vision is not four, but one. In Chapter 6 we will discuss in greater detail the time course of this effect (the length of time required to "see" an object in this sense). Box 5.2 presents a demonstration. It suggests that even our vision of a single object is not uniformly rich in detail.

WHAT IS A VISUAL OBJECT?

If detailed vision is limited to only one object at a time, and sometimes even less than that, it becomes important to determine what vision deems to be an object. But this is not easy to do. Just as we saw in Chapter 3, where the definition of color could not be mapped directly to a physical property of light (wavelength), it is impossible to define an "object" for the visual system by appealing directly to the physical world. In the world of solid objects, molecules that adhere together and move together may be good starting points for a definition of "object." However, in the world of reflected light, "object" must be defined solely on the basis of visible properties—properties that can be conveyed by light. This is more than a philosophical point. It means that our definition of a "visual object" will be unable to distinguish between (1) real objects that give rise to a particular image, and

BOX 5.2

Uneven perception of a single object

Background

Figure 5.11a is the ambiguous wire cube we first saw in Chapter 1. It can be seen as though the side labeled 1 is at the back of the wire cube, in which case the cube is being viewed from above. But it can also be seen as though the same side is at the front of a wire cube being viewed from below. Simply viewing the picture usually leads to spontaneous shifts between these two interpretations.

Instructions

Now take a look at Figure 5.11b. It is a drawing of an unambiguous cube. The side labeled 1 is clearly a solid surface because the lines representing edges that are farther away are not visible behind it. As such, the cube in the drawing is being viewed unambiguously from below. Now look at location 2 for a few moments, and note what you see.

Analysis

Most viewers report that when they look directly at location 2, they seem to view the cube from above—at least that is their interpretation of the corners near location 2. Viewers can still "see" the corners at location 1 even though they are no longer at the center of their gaze. Yet the corner there seems to have much less influence on their interpretation of the cube than it did when it was the center of fixation. This indicates that even for a single, static view of an unambiguous object, perception is not uniformly detailed.

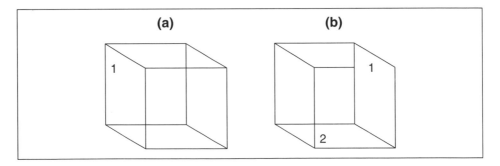

FIGURE 5.11   (a) the ambiguous wire cube and (b) one of its partners, an unambiguous wire cube with a solid side that nevertheless "flips" to a different orientation when the eyes shift from location 1 to location 2.

(2) virtual objects as seen in pictures and movies, provided they give rise to the same image. At the same time, this does not mean we can reduce our discussion of visual objects to the level of two-dimensional images. As we have seen many times already, vision concerns the conscious experience of, and action upon, objects that are "out there." Image processing is an important aspect of vision because our visual system is organized around a rich variety of topographic maps of the visual field, but all these images enable us to see objects in the external world. This is the sense in which the visual system sees objects and not merely images.

Visual objects are notoriously difficult to define. At the moment, no definition of "object" satisfies all vision scientists. Yet as we saw in our discussion of transaccadic memory, there is something importantly "thing-like" about certain kinds of information that helps to organize and place limits on our visual functioning. In this section, we will consider various ways of thinking about what a visual object is. There seems to be enough truth in each approach to suggest that when a coherent definition of a visual object is finally available, it will include in some way all these ideas about the "visual object."

Spatial attention

As mentioned earlier, when we view a typical scene we make a series of eye movements to acquire details from its various regions (Figure 5.1). Yet even when we are prevented from making physical changes in eye position over time—either because we are instructed to maintain fixation in the center of the picture or because the picture flashes on and off before our eyes have a chance to move—there is still a sense in which we can choose to view one object and not another. This mental selection process, called *covert spatial orienting*, is different from the *overt spatial orienting* involved in making eye movements. We use the covert process when we want to inspect someone or something in our visual field without letting others know where we are looking. Athletes in many team sports are experts in this skill, which enables them to pass to teammates without looking directly at them and to avoid opponents who are approaching without losing sight of the ball or the puck.

Studies have shown that covert spatial orienting results in visual benefits for the objects that are attended, and that we see less well the objects that are not the focus of covert orienting. In early studies on this topic, researchers regarded the mental processes of covert orienting as being similar to a flashlight or spotlight that could shine on a region of the visual field and increase the visible detail of objects located there. However, more recent studies demonstrate that the enhancement of vision for attended regions of the visual field applies to something that resembles an object more than it does a region of space.

For example, in some studies of covert orienting the visual sequence consisted of the displays shown in Figure 5.12. The displays showed a pair of rectangles that

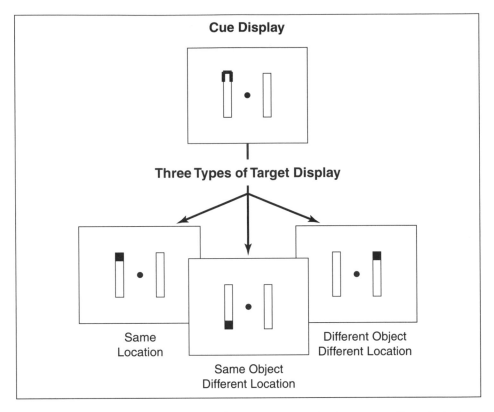

FIGURE 5.12   The display sequence for testing covert orienting to one of four display locations. Not only does the upside-down U-shape in the cue display speed the perception of a
square target that appears in the same location, but it also speeds the perception of the square
when it appears elsewhere within the same rectangle.

could be oriented vertically or horizontally. At the beginning of each sequence
there was a cue display consisting of a brief brightening of one end of one rectangle. This was followed after a brief interval by the presentation of a dark square in
one of the four ends of the rectangles. The viewer's task was to respond as rapidly
as possible to the onset of the dark square by pressing a computer key.

Targets that appeared in the same location as the briefly presented cue were
detected more rapidly than targets in one of the three other non-cued locations.
This is the standard visibility benefit that accompanies successful covert orienting. However, the important result for our present question about object perception was that there was also a benefit for targets that appeared in the same
rectangle as the cue but at another location. If covert orienting worked strictly
like the beam of a flashlight, then targets that appeared at the other end of the
cued rectangle and targets that appeared in an adjacent location to the cued rec-

tangle should have been responded to equally slowly. This object-defined bene-fit of covert orienting suggests that at a minimum, the definition of an object for vision must include a collection of visual features—such as edges, in this case—that are connected.

Studies in this vein by Cathleen Moore and colleagues (Moore, Yantis, & Vaughan, 1998) have demonstrated that the "connection" among edges need not be image-based for these benefits of covert orienting to occur. For exam-ple, when a nearer object partially occludes the rectangles in Figure 5.12 so that the rectangles appear to extend behind the nearer object, the benefits of "same-object" cueing are still obtained. Studies that segment the visual display into different depth planes using stereo viewing or motion parallax (Chapter 7) have also found that the benefits of covert orienting extend to collections of edges that appear to belong to the same object. From the perspective of spatial orienting, the "object" seems to be the perceptual unit around which the con-cept of attention is based. Aspects of the world that can be attended to together because they are attached to one another constitute a good starting point for a definition of "object."

Figure-ground organization

A glance at any image leaves us with the impression that some of the regions have a definite shape and other regions are less well defined. A highly simplified image like this is shown in Figure 5.13. The black regions resemble two sides of the face of a person in profile, whereas the white region seems to extend indef-initely behind the black profiles. Clearly, the white-black edge is not perceptu-ally neutral with respect to the shapes on each side of it. When we see the profiles of faces, it is being assigned by the visual system to the black region and therefore does not belong in the same sense to the white region. When we see the white vase in the center, the edge is being assigned to the white region. *Figure* is the term vision scientists use to describe the shape that has "owner-ship" of the edge at an image boundary; *ground* is the term they use to describe the shape whose visible boundaries are defined by the "accident" of one object occluding another.

These biases of figure-ground organization in human vision have been the focus of research for more than one hundred years. They can be described and il-lustrated in simple terms with respect to two shapes in the image that share a lumi-nance edge. Of the two shapes, the one that viewers will more likely see as the figure (all other factors being equal) is the one that is more enclosed by the other, that is smaller, that has a greater contrast with the background, that is more con-vex, that has a greater number of parallel edges, that is more symmetric, that is more three-dimensional, that has a straight-edged base, and that is of greater fa-miliarity to the viewers.

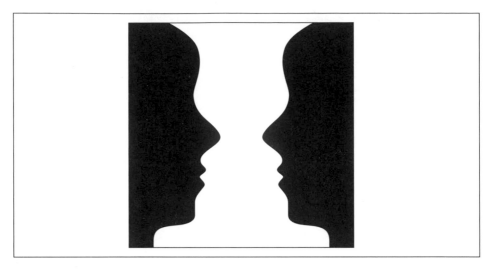

FIGURE 5.13   An image that can be seen either as a pair of black *figures* (profiles of faces) against a white *ground* (vase) or a single white *figure* (vase) against a continuous black *ground* (profiles of faces).

Many of these factors usually work in concert to define regions of an image that correspond to objects in the scene. Thus these factors help determine which side of an edge will take ownership in the interpretation of the image as having figure and ground regions. In addition to the benefits of edge-ownership, which reduces the inherent ambiguity at an edge, there are helpful and automatic benefits of figure-ground organization. For instance, overt and covert spatial attention is automatically directed to figure regions of an image rather than to ground regions. There is also improved memory for figure than for ground shapes. From this perspective, the "objects" of vision correspond to those regions of the image that viewers assign as "figure" rather than "ground."

Parsing at regions of deep concavity

Compare the shape in Figure 5.14a with the two shapes in Figure 5.14b. Which of the two shapes appears to be more similar to the one in Figure 5.14a? Most viewers choose the lower shape as the more similar one.

Now let's examine these shapes in a little more detail. A careful inspection shows that only the upper shape in Figure 5.14b has the same rough edge as the shape in Figure 5.14a. In fact, these two shapes are exact complements of one another; they fit together like interlocking puzzle pieces. The lower shape, however, is not the same as Figure 5.14a. At first glance it may appear to be the mirror image of the original shape, but a closer look reveals that two of its lower

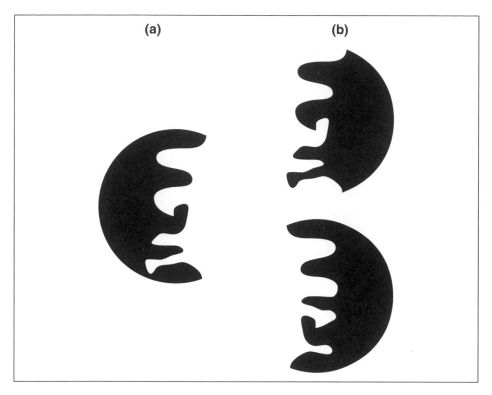

FIGURE 5.14   The shape in **(a)** is most similar to which of the two shapes in **(b)**?

bulging regions have been swapped. What makes these two shapes with different edges appear to be more similar than the complementary shapes with the identical edges?

Some researchers think this confusion illustrates a tendency for the visual system to organize scenes into regions of maximum convexity. Each region of maximum convexity can be considered a *part*, with the region of deepest concavity between parts representing the place where parts are joined. This would mean that a shape such as Figure 5.14a actually consists of five parts (bulges), whereas the upper shape in Figure 5.14b consists of four parts (bulges). In contrast, the lower shape has the same number and rough location of the parts in Figure 5.14a, so it has greater overall similarity. According to this view, a visual object is a collection of interconnected parts of this kind. Presumably, the factors that unify any given collection of parts would be similar to the factors that might unify a collection of edges. They would likely include contact (touching) and similarity in luminance, hue, texture, and motion. However, the important difference from the edge-based view of objects would be that "object belongingness" would be calculated in terms of regions of maximum convexity, which is a property of shape, rather than in terms of similarity of edges without any regard for overall shape.

It is noteworthy that we can extend the definition of "object" based on convex parts into vision of the third dimension. Take a look at the display in Figure 5.15, first in the orientation in which it appears on the page and then with the book turned upside down. In the upright orientation, the corrugated surface seems to consist of a center bump and two concentric ridges—three convex parts in all. The dotted lines lie in the valleys between the parts. When the book is turned upside down, the same display consists of a central donut-shaped ring and one and a half concentric ridges—a half of a part has gone missing. Consistent with this interpretation, the dotted lines now lie on the tops of the ridges and the outermost ridge can be seen as incomplete.

Problems of hierarchical structure and scale

A glaring problem with any simple definition of a visual object is that the world is structured at more than one level. Human vision is flexible enough to interact with this world at different levels. For example, most visual scenes can be examined for either (1) the broad characteristics found in the lower spatial frequencies of an image (Chapter 4), which correspond roughly to the coarse shapes that one sees if one blurs the image entering the eye, or (2) the detail found in the high spatial frequencies, the kind only visible with properly corrected visual acuity. Visual objects defined at one level of structure in the scene may or may not correspond to visual objects defined at another level.

Vision researchers have addressed this problem by examining the perception of stimuli that are carefully constructed to contain different kinds of information at each of several levels. These are called *compound stimuli* because the objects defined at one level of structure can be artificially manipulated so that they are independent of the objects defined at the other level of structure. For example, look at the displays in Figure 5.16 and try to determine, as quickly as you can, whether there is a target letter H in each cluster of elements. Did you find them all? Did you miss any H's? Did some take longer to find than others? If you look again, you will see that the target letter H appears at least once in each cluster.

Research with displays such as these has shown that within certain limits of scale, viewers find target objects faster at the global level of structure than at the local level of structure. You likely are able to find the target letter H more quickly when it forms the larger pattern than when it is contained at the level of the individual elements. This is true even though the local level of structure contains multiple copies of the same information. One reason you can see the global structure more quickly is that low spatial frequency information is transmitted through

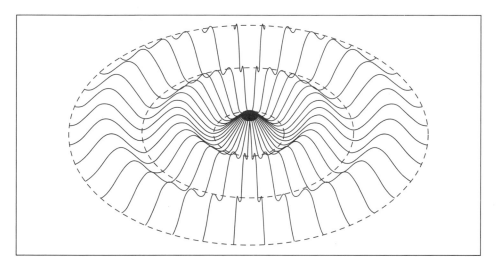

FIGURE 5.15 Are the dashed lines lying on the border between "parts" or in the center of the "parts" in this three-dimensional object? Now turn the book upside down and answer the same question.

the visual system more rapidly than high spatial frequency information. It can be carried on the rapid magnocellular or M-stream of processing we discussed in Chapter 2 (magno neurons).

But other factors also come into play. If the patterns are very large, so that the smallest details at the local level are large enough to activate the M-stream system and the global level of structure falls outside the normal bounds of these receptive fields, then viewers will see targets at the local level of structure first. You may have experienced this effect when searching for the H in the larger patterns.

A complete definition of a visual object has to take into account the hierarchical nature of most scenes. This is evident in the question of whether the whole human body, the face, or some specific facial feature corresponds to the visual "object." The answer is clearly "it depends." For some tasks, such as lip-reading, the appropriate level that corresponds to the visual object is undoubtedly the mouth. For other tasks, such as reading someone's emotional expression or determining her identity, the appropriate level for the visual object is the whole face. Recognizing someone by their gait from a distance is an example in which the whole body is the object of analysis.

THE PROBLEM OF SHAPE: RECOVERING THE THIRD DIMENSION

The visual world we experience and act upon consists of objects such as trees, buildings, people, and coffee cups, to name only a few. The only information we

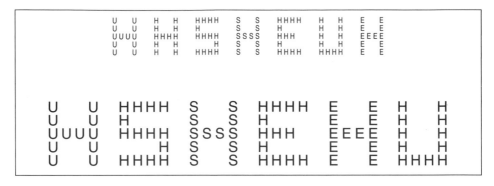

FIGURE 5.16   For each cluster of elements, try to determine as quickly as you can whether it contains a target letter H. The target letter may be either at the local element level or at the level of the global pattern.

receive about these objects through vision lies in the pattern of light they reflect. This pattern of light, called the *image*, consists of a two-dimensional array in which each point in the image can be further specified in terms of its total amount of light (*intensity*) and its wavelength (*hue*). You might be tempted to think of this as the retinal image, but as we saw in Chapter 2 this perspective gets complicated by the uneven way the retina records light across its surface. Instead, it is better at this point to think of the image as an abstraction: as the potential image that could be registered by a photographic retina, if such a retina existed. The image would be formed by a three-dimensional object that receives a bombardment of light from one or more light sources and reflects some of that light into the eye.

The object and its light sources constitute the *scene*. This statement leads to one of the most fundamental problems in vision: How can the three-dimensional shape of an object be determined from the two-dimensional pattern of light that reaches the retina? How can the missing third dimension be recovered so that we see not only the silhouette and interior edges of a shape in pictorial form, but also the form of the object in all three dimensions?

To understand this problem and its possible solutions, we must first appreciate the imbalance between the *geometry* and the *perception* of the physical world. The geometry is, for the most part, quite straightforward. As Figure 5.17 shows, there are four general aspects of the world of solid objects (the scene) that determine the pattern of light (the image) that will fall on our eyes when we view an object.

The first is the light source or sources. In the natural world there is only one primary light source, the sun; but if there are other highly reflective surfaces in the environment, such as water or light-colored stones, then these will constitute

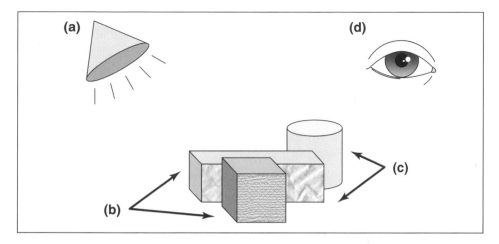

FIGURE 5.17 There are four types of information that together determine the nature of the retinal image an eye will receive when looking at a scene: **(a)** the number and location of light sources, **(b)** the reflectance properties of each object surface, **(c)** the orientation of each object surface, and **(d)** the viewing position of the eye.

secondary sources of light shining onto the object as well. The orientation of the light shining from these sources onto the object surfaces will influence how much light is reflected from the object to our eyes. In general, light sources may be positioned with respect to object surfaces so that light is either (1) reflected back toward the light source or toward our eyes, or (2) unable to make contact with any surface at all because the surface falls in the shadow of another surface closer to the light source.

The second influence on the retinal image of an object is the surface reflectance of the object. As we saw in Chapter 3, surfaces differ in their responsiveness to light of different wavelengths. The intrinsic hue (color) of a surface will depend on which wavelengths of light are reflected most strongly. Now, we can note that surfaces also differ in whether they reflect light in only one direction (as in a mirror) or whether they scatter light in all directions (as in matte construction paper). The intrinsic texture, or smoothness, of a surface will therefore determine how much that light is scattered as it moves from the surface to the eye.

The third influence on the retinal image is the relative orientation of each of the object's surfaces. Surfaces that are properly angled with respect to the light source and the eye will reflect the maximum possible amount of light. If the surfaces are also very smooth they will generate a specular highlight, which is the glint we often see on sunny days reflecting from a car bumper or other shiny surfaces. Surfaces that are oriented more or less sharply with respect to the light will reflect correspondingly less light in the direction of the eye.

The fourth general influence is the position of the eye with respect to the rest of the scene. Just as moving the primary light source will alter the image formed at the eye, so too will movement of the eye itself. In fact, all four general influences on the image form an interconnected web. If any three aspects are fixed and known (or measurable), then the fourth aspect can be determined according to the laws of geometry. This is what computer vision scientists mean when they say that the process of image formation is a *well-formed problem*. Given complete information about all four factors, only one image can be the result. If one factor is not specified but the other three are known along with the image, then the missing fourth factor can be found by simply performing the right calculations.

In contrast to the geometrical neatness of the process of image formation, the process of object perception is what computer vision scientists call an *ill-posed problem*. This means that there are many—in theory, an infinity of—reasonable answers to the question *What object gave rise to this image?* Because of the ambiguity of this problem, attempts to create artificial general-purpose "seeing" machines have failed. There are simply too many possible scenes for every possible image to enable those machines to settle on a reasonable solution very quickly. To speed them up so that they generate a useful hypothesis in real time, one must program in a very large number of constraints. This leaves them in the position of being experts at seeing a very limited class of objects—for example, the shapes of certain widgets on an assembly line. But these constraints also leave them blind to any other objects. The marvel of human vision is that we are able to see such a wide range of objects, and all so quickly. What are the tricks and clues we use to narrow down the possibilities so quickly?

Although human vision does appear to be a general-purpose vision system— at least in comparison to "seeing" machines—it is not nearly the general system we assume it to be when it is at work in the everyday world. Its idiosyncrasies are apparent when we study visual illusions. As I pointed out earlier, however, it is more helpful to consider these illusions as evidence of the constraints vision uses to interpret ambiguous retinal images than as mistakes made by a less-than-perfect visual system. "Perfection" in this case may in fact be the optimal balance between the speed of object recognition and an acceptable level of error or illusion in return for such speed. It is also worth reminding ourselves that the prejudices of human vision reflect the constraints of living and seeing in a three-dimensional environment. It is an environment that is dominated by gravity, that is illuminated by a sun at day and a moon at night, that consists of largely opaque and rigid objects, and in which light is reflected through a medium that tends to be disproportionately scatter short wavelength light (blue). We can only imagine what our vision would be like if it had evolved in a very different environment.

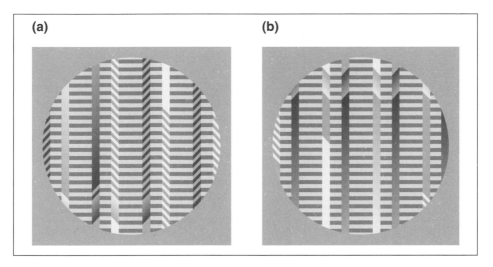

FIGURE 5.18   Viewers tend to see these displays as depicting **(a)** thin corrugated ridges between wide spaces and **(b)** wide corrugated ridges between thin spaces. Turning the book upside down reverses the interpretations. The human viewer assumes that light shines from above.

Light shines from above

Smooth variation in the luminance of an image is called *shading*. Without considering the larger context, a local region of shading can occur for a number of reasons. First, some parts of a curved surface might reflect more light than others. Second, some parts of a surface with graded pigment might be darker than others. Third, parts of a surface within a shadow cast by another object will be darker than others.

As Figure 5.18 shows, we generally interpret shading with the assumption that light shines from above the scene. This resolves one of the inherent ambiguities of shading: whether to interpret the shaded region as bending away or toward the viewer. If a scene is lit from above, then the gradient of luminance that runs from light to dark must represent a surface curvature that is bulging toward the viewer. Vision researchers call this a *convexity* and the opposite direction of bulging a *concavity*.

Surfaces are generally convex

We generally interpret drawings of surfaces with very few cues for three-dimensional shape as convex. Figure 5.19 reveals this bias through images of common objects such as potatoes and faces. Even though the object may be a hollow cast (generally concave), its image looks solid (generally convex). This bias overrides the assumption that light shines from above. A picture of a face that is actually

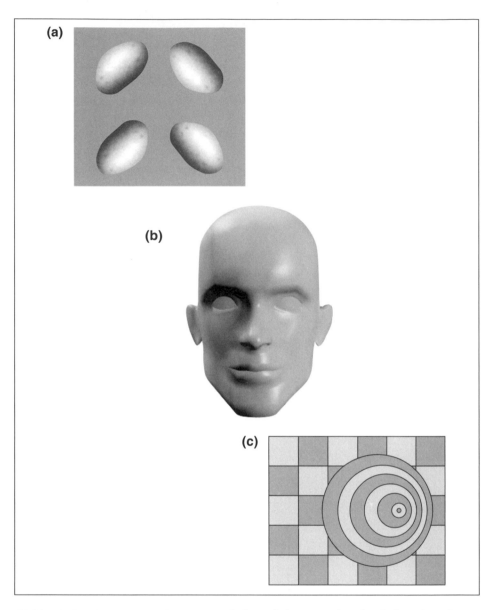

FIGURE 5.19 Pictures of **(a)** potatoes lit from all directions, **(b)** a face lit from the side, and **(c)** texture gradients with no shading. All these surfaces appear to be generally convex even though the geometry of the situation could just as accurately specify pictures of hollow casts of these objects and surfaces.

a hollow mask lit from above will appear as a convex face when lit from below. This bias extends to arbitrary texture gradients depicting surfaces where no shading is involved. The texture shown in Figure 5.19c appears to bulge toward the viewer rather than bend back into the page.

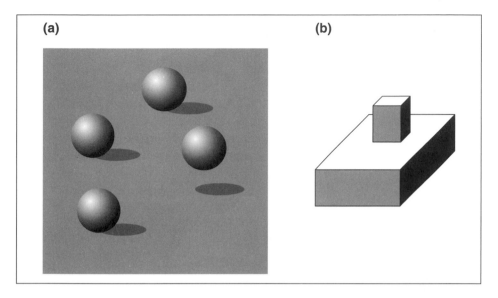

FIGURE 5.20 (a) Objects are seen as resting on surfaces even when only shadows but not surfaces are depicted. The sphere that is displaced from its shadow appears to hover above the implied surface. **(b)** The bias toward surface attachment makes it appear as though the small cube is attached to the center of the large block, not hovering above the front right corner.

Objects are attached to surfaces

Human vision tends to see objects as resting on other surfaces even when those surfaces are not depicted. For example, in Figure 5.20a the spheres appear to rest on a surface that is not shown. We interpret the gray ovals below the spheres as shadows cast by the spheres onto this surface. When one of the shadows is displaced from the sphere, the surface does not seem to dip. Rather, the sphere now appears to be suspended above the unseen surface. Figure 5.20b appears to show a small cube attached to the center of a large block even though it could just as easily be floating a short distance above the block, with its front and right edges aligned with those of the block.

Objects are generally viewed from above

There is a strong bias in human vision to interpret objects as seen from above rather than from below. This bias is evident in the Schroeder stairs illusion, as shown in Figure 5.21. The most frequent interpretation of this picture is that of a set of stairs in which wall A is nearest to the viewer, which means that the triangle is on the first riser and the disc is on the first tread. But another interpretation is possible. Wall B can be seen as the surface nearest to the viewer, in which case the stairs are being viewed from below and the triangle is now on the first tread and the disc on the first

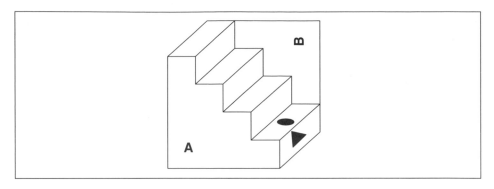

FIGURE 5.21   The Schroeder stairs illusion is an ambiguous picture in which the set of stairs can be viewed from above (making wall A nearest to the viewer or from below (making wall B nearest to the viewer). The first interpretation occurs more frequently, reflecting the bias in human vision to view objects and surfaces from above.

riser. If you find it difficult to see this interpretation because of the natural bias to view surfaces from above, simply rotate your head (or the book) so that the letter B is upright on your retina. Now, slowly rotate your head (or the book) back to the original viewing position and see if you can maintain that interpretation. Most people find it difficult to do so because of the bias to view surfaces from above.

A generic viewpoint

One of the most general biases of human vision is to interpret a relation between two or more edges as though it will hold for a variety of viewpoints. For example, consider the three lines that meet at a junction in Figure 5.22a. It might be a coincidence that for the vantage point from which the picture was taken, the three edges meet at the same place. If that were the case, then a simple movement of the head in one direction or another would reveal that in fact the three edges do not meet at the same place, as in Figure 5.22b. Human vision ignores these low-probability alternatives and assumes instead that the edge relations shown in Figure 5.22a are true. This is the *general viewpoint* bias.

An important bias with respect to the relations among edges is to interpret the meeting of three or more edges as corresponding to the meeting of surfaces in a scene. As shown in Figure 5.23, junctions of three edges that meet are interpreted as corners of objects with convex surfaces. If the three angles among these edges are all greater than 90 degrees in the image and none of them is greater than 180 degrees, then the junction is interpreted as the corner of an object where three surfaces meet (Figure 5.23a). There is a strong bias to interpret these *Y-junctions* as corresponding to convex corners. But this is a bias of our vision, not something contained in the geometry. The Y-junction could just as ac-

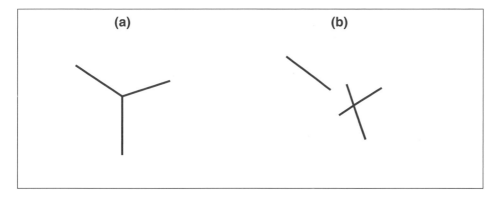

FIGURE 5.22 Generic viewpoint of edges. **(a)** The three lines are assumed to correspond to three edges that meet at a single point in the scene. **(b)** If movement of the head or the scene were to reveal the line relations shown here, we would be genuinely surprised.

curately depict a concave corner. A closely related bias involves interpreting all the corners as right-angled ones. This leads to the interpretation of a "cube" for a wide range of pictures that could, as far as the geometry is concerned, actually be skewed solids.

When one of the angles between three edges is exactly 180 degrees, another specialized interpretation occurs, as shown in Figure 5.23b. This is referred to as a *T-junction*; its interpretations is that the crossbar of the T is nearer to the viewer and partially occluding a full view of the edge corresponding to the stem of the T. Again, the T-junction could occur because several shapes have been placed side by side in a mosaic pattern, as shown in the last image in the panel of Figure 5.23b; but as far as human vision is concerned, this is a less than generic interpretation.

When one of the angles between the three edges is larger than 180 degrees, an *arrow-junction* is formed, as shown in Figure 5.23c. The default interpretation of this three-edged junction is of a convex corner. It differs from the interpretation of the Y-junction in that only two of the three surfaces that meet at this junction are visible. But again, note that an arrow-junction could equally well, in theory, represent a concave corner, as shown in the last image in the panel of Figure 5.23c. Yet the default interpretation, without any additional information, is for convexity.

The assumptions of lighting from above, surface convexity, surface attachment, viewing from above, and a generic viewpoint can readily extend beyond local shading and edge interactions to the interpretation of objects and entire scenes. Consider the picture in Figure 5.24a. It depicts a scene containing three-dimensional objects of specific shapes in a particular spatial arrangement even though the shapes are all silhouettes containing no interior detail. None of the shapes occludes another, though the two large shapes partially occlude the horizon. Under the

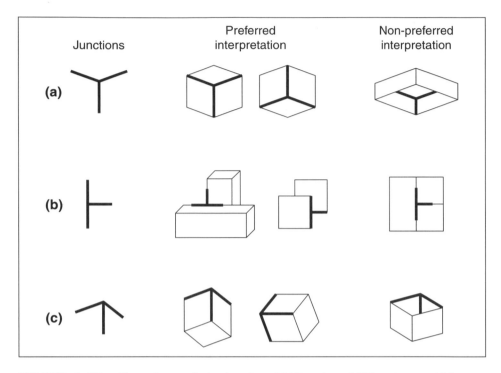

FIGURE 5.23   Three classes of edge junctions: **(a)** Y-junctions, **(b)** T-junctions, and **(c)** arrow junctions. These junctions are each shown in two preferred scene interpretations and one non-preferred scene interpretation.

surface convexity assumption, the depicted shapes are blobs and not holes. Under the surface attachment assumption, the blobs are resting on a surface that helps determine the shapes of their lower edges. Under the generic viewpoint assumption, the remaining round edges of the blobs would continue to be round if the viewpoint on the scene were shifted.

The two largest black blobs are especially interesting because they seem to have indentations and bulges that are nowhere specified by shading, texture, or occlusion. From what does their three-dimensional shape derive? Figure 5.24b illustrates the equal elevation contours of these blobs under the assumption that they are resting on the same surface. Clearly, they are very different three-dimensional shapes under this assumption. However, now imagine one of the blobs rotated onto its side: You will realize that both blobs' exterior outlines are identical. This difference in three-dimensional appearance, despite the identical nature of the two-dimensional silhouettes, illustrates the power of interpretation based on the principles of surface attachment and generic viewpoint. These assumptions take no apparent mental effort on our part.

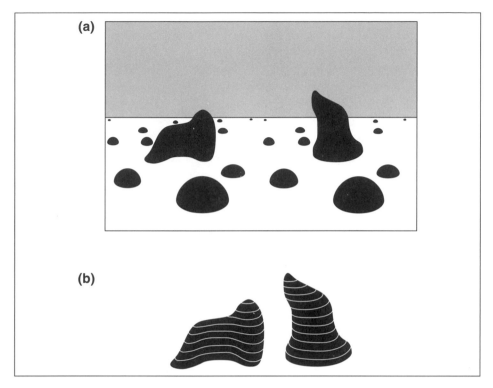

FIGURE 5.24 **(a)** An image of solid blobs that appears to depict a three-dimensional scene. **(b)** Equal elevation contours show how different these two blobs are in a three-dimensional interpretation even though they have the same image dimensions. Rotate the page by 90 degrees to see their similar outline shapes.

OBJECT RECOGNITION

The perception of an object's shape, color, and texture is one thing. After all, these properties tell us a lot about an object. But understanding the object's use, how it relates to other objects, and whether we have seen it before is quite another thing. This distinction is not only an intellectually formal one, in that it helps us understand all the operations we must perform in order to "see" as opposed to "know" that object. But it is also a physiologically real one, in that "seeing" or "knowing" can be impaired through brain damage while the other ability remains more or less intact.

An individual who has lost the ability to see the shapes of objects while still being able to make fine-grained discriminations on the basis of color, luminance, and motion is an *apperceptive agnosic*. Often the cause of the brain damage leading to this condition is carbon monoxide poisoning or a prolonged lack of oxygen. Simple shape-matching tasks and perceptual grouping tasks are very difficult, if not impossible, for these individuals. What they do see appears to consist of fragmented elements of the normal scene. When asked to find matching shapes that are similar in color, the individuals often base their responses on localized edges, leading to false matches between a triangle and a diamond on the grounds that they both have a slanting edge. These people often match objects of assorted colors on the basis of color rather than shape, leading to false matches between a safety pin and a nail clipper because they are both silver. However, these individuals' object identification based on other senses seems to be fully preserved. Apperceptive agnosics have no trouble identifying and naming objects on the basis of touch, hearing, or smell.

An *associative agnosic* has a very different problem. Although the cause of this individual's brain damage may be similar to that of the apperceptive agnosic—prolonged lack of oxygen to diffuse regions of the visual cortex—the functional manifestation is very different. An associative agnosic has no trouble seeing, matching, and drawing shapes and objects. When asked to give a verbal description of an object, he can characterize it in great detail to the extent that anyone listening will know what he is describing. For example, when looking at a picture of a leather glove, the associative agnosic might describe it as "a leather bag with an opening at one end and five distinct and long bulges protruding from it. These bulges each appear large enough to contain a roll of coins. The middle bulges are somewhat longer than the bulges on the end."

Associative agnosics' drawings can be equally detailed, such that anyone viewing them will recognize the drawn objects with almost perfect accuracy. Yet the agnosics have no apparent understanding of these objects' names, uses, or meanings. The problem is not one of object naming and understanding in general, because when the agnosics encounter the same objects by touch or hearing, they readily recognize them. Rather, the normal link between object shape and meaning seems to have disappeared.

The problem of object constancy

When vision fails, as it does for agnosics, it gives us insight into some of the deep problems being solved every waking moment by the healthy brain viewing everyday scenes. Seeing does not consist of simply opening the eyes and recording "the picture." Instead, it involves solving very difficult problems on a moment-by-moment basis. One of the most difficult—as measured by the volume of literature written about it over the years and by the elusiveness of its solution for artificial vision systems—is the problem of *object constancy*. How do we know what an object is, based on the view we are currently seeing? It is likely that we have never seen this object before under exactly these lighting conditions, in this orientation, from this vantage point, and at this distance. We may have never seen this particular instance of a well-known category, such as this year's latest car model or a new neighbor. Yet our vision works well under all these conditions to let us know, instantaneously, what we are looking at.

As you may be guessing by now, vision scientists do not take these kinds of armchair arguments as evidence. How is object recognition affected by the various ways in which we can see an object? What does the study of object recognition tell us about the processes by which we are able to rapidly find a link between an object's image and its meaning? To understand the current answers to these questions, we need a brief overview of the two approaches taken so far in trying to understand how object constancy can be achieved.

Recognition by parts

A popular approach to the problem of object constancy begins with the assumption that an image is understood through an attempt to match models of three-dimensional objects to the visual features in the image. This approach enables us to divide object recognition into several discrete subproblems that can each be solved independently of the others. The subproblems include:

- segmenting the image into candidate regions for model matching
- determining the "alphabet" or "library" for the underlying three-dimensional models that are matched to the image
- linking the model found in the image to a meaning stored in long-term memory

The most common approach to the first subproblem, image segmentation, involves identifying and labeling edges in the image (Chapter 4), followed by grouping them into candidate regions that correspond to objects in the model "library." The grouping of edges follows the kinds of rules outlined in the previous section. Of the three subproblems this one seems the most straightforward, although computer vision experts will quickly tell you that no general-purpose solutions have yet been found. Nonetheless, they would probably agree that it's an easier subproblem than the remaining two.

Selecting the right model to match the candidate regions is fraught with difficulty. At one extreme might be a library of three-dimensional models where each entry consists of a different object. Rough calculations of the number of objects a typical human will recognize over a lifetime, however, soon leads to the realization that even though a large number of neurons in the brain might be devoted to object recognition, their number would be no match for the vast array of objects a human will ever see. At the other extreme might be a library of a much smaller set of three-dimensional model parts such that any object, including a

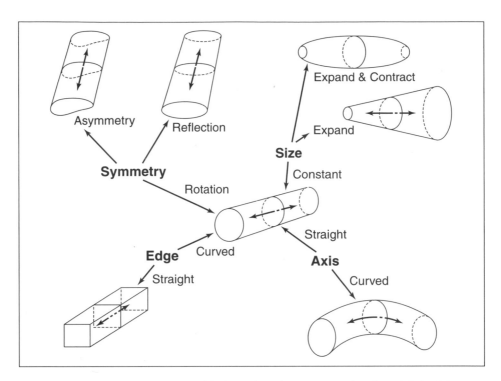

FIGURE 5.25   Simple convex solid objects have been proposed as the "alphabet" for recognizing three-dimensional objects. They are derived from combinations of axis elongation (straight, curved) and three features of the cross-section: edge (straight, curved), symmetry (asymmetry, reflection, rotation), and size change (constant, expand, contract).

newly encountered one, could be modeled quickly by assembling the necessary parts into the correct spatial arrangement. Now the problem becomes: *which parts?* Selecting too few parts or the wrong parts would leave many objects unrecognizable. Selecting too many parts would lead to the same problem that occurred when each object was represented by its own model.

One set of parts that might work—as documented by computer efforts to achieve vision and by human performance on object recognition tasks—are of a type shown in Figure 5.25. These are simple convex solids that consist of a main axis of elongation and a cross-section. Both aspects of a simple solid can be varied along a few well-chosen dimensions, so that from the combination of two basic types of axes (straight, curved), two types of cross-section (straight, curved), three types of cross-section symmetry (asymmetry, reflection symmetry, rotational symmetry), and three types of cross-section change across the axis (constant, expanding, contracting), it is possible to generate thirty-six simple solids to form the basic set of the three-dimensional library.

FIGURE 5.26 Several common objects in their ideal form according to a simple, solid, and convex part description.

The final step in this approach to object recognition involves linking the objects found in the image to a long-term memory in which known objects have been catalogued on the basis of their description in terms of the thirty-six parts. Consider a simple pail, for example, as illustrated in Figure 5.26. Past experience with pails has taught us that this class of objects consists of a wide cylinder in vertical orientation topped by a long thin cylinder with a curved axis of elongation. This object may have the same parts as another object such as a coffee mug, but it is critically different in the way in which the two parts are related spatially. A pail's handle is on top over the opening, whereas the mug's is on the side. This kind of object recognition scheme can be readily used to model lamps, suitcases, and drawers, among other objects.

One strength of this approach is that it strikes a good balance between a well-defined system and an open-ended one. It is well defined in that the proposed parts have clear definitions and are of a manageable number. It is open ended in that the possibility always exists to add new objects to the memory store of known objects without having to increase the basic set of model parts. Long-term memory needs to store the specific parts comprising an object and their spatial relations to each other.

Another strength is that it accounts in a natural way for the problem of object constancy. The constant or invariant aspects of objects captured by this approach are their descriptions in terms of the model parts. Given sufficient clues in the image to the presence of the appropriate parts, object recognition can proceed regardless of lighting conditions, object orientation, viewing angle, and viewing distance.

A weakness of this approach is that it can be applied more readily to certain classes of objects and for certain object recognition tasks than to or for others. Indeed, certain objects cannot be easily modeled by simple convex solids: crumpled newspapers, clothes, human faces, and trees, for example. In response to this criticism, advocates of this approach point out that complications of scale and detail can be worked out with a little extra effort. For example, from a distance it may be appropriate to model a crumpled newspaper as a lumpy but generally spherical solid object. For greater detail, each roughly planar surface in the crumple can be modeled as a separate solid. But, as this example shows, modeling the right level of detail is only half the problem. How is long-term memory supposed to know that a newspaper can be modeled as either of these possibilities? Invoking past experience leads to the slippery slope where single objects with the same name have many entries in the library of known objects. How are all these entries to be related? Distinguishing them on the basis of the spatial relations among their parts is no longer a simple solution.

Recognition by views

Partly in response to the problems mentioned above and partly in response to data on human performance that we will discuss in the next section, a very different approach to the problem of object constancy has been gaining popularity. It builds on a known strength of the human brain: the capacity to store and retrieve large numbers of different patterns. What if objects were stored in long-term memory according to a collection of views acquired over time? These views would not have to be photographic; rather, they could be abstract structural descriptions—schemas, if you will. The important difference from the "recognition-by-parts" approach is that these descriptions would represent views of an object from a certain vantage point and distance. Together, the various views of a known object would be stored in something like a photo album, and many albums would be linked in a giant web of connections representing potential relations among objects.

Of course, a single view of each object would be insufficient to achieve object constancy. To correctly match an object to its proper "photo album," multiple views would have to be included. But not all possible views would be needed. Novel views of an object would still permit recognition if a mechanism was in place for rapidly calculating the similarity between views. Indeed, the human brain seems particularly adept at making pattern comparisons involving a large set.

A strength of this approach is that it achieves object constancy without involv-ing the computationally expensive and time-consuming steps (at least when per-formed by machines) of constructing a model of the three-dimensional objects in the scene. The main computations now involve searching for and matching two-dimensional patterns that consist of schematic descriptions of objects seen from particular vantage points. When a good match is found between an existing view and a stored one, object recognition can take place. The unknown piece in the puzzle is the nature of the structural descriptions that form the patterns to be searched through and compared. Is there a scheme for identifying and describing those features of an image that will be useful in its later recognition from another image? Does this scheme involve a decomposition into object parts? These ques-tions will provide work in vision science well into the next generation.

One weakness of this approach is that it does not easily account for the fact that human vision is very adept in responding to objects in three-dimensional space. Especially in terms of action toward objects, vision is capable of comput-ing very precise three-dimensional relations. We seem to know instantly how to hold our hands in order to grasp a new object. But it is not clear how vision ac-complishes this by using a large number of discrete views. Another weakness is that there is no obvious way in which to capture the part structure of objects in a multiple-view theory of object recognition. There seem to be no "parts" in this approach.

So what are the vision scientists on each side of this debate arguing about? Given the primitive state of understanding associated with both approaches, you may wonder if it is worth trying to decide which one is better. Both ap-proaches seem to have a long way to go before becoming testable theories in the sense of making predictions that are strongly consistent or inconsistent with human behavior. Both may turn out to be flawed. Each one may turn out to be correct in accounting for a certain aspect of human vision. Regardless of the ul-timate outcome, they both merit analysis in terms of the broader context of human behavior.

Canonical object views

One of the most reliable findings in studies of object recognition is that the time required to name an object is related to the perspective from which it is viewed. For example, as Figure 5.27 illustrates, we identify horses most rapidly in three-quarter view from the side and tricycles in three-quarter views from slightly above. We identify clocks, which are not shown, most rapidly face-on. When some partic-ipants in a study by Steven Palmer and his colleagues (Palmer, Rosch, & Chase, 1981) were asked to rate pictures for how well they represented certain objects and other participants were asked to name the objects as rapidly as possible, there

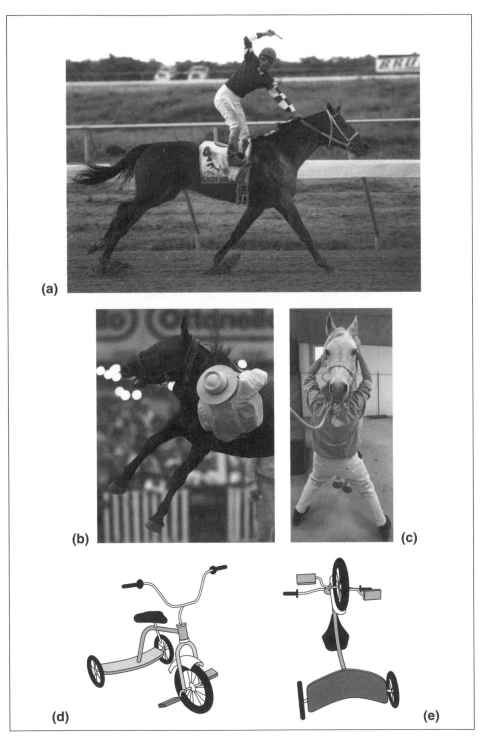

FIGURE 5.27 Pictures of objects in speeded naming tasks. Naming speed is influenced by viewing perspective and object orientation.

was a very strong correlation between the ratings of *canonicality* (the "simple ideal") and naming speed. That is, most common objects have an ideal viewing perspective for optimal recognition.

At first, this finding might seem to be indisputable support for recognition by views, since some views are favored in the recognition process over others. Canonical views could be (1) the views that participants had seen most frequently, making them well represented in the participants' mental "photo album," or (2) the views with the greatest similarity to "photos in the album" for that object as a whole. However, recognition by parts can also explain this aspect of human performance. It predicts that canonical views are the ones in which model parts that are critical for identifying an object can be matched most efficiently to the image. This speeds the process of model matching. Clearly, more details must be specified for each theory to resolve this issue.

Viewing orientation and distance

Many studies of object naming show that when a picture of an object is shown at orientations other than upright, naming speed increases as a function of the difference in orientation from the upright. Similar results have been reported for the relation between the sizes of two shapes being compared and matching speed. Comparisons are made the fastest when the shapes are the same size.

These orientation-specific and size-specific effects on object naming seem to support recognition from views rather than recognition from parts, since it should be possible to match three-dimensional models to an image regardless of the image orientation or size. The similarity of a given view to stored views, however, should vary with changes in orientation and size, leading to the prediction of these effects. Once again, though, the recognition-by-parts theory is not as inappropriate as you might think. If objects are indeed identified on the basis of the relations between parts, as this theory claims, then mis-orienting the parts in the image should slow down the naming speed, as it does for recognition by views. Also, there may be an optimal image size for matching model parts, so variation along this dimension should slow down the process as well.

Representing the third dimension in vision and action

As we have seen many times already, human vision often gives a strong and reliable sense of the three-dimensional shape of an object. This is not just a fanciful hallucination. Our actions can prove it, as they often do when we reach toward and manipulate objects with our hands.

On the face of it, this observation favors recognition by parts, which attributes a three-dimensional quality to vision. It is a little more difficult to understand how recognition by views can support the same functions of vision and action in the third dimension. One solution to this dilemma for recognition by views is to propose that human vision uses a three-dimensional model, but not in the long-term storage of visual information. Instead, human vision may use multiple views of an object to create fleeting three-dimensional models that are only used "on-line," or in the moment, to support ongoing vision and action. Of course, this proposal requires more detail on the nature of the dynamic three-dimensional models.

Recognizing an object's class versus its identity

What is a study participant doing when he or she successfully names an object? Does naming one of the pictures in Figure 5.27 as "horse" involve the same processes as those involved in naming your friend "Fred" when you see a photo of him? Careful consideration of the differences between these two tasks will reveal that the first case involves labeling the object by its general class (often called the *basic level* object by vision scientists) and the second case involves labeling the object by its unique and individual name (the *subordinate level*). Very different kinds of discrimination appear to be involved in these two cases. For example, identifying an object as belonging to a general class involves generalizing across many different objects, or *exemplars.* Identifying an object as being a specific individual involves discriminating him from among all the other individuals, or exemplars, of the same class (e.g., male friends).

Upon closer examination, one can make the case that the two approaches we have been discussing are specialized for these kinds of object recognition. In particular, recognition by parts seems ready-made for distinguishing general classes of objects such as pails and coffee mugs. It is much more difficult to imagine using that approach to discriminate my coffee cup from yours, which probably differ not in their parts but in their surface markings. However, recognition by views seems suited to distinguishing "Fred" from "George." As we have seen, that approach does not have a ready-made way to distinguish among general classes of objects as distinct from specific exemplars of a class.

SCENE PERCEPTION

The study of *object perception* (seeing the properties of an object) addresses the mental representations that we form of individual objects seen at a glance in a larger scene. The study of *object recognition* (knowing the meaning of an object) addresses our understanding of how an object is identified in relative isolation. Here in the last section of this chapter, we will return to the larger question of *scene perception* (understanding the larger context in which individual objects are seen). Studies reveal that two important kinds of information are gained in a glance at a scene, in addition to visual details of the few objects at the focus of our attention. One kind of information is the meaningful context in which the attended objects are presented; this is the *gist* of a scene. A second kind is the overall spatial arrangement of the objects, or the *layout.*

Gist

The speed with which the general meaning of a scene can be determined was revealed in a very elegant way by studies conducted in the 1970s on the perception of rapid-fire sequences of images. For example, Molly Potter (1976) presented viewers with brief glimpses of fifteen or more images in a row under two different viewing instructions. In one condition, the *category detection* task, viewers were given a verbal category such as "a picnic" or "a classroom" before seeing the sequence of images. Their task at the end of the sequence of views was to indicate whether any picture matched that category. In a second condition, the *new-old recognition* task, viewers were first shown the same sequence and then shown either (1) one of the original images in the sequence (called an *old* picture), or (2) an image that had not been presented (called a *new* picture). They were again given a choice: *Was this picture one of those that appeared in the original series?* Think about these two tasks for a moment. Which do you think would be easier to do: preparing yourself to see an unpredictable picture of a general type, or simply matching two copies of the identical image?

An interesting finding was that the new-old recognition task is much harder than the category detection task when the images are shown at high speeds. When the images were flashed at a rate of ten per second (100 ms per image), viewers' accuracy in category detection was over 80 percent, which is reasonably good performance given the high speeds. However, their new-old recognition accuracy was only a little more than 50 percent, which is near the chance level of performance. Thus we can infer that humans are able to use vision to comprehend the meaning of pictures shown at this rate—in this case, to assign them correctly to an abstract verbal category—but are unable at the same time to form a short-lived memory of the picture that can survive the second or two intervening between the presentation of the original picture and the test picture. You may have had a similar experience when viewing a rapid-fire sequence of images in a music video or a television commercial. Each image appeared vividly and clearly, but a second later you may have been unable to recall the specific content of more than one image.

What prevents the visual system from forming longer-lasting memories of rapid-fire images? We find an important clue when examining recognition accuracy separately for each picture in the series. New-old recognition accuracy is at chance levels for each picture except the last one viewed. The last picture viewed can be matched very accurately to the test picture even though it is shown for the same 100 ms as the preceding pictures. Thus the short time each picture is displayed is not the critical factor in the poor memory. Rather, the problem is that before the contents of each picture can be formed into a lasting representation, visual details from a new picture override the sensory information from the old picture. Apparently, it takes longer than one-tenth of a second to form lasting memories of unpredictable pictures. We will consider this topic in greater detail in Chapter 6. At the same time, a glimpse that is shorter than one-tenth of a second is enough to permit a preexisting idea, such as a verbal picture category, to be matched against the information in the glimpse. As we will also see in Chapter 6, there are severe limits on this process. After one successful match of a verbal label to a picture in a rapid-fire sequence, there is a period of up to one-half of a second in which the viewer is essentially blind to images that follow. This is the *attentional blink*, and we will consider it in greater detail in the next chapter.

One effective approach to studying the way the visual system represents the gist of a scene is to measure viewers' sensitivity to various kinds of changes in a scene following an interruption in viewing—such as an eye movement, a change in viewpoint, or a brief blanking and redisplaying of the scene. Consider once again the card trick described in Box 5.1. Imagine what would happen if you replaced the original six cards with five different objects such as snapshots or coffee holders. Needless to say, your card trick would be a complete flop because the audience would know you had removed all the original cards. The reason they didn't notice this the first time is that you preserved the gist of the scene between views. Both the original six cards and the replaced five cards were of the category "face cards." By carefully manipulating changes between views without alerting the viewers to these changes, researchers are starting to understand how the gist of a scene is represented.

In one study by John Henderson and Andrew Hollingworth (2002), viewers were shown typical indoor scenes (e.g., offices, kitchens) under the instruction that these pictures would appear again later in a memory test and that some of the objects in the picture might change unexpectedly. Viewers were to immediately report any such change that they noticed. The experimenters designated certain objects in the scenes as "target objects" and changed them in the following ways during the viewers' execution of an eye movement while inspecting the scene. For example, for a target object that consisted of a book lying on a desk, at some point during the viewing the book might be completely *deleted* (replaced by the background of the desk), replaced with an object of *another type* (a coffee mug), replaced with an object of the *same type* (a book of different dimensions and color), or replaced with the *same object rotated* by 90 degrees. The viewers detected object deletions most frequently, followed by replacements of another type. Both types of changes affected the meaning of the scene. Replacements of the same type, as well as by the same object rotated, did not change the scene's gist; viewers detected these types of changes much less frequently, as you might expect from thinking about the card trick.

The meaning of a scene also serves to rapidly focus attention on particular objects in the scene and to influence the particular properties of a single object that are attended to. In a study similar to the previous one (Hollingworth & Henderson, 2003), target objects were either semantically *consistent* with the scene (e.g., a microscope in a laboratory) or semantically *inconsistent* (e.g., a teddy bear in a laboratory). If each object in a scene contributed to the overall meaning, then a semantically inconsistent object would draw the viewers' attention, and they would notice any subsequent change in it more readily than the same change in a semantically consistent object. This is exactly what happened.

Not only does the semantic analysis of a scene occur rapidly, helping to guide the more detailed attentional processes to specific objects, but it also leads to the formation of stable long-term memories for scenes. However, we must remember that these memories are removed from the specific details in the scenes. The apparent price of this long-term and stable memory for scenes is a level of abstraction that is not sensitive to the particulars of most objects in the scene. Many vision scientists call this level of abstraction *schematic memory* because it is rich in meaning but impoverished in terms of its retention of details incidental to the meaning.

Humans' amazing memory for scene gist was first documented in the 1960s, when Ralph Haber and Lionel Standing showed study participants hundreds of typical "summer vacation" photographs, each for only a few seconds, and then tested participants' memory by using the new-old recognition task (Shepard, 1967; Standing, Conezio, & Haber, 1970; Standing, 1973). The researchers divided a given set of photos in half, showed one-half as pictures to be remembered, and then tested on the full set. A chance level of accuracy in such a test is 50 percent. Recognition accuracy was well over 90 percent when memory was tested on the same day. Some studies found accuracy to be over 70 percent several days and weeks later. Thus we can infer that visual scenes can be retained for long periods as measured by recognition accuracy.

The abstract nature of the memory involved is evident from results of other studies that examined sensitivity to more subtle differences in a given picture than merely whether it belonged to an original and haphazard set of vacation slides. In one especially revealing study by Molly Potter and her colleagues (Potter, O'Connor, & Oliva, 2002), participants viewed sets of slides taken in a panoramic series at a city intersection (an intersection they had never seen before) in order to determine where the camera had been placed in the intersection. When participants were later tested with a new set of pictures displaced laterally by 30 degrees from the original views, they had no trouble correctly indicating where the camera had been placed. In other words, they were now familiar with the scene and had specific metric information about it.

Yet in a new-old recognition test, the same participants were unable to discriminate the new slides from the old slides at a better-than-chance level. What the participants apparently learned from the original set of slides was a detailed mental map of the city intersection. Specific images in the slides, however, had not been committed to a form of memory that permitted the participants to detect which slides from among all the views had been presented during the learning phase.

This process of abstraction does not only happen over time, similar to the fading of a photo left too long in the sun. Rather, it can occur as soon as the picture is presented. The exercise in Box 5.3 will enable you to experience the process of

BOX 5.3

How detailed is your picture memory?

In this demonstration you will examine a picture for only a few seconds in order to form as detailed a memory of it as possible. Once you have completed the demonstration, you may also want to test it out on one or two friends to see how reliable it is.

Materials

The picture in Figure 5.28 and a clean sheet of paper on which you will draw as detailed a picture of it as you can.

Instructions

Examine the picture in Figure 5.28 carefully. Do so for only a few seconds, but study it with an eye for remembering as many details as you can. Then close the book and draw the picture to the best of your ability.

Analysis

Once you have completed the drawing, score it for the following details: how many trashcans you drew; how many fence pickets you drew. The typical finding in studies of this task by Helene Intraub (1977) is that participants are accurate in drawing the central objects in pictures such as these. However, they often draw more background items than were actually shown—in this case, pickets in the picket fence. The tendency to fill in extra detail about the background is called *scene boundary extension*. It occurs not only in drawing but also in new-old recognition tasks conducted immediately after a picture is presented. In this case, participants select as "old" pictures that contain more of the background than was actually shown. The illusion is an example of the viewer's vision "going beyond" what was seen in the picture.

abstraction for yourself. I encourage you to try this demonstration before reading further in order to benefit from the full impact of the experience.

The illusion of *scene boundary extension* illustrated in Box 5.3 has occurred under a wide variety of testing conditions and retention intervals. It appears to involve an adaptive process of inferring the context of a scene beyond the boundaries of what is actually presented to the eyes. Presumably, we do this every day. We look out a window and assume that the world extends beyond what we see within the window frame. But this assumption goes beyond a straightforward cognitive belief like the kind that says, "There is a potential scene to be viewed behind my head." It involves the construction of a visual schema that includes more of the

FIGURE 5.28   Study this common scene briefly, and then cover it before drawing all the shapes in as much detail as you can remember.

background and therefore can be fooled by test pictures that include more of the background. As such, this illusion contributes to the continuity of perception from glance to glance.

One proof that this illusion is really driven by our schematic visual processes and not just a byproduct of viewing all pictures is evident in similar tests with very wide-angled scenes or with scenes containing outline drawings of central objects (no drawn background). In both cases, the scene boundary extension effect does not occur. However, the effect can be reinstated for the drawings consisting only of outline objects by instructing participants to "imagine" a particular kind of background and then drawing it in the remembered scene. In this case, the outline objects drawn at the time of the test are significantly smaller than the same objects drawn when no background items were imagined.

Layout

The layout of a scene involves the relative locations of objects and surfaces in it. Along with some details of the attended objects and the general gist, a glance at a scene leaves the visual system with rich information about the relative locations of objects. Often, viewers can remember these locations as having been occupied or "filled" by an object even though they cannot remember the identity or other features of a given object at a given location.

A relatively straightforward way to study short-term memory for spatial layout involves the methods described earlier in this chapter for measuring the capacity of memory for objects (see Figures 5.6 and 5.7). However, instead of using different items and asking participants to indicate whether one has changed in identity, researchers can use all the same items in a spatial layout experiment and have the change involve items being in a different location in one of the pictures. Figure 5.29 shows an example of such a display sequence.

Experiments by Tom Sanocki (2003) that measure short-term memory for these kinds of displays point to a capacity limit of about ten to twenty items. This is a significant increase in capacity over the limit of four items in the memory for object properties. It indicates that the spatial location of objects is not coded in the same way as the other properties of an object such as color, shape, and texture. Spatial layout seems to be a special kind of visual property.

One of the main reasons the spatial layout of a scene can be seen and responded to independently of the objects that constitute it, as well as their meaning, is that specialized brain regions are apparently devoted to little else other than the representation of the positions of objects in space. This is evident in the expression of many neuropsychological conditions. For instance, individuals who have had a stroke that has damaged tissue in the temporal lobes (Chapter 2) may be unable to recognize objects even though they have no doubt about where these objects are positioned in space. One such case was described vividly by Oliver Sacks in his book *The Man Who Mistook His Wife for a Hat* (1987). This man was leaving the doctor's office one day when he casually reached over to his wife's head, rather than to the coat rack, in an effort to grasp his hat. Formal testing revealed that he had the spared visual ability to see where objects were located in space. His reach and grasp were appropriate to the distance and shape of these objects. What he had lost was the ability to identify the meaning of the objects he could locate in space. As described in Chapter 2, other individuals with damage to the parietal lobes have lost the ability to locate objects in space even though they have no trouble correctly identifying these objects.

Spatial layout is a visual property of scenes and objects that we learn even when we are not consciously aware of it. Marvin Chun and his colleagues (Chun & Jiang, 1998) have conducted studies making this point in a very convincing way. They begin with a typical visual search task of moderate difficulty. It involves the presentation of a target shape (e.g., a T in one of four orientations) among a large number of distractor shapes (e.g., L's in any one of four orientations) in a random configuration or layout. The experimental factor is whether these layouts, which are initially determined at random, are repeated during the course of the experiment. The finding is that when as many as twelve random layouts are repeated, the search for the target is much faster and more accurate than when the same layouts are generated from scratch on each trial. In the same experiment a new-old recognition test of the repeated layouts, administered after the search task, showed that

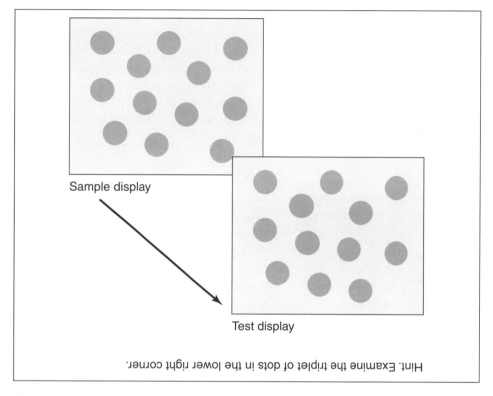

Sample display

Test display

Hint. Examine the triplet of dots in the lower right corner.

FIGURE 5.29 A sequence of displays used for studying short-term memory for spatial layout. Can you find the difference in the two pictures?

participants were only at chance levels in guessing which layouts had been repeated and which had never been presented in the search task.

Spatial layout can also play a strong role in modulating the influence of emotional content. This can happen without any awareness on the part of the viewer of the link between the spatial layout of pictures and their emotional content. In one study (Crawford & Cacioppo, 2002), participants were presented with almost two hundred pictures of both emotionally upsetting and emotionally pleasing scenes. The upsetting pictures included scenes of snakes, spiders, weapons, and injured people. The pleasing pictures were images of nature scenes, romantic scenes, and smiling people. When these pictures were presented in a random order, participants were simply told to look at each picture and to think about how each scene made them feel. The experimenters varied the screen locations of the emotionally positive and negative pictures. In one condition, experimenters introduced only a weak correlation between the screen location and the emotional content of the images; in the other condition, they created a stronger, though not perfect, correlation. When participants were asked in a second phase of the study to place pictures on the screen that they had never seen before, they tended to position them in locations that corresponded to where they had seen similar emotional content earlier. Participants seemed unaware that there was any order to their choices for picture locations. This tendency was also stronger for pictures with negative emotional content than for those with positive content—a finding consistent with the proposed existence of a specialized visual circuit for processing visual images of fear and threat. I will have more to say about this circuit in Chapter 9.

VISION FOR IMAGES OR OBJECTS?

This chapter's discussion of vision of objects and scenes has answered many questions and left us with many new ones. We still have a long way to go to put object vision on the same solid foundation that we have for color vision and edge perception. Some of the uncertainty stems from our limited understanding of the neural processes involved in object perception. In comparison, we seem to be much farther ahead in understanding the vision of object properties such as location in space, color, and shape.

Other aspects of the uncertainty stem from the inherent slipperiness of trying to study something that never stands still. The ongoing eye movements during scene perception, the changing views of a scene caused by the motion of ourselves and other objects, and the changes in the moment-to-moment goals and expectations of the viewer all mean that perception of an object is rarely stable long enough for us to get a proper measure of it. Perhaps trying to get a fix on an inherently dynamic process is the wrong goal. Perhaps we need new tools to study the dynamic systems involved in object perception. Yet another aspect of our uncertainty stems from our limited understanding of the role of consciousness in perception—but more on that will appear in Chapter 9.

The mystery with which we began this chapter still remains. I have the experience of a richly detailed visual world, and I benefit from long-lasting memories of specific scenes, at the same time that I suffer from a severe amnesia of the details seen in the previous glance. The solution to this dilemma will almost certainly involve an answer similar to the one we encountered in earlier chapters and will encounter again in future chapters. The solution must begin with an understanding that vision is primarily designed for seeing objects and surfaces "out there" in the world and "at a distance." It is not designed for seeing the patterns of light and the images that emanate from these objects and surfaces. To adapt a well-worn metaphor, in vision the medium is *not* the message. The image is only a vehicle by which we gain access to the objects and their relation to us. No wonder our perception and memory of image properties is so poor! But this answer merely points the way. It does not tell us how our brains are able to construct these models of objects and their properties by using only the information gained from the images.

FURTHER READING

Albert, M. K. (2001). Surface perception and the generic view principle. *Trends in Cognitive Science, 5*, 197–203.

Biederman, I. (1987). Recognition-by-components: A theory of human image understanding. *Psychological Review, 94*, 115–147.

Hochberg, J. (1978). *Perception* (2nd ed.). Englewood Cliffs, NJ: Prentice-Hall.

Hock, H. S., & Schmetzkopf, K. R. (1980). The abstraction of schematic representations from photographs of real-world scenes. *Memory & Cognition, 8*, 543–554.

Hoffman, D. D. (1998). *Visual intelligence.* New York: Norton.

Rensink, R. A. (2001). Change blindness: Implications for the nature of visual attention. In M. Jenkins & L. Harris (Eds)., *Vision and attention* (pp. 169–188). New York: Springer.

Rensink, R. A. (2002). Change detection. *Annual Review of Psychology, 53*, 245–277.

Sacks, O. (1987). *The man who mistook his wife for a hat.* New York: Summit.

Simons, D. J., & Levin, D. T. (1997). Change blindness. *Trends in Cognitive Science, 1*, 261–267.

Tarr, M. J., & Bülthoff, H. H. (1998). Image-based object recognition in man, monkey, and machine. *Cognition, 67*, 1–20.

6 TIME

FUNDAMENTAL QUESTIONS

- How long does it take to see something?
- What are the smallest time differences that can be detected among visual events?
- How does the visual brain handle the feature of time?
- What are some revealing illusions of time perception?
- How long does it take to switch attention from one object to another?
- Does vision merely record correlations among events, or does it also assign causal blame?

TEMPORAL RESOLUTION AND THE SPEED OF SIGHT

Human vision is exquisitely sensitive to the physical dimension of time. The order in which two objects appear or disappear from view can be judged very accurately when they differ by as little as 30 milliseconds. To get a sense of how small a unit of time this is, remind yourself that there are more than 33 of these units in a single second (1 second = 1,000 milliseconds). Thus if two race cars were approaching the same finish line from different directions, each traveling at 200 miles per hour, you would be able to see which one arrived first if one led the other by as little as 9 feet. This may seem like a large lead until you consider that in the last period of 1 second, each car would have covered almost 300 feet—the length of a football field. On a baseball field, where the absolute speeds would not be as high because human movement is the limiting factor, a similar race to first base between two players traveling at 30 miles per hour would permit you to determine the winner by a separation of around 16 inches.

Cycling patterns of visual events that recur over very short periods can be used effectively to organize a display into "figure" and "ground." For example, in one study (Alais, Blake, & Lee, 1998) observers were shown displays containing many small bars in many orientations, with each bar moving independently in a different direction. At unpredictable intervals, any single bar would suddenly reverse its direction of motion. These displays look like the random snowstorm you see on your TV when it is not turned to a specific channel. There is no order in the spatial pattern of luminance, edge orientation, or motion direction.

Yet it is easy to create visible order in these displays by adding a pattern that consists entirely of changes over time. If the randomly moving bars in one region, such as a central square, change their directions at the same time, then those bars form a square "figure" that can be seen against the "ground" of the other bars switching directions of motion at random intervals. This is the case even though the many different directions of motion contained in the square are unrelated and the changes in direction occur at random. The changes that occur "in concert," technically called *synchronized changes,* result in a visible shape even when the rate of change is as high as fifty times per second. That corresponds to a reversal in the direction of motion on average every 20 ms. Despite the short-lived and unpredictable nature of each event, observers can see the geometric form defined by these correlated changes in time quite easily and accurately.

The acuity of the visual system for events over time is called its *temporal resolution.* Box 6.1 will help you experience some of the limits of temporal resolution in human vision. As these demonstrations and the previous examples show, the temporal resolution of vision is generally very high, meaning that small differences in luminance over time, edge orientation over time, or motion over time can be detected reliably. It is tempting to jump from this finding to the conclusion that vision occurs very quickly; that we see the world with only a small delay between the time our retina is stimulated with light to the time we become conscious of the objects revealed by that light or are able to act upon them. This aspect of vision can be called the *speed of sight.* But such a conclusion linking temporal resolution and visual speed falsely assumes that vision for relative time differences (the only requirement for temporal resolution is a time difference between two events) is directly related to vision in absolute time (the time that elapses between a physical event and our perception of it). When the speed of vision is measured with respect to a physical reference point, seeing always takes much longer than 30 ms from the onset of retinal stimulation.

To get a sense of some of the issues involved in measuring the speed of sight, consider the simple visual task illustrated in Figure 6.1. In this display a bar rotates smoothly around its center, and observers fix their gaze on the center. The bar continues to rotate at a constant speed of about one full revolution every halfsecond. Every now and then, each of the two extensions of the bar flashes briefly while the bar continues to rotate. If perception occurred instantaneously and was faithful to the physical timing of the display, then the flashed bar extensions would be seen in their actual locations and for a brief period the bar would appear to be longer than it is most of the time.

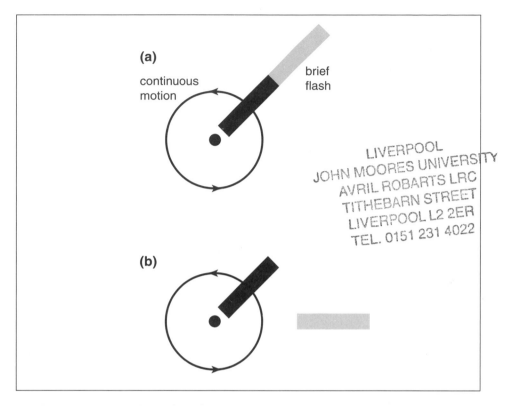

FIGURE 6.1 (a) The sequence of visual displays used to study the flash-lag effect. (b) What observers see when shown this display?

Even if perception lags behind the physical events by a constant amount, as it must to some extent because of the time required for neurons to carry the visual signal from the eye to the brain, the flashed bar extensions would be seen in their proper locations. That is, perception might be delayed overall, but the delay would be the same for the central bar and the extension. But this is not what we see. What observers see differs both from the assumption that perception is instantaneous and from the assumption that perception is delayed by a constant amount. The briefly flashed extensions of the bar are seen to consistently lag behind the location of the smoothly rotating center bar. The lag may be as much as 10 degrees, which corresponds to a temporal lag of over 50 ms. This illusion, the *flash-lag effect,* is currently at the center of a lively debate among vision scientists because of its implications about the way that time is represented in human vision.

We will return to the flash-lag effect later in this chapter after considering some background that is needed to understand what the vision scientists are arguing

Critical flicker fusion

Materials

A lamp with a fluorescent light bulb or a personal computer monitor on which you can set the flicker rate to at least 60 cycles per second (the *hertz rate,* or Hz) or lower. Several sheets of transparency in different colors (yellow and blue are ideal). A recording sheet labeled with experimental conditions 1–6.

Instructions

View the light source (lamp or computer screen), first under normal room lighting conditions and then in a darkened room. Give each of the following conditions a rating of 0 to 3, where 0 means you can detect no flicker at all and a 3 means there is a clear and undeniable flicker:

1. Gaze directly at the light source.
2. Look at the light out of the corner of your eye.
3. Gaze directly at the light, but through a transparent overlay that blocks short wavelength light (yellow is ideal).
4. Look out of the corner of your eye through an overlay that blocks short wavelength light (yellow is ideal).
5. Gaze directly at the light through an overlay that blocks long wavelength light (blue is ideal).
6. Look out of the corner of your eye through an overlay that blocks long wavelength light (blue is ideal).

Use your recorded results to answer these questions: Under which conditions was the flicker most obvious? Under which conditions was it best hidden?

Analysis

A fluorescent bulb is a light source that turns on and off many times each second. We normally see this as a steady source of light, not as a flickering one, because it flickers at rates that are higher than our temporal resolution. The lowest rate of flicker that we are able to see as a steady source of light is called our *critical flicker fusion.* It can be as high as 60 cycles per second (8.3-millisecond periods of on and off) and as low as 10 cycles per second (50-millisecond periods of on and off), depending on both the condition of the environment and the portion of our eye that we use to detect it. The bulb in a standard fluorescent desk lamp cycles at 60 cycles per second, which is very near to our maximum temporal resolution. Normally, we cannot see it flicker except when we view it under fairly bright lighting conditions and out of the corner of our eye.

When we view the lamp in an otherwise dark room, we will not be able to detect any flicker because under dimly illuminated conditions our rods become active. Rods have a much slower response to changes over time than cones, so their critical fusion frequency is lower. Thus whether we view the lamp in the dark out of the corner of our eye or directly, it will likely appear to be a steady source of light. Flicker is more readily detectable in the light because cones have the ability to turn on and off more rapidly than rods. Even among the three cone types there are differences in critical flicker fusion, with L-type (red) and M-type (green) cones responding with greater temporal resolution than S-type (blue) cones.

When we view a flickering light in a fairly bright room, we can see it flicker more strongly out of the corner of our eye than when we view it directly. This is because there are relatively more rapidly responding magno ganglion neurons in the visual periphery of our eye than the sluggish parvo neurons. Magno ganglion cells are better able than parvo neurons to detect differences in light levels over such short periods as 16 ms. You will therefore see the most flicker when the light is of a medium to long wavelength (not blue) and viewed out of the corner of your eye. The best color choice (yellow overlay) helps to ensure that your long and medium cones are stimulated. Looking at the light through the corner of your eye places the light on a retinal location (the visual periphery) where the magno system is stimulated more than the parvo system.

about. However, even at this point it is clear that the fine-grained temporal resolution of vision does not in itself guarantee that perception will occur quickly. We will always see some aspects of the visual world later than other aspects, even when they occur at the same point in physical time.

SEEING TAKES TIME

Because of the physiological limits of the brain, such as the time needed for a neuron to signal another neuron, seeing takes time. As we saw in Chapter 2, individual neurons operating at their best can fire (undergo a cycle of activation and deactivation) only once every few ms. We also saw in that chapter that there is a temporal hierarchy of visually sensitive regions of the brain, such that some regions are activated only after others. Even if we consider the earliest cortical sites of visual activation, such as areas V1, MT (the middle temporal area), and FEF (the frontal eye fields), an average of 40 ms has elapsed from the time that the retinal receptors are stimulated by light to the time that these earliest cortical regions are activated. If we now consider any rudimentary visual analysis of the object—the kind needed to determine, for example, its spatial location, color, or orientation—even more time will have elapsed. This is because for almost every visual task, two more time-consuming classes of neural events must occur.

First, neural activity within a brain region must continue for some time before a pattern of activity emerges that is differentiated for the object of perception as opposed to the visual background to that object. These are often referred to as *neural oscillations,* and they take 50 to 100 ms to emerge. The oscillations usually involve horizontal connections within a brain region and feedback connections between a brain region and other brain regions activated earlier in the temporal hierarchy (see Chapters 2 and 4).

Second, brain regions that are farther along in the temporal hierarchy must be activated. For example, in order to respond to the color of an object at a given location, some color analysis will likely be required from area V4, and this information will have to be coordinated with the location information contained in MT and sent to regions of the parietal cortex. These are only the minimal requirements for "seeing" the color of an object at a given location. If a response is required to the same object, even more time will elapse before the motor commands to the finger or voice can be selected and performed.

These considerations mean that under the most ideal circumstances, it will take at least 200 ms for a visual signal to complete the circuit from retinal stimulation to appropriate action. We can apply these estimates to an everyday action: For example, when a conscientious driver depresses the brake pedal in response to a red light, well over half of this time is taken up in the visual analysis of the light itself. It may easily take 40 ms for the red light to reach the lateral geniculate nucleus, another 20 ms for it to reach area V1, another 20 ms for it to reach the color area V4, and then another 40 ms for this information to reach centers in the frontal parts of the brain responsible for action, planning, and perhaps even consciousness. So at this point 120 ms have elapsed and the light has only been "seen." No signal has yet been sent to the motor regions of the brain to begin the process of initiating the appropriate response of the foot. That process may take another 60 ms, leaving 20 ms for the activation of the appropriate muscles.

At this point 200 ms have elapsed, the car has continued to travel at the same speed, and the driver is only beginning to depress the brake pedal. At the typical highway speed of 65 miles per hour, the vehicle will have traveled more than a full car length before the driver initiates any response to begin slowing the car. Of course, even once the brake has been depressed, the car will have its own time course of coming to a halt. As we often hear, "individual results will vary." This warning applies equally well to the momentary condition of the driver and to the condition of the car. The larger point is that the speed of perception, for even the simplest visual analyses, can be surprisingly slow—at least when compared to our subjective experiences of seeing the visual world unfold in what appears to be "real time." When measured with respect to physical time, it turns out that we experience the world in a way that bears a greater resemblance to "instant replay" than to "live action."

The conclusion that we live in the "near past" in terms of our visual experiences raises puzzles of its own. Some of them are deeply philosophical, such as whether we can ever have an experience in the "physical present." Many philosophers have concluded that we cannot, and they refer to our immediate experiences as occurring in the "specious present"—that short period of time of which we are aware at any given moment. This period can vary from a few seconds to several minutes, and the contents of this consciousness are often thought to be synonymous with short-term memory. But regardless of how we define this "moment," it seems doomed to be about the past rather than the actual present. Other aspects of the puzzle of living in the "near past" are more practical and therefore of immediate interest to vision scientists. For instance, why don't we walk into dangerous, fast-moving traffic? What visual signals are we using when we duck unconsciously to avoid being hit in the head by projectiles?

Neural chaos in a stable world

As we learned when we considered object perception in Chapter 5, human vision takes advantage of the fact that the physical world is generally a quiet place. When we think of the time domain, the various visual features of an object in our visual field generally do not change quickly or drastically over time. From moment to moment and from glance to glance, we are usually safe in assuming that the physical world is relatively stable. Even when objects' visual features do change—as, for example, when the location of an object changes because it is in motion, or when its color changes because of shadows—these changes tend to be gradual and continuous. This overall quietness of the world can be contrasted with the many abrupt changes that occur to the images on our retina when our eyes move from one gaze location to another. As we have seen many times already, it is usually in our interest to ignore these image changes in an effort to see the stable world. Most of the time, vision is working to accomplish this.

The physical world also tends to be coherent. That is, there is a high correlation between specific clusters of features and their locations and movement patterns. Trees are tall thin green structures that tend to be attached to the ground, they often occur in clusters and rows, and they have a distinctive shape. Houses are generally long, low, and stationary and have a different class of shape and size from trees. People have semi-rigid shapes, move in distinctive ways, and come in predictable sizes. This inherent coherence of the visual world, like its stability, turns out to be beneficial when we consider how the visual system is able to combine the appropriate visual features of an object in the time domain.

To understand the problem facing the visual system in the realm of time, it is helpful to contrast the coherence and stability of the physical world with the variability and segregation that exists for the corresponding visual signals in the brain. Take, for example, the sudden appearance of a common object such as a cat in your field of view. The magno ganglion neurons in your retina will initiate activity in the superior colliculus and in areas V1, MT, and FEF very quickly (see Figure 2.11 in the color appendix). This early-arriving information will be relatively crude with respect to color and shape but will be informative with regard to the specific location of the object in your visual field, its movement patterns, and its approximate size. This is the kind of information contained in the dorsal stream of visual processing (see Figure 2.10 in Chapter 2). Later-arriving information in area V1 and eventually in the temporal cortex will contain more detail on color and shape. Cells in the temporal cortex, part of the ventral stream discussed in Chapter 2, will be able to recognize the object class ("cat") and even the specific member of that class (my cat "Shadow"). These cells will likely be receiving information quite early from regions of the rapidly responding dorsal stream and only later from brain regions that are considered to be part of the feedforward ventral stream. Box 6.2 will help you experience some of the differences in the speed with which different visual attributes can be seen.

The result of considerations such as these is that the temporal coherence of the "cat" in the physical world (all visual aspects of the cat arrived on the retina at the same time) has become a chaos of temporal events when considered from the perspective of the brain events involved. How does the brain put the visual features of the cat back together again so that we are able to see all aspects of the cat's appearance as belonging to the same "slice" in time? Vision scientists have been actively pursuing this question for the past several years, and there is not yet a single dominant answer on the horizon. However, it is becoming clear that at least two factors contribute to our experience of temporal coherence. One factor is a brain mechanism that unifies the activity of widely separated regions of the brain. The other factor is a visual system that assumes temporal coherence in the physical world and uses this assumption as a starting point in generating hypotheses. We will discuss each of these factors in turn in the following sections.

TEMPORAL BINDING IN THE BRAIN

At the beginning of this chapter, we noted that human vision is exquisitely sensitive to the physical dimension of time. This sensitivity is remarkable when we stop to consider that there are no known receptors in the brain specifically responsible for recording the "time" of a visual event. This makes the temporal features of vision different in some sense from the spatial features. In previous chapters, we encountered many cells with receptive fields specialized for such spatial features as luminance gradients, color differences, and the detection of complex shapes. In

BOX 6.2

Seeing "where" before seeing "what"

There are many situations in the everyday world that enable us to see some visual attributes of an object before other attributes. Think of this the next time you try to:

- identify an approaching vehicle from a great distance on an open road
- identify a bird from a distance
- find your friend in a busy airport

In each circumstance, you will know "where" something is with considerable precision long before you are able to identify "what" it is. For example, from a distance the approaching vehicle may be a truck or a car. You will likely know in which lane it is traveling well in advance of seeing its specific make. It is a general principle of vision that an object's location in space can be determined well ahead of its color and shape.

Because the motion characteristics of an object involve changes in spatial position over time, distinctive motion features can often be detected before distinctive shape and color features. Expert bird watchers know this and often use the movement pattern of the bird as a more reliable indicator of its species than either its color or shape, which may be hard to determine from a distance.

The same principles hold true for finding your friend at an airport. You will be able to determine where people are well in advance of knowing who they are. From a distance, the movements your friend makes in walking and gesturing may well be a more rapidly discerned clue to her identity than her facial features.

contrast, the processing of temporal events occurs as a side effect or byproduct of the way that neurons behave, both individually and in groups.

Many typical single neurons respond to the onset of an event for which their receptive field is specialized with a short-lived and rapid-fire burst of activity. When the same stimulus disappears from the receptive field, the same neuron may not even note its disappearance; if it does, it will note it with a second, weaker burst of activity. These neurons simply respond to the change that occurs when a visual "trigger feature" either enters or exits their receptive field (their individual field of view). In fact, this is a fair account of the behavior of the magno ganglion cells in the retina that we discussed in Chapters 2 and 4. As such, these neurons are incapable of keeping any record of time on their own because they have no way of marking the time that elapses between the burst associated with the onset and the offset of the trigger feature.

Other neurons respond with a similar burst of activity to the onset of a trigger feature, but then they continue to be active above their resting level for some time if the trigger feature remains in view. The parvo ganglion cells of the retina are an example of neurons with this kind of response to sustained visual input (Chapters 2 and 4). In contrast to magno neurons, these neurons carry some aspects of timing, in a limited way, by continuing to fire while their trigger feature is in view. For example, two brief events that differ only in duration could, in theory, be discriminated by a comparison of the sustained neural activity associated with each of them.

But a closer examination of the behavior of these neurons reveals complicating factors. For example, both the overall rate of neural activity and the extent of its duration are influenced by factors other than the passage of time. If the trigger feature is closer to the ideal for that neuron, both the overall rate of activity and the temporal extent of the activity will be greater. If the intensity of the signal from the trigger feature is greater—for example, because of a greater contrast with the background—it will also result in more activity. These factors make the duration of neural activity a poor index of the elapsed time of visual events. Trying to link neural activity in different parts of the brain on the basis of this kind of information would be a hopeless task.

There is a feature of neural activity, however, besides the rate and duration of firing, that is much more ideally suited for coordinating brain events occurring near the same place in time. This is the general tendency for neurons, when they fire, to cause other neurons with which they communicate to fire with precisely the same temporal pattern. That is, not only can neurons initiate activity in other neurons they contact, but they also initiate a pattern of activity similar in temporal microstructure. Neuroscientists call this *neural synchrony*. It means that if a given neuron is firing with some random pattern over time, connected neurons will begin firing with the same random pattern. This synchronous behavior is evident when neural activity patterns are measured in different regions of the brain at the same time and the two traces are compared for coincidental firing. The two regions are said to be in synchrony when for any given small window of time, such as 10 ms, neurons in both regions have a high probability of firing.

An interesting feature of neural synchrony is that the firing coincidences seem to increase and decrease in cycles, creating waves of activation that repeat themselves between twenty and sixty times per second. These waves of coincidence, called *oscillations* by neuroscientists, are increasingly being interpreted as a sign that two brain regions are in communication with each other concerning the same visual object. Fortunately for scientists studying human vision, the oscillations can be measured noninvasively, while the study participant is performing a visual task, by recording small changes in brain voltages from a cap of electrodes worn by the participant. These techniques—known as recordings of event-related potentials, or

ERPs (Chapter 2)—are at present the best way to study the temporal microstructure of brain activity in a noninvasive way.

Many vision scientists now think that neural synchrony and oscillations are the key ingredients for establishing the visual coherence of an object, such as that of a cat entering our field of view. Even though the many visual features of the cat may be processed in brain regions that are anatomically separate from one another, and even though each brain region may initially become active at a different time, because these regions were activated by the same new event their activity will tend to become synchronous. Over a short period (100 ms or more), this synchronous neural activity will have propagated to all brain regions involved in the representation of the cat. Not only will that distinctive pattern of synchronous activity help to distinguish the neural activity corresponding to the cat from the neural activity corresponding to other visual objects forming the background, but there will be a different pattern of neural synchrony for each cat, should two or more of them come into view at the same time. The main role played by synchronous neural activity is to act as a neural "tag," indicating that the various features involved in the synchronous neural activity belong to the same object in both space and time. This unification of signals in diverse regions of the brain is called *neural binding*.

In a recent study by Eugenio Rodriguez and colleagues (Rodriguez et al., 1999) that examined the role of neural oscillations in vision, human participants examined pictures that looked either like faces or like random abstract forms. The faces were versions of the Mooney faces seen in Figure 4.26 in Chapter 4, and the abstract-appearing forms were actually the same faces but shown upside down. The participants were wearing a dense cap of recording electrodes that were sensitive to small changes in voltage across the scalp. The main finding was that when participants saw the faces, there was both a sharp increase in general activity and a measurable increase in neural oscillations in the occipital regions of the brain (area V1 and neighboring visual regions). Viewing the upside-down faces, which had the same number of edges but which looked only like abstract shapes, also caused a sharp increase in neural activity in this region. However, this activity was not the oscillatory kind seen when participants were viewing the recognizable faces.

One interesting feature of the oscillations that occurred in response to the faces was that the oscillations were not tightly coupled in time to the onset of the faces. An initial burst of activity could always be found that was time-locked to the onset of the stimulus (whether recognizable or upside-down). But the oscillations themselves seem to be generated internally to the brain. It is as though the brain establishes neural binding on its own time scale, rather than needing to anchor that timing with regard to any external benchmarks.

Another interesting feature of the oscillations in this study was that they were short-lived, with most of them being over within 300 ms. This is less time than the

600 or so ms that elapsed before the participants began to press the button indicating they had seen a face. In fact, shortly after the face-phase of oscillations had been extinguished, a different phase of oscillations was observed. This one was associated with the finger response (a button press) that participants made to indicate they had seen a face. It was measured most strongly over regions of the brain known to be involved in the planning and execution of actions, which are the frontal lobes and an area called the motor strip. The researchers concluded that these two phases of oscillation corresponded to the two coordinated mental activities required for successful completion of the task on each trial: face recognition, followed by a decision to make the appropriate response.

ILLUSIONS ARISING FROM TEMPORAL CHAOS

If brain activity such as neural synchrony and oscillation accomplishes the temporal coherence of vision, and if these brain activities are designed to take advantage of a generally quiet world, then it shouldn't be too difficult to imagine that a wide variety of visual illusions are possible when the world is artificially constructed to violate the usual temporal serenity. In this section we will consider a number of these illusions. We will begin with some illusions that depend on the irreducible delay between physical events and their neural consequences, and then we will move on to some that depend on the differential times required to see various aspects of the visual world.

Temporal integration

Perhaps the simplest and most easily demonstrated illusion of time is that of *visible persistence,* which was introduced in Chapter 2 in demonstration Box 2.2. To recap briefly, it is very difficult to see accurately the onset, duration, and offset of brief flashes of light because of the imprecise relationship between changes in light intensity over time and the neural activity those changes produce in the brain.

To help understand this point, look at the relationship, shown in Figure 6.2, between a simple visual event and the associated neural activity in a brain region sensitive to this event. The event is a 10-millisecond flash of light. The neural activity associated with it begins after a short delay caused by neural transmission time between the retina and this brain region. But once it starts, the neural activity continues for a much longer time than the duration of the brief flash. A 10-millisecond visual event becomes a 50-millisecond or longer neural event. Also, the neural activity does not end abruptly, like the actual event, but gradually wanes if no other visual events follow, until the neurons return to their normal resting levels.

What happens during this period of neural activity that extends beyond the temporal life of the brief flash? One reason neural activity must extend beyond such brief events is that neural activity is intrinsically a statistical affair. Even at rest,

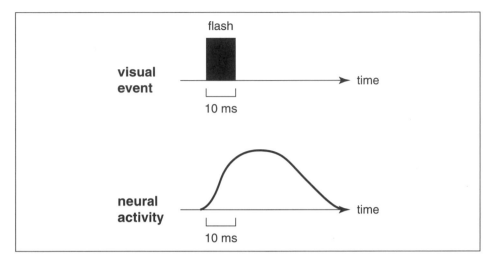

FIGURE 6.2   The relationship between a brief flash of light and the associated activity generated in visually sensitive neurons. The conscious experience of seeing a briefly flashed object for a longer period is called *visible persistence*.

a neuron has a natural level of random activity. Because of this, other neurons that are in contact with any given neuron need to be "convinced" that the increased activity is not just another random increase in firing. Such confirmation requires that the neural events take longer than the physical events, especially if the duration of the physical events is shorter than the time units in which the neurons communicate with one another.

Another reason a neuron remains active longer than a brief physical event that initiates its activity is that it take time for the signal to be propagated around the neural network to which any given neuron is connected. These connections are feedforward, horizontal, and feedbackward, as we learned in Chapter 2. If the entire network is to participate in the temporal binding of the event, then it will also take time to establish synchronous neural activity. In fact, any process of establishing temporal binding is doomed to fail if the originating signal of the process is terminated abruptly before neural synchrony and the associated waves of neural oscillation have been established. The neural events simply have to take time.

Vision scientists have developed some very efficient procedures for studying the consequences of persisting neural activity by designing displays that create illusions in time. Figure 6.3 illustrates these displays. Two patterns of dots flash briefly on a viewing screen, separated by a variable period of time. There are 25 different possible dot positions in all, arranged in 5 equally spaced rows and columns. The first pattern that flashes briefly presents a random pattern of 12 dots. The second pattern presents an equal number of dots, occupying 12 of the 13 positions that were

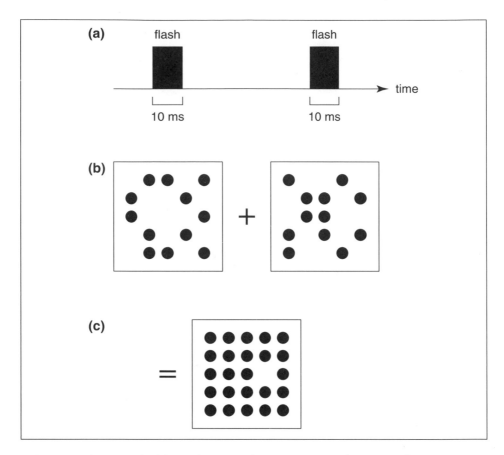

FIGURE 6.3   A method for studying neural persistence using the reports of participants. **(a)** Two brief flashes of 10 ms each are shown on a viewing screen, separated by a variable time period. **(b)** Each flash consists of a random pattern of 12 dots. **(c)** If the two dot patterns are superimposed in space; the missing dot can easily be seen. *Temporal integration* is measured by finding the longest interval between flashes that still permits reliable detection of the missing dot's location.

empty in the first flash. Thus 1 of the 25 possible dot positions remains empty; if the two patterns were superimposed in the same screen, a missing dot would be readily apparent.

Participants in these experiments have the task of trying to find the location of the missing dot. The large number of dots (12 in each pattern), the short time periods, and the randomness of the missing location make it impossible to do this task by using a deliberate strategy such as short-term visual memory. If participants are able to find the missing dot accurately, they can only do so by seeing the entire pattern of 24 dots. The results reveal that this task can be performed accurately when the two brief flashes of 12 dots are separated by 0 to 50 ms. In fact, under these conditions, participants often seem unaware that there are two flashes because they see all 24 dots at the same time. Yet by the time the interval between flashes reaches 100 ms, accuracy in the missing-dot task has dropped to chance levels of guessing. Participants say they can see two distinct groups of dots and cannot combine the two patterns to perform the task.

This task relies on the extended neural activity that accompanies each flash to create the illusion of "simultaneous presence," when in fact the physical flashes are quite separate in time. Because the neural activity generated by each flash overlaps in time, the brain treats the two events as being coincidental in time. Thus we can consider this an illusion of *temporal integration*: The brain has treated discontinuous physical events as though they are contemporaneous.

If we ended our discussion of temporal integration with this experiment, however, it might seem that the visual brain is simply treating time in a sloppy manner. The coarse temporal resolution of neural activity permits physically discrete events to be blurred in time as far as the brain is concerned. But this would be too hasty a conclusion.

Let's look next at the results of an experiment by Vincent Di Lollo (1980), again using the two patterns of 12 dots, but this time examining the consequences of increasing the duration of each flash. Figure 6.4 illustrates the stimulus sequence. When the duration of each pattern is long enough, there comes a point at which no interval remains between the presentations of the two dot patterns. In Figure 6.4 this is illustrated with two patterns that are each presented for 200 ms, such that there is a period of 50 ms in which the 24 dots are present at the same time on the viewing screen. The surprising result is that under these conditions participants are completely unable to locate the missing dot. They see an initial pattern of dots followed by a second pattern of dots in different locations; and when they attempt to report the location of the missing dot, they choose randomly among the 13 positions that remain unoccupied in the second pattern. This implies that they fail to see the period in which the 24 dots are simultaneously presented and instead, as far as their ability to report is concerned see only the locations of the 12 dots in the second pattern. The locations of the dots in the first frame have been masked; although some part of the visual brain may have recorded them, they are unavailable for conscious experience and report by the participants.

How could the visual system fail to see objects that are actually presented simultaneously? Why would vision construct an illusion of discontinuity when presented with the reality of simultaneity? Once again, the only way to understand this is to consider the neural activity initiated by the onset of new visual events. Simply thinking of vision as being a little sloppy with respect to time is not going to help us here. Such sloppiness would only contribute to seeing the 24 simultaneously presented dots as being simultaneous. But the dots are seen as separated in time.

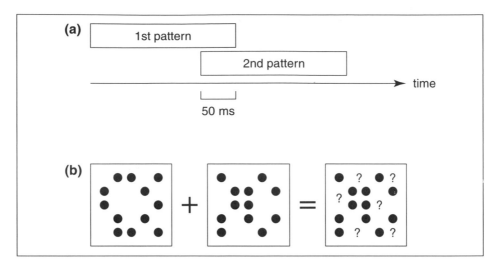

FIGURE 6.4   When two patterns of 12 dots are flashed briefly, each for 200 ms, such that the two patterns are simultaneously present for 50 ms, temporal integration is not possible. This means that when observers are asked which dot was not presented, they must guess among the 13 empty dot locations in the last pattern.

We have to consider the neural events that are constantly at work in trying to bind objects together in time. In the first temporal integration task we considered (Figure 6.3), where the duration of each flash was very brief, we can imagine the processes of neural synchrony and oscillation being initiated by the neural signals generated by the combined activity of the 24 dots. That is, by the time synchrony between two or more brain regions could be established over the course of the first 100 ms, it was based on neural activity generated by both patterns of 12 dots, which for neural purposes were being treated as simultaneous.

What changed in the second temporal integration task (Figure 6.4), where the duration of each flash was much longer, was the amount of time for neural synchrony and oscillations to become established for the first pattern of 12 dots before the second pattern of 12 dots appeared. Therefore, even though there was a 50-ms period in which the 24 dots were physically contemporaneous, in terms of neural binding a 12-dot pattern appeared first and initiated the temporal binding process. This was followed by a second pattern of 12 dots that appeared in roughly the same place in space and had to be bound together by the same neural mechanisms. A simple overlap in time of 50 ms was not sufficiently long for the 12 dots bound together for the first pattern to be "unbound" and integrated into the binding process established for the second pattern. Researchers' present understanding of the time course of temporal binding predicts that at least 100 ms of uninterrupted neural activity would have to elapse before a pattern could be formed that included all 24 dots. The tests that have been conducted so far are consistent with this prediction.

Object formation

The most important lesson illustrated by these examples of temporal integration is that the process of visual object formation takes time. The initiation of neural events is not the same thing as seeing those events. To see an "object" requires the completion of an important period of consolidation involving the neural processes of synchrony and oscillations between distributed regions of the brain. This appears to take 100 ms or more. If these processes are interrupted before an object has been fully formed, only fragments of the object may remain represented, and they may then be bound inappropriately—as far as the physical world is concerned—to events that occurred at different points in time.

A time-honored way to study visual object formation involves a method known as *backward masking*. A typical study is illustrated in Figure 6.5. Participants report on the identity of two shapes that are presented in rapid succession. The two shapes in any sequence appear randomly from the same set of five shapes. When the two shapes appear simultaneously, reports are not perfectly accurate because the two shapes camouflage each other. It is not always easy to determine, for example, whether a briefly flashed composite of two shapes is a square and a diamond or two triangles pointing in different directions. With an increasing time interval between the two flashes, however, accuracy in reporting the two shapes begins to deviate markedly. Accuracy for the second shape in the sequence improves steadily with increasing time; after 100 ms, participants can report the second shape with almost perfect accuracy.

Over the same period, accuracy of identifying the first shape in the sequence first plunges to chance levels of guessing (1 in 5, or 20%) at 50 ms before rising gradually to reach high levels of accuracy at around 200 ms of separation. The question, then, is why the first shape in a series of two suffers disproportionately in the competition for object formation. The answer is that before around 100 ms have elapsed, the neural representation of an object has not yet achieved the steady state required for the experience of a temporally coherent object. Such a period of uninterrupted calm is available to the second shape in a sequence, provided no additional shapes appear after it. The first shape, however, does not enjoy the same benefits. Any early attempts to begin synchronous neural activity in a neural network corresponding to that first object have been interrupted, interfered with, and eventually usurped by the neural activity initiated for the object that appears later in time.

One way to see the vivid consequences of incomplete object formation is to study display sequences that alternate rapidly between two views. An example of such a display from a study conducted in my own lab appears in Figure 6.6. One of

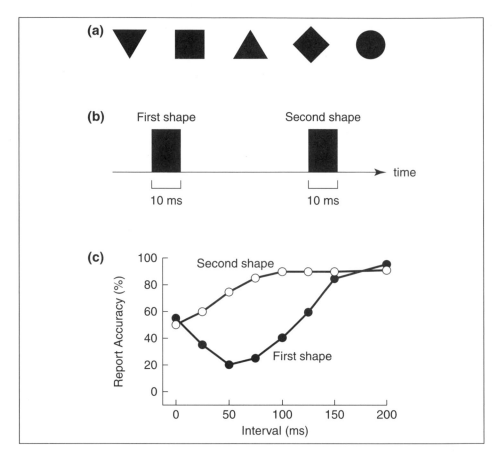

FIGURE 6.5   An illustration of backward masking. **(a)** Shapes are selected randomly from among these five. **(b)** Each of two shapes is flashed for 10 ms, separated by a variable interval between 0 and 200 ms. **(c)** Report accuracy varies predictably over time, with the accuracy for the first shape deviating sharply from the accuracy for second shape.

the frames in the display contains a single vertical bar, whereas the other frame contains two vertical bars that closely surround the single bar in the alternate frame. If the two frames are alternated very rapidly in time—say, at 20 ms per frame (one full cycle = 40 ms)—then all three bars are equally visible as shimmering black bars (Figure 6.6a). Each bar is refreshed in the display before the visible persistence generated by its previous presentation has had a chance to wane completely.

It is interesting to note that something different occurs if the cycle time is a little slower—say, between 50 and 100 ms per frame. At these rates, the frame with the single bar becomes invisible and only the two outer bars are visible as "dancing" in place (Figure 6.6b). This effect is called *standing wave masking* because

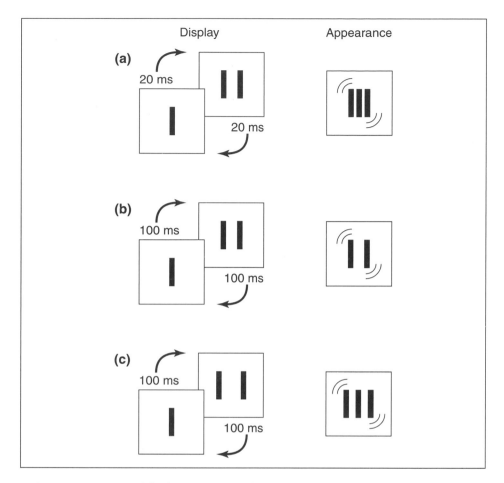

FIGURE 6.6 Typical display sequences in the study of standing wave masking. **(a)** If the two displays are alternated very rapidly, then the rectangular bars in both frames will be seen. **(b)** If the two displays are alternated at a slower rate then only the pair of 'surrounding' bars will be seen; the central bar is invisible. **(c)** Introducing a spatial separation between the bars eliminates standing wave masking; the central bar is visible.

the displays are timed to interrupt the neural activity required for seeing the central bar. Just before the neural activity for that bar is complete on any given cycle, it is interrupted by the neural activity associated with the two outer bars in the alternating display.

An illusion such as this raises an obvious question: Why is the central bar not as visible as the two outer bars when it is presented to the visual system for exactly the same period in alternating frames? The answer is that there is a neural competition among the bars in each frame for the long edges that define the central bar. In one frame, the visual system has evidence (connected edges and common contrast differences) that these edges belong to the central bar; in the other frame, there is evidence that they belong to the outer bars. The visual system is compelled to settle this dispute, and it does so by using the other available evidence: In the frame containing the two bars, there are two long edges (the extreme outer ones) that are not in dispute and that are temporally synchronized with the long inside edges of the same bars. That is enough to give the outer bars the "edge" for control of vision.

Direct evidence of this neural competition can be obtained by introducing a spatial separation, in addition to the temporal one, between the bars in the alternating frame, as shown in Figure 6.6c. Such a spatial separation eliminates the masking of the central bar, allowing all three bars to once again be seen equally well.

Another question is whether there is evidence that the visual system has begun forming a representation of the invisible central bar before that representation has been abandoned in favor of the representation of the outer bars. Again, it is fairly easy to prove. If the center (masked) bar has visual attributes that are slightly different from those of the outer bars, observers of the standing wave illusion report those attributes as "belonging to" the outer bars. For example, as Figure 6.7 shows, a slightly shorter center bar that is made invisible by the appropriate choice of alternation rate will nonetheless cause the outer bars to appear to shrink and expand in length on each cycle. That is, in addition to seeing those bars dance in place, observers now see them change in length on every cycle even though their display frame has not changed at all. *Feature migrations* such as these have also been found to occur for small differences in color and texture between the center (masked) bar and outer visible bars. These feature migrations are direct evidence that visual features (length, color, texture) presented to the brain at one moment in time can be bound together and therefore be seen with features presented at other moments in time. Vision is no less a construction project in time than it is over space.

What happened when?

The fact that visual features presented to the retina at the same point in time can be seen as occurring at different points in time, along with the fact that visual features presented at different points in time can be seen as occurring simultaneously, now makes the flash-lag effect introduced at the beginning of this chapter a little less mysterious. To remind you, this effect involved a smoothly rotating bar on the screen that occasionally also included a brief flash in which the two extensions of the rotating bar appeared. However, rather than seeing these brief flashes as extensions of the rotating bar occurring at precisely the same time as the bar rotating through their positions, observers see the flashed extensions as lagging behind the rotating bar (see Figure 6.1).

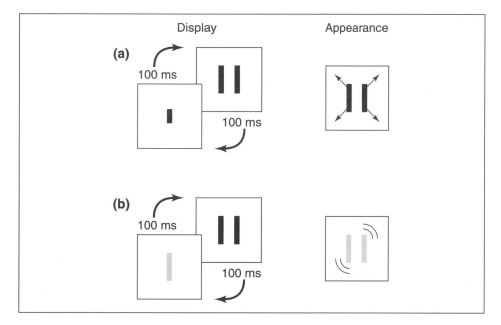

FIGURE 6.7   Displays in a standing wave masking experiment that result in feature migrations. Participants do not see the masked center bar, but they do see features of that bar as belonging to the visible outer bars. **(a)** Shape migration: the flanker bars appear to expand and contract. **(b)** Color migration: the flanker bars take on the color of the invisible central bar.

Vision scientists have spent the past few years examining this effect. They have published dozens of papers on this topic in the most prestigious scientific journals, including *Science* and *Nature*. A brief summary of the ongoing debate is informative because it illustrates what modern vision researchers think is at stake in this effect for their understanding of human vision.

The first idea that researchers pursued was that the flash-lag effect occurs because of differences in the processing of smooth and predictable visual events from the processing of sudden and unpredictable ones. When processing a predictable visual event, such as an object in motion, the brain has time to form a representation of the object in motion, and this representation is thought to involve a network of neurons distributed over several brain regions. The neurons in the network are likely bound together by their synchronous activity. One of the features represented by this network is the direction of the moving object. As such, this representation has the ability to forewarn, or "prime," neurons that will likely become active if the object continues on its current path. This priming would speed the perception of an object in the primed locations, compared to the perception of an object in an unexpected location. Perception of the bar extensions in the flash-lag effect suffers, in this explanation, because their location cannot be predicted in advance.

This is called the *motion extrapolation theory* of the flash lag. It is certainly a reasonable theory, and there is much supporting evidence for it. Neural circuits that can anticipate the location of a moving visual object do exist, and they do speed visual processing. I mentioned some examples of known circuits of this kind in Chapter 4. However, two types of additional findings reduce the likelihood that this is the important factor in the flash-lag effect. (1) Experiments involving random changes in the direction of the moving object in the display show that the perception of a briefly flashed object is just as delayed for motion in random directions as it is when the moving object follows a predictable path. (2) Several experiments have also shown that what happens to the moving object *after the flash has occurred* has a much stronger influence on the delayed perception of the flash event than what happens to the moving object before the flash. For instance, the relative lag in the apparent location of the flashed object is influenced by the overall speed of the moving object, such that a faster moving object creates a larger lag effect. These experiments show that the speed of movement *after* the flash, not *before* the flash, determines the extent of the lag. This finding is not consistent with the motion extrapolation theory.

The second theory of the flash-lag effect, proposed to explain all these findings, is that a moving object can be seen in less time than it takes to see a briefly flashed object. This is called the *differential latency theory*. It builds on the well-supported idea that signals about visual motion get transmitted very rapidly, via magno ganglion neurons, to the dorsal stream that is specialized for motion perception. An abrupt flash will therefore be seen more slowly because of the privileged neural status given to objects in motion.

But this explanation runs into difficulties when new experiments are considered. For example, the flash-lag effect occurs even when there is no movement in the display prior to the onset of the flash. That is, the moving bar and the flashed extension are both initiated at the same time, the only difference being that the center bar continues to rotate smoothly whereas the bar extension flashes once. The initiating event for both objects is therefore a flash-onset. Any differential latency between a moving object and a briefly flashed one would have to come into play after the flash had already occurred.

Another finding that places the differential latency theory in question comes from experiments that compare the perception of smoothly changing objects in a single visual field location with the perception of abrupt flashes of similar objects. If a flash-lag effect occurs under these conditions involving stationary objects, it cannot be blamed on the differential rate at which objects in motion can be seen.

An example of such an experiment conducted by Bhavin Sheth and colleagues (Sheth, Nijhawan, & Shimojo, 2000) is shown in Figure 6.8 (see color appendix). Here, a colored disc on one side of fixation changes gradually from green to red in small steps of color, with the display changing every 75 ms. At some point during this transition, the changing color disc is a particular shade of yellow. At precisely the same time, the identical color is flashed for a 75-ms period in another location an equal distance from where the eye was positioned. The participants' task is to indicate which disc appears as more "red." These reports are always shifted, as far as the changing colored disc is concerned, in the direction in which the colors are changing. That means, in this example, that the changing disc is seen as more "red" or "orange" than the simultaneously flashed and identically colored yellow comparison disc. In order to be seen as equal in color, the flashed disc has to appear over 300 ms before its same-color partner in the gradually changing disc. Clearly, object motion is not a critical feature of the flash-lag effect. The fact that the same effect is found for a stationary object changing only in color means that the dorsal visual stream, thought to be largely color blind, is not even a player in this effect.

The flash-lag effect now appears to many vision scientists to be a consequence of the more general considerations we have already discussed: Namely, that *object perception takes time* (this chapter) and that *only one object can be attended to at a time* (Chapter 5). It does not have to be thought of as a consequence of seeing objects in motion or of seeing unpredictable brief flashes of objects. Considered in this way, the flash-lag effect occurs because the participants' task requires them to process certain visual features only after processing another feature. We can call the first feature the *defining* attribute of the display and the second feature the *report* attribute. In the experiments involving rotating bars, the defining feature is the visual position of the flashed bar. It takes some time for the neural activity from that event to result in a bar visible at a given location. Only once that information has been established, in neural terms, can the report feature be evaluated, which in this case is the current position of the smoothly rotating bar. By the time the position of the flashed bar has been determined, the moving bar has moved along to a new position on the screen.

The same analysis applies to the color-change experiment. The color of the flashed disc is the defining feature in this task. It takes time for participants to evaluate its color; once they have completed this task, their report attribute (color of the changing disc) has changed considerably. It is important to note, too, that changing the order of these processes does not alter the outcome. If the defining attribute is the color of the changing disc at the time the other disc is flashed, by the time the changing disc color has been determined it will be different from the color of the color-constant flashed disc.

Additional support for this explanation of the flash-lag effect comes from studies in which participants are asked a different question about the same displays we have already discussed. For example, in one study of the rotating bars and the flashed extensions by David Eagleman and colleagues (Eagleman & Sejnowski, 2000), a small change was made to the displays so that a different question could be asked. The smoothly rotating bar could come to a halt on the screen, unpredictably, at any point before, during, or after the flashed bar. The participants' task was to indicate which occurred first, the flash or the halt in the rotating bar. It is important to note that this was the same display that caused a flash-lag effect when participants reported on the spatial position of the flashed bar; the only change was that now the rotation would stop at some point.

The results showed that participants could judge the temporal order of these two events very well. Accuracy in this task was very high when one event led the other by as little as 30 ms; more important, there was no bias in judging one or the other of these events as "first." This indicates that the brain has an excellent record of the relative order of the same events for which it reports an incorrect combination of spatial position or color. This leads to the conclusion that there are feature migrations in reports of the objects in the flash-lag displays because object formation takes time. By "object formation" I mean inclusion of the "report" attributes of the object in the synchronous neural assembly that governs perception. As we have already seen, this can take upwards of 100 ms. While the brain is busy doing that, the display in the flash-lag experiment has changed. In this sense, then, the flash-lag effect is not so different from the feature migrations that occurred in the standing wave illusion (see Figures 6.6 and 6.7).

THE MAGICAL NUMBER ONE, AGAIN

This explanation once again begs the question of why only a single object, or maybe even only a single attribute of an object, can be attended to at a given point in time. We encountered this question in Chapter 5, where we merely pointed to the hard reality of the "magical number one" in visual processing. Whenever humans are asked to divide attention among the details of two or more objects, there is a loss in the speed or accuracy of that report, compared to single-minded attention to the attributes of a single object. In the present discussion of the flash-lag effect, this prompts us to ask why the positions of the rotating bars (the smoothly moving one and the flashed one) or the colors of the discs (the gradually changing one and the flashed one) cannot be seen during the same slice of time. Both of these visual attributes were physically available in the same temporal frame of the displays. Some of the attributes, such as the flashed bar extensions and the smoothly rotating bar, could even be considered attributes of the same object. Why was that not enough to prevent an illusion?

A possible answer is that only one synchronous neural assembly can govern control of the visual consciousness of the participant or of the action system of that participant at any point in time. This is only a tentative answer, and there is no direct evidence of it so far, but it is an avenue that some vision researchers are pursuing in an attempt to understand this fundamental "bottleneck" of human vision. Admittedly, this answer only pushes back the problem one step, from being a functional description (humans can only see one thing at a time) to being a neural description (only one circuit of synchronous neural activity can be dominant in the brain at a time). If this answer turns out to be correct, we will probably only be convinced that it is correct after some scientist—perhaps a computationally inclined one—has demonstrated that massively interconnected networks such as the human brain can only support the establishment of a single synchronous assembly of neurons at a time. There might even be a mathematical limit in the behavior of complex networks. But researchers are still not sure. These kinds of hunches and questions are currently guiding researchers interested in the problems of action and consciousness, of which I will have more to say in Chapter 9.

VISUAL ATTENTION OVER TIME

When we discussed object and scene perception in Chapter 5, we noted that certain kinds of visual tasks could be performed very well on rapid-fire sequences of images, whereas other tasks could not. For example, detecting whether any pictures that are flashing by at a rate of ten per second (one every 100 ms) belong to a particular abstract category, such as "a picnic" or "a classroom," is easy, provided that study participants know the category name before the sequence begins to appear. Once the sequence has been shown, it is difficult to accurately match even one image to an identical image presented for comparison. This means that a brief glimpse of 100 ms is sufficiently long for participants to compare a preexisting idea with an image, but it is not long enough to form a representation of the same image when it is unpredicted and therefore must survive the onslaught of subsequent visual images.

Just how long does it take for vision to be able to see an image that is unpredictable and that is followed by other images? The importance of the subsequent images in the sequence for this question is that the new images will act as an ongoing sequence of visual masks. They will terminate the processes devoted to an earlier image and will initiate their own neural processes of object formation. If the earlier image is to survive in the visual brain and form a representation that is stable enough to permit a report at the end of the sequence, it will have to do so in one of two ways. Either it will complete the necessary processes before the next image arrives, or it will fend off the processes that would normally be initiated by the subsequent images in order to complete the processes. Vision scientists often use the term *attention* to refer to these dynamic processes of vision, which are able to select some information at the expense of or to the neglect of other information.

Two modes of attention

One of vision researchers' favorite ways to study the temporal dynamics of visual attention is to show participants a rapid stream of visual information and then to have them perform various tasks on that stream, in order to see what is required for the successful perception of a single image. At the same time, researchers are interested in the consequences of successful target detection for the perception of other images in the stream both before and after the target image.

An example of a typical sequence from one of these experiments (Weichselgartner & Sperling, 1987) is shown in Figure 6.9a. It consists of a single series of twenty-five letters presented at a rate of ten letters per second. One of the letters is surrounded by an outline square. The participants' task is to report the first four letters they can see after they spot the outline square in the sequence. Results show that participants are quite accurate in reporting either the letter that accompanies the square or the one immediately following it. It is interesting that they almost never incorrectly report the letter that precedes the square, showing that recognition of the temporal order of events is good. The fact that they often report the letter immediately following the outline square is likely related to the processes we discussed for the flash-lag effect. It takes a short time for the outline square to be seen, and in that time the stream may have moved on to the next letter in the sequence.

But what about the remaining three letters the participants have to report? Where in the sequence are these letters from? It turns out that there is a period extending from about 100 to 300 ms after the outline square in which letters are not reported. Instead, the next letters reported come from among letters that appear 400 to 700 ms later than the square. It is as though the visual system shuts down briefly after seeing the first one or two letters. This period of insensitivity to images following an initial sensitivity to one or two images in a sequence is the *attentional blink*.

From the results of experiments such as these, researchers have concluded that two major factors contribute to attention to images in a rapid-fire sequence. The first factor corresponds roughly to the detection of a discontinuity in the visual environment. In the sequence shown in Figure 6.9a, the discontinuity is the outline square that suddenly appears amid an ongoing stream of letters. In other experiments it is a sudden flash or the introduction of a distinctive visual feature that is unique amid the ongoing events. These visual discontinuities "pull" vision involuntarily toward the location and objects near them, in both space and time, so that the nearby events are processed at the expense of events immediately before or after. The pulling of attention can occur within 100 ms, as is evident both in this experiment and in previous experiments on the flash-lag effect.

The second factor governing visual attention is an internal one. The momentary goals and expectations of the observer can be used to focus vision on particular events. For the experiment shown in Figure 6.9a, these goals include seeing four letters in all immediately following the outline square. Thus having seen

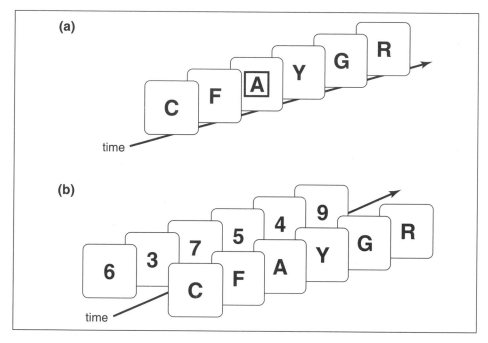

FIGURE 6.9 Rapid-fire sequences of letters and digits are used to study the temporal dynamics of visual attention. **(a)** A sequence of letters in which the sudden appearance of the outline square is a cue to begin reporting the next four letters. **(b)** A simultaneous presentation of digits (*left*) and letters (*right*). A pre-designated digit (e.g., 7) is the cue to report the next four letters.

one or two letters in close proximity to the square already, participants now try to select a few more to complete their report. This second glimpse, the one following the attentional blink, enables them to see additional letters, but only at the expense of missing letters that intervened while the second glimpse was being prepared. Some researchers talk about this voluntary aspect of visual selection as the "push" of attention from within, in contrast to the "pull" of attention from visual discontinuities.

The relatively slow shifts of voluntary attention can be seen quite effectively in experiments involving two simultaneous streams of images, as shown in Figure 6.9b. Here the participants first examine the stream of digits on the left for a critical target digit (7 in the display shown) and then try to report the next four letters they can see on the right. Throughout the sequence of images, the participants keep their eyes locked on the central fixation point so that retinal acuity is the same for the digits and the letters. Participants accomplish the switch in attention from the digit stream to the letter stream without any physical movements of the head or eyes.

The results show that letter report accuracy is highest for letters that follow the target digit by almost half a second (500 ms), with accuracy falling off gradually for letters that come both before and after the peak in performance. This estimate of the time required to switch attention voluntarily from one location or object to another is consistent with many other estimates derived from a wide range of tasks.

Attentional capture

The two modes of visual shifts in attention, the rapid external "pull" and the slow internal "push," represent superb adaptations of human vision. Think about it. Vision is charged with performing two general kinds of functions that are often, on the face of it, in direct conflict with one another. One function is to alert us to the appearance of sudden and unexpected information. For example, if we are driving down a city street and a child darts onto the road, a rapid alerting system must be in operation for us to avoid a collision. We can think of this as a very useful *novelty bias.*

The other, equally important, visual function is to be able to stay on task without distraction until certain tasks are complete. For example, while driving we must pay ongoing attention to cars that are slowing down in front of us. If we are too easily distracted, we may collide with those cars because we momentarily attended to a road sign or someone on the sidewalk. We can think of this ability to stay on task as a *task-set bias.* It is interesting to see how the two biases are coordinated effectively. But first we must see how each is studied in relative isolation.

The novelty bias in vision can be studied quite effectively through *attentional capture,* the involuntary tendency for something unusual in our visual field to attract our attention. Howard Egeth and Steve Yantis (Egeth & Yantis, 1997) have studied this tendency extensively. The effects of attentional capture are readily evident in a visual search task from one of their studies, as Figure 6.10 illustrates. Here, the participants' task is to determine as quickly as possible which of two target shapes is in the display. The target shape is a rectangle that is slightly taller or wider than the other shapes (squares). However, there is one other feature of the display that is hard to ignore: One of the squares is black instead of just being a gray square like all the others. A large color difference like this is a visual discontinuity that "pulls" attention toward it.

We know that attention has been pulled to the black square because we can compare (1) target search times for displays in which the black color coincides with the target rectangle, and (2) search times for displays in which the black color patch is not the target rectangle. To make this a fair test, the displays are designed so that the black color coincides with the target rectangle only by chance. Participants know this, so they try hard to ignore the black color patch. But they simply can't. Search times are much faster when the target rectangle is also black than

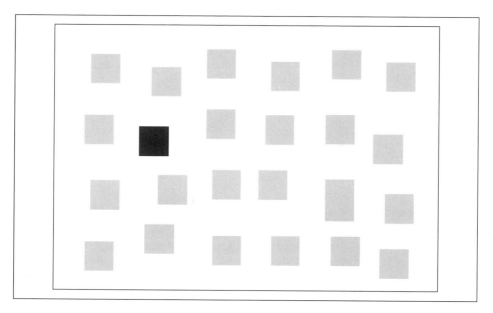

FIGURE 6.10 A visual search task in which the target is a gray rectangle that is either slightly taller or wider than the other squares. The one black item in the display is technically unrelated to the search task, since it coincides with the target shape only by chance. Yet, it is usually impossible to ignore the black item completely while searching for the gray rectangle.

when it is gray. When a nontarget square is black, making the target rectangle gray, search for the target is much slower than when there is no black square in the display. The influence of the task-irrelevant black color patch is therefore a clear indicator of its attention-capturing ability.

The *task-set bias* can be studied by looking to see what visual images can make their way into the visual system once the observer has set his or her goal on the detection of a narrowly defined class or event. In one recent study by Philip Barnard and colleagues (Barnard, Scott, Taylor, May, & Knightly, 2004), participants were told to monitor a rapid sequence of words for a target word that defined "a job that people perform for pay." An example word sequence from this experiment appears in Figure 6.11. Most of the words in the list denote things or events from the natural environment such as *island, snowstorm,* and so on. The target word denotes a job such as *banker* or *waitress.* The critical factor in the experiment is the inclusion of foil words, at variable lags prior to the target word, that are related in similarity of meaning to the target word. For example, some foil words denote human activities for which people usually do not get paid (e.g., *shopper, witness, tourist*), and others merely denote human artifacts (e.g., *television, freezer, park bench*).

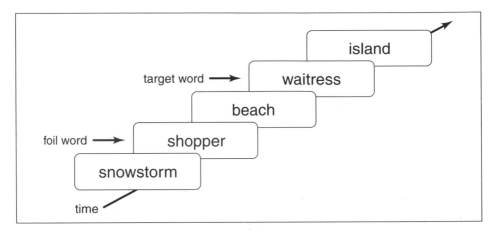

FIGURE 6.11   A sequence of words in an experiment testing the ability of an observer to stay on task. One of several different foil words can be presented prior to the presentation of the target word. If observers attend to the foil words, they will miss detecting the target words that come shortly after.

The extent to which participants are able to form a mental filter that permits only the target word to be detected is measured by looking at target word accuracy as a function of the temporal relationship between the various foil word types and the target. For instance, when all the words prior to the target are from the natural environment, target detection is very high. Participants are able to read the words denoting human occupations equally well at all target word locations. The same is true when a foil word denoting a human artifact is presented. However, when the foil word denotes a human activity that is not associated with pay, target word reading accuracy drops to a very low level for about a half-second. In other words, an attentional blink is associated with the unintended reading of the foil word in this case. Participants are able to set a mental filter to exclude the reading of words that do not denote human activities, but this filter cannot be tuned more finely to select only words denoting human activities for pay.

As noted earlier, an important tension must always be maintained between the bias toward novelty and the bias toward task-set. If novel events always captured attention, or if a task-set bias was perfectly maintained, then we would be in considerable danger for two reasons: We would be unable to maintain focus on a task when it was necessary to do so, and we would be unable to switch our attention to unexpected new information.

This dynamic balancing act of human vision can be seen most effectively in an experimental effect called *contingent attentional capture,* following the lead of Charles Folk and Roger Remington (Folk & Remington, 1998). It refers to the fact that those visual features that are able to "break through" and attract our attention are often only the features for which we have been prepared by our task-set. For example, if it is our intention to search a display for a target defined by a specific feature, such as a specific shape for the search task in Figure 6.10, then whether or not other salient objects will capture our attention involuntarily, such as the black square, depends on how we have set our visual system for the task at hand.

If we have set ourselves to look for "conspicuous discontinuities," which is one effective way to search for the rectangle among the squares, then we will certainly experience the attentional capturing effect of the black square. Similarly, if we believe the black square is a predictive clue to the location of the target rectangle, once again we will find that it has a strong influence on search. However, if we set ourselves to look for specific rectangular shapes rather than "discontinuities," then it is possible to overcome the "pull" of the black square. This effort may require some practice before we are good at it, but many studies now show it to be possible. Whether or not we see the conspicuous black square in this case will depend on how we have described the task to ourselves. I will have more to say about the effects of expectation on vision in Chapter 9 when I discuss consciousness awareness.

TEMPORAL CORRELATION AND PERCEPTUAL CAUSALITY

Another topic to consider in our discussion of time is the perception of cause and effect in visual events. This is an important topic because our perception of causality is governed so strongly by visual processes outside of our awareness. Even though we might like to think we don't "jump to conclusions" in reasoning about the causes and effects of what we see, a few demonstrations can show that this is, in fact, exactly what we do. Our visual systems are designed at the simplest and earliest levels of analysis to draw causal connections. As with any illusion, this one probably works to our advantage most of the time because we live in a world in which effects have causes. But once we are disconnected from this world, through the use of artificial displays such as movies, the processes leading to this illusion can be studied.

Figure 6.12 illustrates a short movie sequence consisting of two discs, beginning with one on the left and one in the center. After a short time the disc on the left moves right, toward the center disc. When it reaches the center disc it stops, and the center disc moves at the same rate toward the right. In this sequence of images there is an objective *correlation* between the motions of the two discs. The disc in the center moves in the same way as the disc on the left, but only after the disc on the left has moved to make contact with the center disc. Given such a correlation, we should reasonably be able to see the events as corresponding to several different scenarios. We might see the discs as each being moved by an outside force (a third factor, in the language of statistics), we might see the two discs as each moving on its own (merely a coincidence or correlation), or we might see the first disc as causing the second disc to move (a causal connection).

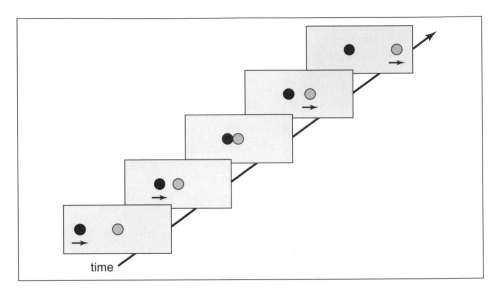

FIGURE 6.12 A short movie sequence that is seen by all humans as involving a ball on the left bumping and then launching a ball on the right.

Observers watching this movie invariably see the left disc as *causing* the center one to move. This perception of causality is compelling and irresistible, even when you know that they are just two discs, programmed by another human, to move on the screen. You know full well that they are not billiard balls or bowling balls. Yet you can't help but see the left disc as "pushing" the center one, according to an unspoken understanding of the laws of physics. Your visual system, and the visual system of every other human that has been tested so far, leaps to this unfounded conclusion about such simple displays. Among people who have been tested are adult participants from non-Western cultures and infants as young as six months of age.

It is certainly possible, knowing that these are simple movies involving inanimate discs, to "reason" in such a way that a causal connection is not drawn. I can tell myself that just because I see one disc bump another and cause it to move, that doesn't mean other factors aren't involved. However, at the same time it is impossible not to "see" the causal link. The cognitive reasoning must, in this case, overcome the compelling sensory information that is screaming "cause" in order to conclude that such a causal link is not necessarily true and that it could be a mere "coincidence."

Other, equally unwarranted and yet equally irresistible conclusions are drawn by the visual system for even more complex causal connections. Several are shown in Figure 6.13. In fact, it is easy to create a movie in which observers see the geometric shapes as "being alive" and having "goals" that they attempt to achieve through a variety of self-selected strategies. For instance, if a small disc moves

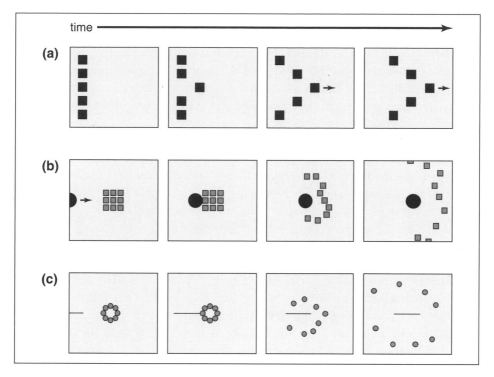

FIGURE 6.13 Short movie sequences that are interpreted as **(a)** the center square pulling the remaining squares, **(b)** the moving disc scattering the small squares, and **(c)** the moving line puncturing and bursting the circle of dots.

around the screen in concert with a large triangle—that is, the disc moves first and the triangle lags behind in both space and time—then observers are sure that the triangle is "pursuing" the disc. This conclusion becomes even more unavoidable if the small disc moves around some larger stationary shapes in such a way that it is no longer in the triangle's "line of sight." Of course, the triangle has no "sight" at all, but that doesn't prevent observers from interpreting its behavior as though it does. If the triangle ceases its "pursuit" every time the disc is behind a larger object, observers see the "hiding" strategy of the disc as being successful and the "seeking" strategy of the triangle as being thwarted by this tactic.

However, some critics find it difficult to believe that these conclusions are the work of the visual system rather than some higher-level reasoning process that simply uses the visual system as its database. For these critics to be convinced that the conclusion of causation is "visual," it is important to demonstrate that it is governed by temporal and geometric aspects of the displays rather than by the thought processes of the observers. One way to demonstrate this involves the displays shown in Figure 6.14, taken from experiments by Brian Scholl and colleagues (Scholl &

Tremoulet, 2000; Scholl & Nakayama, 2002). In Figure 6.14a, the only frame that has been changed is the middle one in the sequence. Instead of touching one another, the two discs are completely overlapped in this frame. In fact, there is now only a single disc on the screen. Yet played as a sequence, these frames result in the perception that the left disc moves continuously across the screen, passing briefly behind the stationary disc in the center. The perception of *launching* (Figure 6.12) has been replaced by the perception of *passing* (Figure 6.14a).

A further small change in this display, however, can once again completely restore the perception of launching to this sequence of images. Simply add a third and fourth disc to the movie, positioned below the original two discs. When the lower two discs follow the launching sequence (Figure 6.14b), the discs above them also appear to be involved in launching, even when only the passing sequence is used for them. When the lower two discs follow the passing sequence, the upper disc on the left once again appears to pass. The context is clearly taken into account in determining which "version of the story" is seen.

Subtle factors of time turn out to be just as important as factors of geometry (seeing one as opposed to two discs in the central frame of the movie) in determining what is seen. For example, if the bottom two discs are shown in motion for 100 ms or less, then their sequences have no influence on what is seen. The contextual motion must be on view for longer than that in order to influence the interpretation of the upper two discs. Also, the window of time in which the lower launching occurs is critical to inducing that perception in the upper two discs in a passing movie sequence. If the launching event in the lower two discs occurs more than 50 ms apart (either before or after), then it will have little influence on the perception of the *passing* movie sequence. Findings such as these make it clear that our visual system has "made up its mind" prior to our slower and more conscious thought processes having any effect on what we have seen.

THE TIMING OF VISUAL EVENTS

I mentioned earlier that the brain does not seem to contain any receptors for the passage of time of visual events—at least not in a comparable way to which it contains receptors for features of space such as edges, area, and extent. Yet we have no trouble assessing the duration of visual events, sensing whether events are simultaneous or successive, seeing the relative order of events, and reaching conclusions on who did what to whom. Of course, some of these impressions are illusory. For example, the perception of simultaneity may indeed correspond to events that are in fact successive. Causation may be seen when only coincidence is warranted. But such illusions do not detract from the point being made here, which is that we have clear perceptions of the temporal flow of visual events despite having no direct visual receptors for time. Studies on the limits of vision in the domain of time, together with studies of neural behavior, have given us hints as to how this sense of visual timing is accomplished.

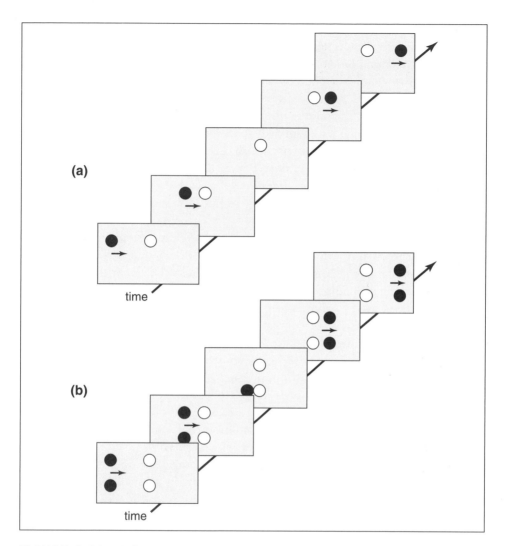

FIGURE 6.14   A short movie sequence seen by all humans as involving a ball on the left passing a stationary ball in the center. The only difference between this movie and the one in Figure 6.12 is the middle frame. **(b)** The *passing* sequence of frames is shown for the upper balls while the lower balls participate in a *launching* sequence.

One hint comes from noting certain temporal intervals that recur in studies of visual timing. These include 30 ms, 100 ms, 500 ms, and 3 seconds. Although these intervals are not always exactly accurate and the longer intervals are generally less accurate than the shorter ones, nonetheless they recur so often in vision studies that they warrant speculation about their functional basis.

The 30-millisecond unit has already shown up several times in our discussion. It is the smallest difference in time that can be discriminated reliably in making judgments of the temporal order of visual events. It is often also the unit representing one cycle when neural oscillations are measured with event-related potential (ERP) techniques. Most recently, it has shown up in studies of eye movements and motor actions made in response to visual events. For example, when distributions of simple motor responses are examined—either of manual responses to signal the onset of a light, or of eye movements in response to a moving target in the visual field—the distributions typically contain a wide range of response times, as shown in Figure 6.15. Some movements are initiated as early as 100 ms whereas others take more than 300 ms, but the bulk of the responses occur in the window of time stretching from 150 to 250 ms.

Several scientists, including Ernst Poeppel (1997) have recently noted a number of smaller peaks superimposed on the larger response-time distributions. The smaller peaks recur every 30 ms or so. It seems likely, then, that the 30-ms unit corresponds to the minimum time that must elapse between peaks in the waves of neural oscillations used to communicate between brain regions. In this account, 30 ms may form the smallest perceptual unit because it is the most irreducible unit of neural communication.

The 100-millisecond unit showed up when we reviewed the processes of object formation, where it seemed to take a minimum of this amount of time to begin to see neural oscillations. This unit also appeared as (1) the maximum time over which temporal integration of two brief flashes was possible, and (2) the minimum time necessary to form an object representation that could withstand backward masking. It also figured in the period over which the flash-lag effect occurred in the rotating bar display, and it figured again in the time needed for attention to be "pulled" involuntarily to a conspicuous discontinuity in a visual image. A reasonable guess is that this is the minimal unit of time needed to broadcast visual information throughout the brain that something new has arrived on the scene, along with some tentative hypotheses about what the new event might be.

The 500-millisecond (or half-second) unit is seen most often when the visual system is "changing its mind." We saw this unit in the attentional blink, where much visual information was lost for this period between preparing some visual information for report (e.g., a first letter in a rapid series of letters) and then preparing some other information for report (e.g., a second letter). It showed up in the time over which the neural oscillations associated with seeing faces occurred. It was also the time that elapsed when the flash-lag effect was measured for discs of gradually changing color. We should also note that when a visual discrimination must be made on the basis of a single feature difference in shape, color, or motion, 500 ms forms the floor of the response time distribution. It is therefore likely that this fundamental unit of time limits voluntary switches of attention between different visual

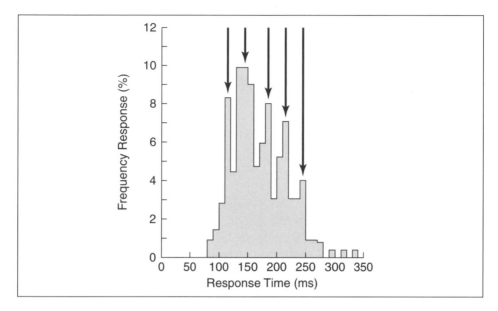

FIGURE 6.15 A typical distribution of response times in a simple manual reaction time task or in an eye movement latency task. The larger distribution of responses is overlaid with peaks every 30 ms or so, as indicated by the arrows.

tasks and conscious decisions among multiple responses. Some scientists have referred to one-half second as the irreducible unit of conscious will or intention. Our minds can't be changed, even by ourselves, in less time.

The final unit of time to consider, 3 seconds, we have not yet encountered because we have focused on the shorter time units involved in visual integration, object formation, and attention switching. The 3-second rule becomes apparent when we ask: *What is the longest visual event that can be accurately reproduced in motor actions?* Several studies have shown that the duration of a simple visual event can be reproduced very faithfully over the period of one-half second to 3 seconds. The function relating duration of response to duration of event is 1-to-1 for up to 3 seconds, as Figure 6.16 shows. After that it begins to fall off sharply. The 3-second rule is also apparent in the duration of perceptual states associated with bistable images, such as the ambiguous cube shown in Figure 1.4 of Chapter 1. Although every observer switches from one percept to the other at different times, the duration of stable states has an average of nearly 3 seconds. Most likely the "near past" of our conscious experience is also linked to this time unit. It is as though every 3 seconds the brain shakes itself off and says, "What's new?" Like the novelty bias discussed earlier, this phenomenon has adaptive benefits for staying flexibly attuned to the visual world.

TIME AFTER TIME

In this chapter we have been forced to confront one of the most difficult puzzles of vision, which is that although our experiences of visual events never coincide exactly with the physical timing of those same events, we are still largely successful in using our visual system to interact with other objects in "real time." The neural activity that must occur for us to behave in response to an event, or to even have an experience of it, takes a measurable period of time. And while this neural activity is unfolding, the physical world has not been standing still. What appears to us to be our immediate experience is in fact a version of our recent past; yet we are able to follow the path of a flying bird with our eyes, catch balls that are thrown to us, and usually avoid collisions with other people.

Before we get too frustrated by this puzzle, let's keep in mind that this is no different from our perception of other aspects of vision, such as those that concern space (edges and objects) or intensity (brightness) or wavelength (color). The perception of each aspect involves "construction," as we have seen. In each case our visual perception is initiated by properties of the physical world (i.e., edges, intensity, wavelength), but by the time our eye and brain have completed their analyses we are experiencing a reality that is both measurably different from the properties themselves and unique to each one of us.

In this chapter we have seen that the same story holds for the physical property of time in vision. Our eyes and brain construct a version of the temporal course of events that is predictably different from the physical time course under many circumstances, as we have discussed. And as with the other aspects of vision, the deviations from temporal reality that we can study as visual illusions of time give us insight into how human vision bridges the gap between the physical "now" and the experienced "now." One of the next great challenges faced by vision scientists will be to link understanding of the temporal aspects of *vision* with an understanding of how our *actions* are timed to interact with the world. We will return to this topic in Chapter 9, when we consider the relationships between human consciousness and visually guided action.

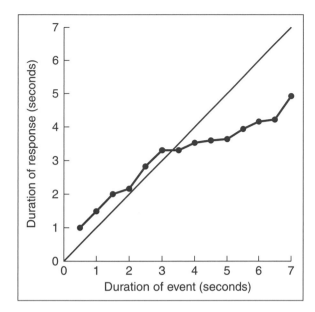

FIGURE 6.16   Visual events lasting between half a second and three seconds can be reproduced quite faithfully. After that there is still an increase in reproduced duration and the actual duration, but the relationship is not as direct. The small constant error of 300–500 ms seen for the duration between ½ and 3 seconds is the time taken to end the action.

FURTHER READING

Bachman, T., & Allik, J. (1976). Integration and interruption in the masking of form by form. *Perception, 5,* 79–97.

Eagleman, D. M., & Holcombe, A. O. (2002, August). Causality and the perception of time. *Trends in Cognitive Sciences, 6,* 323–325.

Eagleman, D. M., & Sejnowski, T. J. (2000, March). Motion integration and postdiction in visual awareness. *Science, 287,* 2036–2038.

Enns, J. T. (2002). Visual binding in the standing wave illusion. *Psychonomic Bulletin and Review, 9,* 489–496.

Nijhawan, R. (1994). Motion extrapolation in catching. *Nature, 370,* 256–257.

7 SPACE

FUNDAMENTAL QUESTIONS

- Why do anti-gravity hills and mystery spots fool us?

- What visual clues calibrate our sense of the upright?

- What do two or more images bring to the problem of constructing a three-dimensional world?

- In what way is our perception of depth an illusion?

- In what way do pictures of realistic scenes have a "dual reality"?

- What do shadows add to our understanding of a scene?

- How can we determine the size of an object in the world? in a picture?

MAGNETIC HILLS AND MYSTERY SPOTS

I grew up in a small town that had a natural wonder just a few miles from the town center. This was one of my favorite places to visit when I was a teenager, especially if I was trying to impress someone from out of town. The natural wonder was an *anti-gravity hill,* a place where the concepts "downhill" and "uphill" don't seem to apply—even to the extent that balls and cars move uphill when left on their own. Using a carpenter's level to make sense of these places doesn't provide us with much insight. The reading on the level simply agrees with the rolling ball, which tells us that what appears to be downhill is actually uphill, and vice versa. Some people have concluded that whatever mysterious force is at work to produce the anti-gravity effect, it exerts its force as readily on the fluid in the carpenter's level as it does on the balls that run uphill.

Getting to the anti-gravity hill in my small town involved a short drive up a twisting mountain road. When the car stopped in the middle of an otherwise innocent-looking straight stretch of road, nestled between two curves and sur-rounded by rolling tree-covered hills, I would pose the critical question to the

257

visiting passenger: *Which way will the car roll if the transmission is placed into neutral, the engine turned off, and the brake released?* The visitor would reply, *Well, that way, of course,* pointing to the slight downhill section lying directly in front of the car. I would then place the car into neutral, turn off the ignition, and release the brake—and slowly but surely the car would begin to roll backward. Spooky stuff!

This eerie demonstration never failed to surprise my visitors. The more curious among them would get out of the car to inspect the site. Certain that the car was pointing downhill even when viewed from a vantage point outside of the car, some visitors would insist on controlling the car themselves to ensure that no driving tricks were happening. Others tried to see in which direction a softball or basketball would roll on the road. The anti-gravity hill never failed: Cars and balls always rolled uphill, picking up speed as they went. What made it fun for local residents like me was that the anti-gravity effects didn't seem to diminish over time, even for those who returned time and again with new visitors.

I later learned that our town was not unique in having an anti-gravity hill. Hills with similar characteristics have been documented in many countries, including several in the United States (Confusion Hill in Ligonier, Pennsylvania; Gravity Hill in northwestern Baltimore County, Maryland; Mystery Spot Road in the Santa Cruz Mountains of California), Canada (Magnetic Hill near Moncton, New Brunswick; my own Gravity Hill near Abbotsford, British Columbia), Scotland (Electric Brae near Ayeshire), Portugal (Mount Penteli), Italy (Ariccia, Martina Franca, Taranto), South Korea (Mount Halla), and Barbados (Morgan Lewis Hill). A photograph of one of the sites is shown in Figure 7.1 (see color appendix).

Although specific aspects of anti-gravity hills always differ, all sites share some general characteristics. First, a clear view of a large portion of the true horizon, such as would be seen when viewing a large body of water or a flat prairie, is never available at these sites. Second, there is more than one surface plane in view in the environment. Third, a local story always accompanies the site, accounting for the fact that gravity fails to operate at this location. Some stories involve ghosts of persons who are thought to have died at the site long ago; others involve alleged local anomalies in the gravitational field of the earth; still others involve strong local magnetic fields that are vestiges of sophisticated civilizations that allegedly resided in the area but long ago became extinct.

Human nature being what it is, the third feature of anti-gravity hills has attracted more attention over the years than the more innocent-sounding first and second features: the absence of a visible true horizon and the presence of multiple surface planes. Indeed, if you think the local stories about anti-gravity hills are a little over the top, a quick trip on the Internet will reveal a host of books and Web sites dealing seriously with the supernatural in these effects.

Recently, vision researchers led by Paola Bressan (Bressan, Garlaschelli, & Barracano, 2003) have become interested in bringing science to bear on the folksy interpretations of anti-gravity hills. They have begun to consider more systematically the role played by the first two characteristics mentioned above. Figure 7.2 illustrates a piece of equipment built in their laboratory that successfully mimics all the important features of anti-gravity hills. This apparatus works, in the sense of creating the eerie effects of balls rolling uphill, regardless of where it is positioned. Its successful functioning dispels all theories based on local gravitational anomalies. Supporters of a magnetic field theory—the third characteristic mentioned above—should take note that it works even though it is made entirely of wood and even when plastic balls (or balls made of other nonmetallic materials) are the rolling objects.

A key to making the demonstration work in the lab is that the viewer must gaze at the series of textured surface planes through a peephole at one end of the apparatus. This has the effect of removing several important clues to what is upright. Normally, there are many clues regarding the direction of *gravitational upright,* meaning the direction pointing away from the pull of gravity. For instance, our bodies must be placed into certain positions if we are to sit down or stand up without falling over. These internal clues coming from our own sense of balance are collectively called *proprioception.* But there are many visual clues as well. One is the sense of depth and distance derived from the fact that each eye has a slightly different viewing angle on any particular scene. This clue is called *stereovision,* and I will say more about how it works later in this chapter. Its absence in the lab demonstration means that the viewer cannot judge the relative orientation of a surface using as a clue the differences between the two images of that surface in each eye.

Another visual clue that is normally available about where surfaces and objects are positioned arises from our ability to move our heads and bodies separately from the objects we are viewing. This is called *structure from motion,* and I will consider it in more detail later on. By looking through a peephole, the viewer loses all the potential information about surfaces that he or she could derive from considering how the surfaces change with respect to his or her body position.

Finally, viewing the artificial scene through the peephole ensures that other reference points to the gravitational upright that might exist in the environment, such as the tabletop or the walls of the room, are eliminated from consideration. The peephole leaves the viewer with the task of judging gravitational upright by using only the internal impressions of balance obtained from his or her proprioceptive senses and any visual clues that remain in the view of the three surfaces in the apparatus.

It is worth considering briefly the proprioceptive sense of upright that we all take for granted. It works well on its own under some conditions, as we can prove by shutting our eyes and trying to remain standing. Box 7.1 will help you investigate its abilities in isolation from the visual sense. As shown by several exercises there, it becomes unreliable after a few moments unless we have more than two points of contact with the earth. Under full viewing conditions, visual clues to the

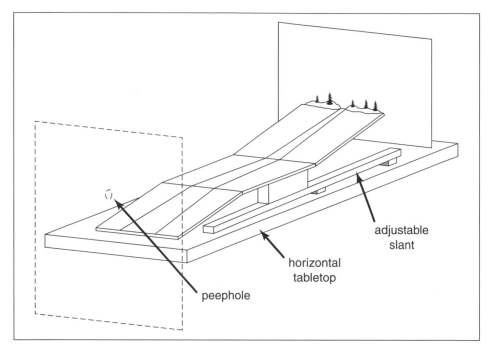

FIGURE 7.2   A tabletop method that mimics the effects of anti-gravity hills.

upright help calibrate this sense. But in combination with limited or restricted visual input, it fails miserably to inform us about the true orientation of surfaces. This is what's happening when we view the surfaces in the tabletop anti-gravity model through the peephole.

Consider, for example, what happens when viewers looking through the peephole judge the situation depicted in Figure 7.2. They see what appears to be a series of three surface planes. The first and third planes are running uphill and away from the viewers, as indicated by the clues derived from perspective, the texture painted on the surfaces, and the fact that the rear portion of each surface is nearer to the upper part of the visual field than the front portion. But what about the orientation of the second, or middle, plane? It is slanted less steeply than the other two; but is it horizontal, is it running slightly uphill, or is it running slightly downhill? The only surfaces that serve as "anchors" for this perceptual judgment are the more steeply slanted first and third surfaces.

Under these conditions, viewers' internal sense of gravity is too weak and unreliable to permit them to sense that the second plane is running uphill (it is actually tilted slightly upward with respect to the horizontal tabletop). Instead, the brain uses the available visual clues to orientation, which are all based on relative, rather

BOX 7.1

Exploring proprioceptive balance

Materials

For this demonstration you will need the cooperation of a friend and a watch with a second hand to measure intervals of less than one minute.

Instructions

Each of these tests is designed to measure the effectiveness of your proprioceptive sense of balance. As such, they must be performed with the participant's eyes firmly closed. First, see how long your friend can balance without shifting the position of his feet (or foot) on the ground under the following four conditions. After you have recorded your friend's times under each condition, have him time you under each one. If you think the first test wasn't representative, try all the conditions again. Rank order the four conditions with regard to which can be done the longest, second longest, and so on. The *relative* time differences among conditions are important, not the *absolute* times.

1. Stand on one foot.
2. Stand on two feet separated by a shoulder width.
3. Stand on two feet with shoes and knees touching one another.
4. Stand on two feet with one foot in front of the other on a straight line, separated by a shoulder width.

Analysis

None of these tests poses much of a problem to a typical young adult whose eyes are open. However, you may have been surprised at how quickly you lost your balance in some of the tests when your eyes were shut. Your proprioceptive sense of balance does not work very well on its own without constant updating from vision or from having more than two points of contact with the ground. Note that when you stood with your feet slightly apart, you were actually in contact with the ground at more than two points because feedback was coming from your heels as well as your toes. When you removed contact with one of the two dimensions of the ground plane—by standing either on one foot or with one foot in front of the other—the proprioceptive sense quickly became unreliable.

than absolute, comparisons. For example, in comparison to the generally steep uphill slants of the first and third surfaces, the slant of the second surface appears to be horizontal or slightly downhill, leaning away from the viewers. But balls placed on the second surface roll toward the viewers, in contradiction to the conclusion made by their visual system. Anti-gravity has been achieved in the lab without the benefit of occult forces or hidden magnets!

Anti-gravity hills, whether in the natural world or in the lab, are illusions that help us understand how we know where we are and where other things are, according to our sense of vision. Indeed, we often take for granted that what we "see" is simply "what is there." Vision is every bit as much a construction project (Chapter 1) for knowing *where* things are as it is for knowing *what* things are (Chapter 5) and *when* events occur (Chapter 6).

A close cousin to the anti-gravity hill is the *mystery spot,* where objects appear to change size from one location to another and heavily weighted pendulums appear to hang in nonvertical orientations. These illusions illustrate not only that our visual perception of upright calibrates our sense of gravity, but also that these calibrations are closely related to objects' apparent size and weight.

A typical mystery spot involves a lopsided wooden cabin built on a steep, forested hillside. According to legend, the cabin accidentally slid down the hill during a rainstorm and ended up as a twisted wreck among the trees. In reality, many such cabins have been purposefully constructed to create roadside tourist attractions in mountainous regions. A search for "mystery spot" on the Internet will guide you to all the details needed to visit them in person. And they are well worth the visit, both for the perceptual effects you will experience there and for the way the attractions are presented to tourists as a folksy mix of local legend, pseudo-science, and a dash of the supernatural. (The anthropology of these accounts, which are often presented in part as examples of "real" science, is as interesting as the visual effects. But here we will stick to the visual effects.)

All the cabins built at mystery spots have surface planes that cause disorientation regarding the effects of gravity. This is achieved by making sure that none of the surfaces is truly horizontal or vertical. As a result, an extended visit in these locations often leads to vertigo and nausea. There is a strong tendency to want to hold on to anything solid in order to keep one's balance. Within this context, two effects are striking. First, in some places in the cabin, people appear to shrink and grow as they move from one location to another. Second, in other places a heavy ball suspended by a cable from the ceiling appears to be oddly oriented to one side, as though a powerful magnet were pulling it. Of course, unless you believe in a local gravitational anomaly or magnetic effect to explain this, you can safely assume the ball is hanging straight down. The mere existence of a "plumb line" (the cable that the ball hangs on) does not, however, act as a "gravity calibration" for your visual system. Just as a carpenter's level would fail to convince your visual system that an anti-gravity uphill is actually a downhill slope, the plumb line provided by the suspended ball fails in the mystery spot context. The visual system insists, instead, on using the frame provided by the angled walls and floor of the cabin as the calibrating signal for "gravity."

Both illusions—the shrink-and-grow effect and the misaligned plumb line—have recently been taken into the lab by vision scientists. In one study, researchers Art Shimamura and Bill Prinzmetal (1999) considered the shrink-and-grow effect in photographs. A photograph provides a much less vivid experience of the illusion, but it preserves the main components. Depending on where an individual is located in the photo, he appears to vary in size, as shown in Figure 7.3.

The size illusion has been studied in the lab many times before, albeit with simpler displays. In one version, two lines of equal length can appear to be of different lengths simply by adding two converging context lines. Shown in Figure 7.4, this is known as the *Ponzo illusion,* named after the scientist who first studied it in detail. Of the numerous contributing factors to the illusion, two of the most significant are (1) the assumption that converging edges are parallel, leading to the conclusion that the "more distant" line is larger, and (2) the phenomenon of local context that leads to visual "averaging," such that the true length of the line near the converging ends of the context lines is misjudged. Both factors would also contribute to the illusion of size changes in individuals at the mystery spot in Figure 7.3.

The basis of the misaligned plumb line has also been studied in a variety of ways. Participants in a study by Bruce Bridgeman (in press) reported that weighted balls actually did seem harder to push in one direction (against the apparent oblique orientation) than in the other (along with the apparent oblique orientation). In the study by Shimamura and Prinzmetal, observers tried to set two dots in a display to be either horizontally or vertically aligned. The critical variable was the orientation of a background set of textured lines that the observers were asked to ignore. Figure 7.5 illustrates some of the conditions in this experiment.

As you might guess from looking at Figure 7.5a the orientation of the background lines can influence your ability to align the dots. In fact, as the data from this experiment show in Figure 7.5b, the largest illusion seems to occur at about 15 degrees away from the true vertical or horizontal frame orientation. Moreover, the illusion is more powerful overall for the vertical axis than for the horizontal one. These findings suggest that the largest "gravity" illusions will likely occur for vertically oriented objects that are misaligned by about 15 degrees from upright. It is interesting to note that mystery spot cabins are usually built with floors and walls differing from the true upright and horizontal by between 15 and 20 degrees.

KNOWING ONE'S PLACE IN THE WORLD

The perception of where we are positioned in space can be subdivided, for purposes of research, into three subproblems: determining orientation in a three-dimensional world, determining the direction of objects with respect to the observer, and determining one's heading while in motion.

Orientation: What's up?

How do we know which way is up? By "up" I am again referring to the direction that points away from the pull of gravity. *How can we tell that an object is about to fall*

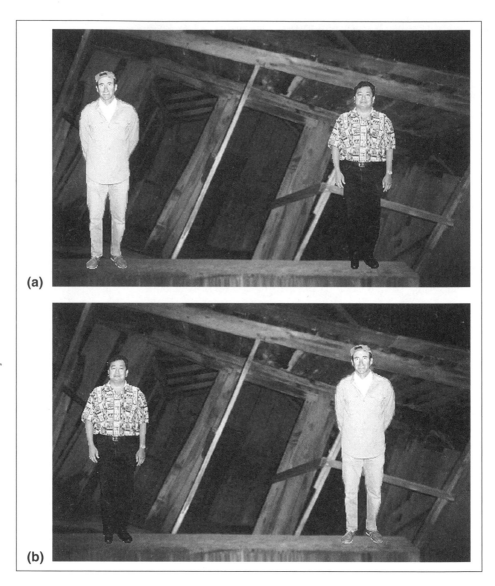

(a)

(b)

FIGURE 7.3   Two photos taken from the same vantage point and of the same scene, with only the locations of the two individuals being switched. Although both men appear similar in height in **(a)**, they look markedly different in height in **(b)**. The background angles in the scene contribute to the illusion. In the real-world setting where these photos were taken, the illusion is more pronounced because observers are disoriented with respect to gravitational upright. Here, the frame of the picture and the page of the book serve as reference to upright that are missing in the mystery spot environment.

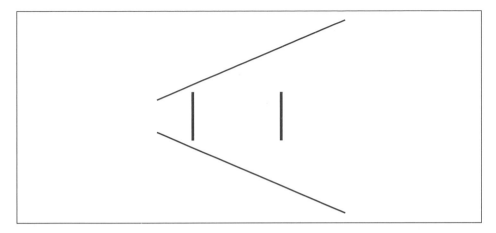

FIGURE 7.4   The Ponzo illusion. The vertical line on the right looks shorter than the line on the left, even though both are equal in length.

over? These questions may seem relatively easy to answer until we consider the wide range of circumstances under which we can determine the orientation of an object. For instance, if you tilt your head from side to side—say, from 30 degrees to the left to 30 degrees to the right—the world doesn't seem to tilt in any way. Rather, you correctly perceive that your head is tilting from side to side. Rocking your head forward and backward also doesn't change the apparent slant of surfaces around you. These observations mean that the basis for "upright" cannot be tied very closely to the orientation of the retina, which is tilting and rocking under these circumstances. Yet if you shut one eye and gently apply rocking pressure to the side of the eye that is open, objects will appear to rock from side to side. This exercise demonstrates that simply "knowing" that the world is stable is also not sufficient to maintain the perception of upright. Instead, changes in orientation on the retina seem to matter.

The perception of orientation is determined by a complex interplay between your internal sense of proprioception (sensing the position of your body in space, as tested in Box 7.1) and certain assumptions that your visual system makes about what it sees. This interplay was the focus of a study in which observers looked through a porthole into a room tilted by 22 degrees and were asked to orient a rod so it would be upright with respect to gravity. As you might guess after reading about the illusion shown in Figure 7.5, the tilt of the room influenced the observers' perception of the upright. They tended to tip the rod 15 degrees away from the vertical, in the direction of the room's tilt. The illusion of upright was not based completely on vision; if it were, the misalignment of the rod would have been by 22 degrees. The proprioceptive sense of upright was still having an influence. However, when the same observers viewed the slanted room while sitting in

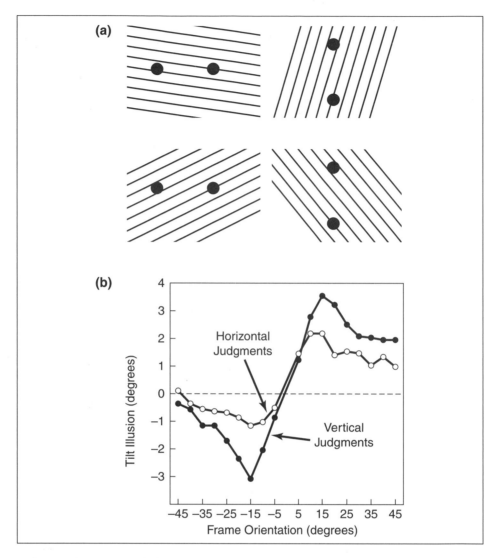

FIGURE 7.5 **(a)** In which way must the dots be moved in order to be aligned, either horizontally or vertically? In fact, each dot pair is perfectly aligned already. If they look misaligned, it is because you were unable to ignore the textured background lines. **(b)** The size of the tilt illusion (in degrees) when observers are asked to horizontally or vertically align a pair of dots seen against a background of lines of varying orientation.

a chair leaning by 30 degrees, they adjusted the slant of the rod to match the room's slant exactly. Sitting in the slanted chair disoriented the proprioceptive contribution to the sense of upright, so now only the visual clues were used.

A hint as to the nature of these visual clues can be found in laboratory studies of a tilted room, as shown in Figure 7.6a. An experimental situation like this pits numerous visual cues from the surfaces in the room against the single visual cue of

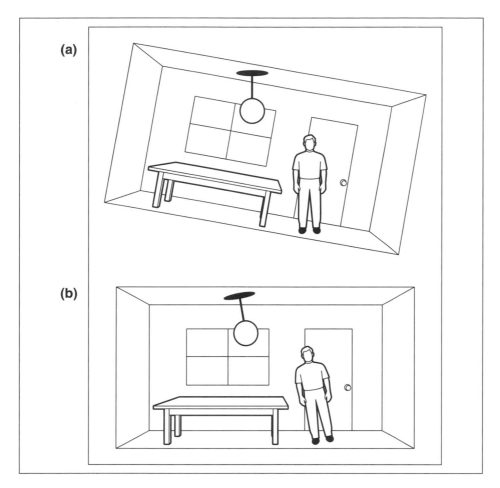

FIGURE 7.6 **(a)** The actual situation in the tilted room illusion. **(b)** What it feels like to be in the room.

the tilted light fixture and the subtle internal cues of the observer's sense of proprioception. The visual cues of the room win under these circumstances, so the light fixture seems to hang crookedly and the observer senses that he or she is slightly off balance.

What is critical is that the room and the frame are rectangular, meaning that the dominant edges in the displays meet at right angles. *Rectilinearity* of this kind turns out to be a highly effective and reliable cue to the upright in the natural world. Objects that fall to the ground, as well as objects that stand on the ground, tend to do so along the vertical dimension because of the ubiquitous effects of gravity. Plants and other objects that are not generally upright eventually fall over if left alone. Surfaces on the earth are generally horizontal unless other forces are raising them up. For objects that are generally upright, the vertical dimension is dominant because of the tendency for less-than-vertical objects to fall over. These considerations result in many right-angled corners between surfaces. Because our visual system has evolved in an environment dominated by gravity, it is no surprise that our vision is guided so strongly by rectangular corners. They are powerful clues to the pull of gravity on objects. But most likely we have never really thought about it much—until we walk into a mystery spot.

The preference of our visual systems for right-angled corners can also be seen in the interpretations it gives to corners that deviate slightly from the rectangular. Drawings of three-edged vertices, where one of the angles is slightly greater or less than 90 degrees, still are seen as right-angled corners. The deviation from rectilinearity is taken as evidence not that the corner is skewed, but that a right-angled object is being seen from a foreshortened perspective, as we discussed in Chapter 5. Needless to say, the rooms in a mystery spot cabin are filled with corners that are close to being rectilinear, but not exactly.

The ultimate domination that our visual system holds over our proprioceptive sense of upright is seen most vividly in the "rotating room" experiments of Ian Howard and colleagues (Howard & Childerson, 1994; Howard & Hu, 2001) and depicted in Figure 7.7. These scientists work on the problem of human orientation for NASA's manned space program. They have found that under certain simple conditions right here on earth, the gravitational pull on subjects' bodies is ignored while their visual system convinces them that they are either upside down or right side up.

Consider the situation shown in Figure 7.7. Here, a subject is sitting in a chair equipped with seat belts and a shoulder harness inside a specially designed chamber in which both the room and the chair can be rotated independently of one another. It is important for this experiment that the room contain many cues to the visual upright, including a strong source of light on the ceiling and objects with a clearly "normal" orientation such as tables, chairs, fruit on the table, a mannequin sitting in a chair, and so on. When the subject's chair is in the upright position but the room slowly rotates until it is upside down, the subject in the chair feels distinctly upside down. This odd sensation occurs even if no seat belts have been used to strap the subject into the chair. If the door of the room is opened suddenly to reveal the larger testing room containing the experimenter and other equipment, the sense of gravitational upright snaps back into place. Also, if the subject shuts his eyes and pays attention to the feeling of sitting in a chair, the sense of sitting upright returns. But if the door to the room is shut again and the eyes are opened, the irresistible feeling returns that one is hanging upside down in an upright room. In this situation, the proprioceptive feelings associated with gravity are not strong enough to overrule all the visual cues in the room contributing to the illusion of hanging upside down.

FIGURE 7.7 A view from inside an experimental rotating room.

Something even more remarkable can happen when both the room and the chair—this time with the seat belts firmly in place—rotate into the upside-down position. At this point, it is common for the subject to think he is sitting upright in an upright room even though his body is tugging against the seat belts, blood is rushing to his face, and his hair is standing on end! All the gravitational cues to the upright that the body can feel are inconsequential in the face of the visual cues that the room is upright. Of course, if not all the objects in the room are fixed in place, other strange things can happen: Objects tied with string to the floor may appear to be hovering eerily in mid-air, and if the subject reaches out his arm it will feel tugged upward. Knowing that gravity is simply doing its regular job is not enough to change the experience that there are mysterious forces raising one's arm heavenward.

Experiments like this reveal how utterly dependent we are on our visual system. Indeed, vision is highly reliable—not only about attributes of the environment such as color and lightness, which are acquired through light, but also about properties that are available through other senses, such as gravitational upright. Our brains have become accustomed to relying on information in the light to inform our other senses about gravity and bodily orientation. As a consequence we now pay the small price of occasionally getting fooled, for example, on the golf course about the orientation of a putting green. In rare situations, we may get fooled when we enter mystery spots, encounter anti-gravity hills, or buy a ticket to a

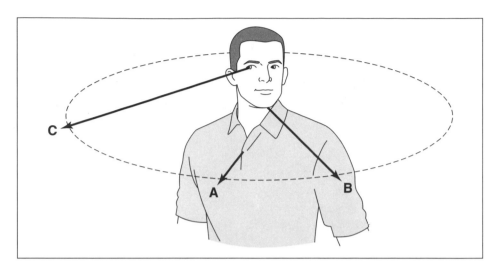

FIGURE 7.8   The distinction among interpretations of "straight ahead" as defined by **(A)** body posture, **(B)** head position, and **(C)** eye direction.

carnival fun house. But for the most part we benefit enormously from having our crude sense of proprioception finely calibrated by interactions with the information gained through our eyes.

Direction: Where is it?

Where are objects positioned on the ground with respect to me? This question seems quite straightforward until we examine certain complexities. For example, our body, head, and eyes can each be aligned somewhat independently with respect to other objects. Consider the diagram in Figure 7.8. Identifying any objects that lie "straight ahead" of this individual depends on which part of his body is the reference. The individual's body is aligned with A, his head with B, and his eyes are directed at a third location, C.

You may remember that when you began to drive a car or learned to ride a bicycle, it was dangerous to move your head and eyes to one side to take in the view. This was because of the strong involuntary tendency for your body to be aligned with the direction of your head and eyes. When you are driving a car or riding a bicycle, your arms tend to move in the direction you are looking, which puts you on a turning trajectory even when you have no intention of turning. As you became a more expert driver, you learned to suppress this tendency. For evidence that the tendency is still there, simply try walking in a straight line with your eyes closed

BOX 7.2

Eyeing a target

Stand in front of a wall at a distance of about 10 feet. Pick a point on the wall directly in front of you. A corner, a small crack, or any other feature of the surface texture will do as your target. Now, make a small diamond-shaped viewing window by bringing the thumb and index finger of each hand to-gether. With both eyes wide open, quickly reach forward with both hands so that you can see the target clearly through the viewing window of your fin-gers. Keep your arms outstretched for this target alignment process. When the target is clearly visible through the viewing window, slowly begin to bring your fingers toward your head. Make sure the target is visible at all times while you are doing this. Also, be sure to keep both eyes open throughout this demonstration. When you have brought the viewing window as close to your head as possible, you will find that you have been sighting the target with only one eye. This is the eye that the viewing window is now in front of. If you now shut that eye, you will see that the other eye has not been in-volved in the target alignment procedure at all. Its view is blocked by one of your hands that are forming the viewing window. The eye that you used to sight and align the target is your *dominant eye*.

and your head turned sharply to one side. (Of course, you should only try this in an open space where you are not likely to trip over any obstacles.) If you try this for ten or twenty paces, you will likely find yourself walking on a curved path even though you have every intention of walking in a straight line (and are quite good at it when your head and body are aligned).

Another complication of determining the direction of objects with respect to ourselves is the fact that we have two eyes. To understand this complication, try the demonstration in Box 7.2 before reading further.

As we will see later in this chapter, the fact that we have two eyes is enormously beneficial for many visual tasks. However, in terms of aligning ourselves with loca-tions in space, the fact that we have two eyes makes the process more complicated than if we only had one. The difficulty arises because each eye can align itself only with one visual target. The fact that our eyes are separated horizontally means that there are, in essence, two visual directions: one for each eye. For many visual tasks—such as lining up a target to throw or shoot at, or pointing at objects accu-rately with one of our fingers—target aiming is best achieved if we ignore one of the eyes and concentrate on only one of the two directions. Most of us favor one particular eye in performing aiming actions of this sort. It is called the *dominant eye*. Many people are not aware that they have a dominant eye until they try aiming with the non-dominant one. They usually report this as feeling "unnatural," in the same way that throwing a ball or signing their name with their non-preferred hand feels strange and uncomfortable.

Yet for other visual tasks, such as moving our bodies in the direction of a goal or moving our heads to one side to avoid an obstacle, it is advantageous to take the average of the two visual directions. By using the average, we ensure that the center of our heads will be perfectly aligned with a visual target. A demonstration of this sort of averaging appears in Box 7.3.

Often when the visual system has to coordinate multiple factors, those factors influence one another. This can be seen in the realm of visual direction perception by making note of a very ordinary and otherwise unremarkable characteristic of people. Have you ever noticed that most people hold their head slightly to one side or the other? Fred Previc and colleagues (Previc, 1994) studied whether the direction in which people tilt their heads is related to the side of their dominant eye, using sighting tasks such as the one described in Box 7.2. They found that individuals with right-eye dominance tend to tilt their heads to the left, whereas those with left-eye dominance tend to tilt their heads to the right. The tendency becomes more pronounced when they are asked to judge the alignment of objects. Individuals seem to be making a compromise between aligning objects with reference to (1) their egocenter, and (2) their dominant eye. Tilting one's head to place the dominant eye close to the center of the head's position in space is apparently an effective way to accomplish this.

Heading: Where am I going?

Just as with the perception of orientation and the location or direction of objects with respect to ourselves, the determination of heading—where we are going—is made largely on visual grounds, even though our proprioceptive sense also plays a role. Think about the last time you were stopped beside a large truck at a traffic light or stop sign on a steep hill. When the truck started to inch forward, your first impression probably was that you were rolling backward. This perception was not based on any proprioceptive signals, since your foot was firmly planted on the brake pedal all along. It was instead based solely on a visual rule concerning motion of the self. That rule can be expressed as follows: *If a large part of my visual field is in motion, then it must be me that is moving.* If you have ever stood on a wharf beside a cruise ship or large car ferry that is leaving the dock, you will also get a vivid sense of this signal. Short of shutting your eyes, you will be unable to sense that the ship or ferry, and not you, is undergoing the motion. These illusions are called *induced self-motion.*

The same rule is at work when we try to judge our motion while flying in an airplane. However, in this case it gives us the illusion of being stationary even though we may be flying through the air at more than 500 miles per hour. Unless we are near some slower-moving or stationary reference points such as clouds, the

BOX 7.3

Acting like Cyclops

Materials

For this demonstration you will need a stiff piece of cardboard (about the size of a regular sheet of paper) and a friend to help you make some measurements. Place one edge of the cardboard in line with your eyes, as shown in Figure 7.9. Have your friend mark the centers of your eyes on the cardboard, when it is held to your face, as carefully as possible. Next, draw straight lines from these two points to the center of the two positions at the other end of the card. The card should now show a long V, with the open end of the V aligned between the centers of your eyes.

Instructions

Hold the card as shown in the figure, and fixate at the point in the V at the far end of the card. What do you see?

Analysis

In addition to the two lines of the V, you will see a single line extending from the point in the V where you are fixating to the middle of your nose. This third line is an illusion, of course, since you only drew two lines on the card. It is your brain's best guess as to origin of the lines that are seen by each eye and that seem to lie in corresponding places in the view of each eye. The illusory line is pointing to the *egocenter*, or to what some vision scientists refer to as the *Cyclopean eye* (named after the mythical ancient character Cyclops, who had a single eye in the center of his forehead).

ground, or other airplanes, flying in an airplane seems motionless. Because the distant ground is not moving perceptibly relative to ourselves, we assume that we are at rest in a stable world.

A similar rule operates in judging the relative motion of other objects in our visual field. Figure 7.10a illustrates a single dot on a computer screen that is moving up and down at the same time that a larger frame is moving from side to side. Consider all the cues in this situation that would indicate the motion of the dot is simply up and down: the stationary room in which the computer sits, the desk, the frame of the computer screen, and even our own eye movements tracking the dot's motion in the vertical direction. Yet despite all this evidence, our visual system arrives at the conclusion that the dot is moving in an oblique direction on the screen (Figure 7.10b), which turns out to be the average of the vertical motion of the dot and the horizontal motion of the frame.

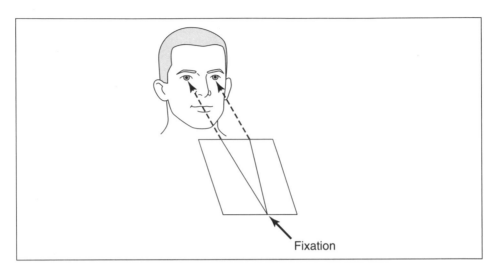

FIGURE 7.9   Looking at the distant point in a V-shaped set of lines will enable you to experience the illusion of *Cyclopean* vision.

A general principle is that the judged motion of smaller bodies, which includes ourselves in the case of induced self-motion, is always made with reference to the motion of larger objects and surfaces in the vicinity.

In terms of *where* we are headed when in motion, a very informative pattern in the motion signals on our retina provides an important clue. It was first studied systematically by J. J. Gibson and other vision researchers (Gibson, Olum, & Rosenblatt, 1955) who were interested in the problem of how to land a plane safely. Apparently, when our eyes move in a given direction, a distinct pattern of relative motion on the retina indicates the precise direction in which we are headed, including the point of impact if we continue in the same direction. This pattern of motion, called *optical flow,* is illustrated in Figure 7.11. Each arrow in the flow pattern represents the viewer's relative rate of speed and direction of motion in relation to each location in the image. As a whole, the pattern looks like a flowing stream of motion signals that emanate from a single location. As the signals get closer to the edge of the image, they become increasingly strong. At the very center of the pattern is the target, which vision scientists call the *focus of expansion.* It's the place where there is no relative motion in the image; it is the precise location that the eye will impact if it stays on its present course.

However, optical flow is by no means the whole story in terms of perceiving one's heading. As mentioned earlier, the eyes, head, and body can move independently, and optical flow on the retina is a reliable signal to heading only when all three parts of our visual apparatus are aligned. If we make eye and head move-

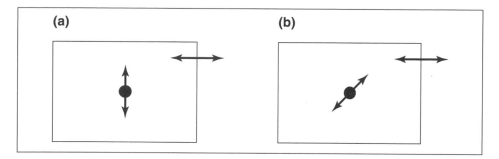

FIGURE 7.10   Illusory oblique motion in a vertically moving dot is induced by having the frame around the dot move from side to side. **(a)** The physical motions of the dot and the frame. **(b)** The perceived motions of the dot and the frame.

ments while in motion, the focus of expansion will appear at many locations on our retinal image. This raises the problem of what visual signals to use to anchor our visual judgments. Once again, it appears that the visual system relies on the assumption that the world is generally stable. Even though we may be making many head and eye movements while our body is in motion, the focus of expansion will continue to emanate from the same location in a stationary three-dimensional scene if we stay on course. A change in course will cause the focus of expansion of the optical flow to emanate from a different location.

CONSTRUCTING THE THIRD DIMENSION

We see and act in a three-dimensional world. When I say this, I am talking about the fact that space consists of an east-west, a north-south, and an elevation dimension. Of course, there are other ways to denote these dimensions: I could speak about the width, height, and depth of objects and spaces, or even of near-far, left-right, and up-down. Regardless of how I label them, there are clearly three different dimensions or directions to my sense of space. Yet all the information I obtain about it through my visual system is two-dimensional.

One of the three dimensions gets lost when the points of light from objects in my space are projected onto the essentially flat retinal surfaces of my eyes. The fact that the retina is actually slightly concave instead of flat like the film in a camera makes no difference in terms of the "lost dimension." It is still an inherently two-dimensional surface as far as the pattern of projected light is concerned. The retina registers only two dimensions, corresponding to left-right and up-down. Near-far has been collapsed in the mapping of light reflecting from surfaces in the external world onto the surface of the retina. This is illustrated in Figure 7.12 by a variety of shapes in different three-dimensional orientations that all correspond to the same image on the retina.

FIGURE 7.11   Optical flow in this airplane cockpit image of a landing scene is illustrated by arrows, which indicate the airplane's direction of motion (orientation of arrow) as well as its relative speed of motion (length of arrow).

One of the most profound problems in vision science is explaining how the brain is able to provide a complete sense of three-dimensional space when it only has two dimensions as its input. At this point in your reading, it is probably no surprise that the human brain "recovers" the missing dimension in vision in a variety of ways. No single brain process or neural operation is responsible for our seeing a three-dimensional world. This is why vision is so "robust," meaning that it accomplishes its goals under such a wide variety of environmental conditions. In Chapter 5 we encountered the problem of recovering the third dimension when there was only a single retinal image. In this section, we will first consider two additional remarkable solutions to the recovery problem that human vision has evolved. One involves combining information from two eyes through *stereovision*. The other solution integrates information over time in order to accomplish *structure from motion*.

The benefits of the second eye

To appreciate some of the benefits of having two eyes, try threading a needle, placing a coin into a vending machine, or reaching for a file in a cabinet with one eye shut. The task can be accomplished, but much more slowly than with both eyes open. The slower speed arises from the feedback required to accomplish the task with only one eye. Feedback about where your limb is positioned in space comes from your visual and touch senses. When both eyes are open, the same task can be done rapidly and with little reliance on feedback. How is the second eye used to make two-eyed reaching so effective?

The answer involves the fact that each eye provides the brain with a slightly different viewpoint on the world. In humans, the horizontal separation between the eyes

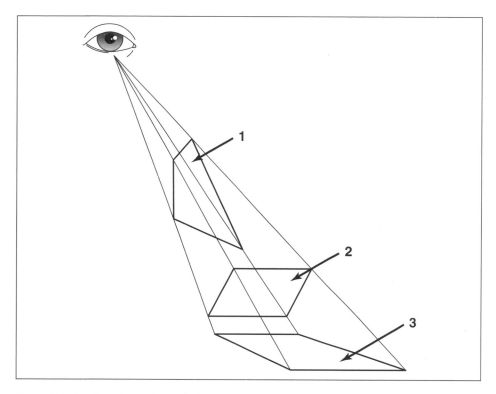

FIGURE 7.12 The ambiguity of retinal images is illustrated in this diagram, showing a variety of three-dimensional shapes that would all generate the same two-dimensional outline in the image formed at the tip of the pyramid of lines (i.e., on the retina).

is around 4 inches, generating a sufficient difference to make images in the two eyes noticeably different for objects within 10 feet. Beyond that distance, the difference in the two eyes' images is negligible. The difference between the two images is called *binocular disparity,* or simply *disparity.* A vision system that uses disparities to determine the near-far dimension is said to have *stereovision.*

Important insights into the process of stereovision can be gained by holding out the index finger on each hand and positioning them to extend in a straight line in front of you. Then, focus your eyes on the nearer finger. If you were to draw a bird's-eye diagram of the situation, it would look as shown in Figure 7.13. The fovea of each eye would be aimed at the nearer finger, so there would be no disparity in the image of the finger in each eye. However, the portions of the image that correspond to the more distant finger would be in different locations in the two eyes. In the left eye, the image of the more distant finger would fall to the right of the fovea (toward the nose); in the right eye, it would fall to the left of the fovea

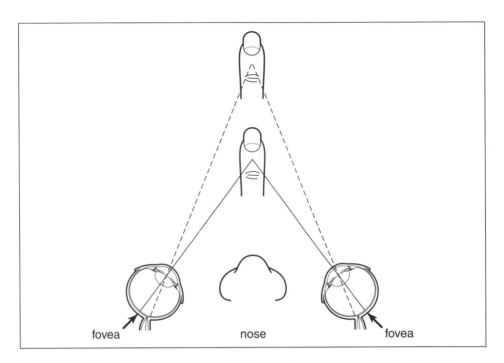

FIGURE 7.13   A bird's-eye diagram of the images formed when we hold out two index fingers in a straight line and fixate our gaze on the nearer one. The image formed by the nearer (fixated) finger appears nearer to the nose in each eye than the image formed by the farther (non-fixated) finger.

(also toward the nose). These "disparate" images can be resolved in two ways. If the more distant finger is not too far away form the near, fixated finger, then it will appear to be a single finger that is a little farther away. However, once it moves beyond a certain point, it will split into a double image—that is, of two fingers. The splitting process can be observed directly if you now place the two fingers side by side. Keep fixating on only one of the fingers, but move the other finger slowly away from you and pay attention to it out of the corner of your eyes. At first, the non-fixated finger will appear to be simply moving backward, but at some point it will seem to split into two distinct images of the same finger.

The narrow band of depth in which disparate images are resolved into objects that are at different locations from the viewer is the *stereofusion region*. Its location depends on where you are fixating. Outside of that narrow and dynamic band of stereovision, the double images in the two eyes are usually ignored. One of the features of our visual system that helps us ignore the double images is the rapid lessening of visual acuity as objects project onto the retina farther away from the fovea. Another helpful feature is the brain's concurrent focus of attention on the

FIGURE 7.14 A repeating wallpaper-like pattern that can lead to the illusion of different depth planes when your eyes converge either in front of or behind the actual depth plane of the surface.

objects and surfaces that are also the focus of gaze in our eyes. Thus what we don't notice doesn't bother us.

The simple insights gained from examining the images of our extended index fingers will help us understand three remarkable illusions involving the process of stereovision. Consider first an illusion that you may have already stumbled across by accident: the wallpaper illusion. An example is shown in Figure 7.14, but any wallpaper-like pattern in which graphical elements are repeated horizontally will do. If you relax your eyes such that they converge at a point either further away from or nearer than the actual surface, strange things will happen. For instance, if you look at the pattern in Figure 7.14 with your eyes slightly crossed (converging on a point in space in front of the pattern), some of the pattern elements will appear to float in front of the other elements. This illusion is so vivid that you can

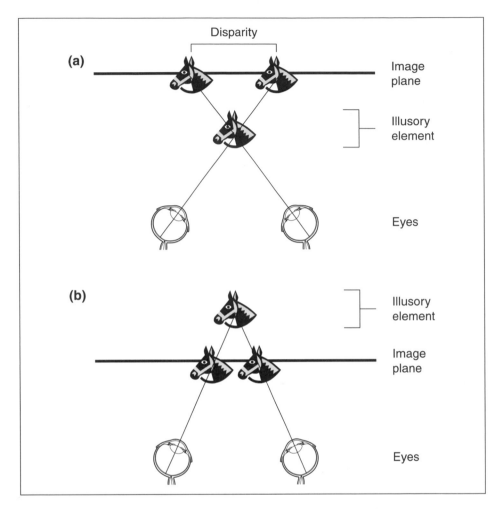

FIGURE 7.15   A bird's-eye view of the wallpaper illusion. **(a)** When the eyes converge on a point that is nearer than the image plane, corresponding disparate images in the two eyes appear to be in front of the image plane. **(b)** When the eyes converge on a farther point, corresponding disparate images in the eyes are seen as farther away.

actually position your finger in space so that it is in the same depth plane as the illusory, floating elements.

Counting the columns of elements in the wallpaper illusion and comparing that number with the number of actual columns of elements on the page gives an important clue as to what is happening. The number of columns floating in the illusion will be smaller than the number on the page. When your eyes converge on the depth plane of the page, you combine the different images in each eye just as when you saw only two fingers in the demonstration in Figure 7.13. However, whether you see the elements floating in front of or behind the page will depend on where your eyes converge. When they converge in front of the page, the elements appear to float in front; when they converge behind the plane of the page, the elements appear to float behind, as illustrated in Figure 7.15. The reason there are fewer columns floating in front of the page than on the page is that two of the page columns have become fused, or one.

If you have understood the wallpaper illusion, you are ready to understand the basis of the "magic eye" posters that were popular in the 1990s. These were interesting two-dimensional abstract patterns when viewed normally, but they sprang to life as three-dimensional relief images when the viewer's eyes converged either in front of or behind the plane of the picture. They were designed to work like the standard wallpaper illusion in that an illusion of stereovision occurred when the eyes converged either in front of or behind the image plane. They were unique in that the disparity between different image elements was carefully controlled so that some regions resulted in strong relief and others in weaker relief. This permitted observers to see three-dimensional shapes defined entirely by differences in binocular disparity. Figure 7.16 presents a simplified "magic eye" illusion. The relation between image disparity and the resulting depth of the illusory elements is shown in Figure 7.17.

It is only one more step from the "magic eye" pictures to another illusion you probably experienced as a child. A popular toy for several decades has been the Viewmaster, which accepts a circular card of small slides seen through a binocular viewing window. The slides create the illusion of a miniature three-dimensional world where some objects are clearly in front of others, as if they were on a small stage. Of course, the small stage is really in your mind, but it appears there because the pairs of photographs were taken from two horizontally separated viewpoints. Figure 7.18 shows a simplified version of two Viewmaster images. You will be able to experience the illusion if you relax your eyes and let them converge on a point in front of the page. This permits the two images to fall on the same place in both eyes. Any remaining image disparities will be interpreted as differences in depth. Can you determine which image element has a different image disparity from the others? If so, you have successfully fused the two images in each eye. Figure 7.19 presents the corresponding bird's-eye view of this situation.

The benefits of motion

The fusion of two spatially separated images, one in each eye, is not the only way to recover the third dimension. An equally good way is to compare information from two images separated in time rather than in space. To experience the rough equivalence of both ways of recovering the third dimension, hold up one index finger in front of your eyes and alternate between views by opening and closing the eyes—one at a time—in rapid succession. You will see a finger in relative

FIGURE 7.16   A repeating wallpaper-like pattern that leads to the illusion of three different depth planes when your eyes are aimed to converge either in front or behind the actual depth plane of the picture.

motion against a background. Whether the finger is seen in motion against a stationary background or the background is seen in motion against the stationary finger is not of great concern. Both can happen. The important point is that the experience of motion can be obtained by comparing two images that occur at different points in time.

This important insight—that two images at different points in time can also give information about the third dimension—enables us to recover the third dimension even when we only have a single eye to work with. To understand this, try the following exercise. Close one eye while trying to thread a needle, place a coin into a vending machine, or reach for a file in a cabinet. But don't keep your head still. While you are trying to do this, rock your head over a range of motion that corre-

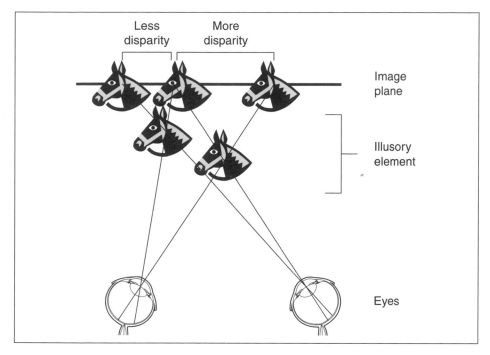

FIGURE 7.17 A bird's-eye view of a simple "magic eye" illusion. Corresponding image elements in the two eyes that are more disparate are seen as nearer to the observer, whereas corresponding images that are less disparate are seen as farther away.

sponds roughly to the separation between your two eyes. In other words, try to recapture what you lose when you shut one eye by regaining two views through the motion of your head. See if the separation of images in time leads to a benefit in three-dimensional perception that is comparable to the separation of images in space that is responsible for stereovision.

Many vision experiments have indicated that these two ways of recovering the third dimension are comparable. You can get some sense of this yourself by repeating the demonstration we conducted earlier in which you held out both index fingers in a straight line in front of you. However, this time, follow the steps with one eye shut and your head rocking slightly from side to side. When you fixate on the nearer of the two fingers, you will note that rocking your head from side to side has a number of effects.

First, the relative apparent movement of the nearer finger is much greater than that of the farther finger. This is consistent with the general principle that objects near us move much more from image to image, relatively speaking, than objects that are farther from us. Instead of retinal disparity being the clue to depth, for a

FIGURE 7.18   Two images that create the appearance of three-dimensional depth when viewed with stereovision. Relax your eyes while fixating on a point between the two frames. The frames will appear to "slide" toward one another. If you are able to put the two frames into alignment, a third frame will emerge in which one of the horse heads appears to be in a different depth plane.

single image in motion, relative motion becomes the clue. Objects undergoing larger position changes from image to image are closer to the viewer.

Second, when you are fixating on the nearer finger with one eye and rocking your head, the motion of the farther finger is in the same direction as the motion of your head. This points to another general principle: Objects that are farther away than our current point of fixation will move, relatively speaking, in the same direction as the movement of the image. Objects that are nearer than those at the current point of fixation will move in the opposite direction to the image. You can confirm this point by fixating on the farther finger while continuing to rock your head. The nearer finger will now be in apparent motion in a direction opposite to the motion of your head. Your current point of fixation is therefore determined by an analysis of the optical flow field created between successive images.

Third, when your head is in motion, some objects disappear from view and other objects come into view. In general, objects that are farther away undergo the greater degree of vanishing and reappearing, simply because they are occluded (blocked from view) by objects that are nearer. The resulting pattern of surface accretion (coming into view) and surface deletion (disappearing from view) is thus a powerful clue to the relative distance of objects.

These clues to the third dimension derived from the analysis of changes in object position across images are collectively referred to as *motion parallax*. Just as the binocular disparity between objects in two spatially separated images provides important input to stereovision, the features of motion parallax provide clues to the relative depth of objects in a scene. In this case, vision scientists call the output

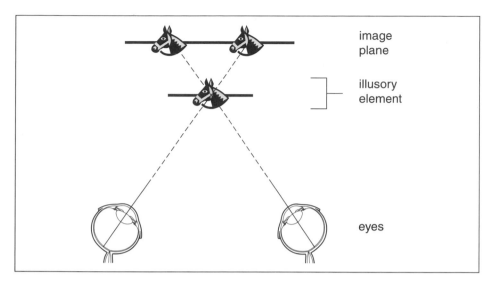

FIGURE 7.19   A bird's-eye view of the stereoimage formed when viewing Figure 7.18.

of such analysis the recovery of *structure from motion*. In this case, *structure* refers to the missing third dimension.

It is important to note that even though the previous demonstrations emphasize the motion of the observer in recovering structure from motion, in fact motion of the object in front of a stationary observer will lead to similar conclusions. This is revealed most dramatically in experiments that use a shadow play technique, as shown in Figure 7.20. For instance, if a haphazardly bent wire is viewed on the shadow screen in a static position, it is very difficult to discern its three-dimensional shape. In fact, it is consistent with an infinite number of possible shadow-casting shapes, and the visual system has no information with which to select among the possibilities. However, shortly after the same shape is in rotary motion behind the screen, casting a series of two-dimensional images, the three-dimensional shape of the wire becomes vividly apparent, enabling a viewer to select the correctly matching bent wire from a gallery of wire shapes.

USING ONLY ONE EYE

From the foregoing discussion it might appear that individuals with only a single working eye, viewing a stationary scene, would have difficulty determining the relative depth of the objects they are viewing. But this is not the case, as you can quickly determine by looking at objects more than 10 feet away from you. Even though at this distance the mechanisms of stereovision contribute nothing to your sense of the third dimension, and even though there may be no scene or viewer

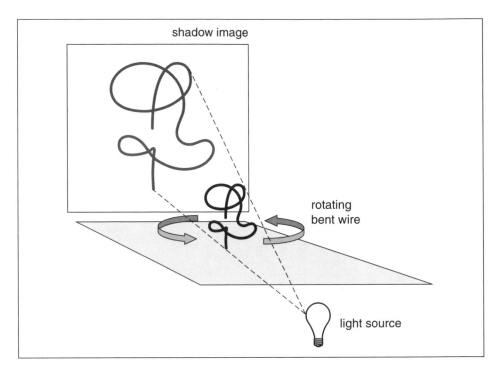

FIGURE 7.20   A vivid three-dimensional impression can be achieved by rotating an object and projecting its shadow against a flat viewing screen.

motion to further differentiate the depth relations, you can still determine a great deal about the relative distance of objects and their position with respect to one another. How is this done?

Seeing distance in pictures

The answer turns out to be the same as when we ask *How do artists and cameras provide us with a perception of depth even though the image they create is entirely flat (i.e., two dimensional)?* Both situations involve recovering the third dimension by inference from a single image. As such, this area of vision is often referred to, respectively, as *monocular* (involving one eye) or *pictorial* (involving pictures) depth perception. It is an area of vision research in which the study of art and artists has contributed a great deal. Of course, there is much more to visual art than the techniques artists sometimes use to "fool the eye." However, for our interest in how the third dimension can be portrayed in a two-dimensional image and how the "scene behind the image" can be recovered by the visual system, it is worthwhile examining the contribution of the visual arts to our understanding of how the human visual system works. One way to begin developing your own insights into the processes of pictorial depth perception is to repeat the exercise you completed in Chapter 4 (Box 4.4: *Using a Window to Create a Line Drawing*), but this time focusing on the rich range of signals that you will find in such a drawing about the depth relations in the picture. This exercise is described in Box 7.4 on the next page.

The drawing exercise in Box 7.4 re-creates an insight that the artist Alberti first described in a formal way in 1436. Because of this, the technique is often referred to as *Alberti's window.* However, some fifty years later Leonardo da Vinci also wrote extensively about this technique, so it is also often called *da Vinci's window.* The main insight is that all the rays of light from a scene pass through many imaginary two-dimensional planes on their way to a fixed viewpoint at the eye. This is illustrated in Figure 7.21. If an artist chooses to represent the rays in one of these two-dimensional planes—preferably one that is at right angles to his or her line of sight—then the representation will be very similar to the two-dimensional image that is projected onto the retinal surface of the eye.

There are, of course, differences between the images in Alberti's window and those on the retina, including differences in orientation (the image on the retina is upside down), in size (the image on the retina is likely to be smaller than the one drawn in Alberti's window), and in clarity (the image on the retina is occluded by blood vessels and blindspots, and it lies on a curved surface). However, the important congruence is that the two images are similar in the geometric sense of being *isomorphic*. This means there is a point-to-point correspondence between the two images. As such, an artist should be able to fool the eye to the extent that the representation made using Alberti's window re-creates the conditions that occur when the retinal image is formed by looking at the same scene.

In our discussion of pictorial depth, we will follow the lead of vision scientists who refer to the pictorial signals about the third dimension as *depth cues*. *Cue* can be traced to a British usage of the term that translates as "signal" or "clue." Perhaps the first cue for depth perception that you will notice in your own drawings of a scene (Box 7.4) is that you are able to draw the outline of some objects in full but others only partially. This is the cue known as *occlusion*. Nearer objects are less likely to be occluded from view than farther objects.

In addition to this coarse level of analysis, occlusion leads to very reliable detailed features of the edges in a drawing. Imagine an inspection of your drawing that relied entirely on a narrow viewing tube that you could sweep back and forth over the picture. If you had to categorize the ways that lines interacted when they came together within the small viewing region of the tube, you would identify many *T-junctions*. These are regions where one end of a line is bounded by another smooth line running roughly at right angles to it. It turns out that

BOX 7.4

Using a window to study depth perception

Materials and setting

You will need a clear plastic transparency, some tape, and an erasable marker. The transparency and the marker can be the kind used with overhead projectors. Now find a window through which you can view a scene. Ideally, the view will contain three or four objects of different sizes and distances from you. Tape the transparency to the window in such a position that you can sit or stand comfortably in front of the window while tracing lines to represent the edges in the scene you think are important.

Instructions

It is very important in making your drawing that your head be kept at a fixed place with respect to the window and that you view the scene with only one eye. This will ensure only one image of the view. Don't try to be artistic in making your drawing; just trace the outlines and edges mechanically that you think are important for someone else to recognize the objects in the scene. When you have finished, place a piece of white paper behind the transparency and make a photocopy of your drawing. Then you can erase the transparency and try another drawing.

Analysis

Examine your line drawing away from the location of the scene. How many clues to object position in the scene (relative depth) can you identify? Prepare a list of all the features of the drawing you think are reliable clues to the third dimension before reading further in this chapter. Then, after you have completed your reading of this section, return to your picture and make a list of all the pictorial clues to the third dimension that you can identify now. Which pictorial signals to depth are missing in your picture? Can you add these to the drawing to improve its representation of the third dimension?

T-junctions can be interpreted reliably by using the simple rule that the surface or edge bounded by the crossbar of the T is nearer to the viewer than the surface or edge bounded by the stem of the T. Proof that the visual system operates according to this rule can be found by drawing haphazard shapes that include T-junctions, such as those shown in Figure 7.22. If you present such drawings to observers and ask them which surfaces appear to be nearer, they will invariably indicate that the surface "owning" the crossbar of the T is nearer to them. Furthermore, observers will see drawings containing inconsistent T-junctions as flat, bistable, or even impossible.

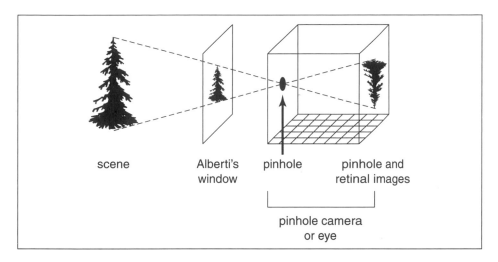

scene   Alberti's   pinhole   pinhole and
           window   retinal images

pinhole camera
or eye

FIGURE 7.21   The relation between the view from *Alberti's window* and the retinal image of the same scene.

Another depth cue in most drawings is the relationship between the position of depicted objects and the horizon. If there is a visible horizon in the scene you drew for the exercise in Box 7.4, you will note that objects closer to the horizon line are the ones that are farther away from your viewing position. This cue is often called *height in the plane* because—at least for objects drawn below the horizon— proximity to the horizon tends to be associated with a greater distance in the scene. However, for any objects drawn above the horizon—such as clouds, trees, and birds—the relationship between distance from the horizon and depth in the scene is reversed. Now, the higher you go above the horizon in the picture, the relatively nearer to you the objects are. Thus it is best to refer to this pictorial depth cue as *proximity to the horizon*.

Once you examine pictures with *proximity to the horizon* in mind, you will find certain ones in which no horizon line is shown. This may be because it is an indoor scene (in which the environmental horizon could not possibly be visible) or an outdoor scene filled with objects that occlude a view of the horizon. Yet at the same time you will notice a relation between the position of objects in the scene and their apparent distance from you. What signals are you using to infer the position of a horizon line that is not even visible?

You will begin to understand these additional cues if you use a ruler to examine one of the pictures you drew for the Exercise in Box 7.4. First, find the location in the picture that depicts a point in the scene farthest from you. To help you do this in your own drawing, look at the example of a simple drawing

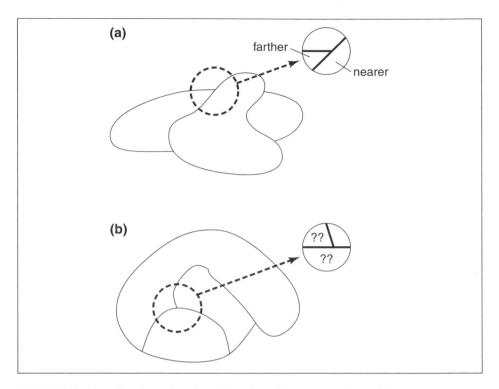

FIGURE 7.22   Depth relations from T-junctions. **(a)** A haphazard set of lines containing T-junctions that can be labeled consistently for edges that are either nearer or farther. **(b)** A haphazard set of lines that cannot be labeled consistently for depth.

provided in Figure 7.23a. In that picture the farthest depicted point is near the center. Now draw a straight line from this "most distant" point in your picture to the edge of a surface on the nearest object depicted in the scene. In Figure 7.23a this "nearest surface" could be the base of the tree trunks on either the left or the right side, near the bottom. Draw the same straight line for any other objects that are at the same depicted distance as this first object. In Figure 7.23a this would be the base of the trees on the other side of the picture. Note that the points you have connected with a line in the picture are collinear (in a straight line) in the scene.

As you continue to do this, you will find that surfaces and objects lying along these lines in the picture are parallel with one another in the depicted scene. This relationship between positions in the scene and their depicted positions is known as the *perspective* cue to pictorial depth. It is a record of the fact that

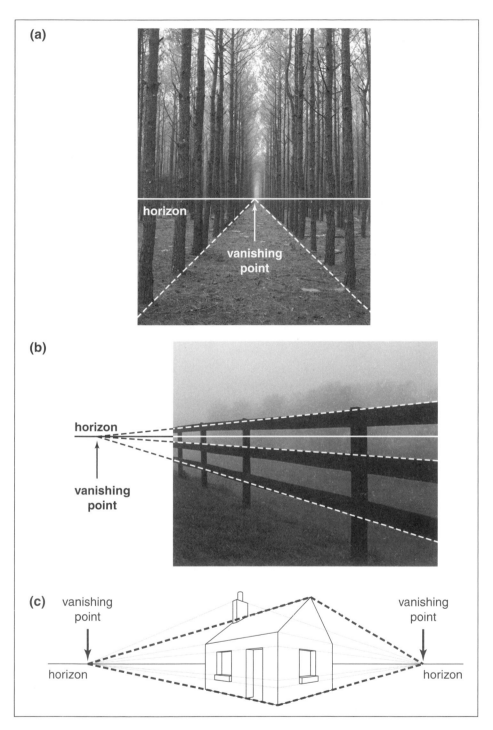

FIGURE 7.23 The pictorial depth cue of perspective involves the fact that parallel surfaces in a depicted scene project to lines that converge to a vanishing point on the horizon. **(a)** A picture with a visible vanishing point and horizon. **(b)** A picture with an implied vanishing point and horizon outside the bounds of the frame. Dotted lines are referred to in the text. **(c)** A picture with two vanishing points.

points that are parallel with one another in a scene are drawn as converging in a picture of the scene. This also means that equal distances in the scene becoming vanishingly small in the picture as the distance between scene objects and a viewer increases. The point in the picture at which distances between surfaces are no longer perceptible is therefore called the *vanishing point*.

Sometimes no vanishing point is depicted within the frame of the picture. This will occur if the drawing you have made did not include the position of the true horizon within its boundaries. For example, your line of sight for the picture may have been either above or below the horizon. You will discover this in your picture if the perspective lines you draw to connect collinear points in the scene converge outside of the picture frame. A simple drawing of this situation is provided in Figure 7.23b.

Other times there may be more than one vanishing point in a picture. This can occur, as shown in Figure 7.23c, when the nearest surface in the picture is near the center. In that case the perspective lines will converge in two different directions, but the points of convergence will still fall on the same imaginary line representing the horizon. Note again that the horizon may be included in the scene, as shown in Figure 7.23c, or only implied because it is outside the picture frame.

Our analysis of perspective has so far made no assumptions about the relative sizes of the depicted objects. The perspective lines we have considered are merely abstract references, thought to be connecting collinear points in the scene. If we now introduce an additional assumption—namely, that objects or surface markings in a picture are all physically similar in size—then an additional pictorial depth cue can be defined: the *texture gradient*. Visual texture involves a repeating pattern, of which there are many, in both our natural and artificial environments. A gradient involves a change of a gradual nature. The pictorial depth cue of a texture gradient therefore involves the way that depicted texture elements change size, shape, and spacing in gradual ways as a function of their distance from the viewing position. Figure 7.24 shows several examples of texture gradients.

Computational vision scientists have shown that the information about surface slant in a texture gradient can be subdivided into two components. One of these, *texture perspective,* corresponds closely to the more general depth cue of perspective we have just discussed. An analysis of the relative size and horizontal distance between texture elements corresponds to an analysis of the implicit perspective lines in a picture and therefore provides useful information about the relative depth in the picture of various points on a surface. An analysis of the vertical distance between texture elements, however, provides information about the shape of the surface that is receding in depth. This component of a texture gradient, called *texture compression,* is closely related to what artists refer to as *foreshortening.* For instance, if the vertical separation between texture elements stops changing altogether, it does so because the surface is vertical with respect to the viewer. In

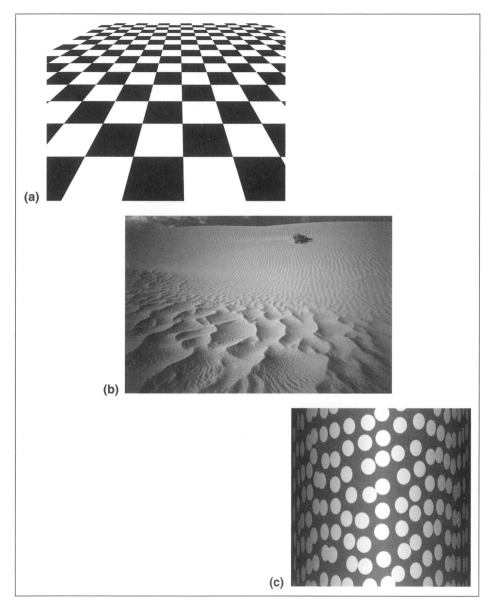

FIGURE 7.24   A variety of textured gradients.

contrast, if the distance between texture elements grows smaller rather abruptly, it indicates that the surface is receding rapidly from the viewer. The more rapidly a surface recedes from view, the more foreshortened is the view and the more compressed is the depicted texture that remains in view.

There is much more to a picture than an analysis of the hard edges at the boundaries of objects. Some of the most evocative cues to depth in a picture involve the gradual changes in luminance that occur as a result of shading and shadows. The technical definition of *shading* refers to a change in light levels in a picture that occurs because of a change in the orientation of a light-reflecting surface with respect to the light source. You may recall that photons behave roughly like billiard balls. Thus if a surface is angled in such a way that the incoming light bounces off the surface at an angle that maximizes the number of photons reaching the eye, that point in a picture of the surface will be brightest. However, if a surface is angled so that most of the light is reflected away from the viewing position, then the picture will be relatively dim at that location.

Figure 7.25 illustrates how shading can alter the apparent depth of a surface. Be careful, however, not to underestimate the problem of interpreting depth as a function of shading. The patterns in Figure 7.25 could be depicting a series of convexities and concavities (pimples and dimples) that are lit with overhead lighting, but they could also be depicting concavities and convexities (dimples and pimples). If you don't find the two interpretations to be equally plausible, simply view the same figure by holding the book upside down. You might want to refer back to our more extensive discussion of the ambiguity of perception in Chapter 5.

The last depth cue we will consider in this discussion of picture perception is the three-dimensional information provided by *shadows*. Technically, a shadow is a three-dimensional region (a volume) in the scene that receives less light than other regions because some object has prevented light from shining directly into it. An appropriate label for such a volume in a scene would be *shade*. However, only the outline shape of the shaded region—the one in contact with another surface—is visible, and so vision scientists tend to refer to it as the shadow. As such, a shadow is probably best thought of as a two-dimensional surface, albeit one that can be "wrapped" onto a three-dimensional surface under certain conditions.

Shadows in pictures are regions that are darker than surrounding regions. They are bounded by an edge that is less abrupt (fuzzier) than the edges of other objects in the picture. The "darker-than-usual" feature of a pictured shadow is caused by the occlusion of light in the scene. The occlusion can result in either an *attached shadow*, referring to a portion of an object that receives less light because it is blocked by another portion of the same object, or a *cast shadow*, referring to a region on a surface other than the shadow-casting object that is occluded from receiving the same light as its surroundings. The fuzzy edge of a typical shadow is the result of the way the edge of a volume occludes light in a graduated fashion from light sources that are extended in space. Sharp-edged shadows are possible, but they only occur under the special circumstance of a scene that is lit by a single small and high-intensity light source (a *point source*). Figure 7.26 illustrates these two types of shadow.

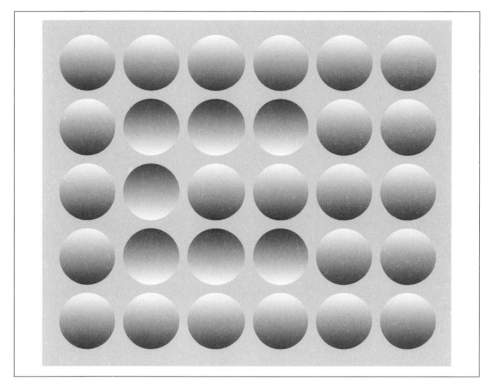

FIGURE 7.25   Shading specifies surface curvature, but only once you have settled on an assumed direction of lighting. Hold the book upside down to view an alternative interpretation of the surface.

Pictured shadows contain rich information about the three-dimensional scene. For instance, there is a predictable relationship between the shape of a shadow and the shape of the object casting the shadow. At one extreme, when the light source is at right angles to the scene and in line with the viewing position, the shape of a shadow is identical to the outline border, or silhouette, of the object being shadowed. This is the basis of the "shadow play" you may have tried as a child. You may also recall that we discussed the richness of an object's outline edges in Chapter 4.

Under other conditions of lighting and viewpoint, however, the shape of a shadow conveys little information about an object's shape. For example, consider shadows cast on the ground by the noonday sun in tropical climates. Here shadows are little more than a fuzzy patch on the ground beside an object facing the sun. The value of shadow shape as a clue to object shape therefore depends critically on lighting and viewing conditions.

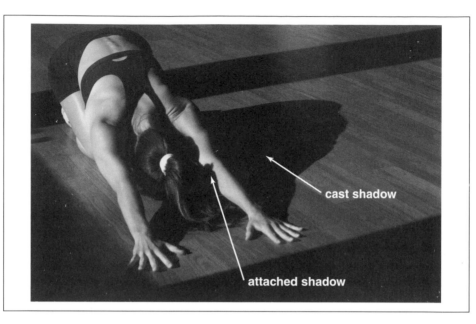

FIGURE 7.26   Types of shadow.

Other properties of a scene are expressed with much greater reliability in shadow features. One of the most reliable is the link between the direction of light in a scene and the direction in which a cast shadow falls from an object. It is not surprising that human observers can use shadows with considerable precision to locate a hidden light source in a scene. Another very reliable scene property conveyed by cast shadows is the distance between an object and the surface on which its shadow is cast.

Of course, these properties can only be seen in a picture if a shadow region has been correctly labeled. For a region to be identified as a shadow, you must determine that it is not merely a surface marking (such as a region of dark paint on an otherwise light surface) or another object (such as a blanket or a piece of cardboard). Among the most definitive clues is a match between the shape of the shadow-casting object and that of the shadow itself. Yet tests of human observers have shown that they do not notice mismatching object and shadow shapes. On the other hand, human observers are much more sensitive to the general direction of a shadow than to its shape.

Many vision scientists agree that shadows represent one of the deepest mysteries of perception. Much of the intrigue and mystery surrounding shadow perception derives from the *shadow paradox:* Shadows are simultaneously (1) the most powerful cue to depth in pictures, and (2) the least noticed of all depth cues by human observers, including vision scientists and visual artists (Casati, 2004).

Figure 7.27 presents some vivid examples of the way shadows alter the perception of a picture. Shadows can (1) make objects appear to hover in space, (2) resolve ambiguities about the relative positions of multiple objects, (3) hold rich clues to the location of the lighting in a scene, and (4) convey critical information about the shape and volume of an object. Artificially removing all the shadows from a picture alters the scene in dramatic ways. Toying around with the natural properties of shadows, such as giving them "impossible" colors or drawing outlines around their borders, can also have the effect of abruptly transforming their perceptual status into "non-shadows."

Yet when observers are asked to indicate the features of pictures that contribute to the appearance of depth, they rarely mention shadows, if at all. As noted, even shadows that are incongruous with the shapes of the objects casting them are rarely noticed, not unless the observers have been asked to inspect the relations between object and shadow shape. Shadow perception therefore seems to represent a perfect natural laboratory in which to study the development, formation, and use of "unconscious inference." Yet there have been no more than twenty-five or so studies of the contribution of shadows to picture and object perception over the past half-century. Clearly, much work remains for vision scientists of the next generation.

Art and illusion

Pictures of three-dimensional scenes represent the earliest recorded form of virtual reality. The oldest human pictures are cave drawings, many discovered by the modern world only within the past one hundred years but made originally many thousands of years ago. They reveal that humans have been engaged in the creation of virtual realities for a long time, perhaps longer even than they have spent trying to speak to one another in an oral form of language. I insist on calling pictures a "virtual" form of reality because of their inherently dual nature. Pictures are often, on the one hand, a pointer to something in the three-dimensional world. On the other, they are also a two-dimensional facsimile of such a reality. The third dimension may be signaled or indicated, but it is not realized on the page. To the extent that it evokes the perception of a three-dimensional scene, a "virtual reality" has been achieved.

The dual nature of pictures is summed up beautifully in the story about a critic of Pablo Picasso who asked the artist why he insisted on drawing people in such unusual ways. "That's not what women look like," the critic allegedly said. "If you want to see women the way they really are, take a look at this. It's my wife." The critic produced a wallet photo of his wife, which Picasso proceeded to study for a brief time. "She is very small . . . and quite flat," commented Picasso, handing the photo back to the critic. What Picasso understood—and what seems to have eluded the critic—is that all pictorial art is composed of a dual reality. The visual

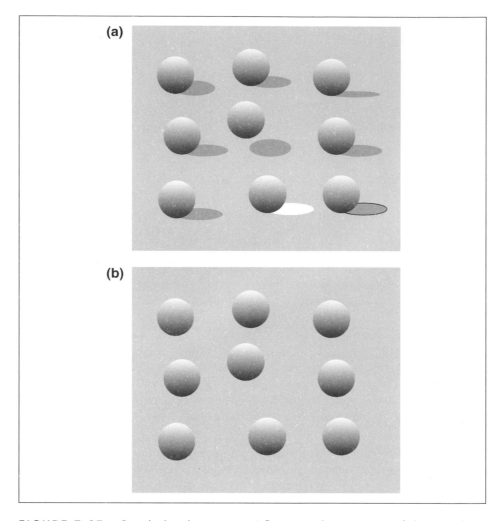

FIGURE 7.27   Cast shadows have a strong influence on the appearance of objects and their relationship to one another in the scene. **(a)** Shadows for the top row of spheres indicate differences in surface slant, shadows in the middle row indicate differences in object distance from the surface, and in the bottom row only the leftmost sphere has a proper shadow. **(b)** The same scenes of spheres without shadows has a reduced three-dimensional structure.

artist has no choice about the number of dimensions that will appear on the canvas: It will always be two. Furthermore, the nonpictorial signals about depth, such as stereovision and structure from motion, directly indicate that the picture is flat. Yet the artist can use pictorial cues to create a virtual reality. In doing so, he has complete control over the aspects and pieces of information to be conveyed within the two spatial dimensions. To understand the nature of the compromise that the artist continually faces, try the exercise in Box 7.5 before reading further.

The exercise described in Box 7.5 has been administered to North American college students many times with fairly consistent results. A majority of students draw houses depicting frontal or unfolded views. Only 10 to 15 percent make drawings involving orthogonal projection, and 2 to 5 percent draw features of a perspective projection.

Yet when the same students are asked to indicate which drawing type is the "best," the vast majority select category 4. Thus one can infer that human observers prefer drawings of houses that most are unable to render on their own. This ability is what most students are referring to when they say of themselves "I can't draw very well" and of the few who make perspective drawings "You have a knack for art."

A closer examination of all four kinds of drawings, however—from the perspective of the "lost third dimension" in drawings—reveals that each style represents a compromise. At one extreme, a drawing can faithfully represent the relations among important features of the objects in the scene. In houses, these features are the edges of the walls and surfaces. The frontal view, which in many senses is the "simplest" form of art, does the best job of preserving the scene relations. Parallel edges in the walls really are parallel in the drawing. Oblique angles in the roofline can be determined by measuring the angles in the drawing. Only a scaling factor separates the drawing of one side of the house from the dimensions of an actual house. What is *not* represented in such a drawing are the relations among the edges of the house when viewed from any position other than head-on.

At another extreme, a drawing can provide a glimpse into the retinal image of a house from another viewpoint. Drawings in category 4 in many ways facilitate the recovery of the third dimension by simulating the pattern of retinal input that would occur if a house was viewed from a viewpoint not directly in line with any major surfaces of the house. Because of this avoidance of "accidental alignments" of the line of sight with any of the surfaces, these drawings represent a "generic" viewpoint. The implicit working agreement between the artist and the viewer is that there would not likely be surprises (hidden features of the house) in another drawing made from a slightly different viewpoint. What is *not* preserved in these drawings, however, are the actual relations among the edges in the depicted surfaces. If the viewer assumes that the corners joining the walls are at right angles and that the converging lines in the drawing represent parallel edges in the scene, then much recovery of the three-dimensional shape is possible. However, if these assumptions are not met—perhaps because the depicted objects are unfamiliar or are not as rectangular as the viewer has assumed—then the recovery process can go astray. In fact, this happens in many pictorial illusions. The rules of perspective viewing that work most of the time in the everyday world are misapplied to picture viewing. This also occurs in the three-dimensional viewing of cabins built at mystery spots, discussed earlier in this chapter.

BOX 7.5

What's your drawing style?

Materials

A pencil and a blank piece of paper.

Instructions

Your task is to draw a house. Without reading further or consulting any other books or your friends, simply do your best to make a drawing of a house that others will recognize as such. It need not be a complicated house. The only requirement is that you show at least one door and one window. That will make your drawing easy to compare with drawings of houses that others have made when given this task.

Analysis

After you finished, identify your drawing according to one of the following categories, using the schematic drawings of houses in Figure 7.28 for reference:

1. *Frontal view:* shows only one wall of the house, with both the door and the window on this wall.
2. *Unfolded view:* shows two walls of the house, with the sides of the two walls lying continuous with one another on the page.
3. *Orthogonal projection:* shows two walls with nonparallel lines at their base, but each side of a single wall and the vertical edges of each wall are still all running parallel with one another.
4. *Perspective projection:* parallel edges converge as the distance from the viewer increases. The quality of this drawing increases, for the purpose of this exercise, if the edges of any given wall converge at a common vanishing point, either on the page or beyond it.

The most important lesson of this exercise is that pictures (two-dimensional drawings) always involve a compromise between preserving the true relations among edges in the scene and preserving the true relations among the edges within Alberti's window (or the retinal image). Drawings that fall into categories 1 and 2 favor the preservation of scene relations; those that fall into categories 3 and 4 favor the preservation of image relations.

Why the moon changes size

Is it possible to tell how large something is simply by looking only at it? When we are drawing a picture, how should we portray the relative sizes of objects? These questions concern something that vision scientists call *size constancy scaling*. In this section, we will discuss the operation of size constancy in everyday perception be-

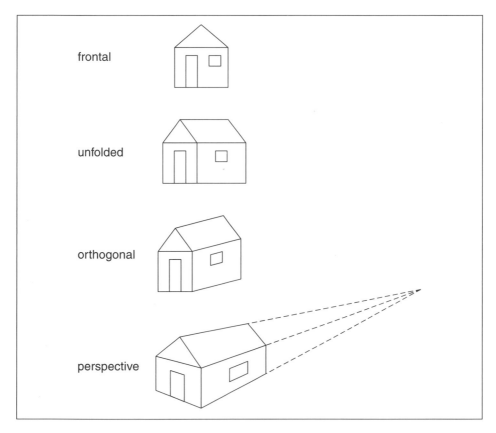

FIGURE 7.28   Four commonly used styles from the exercise in Box 7.5.

fore turning to the question of how these visual processes are applied to the perception of pictures.

Size constancy refers to an important aspect of our experience when viewing objects from a variety of distances: mainly, that objects do not appear to shrink as they move away from us—at least, not until they are really far away, as when we view a scene from an airplane or skyscraper. The fact that objects appear to stay the same size may not seem to be a very important aspect of vision until we examine what viewing distance does to the size of objects projected onto the retina. Figure 7.29a shows a graph on which visual size, measured in *degrees of visual angle* (Chapter 1), has been plotted for an object of actual size 1 as a function of a range of viewing distances from 0 to 30 units. The units used to measure both size and distance are arbitrary: They could be inches, feet, or even miles. The only constraint is that size and distance be measured in the same units.

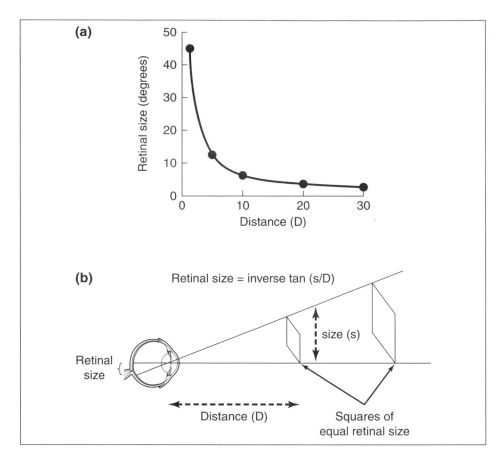

FIGURE 7.29 **(a)** The relationship between the projected size of an object in the eye as a function of the eye's distance from the object. **(b)** How this relationship is calculated. The inverse tan function in the equation can be found as a button press or two on most calculators.

A striking feature of the graph (Figure 7.29a) is how rapidly the curve descends as the distance between the viewer and the object increases. Let's take the size (actually, the height) of your friend's head and neck as an example. If the top of your friend's head is roughly 1 foot above her shoulders and you are speaking to her at a distance of 1 foot, then her head will occupy about 45 degrees of visual angle in the retina of your eye. If she steps back from you so that she is 5 feet away, the projected size of her head will shrink to only 12 degrees. That's a little more than one-quarter of her former size. If she steps back another 5 feet, she is only 10 feet away (the distance between walls in a small room) and yet the image of her will shrink to less than 6 degrees. If she walks away and looks at you from 30 feet, which is still close enough to see the direction of her gaze and the details of her facial expres-

sion, her head will occupy less than 2 degrees of visual angle. That's similar in projected size to the width of your thumb held at arm's length.

Why does the real size of your friend not appear to shrink along with her projected size as she moves away from you? Because your visual system does not judge
size on the basis of the retinal area occupied by an object's projected size. Instead,
it gauges size in a relative fashion, using the differences between the size of objects
judged to be at a similar distance from you. This approach to the perceived size of
objects should remind you of the visual system's approach to the perceived color
of surfaces under a variety of lighting conditions (Chapter 3). Surface color is
judged not on the basis of the dominant wavelength reaching the eye, but on the
differences in wavelength that reach the eye from adjacent surfaces. The perceived
size of objects is determined by following a similar approach.

But this approach also has pitfalls. What if the judged distance of an object from
the viewer is inaccurate? What if the retinal size of an object is used to determine
not only its size but also its distance from us? This inquiry may get us mired in
some hopeless ambiguities, resulting in the perceived size of an object being
different depending on assumptions regarding its distance. This is exactly what
happens, especially when perceived distance becomes uncertain.

The *moon illusion* is one of the best-known real-world consequences of this approach to the perceived size of objects. You have probably seen a full moon
emerge over the horizon early in the evening and been struck by how large it
seemed. Yet later that night when the moon was higher, it appeared to be much
smaller. Surely neither the actual size of the moon nor its distance from you
changed between these two experiences. Time-lapse photographs of a full moon
will confirm that even the retinal image of the moon is unchanging during this period. The moon in these photographs traces perfectly parallel edges over the entire
period of the night. This leaves only one candidate for what may have changed:
Your visual system changed its conclusion about the real size of the moon on the
basis of the same-size retinal image of it. But why?

The diagram in Figure 7.30 demonstrates how the judged distance between
you and the moon may have changed over the course of the evening. The actual
path, or arc, of the moon during the night is indicated by the solid line. Because
the moon revolves around the earth, it is equal in distance to any point on the
earth at all times. The actual size of the moon in the diagram is indicated by the
size of the solid disc on the horizon and at the zenith. The retinal size of the moon
is indicated within the two sets of rays emanating from the eye, which is positioned
at a common viewing position. The key insight is that if the moon appeared to tra-
verse the sky in the shape of a flattened arc, indicated by the dotted line, rather
than in a full circle, then the judged size of the moon would vary as indicated by
the outline disc on the horizon and at zenith. These sizes are much more in line
with the (illusory) changing size of the moon that we actually experience.

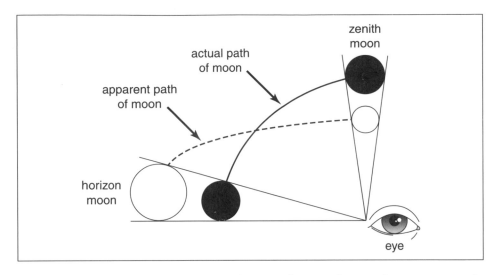

FIGURE 7.30   The moon illusion occurs because of a misapplication of size constancy scaling. The actual size of the moon and the distance of the moon from the Earth are constant at all viewing angles. The perceived difference in size occurs because of a visual underestimation of the distance of the moon when it is in its zenith position. Solid lines indicate the constant retinal size of the moon in all positions.

This interpretation of the moon illusion depends on the consistent misjudging of the distance of the moon from us. Is there any evidence of that? Yes, plenty. First, consider that our visual system has no way of determining the actual size of objects in the sky. The only way it can begin to judge their size is to make assumptions about where they are. In the zenith of the night sky, the only objects that serve as references are the stars—and as far as our visual system is concerned, these pinpricks of light could be anywhere. A different situation holds for the judged distance of the horizon moon. Regardless of where we are viewing the rising moon, it will always appear to be farther away than the most distant point we can see. The horizon moon therefore becomes an object that is farther from us than any other visible object. Against this relatively rich context of comparison objects on the horizon, combined with the absence of similar comparison objects in the night sky, it is less of a surprise that our visual system opts to resolve the ambiguity of the horizon moon in favor of it being farther away than the zenith moon.

More detailed evidence for this interpretation of the moon illusion arises by comparing the magnitude of the illusion in different conditions. By far the largest horizon moons are seen at sea or on the flat prairie, where a very distant horizon is still visible as a comparison reference point. Among artificial environments, such as cityscapes, the moon illusion becomes larger as the variety and distance of nearby comparison objects increase. Simply viewing the moon emerging over the edge of a skyscraper is not sufficient to generate much of an illusion. However, viewing the same moon at the end of a long city street, filled with buildings, street lights, and the cues to perspective given by trolley wires and street markings, can make for a magnificent, and even poetry-evoking, moon.

Now that we understand how visual size judgments are made, we can return to the question of how to depict the size of an object in a picture. Two main issues follow from our discussion of size constancy more generally. The first issue concerns how we will signal apparent distance in the picture. This is important because, as we have seen, the apparent distance and size of an object are interdependent. The second issue concerns the relative size difference between our object of interest and neighboring objects at the same distance from us. To understand how the two issues are related, try the exercise in Box 7.6.

The exercise in Box 7.6 usually produces two main findings. First, the judged size of the target objects in *far* locations is larger than that of the same target objects in *near* locations. This result is consistent with what we learned about the perception of size from the moon illusion. If two objects of the same retinal size appear to be at different distances, then the farther one will appear to be larger. This is a consequence of the inherent link between perceived distance and perceived size. Vision scientists refer to it as an illusion involving *pictorial size constancy*. Its only difference from the moon illusion is a subtle one: The judgment of distance in pictured scenes is based explicitly on pictorial cues to depth. This means that the dual nature of the picture is in plain view; you are judging the size of an object on a clearly flat surface as indicated by stereovision and motion processing. In the moon illusion, the depth cues are also monocular because the moon and most of the relevant comparison objects are too far away for their perceived distance to be influenced by stereovision and motion processing. Yet in the real-world setting, there are no obvious hints that monocular depth cues are the only ones of any consequence.

Second, the pictorial size constancy illusion tends to be larger for the meaningfully consistent pairings of target and background pictures than for the inconsistent pairings. You may have noticed this in your own pictures; inconsistent targets may simply appear to hover above the scene rather than become visually integrated with the other objects. For inconsistent picture pairing, the target object was not seen to be at the *near* and *far* picture locations with the same degree of confidence. As a consequence, the pictorial cues to distance in the scene were not applied to the judged size of the inconsistent objects in the same way that they were applied to the size of the consistent ones. It is fortunate for us that under most visual conditions the complex interplay of factors is sorted out for us without our being aware of the many decisions that determine the construction project we call vision.

BOX 7.6
_____

Size constancy scaling in pictures

Materials

Find four magazine pictures depicting everyday scenes. Try to select pictures that contain a rich variety of cues to depth in the scene. We will call these *background scenes*. Using other magazine pictures, carefully cut around the outline of an object that fits visually and conceptually into one of the background scenes. We will call this a *target object*. Cut out one target object for each background scene. You will also need a ruler and thirty-two small slips of paper on which to record the judged visual extents of the target objects in the background pictures. Finally, construct a chart for recording your results that looks like the one below. The labels *A, B, C,* and *D* refer to the four background scenes. Labels *a, b, c,* and *d* refer to the target objects that match the four background scenes.

Target Object

	a far near	b far near	c far near	d far near
A				
B				
C				
D				

Instructions

Beginning with scene A, place the target object *a* in a location that appears to be quite distant in the picture. Judge the visual size of this target by drawing a line on a slip of paper that corresponds to the horizontal extent of the target at that location. *Draw this line by eye.* Don't overlay the slip of paper or use any sort of ruler or measuring device. Label the slip of paper *A-a far.* Now place the same cutout object in a picture location that appears to be very near in the picture. Record the judged size of the target in this location, and label it *A-a near.* Do the same for each combination of target, background scene, and relative location.

Analysis

Carefully measure the length of each of the lines on the thirty-two slips of paper (preferably in millimeters, to preserve as much precision as possible), and enter those numbers in the chart. Now you are ready to compute some average sizes to see if the judged size of the target objects was influenced by their location in the picture and by the conceptual relatedness of the neighboring objects.

Summarize your results by answering the following questions:

1. Find the average of all sixteen *far* lengths, and compare it to the average of all sixteen *near* lengths in the chart. Use the two numbers to answer these questions: Is there a difference in the judged size of objects placed in apparently *far* as opposed to *near* locations in the pictures? In which location do the targets look bigger?
2. Find the average *near* and *far* judgments of the four *consistent* target-background pairings *(A-a, B-b, C-c, D-d)*. Compare these with the average *near* and *far* judgments of the twelve *inconsistent* target-background pairings *(A-b, A-c, A-d, B-a, B-b,* etc.) Is the difference between *near* and *far* judgments larger for *consistent* or *inconsistent* picture pairings?

PUTTING IT ALL TOGETHER

Our perception of where "up" is, where we are in the world, and where we are heading is based on the constructed reality of our brains, just as much as our perception of an object's color, shape, and position over time. In the case of space perception, we have seen that this construction involves the coordination of many different sources of information. Some of these sources lie outside the realm of vision, such as our proprioceptive sense of balance that informs us about gravitational upright. Other sources are visual, but they derive from comparisons among images separated in space (stereovision) or among images separated in time (motion parallax, structure from motion). Still other sources can be found in the clues left by the light from a scene falling onto a two-dimensional surface (monocular or pictorial cues to depth). One of the real wonders of human vision is how these many sources of information are combined so effortlessly under everyday circumstances to provide us with the seamless experience of knowing where we are positioned in three-dimensional space.

Yet, if you are attentive, you will be able to detect hints all around you that this seamless experience is only the tip of an iceberg of processes that go on without your awareness. This chapter has introduced many of them. So, the next time your sense of balance is deceived by oriented edges that extend far into your visual periphery, or the sense of your own body in motion is deceived by a large field of motion, remind yourself that these are the same cues you use every day to stand up straight and to move in the direction you intend. We are generally not aware of them because most of the time these cues are all in agreement. Also, the next time you stop to admire a realistic painting, remind yourself that your appreciation of the volume and spatial layout in the picture is possible only because you are using exactly the same kind of information every day in the real world. Understanding the spatial layout in a picture depends on the same processes, albeit a reduced number, that are used to see the layout of the world around us.

FURTHER READING

Casati, R. (2004). *Shadows: Unlocking their secrets, from Plato to our time.* New York: Vintage.

Hagen, M. A. (1986). *Varieties of realism: Geometries of representational art.* New York: Cambridge University Press.

Hagen, M. A. (Ed.). (1980). *The perception of pictures I: Alberti's window: The projective model of pictures.* New York: Academic Press.

Hagen, M. A. (Ed.). (1981). *The perception of pictures II: Durer's devices: Beyond the projective model of pictures.* New York: Academic Press.

Hershenson, M. (Ed.). (1989). *The moon illusion.* Hillsdale, NJ: Erlbaum.

Howard, I. P. (1982). *Human visual orientation.* New York: Wiley.

Kubovy, M. (1986). *The psychology of perspective and Renaissance art.* New York: Cambridge University Press.

8 IMAGINATION

FUNDAMENTAL QUESTIONS

- How much time does it take for a thought to influence a visual image?

- Do visual perception and imagery use the same neural machinery?

- How does visual imagination differ from perception?

- Why is our short-term memory for visual details so poor even though our long-term memory for meaning is so good?

- How does a single experience change our brain?

- Why does visual familiarity lead to liking rather than contempt?

- How does the vision of an expert differ from that of a novice?

- Why are solutions to problems often limited by what we can see?

VISUAL IMAGERY

A vast portion of our everyday thinking makes use of visual images. Yet these images do not bear any direct relationship to the pattern of light bombarding our eyes. They are images we manufacture for ourselves in order to think clearly: they form the basis of what we often call the *imagination*. Imagine, for example, that within the next hour you will have to go to an interior design center or a home decor store to buy blinds and shades for all the windows in your home. Even though you cannot return home to check the details before you get to the store, you will still have a precise idea of the number of windows to be covered, you will be able to provide a lot of detail about their approximate sizes, and you will know the colors of the surrounding furnishings and walls. This knowledge will be available without any prior intention to remember such details, and it will be distinctively visual in form. The colors of the walls, for instance, could not have been acquired in any other way.

This ability to form a mental image of a familiar scene is truly wonderful. To really appreciate it, think how difficult the home-decorating task would be if you were unable to form such mental images. You would probably have to return home to record all the details in a drawing or a list before going to the store. Once there, you would probably realize you had failed to record some of the relevant details and would likely have to return home several times for more information. Details that you did not intentionally note in these records would never be factored into your planning. In contrast, consulting a mental image of these familiar scenes could revive your memory, reminding you of details you would not otherwise consider.

But our imagination has abilities that are far more sophisticated than this. It enables us to form mental images of scenes, objects, and events we have never witnessed. We can use our imagination to play out scenarios to test the possible outcomes of our actions and decisions. *What would the inside of your apartment look like if you had a floor-to-ceiling window on one of the walls that now has no windows? What if you removed the wall between your kitchen and dining room? What would it look like if you placed your couch against the opposite wall?* Our ability to answer these questions by "seeing" the results in our mind's eye reveals that the brain can manufacture images of things we have never seen or contemplated before. This aspect of our imagination might even form a critical portion of the cognitive abilities that distinguish us from other animals.

Mental transformations

Vision scientists began to study humans' visual imaginative abilities rather recently. Before the 1970s, the concept of visual imagery had never been put to an objective test. Although scientists were well aware of their own mental images, imagination was considered to be too private and too subjective a topic to merit scientific study. This perspective changed with the publication of a remarkable study in the journal *Science* in 1971.

A short paper by Roger Shepard and Jacqueline Metzler appeared under the simple title "Mental Rotation of Three Dimensional Objects" (1971). It reported that observers were asked to answer the question *Are the two objects pictured in [Figure 8.1] identical in their three-dimensional shape, or is one a mirror image of the other object?* Most people can answer this question after thinking about the problem for a little while; when asked what they do to solve the problem, most respond that they manipulate one of the objects in their mind to see if they can get it to look like the other object. To do this, they mentally rotate the object in one direction or the other until both objects either look similar or are mirror images of each another. To understand what a mirror-image object looks like, simply look at your own two hands. They are, of course, very similar, but no amount of rotation of wrist or arm will align them so that they are exact copies of one another. They will always be *mirror copies* of each other.

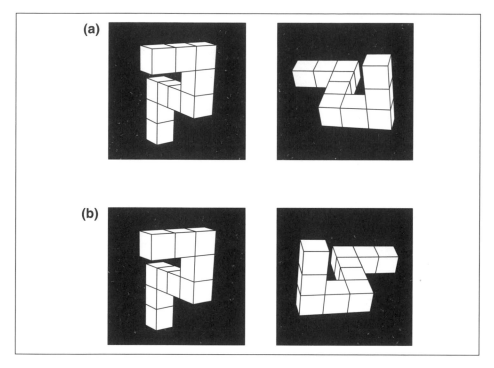

FIGURE 8.1 Pictures used to study the mental rotation of objects. **(a)** Some pairs of objects have exactly the same shape but are shown from a different vantage point. **(b)** Other pairs of objects are similar in overall shape but are actually mirror copies of each other.

What made this paper notable was not its attention to the concept of imagery. Philosophers had been writing about that for hundreds of years. Rather, the paper reported a very simple procedure for measuring the time needed for humans to perform an entirely mental operation—in this case, mentally rotating or repositioning an object in space. Observers' responses were timed in answer to the question *Are these the same objects or merely mirror copies?* for pairs of pictures such as those in Figure 8.1. The main experimental factor was the difference between each set of two pictured objects, measured in the degree of rotation that would have to be completed if one of the objects was to be congruent with the other. No real objects were moved. Observers simply looked at the still pictures and moved them in their mind's eye. The main finding was also not about the total time needed to answer the question. This varied quite a lot among observers.

The most striking aspect of the time measurements was their direct connection to the angular difference between the objects pictured. For every degree of difference in angular separation between the objects, response times increased by 25 to 30 milliseconds. These results are shown in Figure 8.2. The fact that response

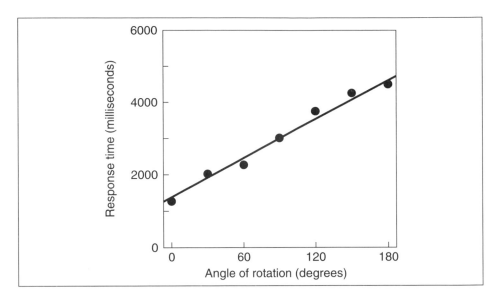

FIGURE 8.2   Typical results for an experiment involving mental rotation. Response time increases linearly with the angle of rotation that separates the two objects in three-dimensional space.

times increased along a straight line suggests that the cognitive operations required to perform mental rotation have a 1-to-1 relationship with the physical operations that would be required if the objects were real and actually had to be rotated in three-dimensional space.

These results did not silence all criticism about the possibility of studying mental images in a scientific way. Some researchers thought, for example, that the results might be the product of imageless but cooperative observers who were trying to produce results that the experimenters wanted. One way to do this would be to simply respond quickly when the angle of rotation was small and to wait longer as the angular separation became larger. This possibility is not altogether farfetched, since human participants in experiments are well known for being very cooperative, wanting to be as helpful to the experimenters as possible.

A variation on the original experiment, however, soon put this possibility to rest. Observers were shown only one object at a time, each for a brief period, and were asked to rotate each object as quickly as possible to the right or the left. After a brief interval in which the screen was blank, a comparison object appeared. It was either the original object rotated by a certain amount, or a mirror-imaged object, and observers had to answer the same question as before: *Are the two objects identical or mirror copies?* The results showed that when the appropriately rotated comparison object appeared at the time predicted by the response time function calculated in Figure 8.2, the response time was not related to the angular separation between the two objects. It was as though the observers' mental image could be compared directly to the comparison object shown on the screen. Because these were already in alignment, responses to all the comparison objects could be made rapidly and accurately. It was difficult to imagine that willing participants could fake these results because they had no way of knowing when the comparison image would appear on the screen.

Since these original experiments on the mental rotation of three-dimensional objects, many other studies have explored the visual images we form in our minds. Some have examined the time required to consult landmarks on mental maps that observers committed to memory. Other studies have addressed the factors of (1) relative size, and (2) mental rotation in the picture plane as opposed to mental rotation in depth along the vertical or horizontal axis. Still others have explored the links between the spatial resolution of observers' mental images and the size of the objects being imagined. In general, mental images of smaller objects contain details that are less clear and therefore take longer to "see" than details in the mental images of larger objects. This is exactly what one would expect while examining relatively small and large objects in a photograph. In all the studies, the amount of time needed for observers to make decisions about the objects they were imagining could be linked to the physical transformations these objects would have to undergo to become similar or congruent to one another. Thus whatever the brain does to give us the experience of seeing things in our mind's eye, it enables the constraints of the physical world to be simulated in our mental re-creations of the world we know through sight.

Unavoidable mental images

Not only are mental images available to us when we solve problems involving spatial relations among imagined objects, but these images often intrude into our thought processes even when they are unnecessary for solving a problem. This is easy to see in experiments that seem to require a verbal, but not a visual, form of memory. For example, imagine participating in a study in which your task is to study and recall a list of words. If some of the words are nouns, naming objects with concrete features for which it is easy to form images (e.g., *house*, *robin*), you will be able to recall them at a much higher level of accuracy than either verbs (e.g., *run*, *strike*) or nouns that are less concrete and for which it is harder to form images (e.g., *idea*, *justice*). This is true even if you receive no instructions to form mental images of the words. It is not surprising, then, that if the experimenter now gives you instructions to remember certain words by forming simple images at the time of study, your recall will again be much better for the words you imagined in your mind's eye than for the other words for which you did not form images intentionally at the time of study.

Even when we are learning about a category of objects for the first time, there is every indication that we accomplish the initial stages of learning by forming rigid images of the objects we are trying to learn. In many ways this resembles the "imprinting" of young animals to the first objects they encounter visually. In the case of humans, these mental images can lead to predictable mistakes when participants are tested for their understanding of a new category with object "foils" that resemble the previously learned objects but do not satisfy a related rule that the participants have learned. Even though participants may have been given an explicit rule to follow for object categorization—a rule that they know well and can state verbally—they can still be fooled by objects that "look like" the ones they have just learned.

In one study of this kind (Allen & Brooks, 1991), participants had to learn artificially constructed categories consisting of cartoon pictures of fictional animals. Figure 8.3 presents several examples. One group of animals was labeled "builders" and the other "diggers" because of the way they were said to build nests in their respective environments. Participants were told that each animal had at least two of three well-defined features. All the animals consisted of some combination of angular or rounded body shape, spotted or smooth skin, short or long legs, short or long neck, and two or four legs. Only three of these dimensions were relevant for classification, and the animals were always depicted against one of several different outdoor environments. The reason for having variation in more features than were relevant to the task was to see the effect of visual similarity on performance.

The rule for builders was that they had at least two of the following features: angular body, spotted skin, long legs. In a training phase of the study, participants were shown sixteen animals in all, including eight builders and eight diggers. These were shown to the participants until they could classify the animals with a high degree of accuracy. In a subsequent testing phase, the participants were shown the animals again, along with foils that resembled the learned animals but did not satisfy the learned rule for builders. Categorization accuracy on these visually similar but non-member foils was only 55 percent, much lower than the 80 percent accuracy attained on other test items that participants had not seen previously but that did not resemble the learned animals. These findings are a strong indication that in the early stages of visual category learning, humans form images of the objects that retain as much visual information as possible. Moreover, they do this even when there is no formal need to do it.

Once you are aware of this tendency in human visual categorization, you will begin to recognize it all around you. For example, if you are looking for a friend in a crowded airport and you know your friend is wearing a distinctive hat, you will find yourself inspecting people who resemble your friend even when they are not wearing any hat. The long-term visual template you have formed for your friend has a much stronger influence on your search strategy than the recently acquired and precisely diagnostic information that your friend is wearing a specific hat. As

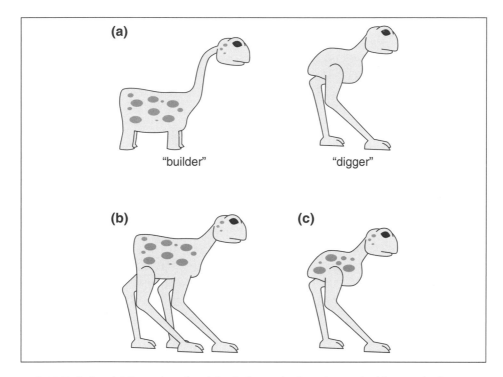

FIGURE 8.3 **(a)** Examples of each kind of animal referred to as "builders" and "diggers." Builders are defined as having *at least two* of the following features: angular body, spotted skin, long legs. All other animals are diggers. **(b)** An example of a builder that looks similar to other builders. **(c)** An example of a builder that looks more similar to the digger family.

another example, doctors given the task of diagnosing a skin disorder will have a higher rate of accuracy when the case they are examining is visually similar to one they have just seen, even when the similarity is based on attributes that are irrelevant for the diagnosis.

Images in the brain

What parts of the brain are active when we form mental images of scenes or objects that are different from the visual images before our eyes? One reasonable possibility is that only so-called higher-order brain areas are involved. These would include the frontal, parietal, and temporal lobes. The reason these areas would be involved is that mental images require access to the stores of scenes and objects in our long-term memories. Patterns of brain damage in neuropsychological patients have shown that these memories are almost certainly housed in the higher-order regions. If these regions are also the sites of mental imagery, then mental images could be formed in these areas, leaving the lower-order regions such as area V1 devoted to the analysis of visual images coming from the eyes.

Although this may sound like a neat way to divide the labor in the brain, it is also unrealistic. First, we have already encountered in this book the principle that seeing depends as much on the higher-order brain centers as on the lower, so-called sensory regions. Thus any hope of keeping mental imagery distinct from vision by relegating these functions to different brain areas has been lost. Second, mental imagery depends on the very functions that are served by the lower visual regions of the brain. In order for (1) mental images to have an adequate degree of spatial resolution, and (2) the spatial relations among objects in a scene to be preserved in our mental images, they will require the functions that can only be performed by the lower regions.

These considerations suggest that we experience mental imagery only when aspects of our long-term memories are used to create a pattern of activity in the lowest-level cortical areas of the brain, including area V1. What we experience as imagery is not the long-term memory representations themselves, but a new pattern of activity in area V1 that is very much like the pattern of activity caused by a scene before our eyes. The main difference is that the origin of the "scene" in our imagination is the re-entrant, or feedback, neural connections from brain sites of long-term memory, rather than the feedforward neural connections coming from a pattern of light falling on our eyes. Area V1 and its neighbors may simply be the sketchpad or screen on which detailed visual functions of all sorts play out, regardless of whether those visual functions are driven by new incoming sensory signals or old signals based on stored memories. This answer to the question *Where in the brain are mental images?* raises another host of questions about how the brain is able to keep mental images distinct from visual ones. We will return to this question after considering the evidence that vision and mental imagery do rely on some of the same parts of the lower-level visual system.

One way to demonstrate the link between imagery and perception is to try to answer the following question from memory taken from a study by Stephen Kosslyn and colleagues (Kosslyn & Rabin, 1999): *Does Abraham Lincoln face to the left or to the right on the "heads" side of an American penny?* (If you live in Canada, try answering this question for the facing direction of Queen Elizabeth on the penny.) Many people are unable to answer this question correctly, though, on average, accuracy among college students is well above chance levels. Now look at the two images of an American penny in Figure 8.4. Which drawing corresponds to an actual American penny? It turns out that when college students try to answer this question while *looking* at the two alternatives, they are unable to rise above a chance level of accuracy. Apparently, the presence of sensory information from the eyes interferes with the ability of the same participants to consult their long-term memories for the facing direction of the image on the penny.

FIGURE 8.4   Which outline corresponds to an actual American penny? The correct answer might surprise you. Abraham Lincoln faces toward the right. One reason that people get this answer wrong is that the penny is an exception in American coinage: The "heads" on all other coins face toward the left.

This demonstration points out several interesting features of our visual memory and image-making capabilities. First, the long-term store of information about the penny must contain some information about the facing direction of Abraham Lincoln. Otherwise, study participants would be unable to answer the first question, strictly from memory, at above-chance levels of accuracy. Second, the information must be coded in a spatial—or at least a nonverbal—form, since it is unlikely that all the participants who answer correctly would have studied the answer and committed it to memory in the past. Rather, the above-chance performance indicates memory for an incidentally learned feature of the penny. Third, some of the neural machinery used to answer the question from memory must be the same as the neural machinery used to see the drawings in Figure 8.4. Otherwise, the mere presence of the drawings should not have a negative influence on the ability to recall the facing direction.

In this case of memory for the common penny, just as in the case of visual backward masking discussed in Chapters 6 and 9, the visual parts of the brain tend to resolve conflicts between top-down (re-entrant) and bottom-up (sensory input) signals in favor of the immediate sensory input. Having a bias in this direction is probably greatly to our advantage most of the time. For example, it permits us to see what is actually on view rather than what is only on our minds. At the same time, as demonstrated for the penny, it can wreak havoc with our ability to access memories with a strongly visual component. It is probably no accident, then, that many people prefer to shut their eyes when they are in a busy visual environment and are required to solve a difficult visual or spatial problem from memory. Closing the eyes is a highly effective means of blocking the feedforward stream of neural signals that would otherwise compete with the descending stream of signals concerning the problem to be solved.

Another way to demonstrate the link between imagery and perception involves studying the pattern of dysfunction in individuals with brain injury. Many people who suffer from cortical blindness—that is, they have sustained damage to visual area V1 and therefore no longer can have conscious visual experiences—report that they also no longer can form mental images of scenes and objects they know well. In individuals with damage to brain regions farther along in the anatomical hierarchy, similar links can be seen. Those with agnosias that are specific to certain classes of visual events, such as prosopagnosia (face blindness) or achromatopsia (color blindness), often also report that they are no longer able to form mental images of these visual features. Individuals suffering from neglect of one side of space tend to neglect not only the visual world on that side but also the same side of the visual images they are able to form from memory.

Brain imaging of healthy study participants is an even more direct way to determine the links between imagery and perception. A typical approach involves comparing the pattern of brain activity associated with the perception of simple scenes that are easy to remember with the later imagination of the same scenes evoked solely from memory. The measure on which the two tasks are compared is the activity map obtained from a technique such as positron emission tomography (PET), functional magnetic resonance imaging (fMRI), or magno-encephalography (MEG) (Chapter 2). In one of the first studies of this kind by Stephen Kosslyn and colleagues (Kosslyn et al., 1993), participants either (1) looked at a large grid in which letters appeared in some cells, or (2) imagined letters in the same cell locations. This study found—and subsequent studies have found consistently—that the "imagination" condition revealed neural activity in area V1 that is similar in many respects to the activity that occurs there under actual "viewing" conditions of the same scenes.

An important clue indicating that this activity of the mind's eye is similar to that which is recorded when participants actually use their eyes is that the location of activity varies systematically with the size of the objects seen or imagined. For example, when participants imagine very small objects near the center of their gaze, the activity measured from the brain imaging technique is largest at the back of the brain and near the center of the topographic map for area V1. In contrast, when large objects and scenes are imagined, a much larger region of activity is evident in the activity maps of the brain; this region extends to the more forward parts of area V1. These parts correspond to peripheral retinal locations, the very same ones in which activity is recorded when participants look at large objects.

Keeping our images straight

The fact that mental imaging involves much of the same neural machinery as seeing solves some difficult problems, such as how we can form detailed images in our minds in the first place. But it also raises other issues, such as how we can distinguish between the two forms of visualization. If complete overlap occurred in the processes of imaging and seeing, we would be unable to distinguish our fantasies from reality.

One of the first clues to the separateness of imagery from perception can be seen in individuals with visually specific brain damage. In some subsets of these individuals, there is a deficit in either perception or imagery, but not in both. The brain imaging studies furnish additional evidence that the overlap in perception and imagery is not complete. There is an estimated two-thirds overlap in the brain regions that are typically active in both imagery and perception. Thus the distinction between these functions in our own experience and in that of brain-damaged individuals might arise from the specialized functions of the non-overlapping regions. At this point it is not possible to definitively identify the non-overlapping regions of the brain, but the rate of current research progress promises many answers in the near future.

At the moment, the best clues about how imagery and perception are kept distinct come from observing the behavior of healthy and brain-damaged study participants. One recurring general theme of studies comparing imagery and perception is that mental imagery is considerably more inflexible and limited than actual perception. The demonstration in Box 8.1 and Figure 8.5 will help you experience a limitation of mental imagery.

Several studies have examined the use of mental images as ambiguous stimuli. For example, look at the well-known ambiguous drawings in Figure 8.6. If mental images of these drawings behaved in the same way as seen images, then one would expect reversals of interpretation to occur in a similar way. That is, their appearance would change spontaneously from one interpretation to the next, even when only examining the mental images of the drawings. But, in fact, reversals of this kind are much less frequent in mental imagery than in perception of the same drawings. For example, in one study participants rehearsed an image like Figure 8.6a until they were able to draw it accurately from memory. The critical factor was whether they had been told they were memorizing a picture of a duck or a rabbit. However, almost no one who imagined the picture after learning it was able to see it as anything else, even when prompted in a variety of ways. Yet after once again drawing the picture they were imagining and then being asked whether it looked like anything else, almost everyone spontaneously reported seeing the alternate interpretation. Findings such as these challenge the view that imagery is as rich and vivid as perception.

BOX 8.1

Limitations of mental images

Imaging the cube

A cube is one of the simplest three-dimensional volumes we can imagine and also one of the volumes with which we have the most experience. Simply think of all the objects in your world that are roughly cube-like, from toy blocks to sugar cubes to clock radios to buildings. We know the shape of the cube very well. Your task in this demonstration is to imagine the shape that would be formed in a patch of sand if you dipped a cube into that sand and then removed it. But make sure that in your imagination you dip the cube into the sand in a very specific way. Do this by holding the cube obliquely, so that it would stand in the sand on only one vertex if you were to let go. Have you formed that image? If so, then what is the *shape of the outline* you would see in the sand after you have withdrawn the cube? Is it a diamond, a triangle, or some other shape?

Most people respond to this question by saying the shape would be a diamond. But they are wrong. To see how they are wrong, examine the drawing of the cube and its outline in the sand shown in Figure 8.5. Perception apparently makes some information available about a well-known object that is less available to mental images of the same object.

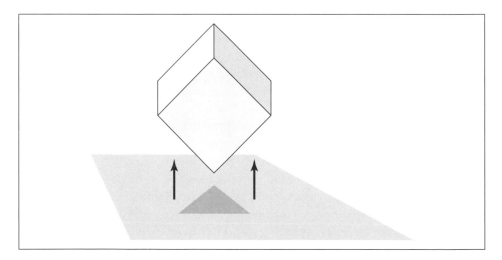

FIGURE 8.5   A cube dipped into sand and then withdrawn will make a triangular shape in the sand. This is easy to see when using an actual cube, but hard when answering the question using only your imagination.

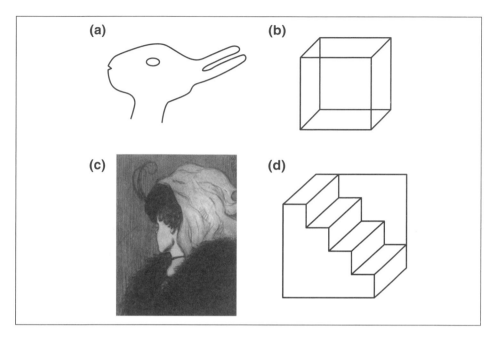

FIGURE 8.6   Ambiguous pictures that spontaneously reverse in their interpretation from time to time. Mental images of these pictures do not seem to reverse as readily. **(a)** duck—rabbit **(b)** cube tilted up—cube tilted down **(c)** young woman—old woman **(d)** stairs on floor—stairs on ceiling

VISUAL MEMORY

In discussing our ability to imagine objects and events that are not currently in front of our eyes, we have sidestepped questions about the nature of memory for sights seen in the past. We will turn to those questions now, since understanding the nature of visual memories more generally will ground our understanding of our visual imaginative abilities as well as our immediate perceptual abilities. Visual memory researchers have found many times, and in many different ways, that our ability to remember a visual scene is both marvelously rich and frustratingly impoverished. Let's examine this apparent contradiction.

The amazing richness of our visual memory is evident in studies in which participants are shown hundreds, sometimes thousands, of different scenes at a regular rate. For example, imagine taking the recent vacation slides of ten of your friends and randomly dividing them into two piles. Next, imagine viewing one pile in a random order at a rate of one new picture every 2 seconds. How many slides would you later be able to correctly classify as "old" (meaning you had seen them before) versus "new" (meaning you had not viewed them already)? If the chance level of guessing was 50 percent because the test involved an equal number of "old" and "new" slides, would you be able to categorize 75 percent of the test slides correctly? More? For how long? A few hours? Days? Months?

In many studies of this kind, the consistent finding is that participants are able to recognize over 90 percent of the "old" slides—even after many days and weeks. Recognition accuracy falls off a little, but in some studies the overall recognition rate is still over 75 percent after six months. This points to a truly amazing ability to commit large amounts of new visual information to memory in relatively little time and with relatively little effort. We are all "visual learners" of this kind. Some people even claim to have photographic memory, pointing to these kinds of feats as evidence.

The counterpoint to this apparent richness in our visual memory is evident in the change-blindness demonstrations we encountered in Chapter 5. Such demonstrations, and other related studies, show compellingly that even people who claim to have photographic memory are "blind" to most details in a scene taken in at a glance. At least they are blind in the sense that they cannot detect major changes to a scene, provided that (1) their view of the scene was briefly interrupted, (2) the change did not alter the overall gist of the scene, and (3) the change did not occur to an object or attribute at the center of their attentional focus. How can we reconcile this poverty in human visual memory with the richness displayed in studies of long-term memory for random photographs?

Part of the answer is that the formation of a detailed visual memory takes time—more time than the brief period between alternating views in a study of change-blindness allows. This point was made very elegantly in a recent study of visual memory (Brockmole, Irwin, & Wang, 2002) where the patterns to be remembered were random patterns of dots used traditionally to study visible persistence (Chapter 6). These are illustrated once again in Figure 8.7. Recall that accuracy in reporting the missing dot in the matrix when the two patterns were superimposed fell off rapidly as the time interval between the two flashed patterns increased to 100 milliseconds. This might indicate that the neural activity associated with the first pattern was no longer sufficiently high to permit the formation of a single mental image involving the neural activity of both patterns.

However, the researchers found that if they allowed more time between the presentation of the two dot patterns, accuracy in the missing dot task began to rise again. After 1.5 seconds, accuracy was equal to or higher than the accuracy obtained when a very brief period separated the patterns. Moreover, accuracy remained high even after 5 seconds had elapsed between presenting the two patterns. Clearly this is a different form of memory from the short-lived one that permitted temporal integration to occur over 50 to 100 ms. I make this claim for two reasons.

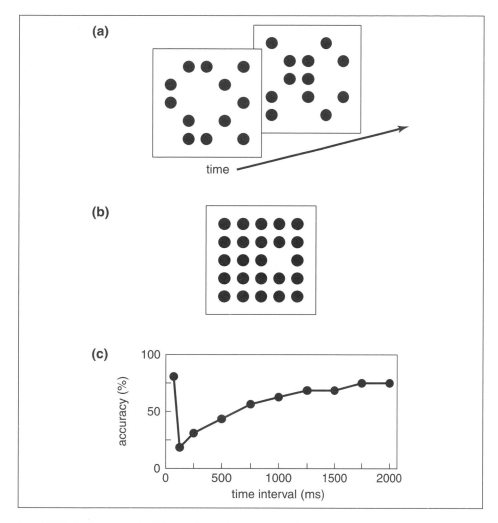

FIGURE 8.7 A method for studying the interaction between visual images and visual precepts. **(a)** Two random dot patterns are flashed briefly, separated by a variable time period. **(b)** If the two patterns are superimposed in space, the missing dot is easy to see. **(c)** Accuracy in reporting the missing dot follows a V-shaped curve, with the initial decline in accuracy being attributable to the decay of visible persistence. The subsequent upswing in accuracy reflects the study participant's ability to compare a mental image of the first pattern with their perception of the second pattern.

First, the memory involved in the long-term "temporal integration" task is capable of surviving a brief interruption in view or a spatial shift in the position of the second pattern. Both factors are detrimental to accuracy in the temporal integration of patterns in the 0- to 100-ms period. Second, there appears to be a limit of about ten on the number of dots that can be remembered for long-term integration. This is a larger number of items than is usually considered as the capacity of short-term visual memory (Chapter 6), but it is smaller than the capacity of visual memory implied by the random photograph studies. A widespread interpretation of this finding on the part of many vision scientists is that our long-term memories of visual scenes reflect a type of *structural description* rather than a *photograph*.

The term *structural description*, when used by vision scientists, can have many meanings, so it is not possible to provide a strict definition by consensus. However, all usages of the term share the idea that visual memory for a scene involves some kind of hierarchical description; that is, an "interpreted" or conceptual understanding of the scene enables it to be categorized at several meaningful levels. An example of a scene and a possible structural description of it are illustrated in Figure 8.8. At the highest level, the scene is recognized as belonging to the general class of doctors' offices. More specifically, in this doctor's office, there is a window covered by blinds on the back wall, cupboards to the right, a cart and a lamp on the left and an examining table and a stool in the center. The examining table consists of a mattress and a base. The stool has a round seat and four legs. This sort of description can go on indefinitely in increasing detail, depending on its purpose. For most purposes, however, a crude analysis involving only the top level is necessary.

From this perspective, the apparent contradiction between our amazing memory for random photographs and our poor memory for details begins to make more sense. When we first encounter a scene, we interpret it in terms of a specific structural description, assigning a level of detail only to the depth required for the task at hand and only to the depth possible given the time restrictions on viewing the scene. One reason we do not need to store the details with great precision is that a subsequent view of the scene will provide a connection between the stored structural description and the details then on view. Provided the structural description does not change between "study" and "test," many details can be changed without our noticing. Indeed, memory is highly adaptive in working in this way, since changes in viewpoint and lighting that occur naturally are usually superficial to the scene's meaning but salient in terms of analyzing the scene on the basis of its features. Attending to feature changes would therefore be counterproductive to understanding the meaning of the scene.

As you can see, visual memory is a complex and poorly understood topic largely because of the bidirectional relationship between vision and memory. Not only are our memories shaped by the processes of vision, but they influence the processes of perception as well. In the sections that follow, we will proceed farther down this "two-way street" by examining the consequences of our past experience in vision.

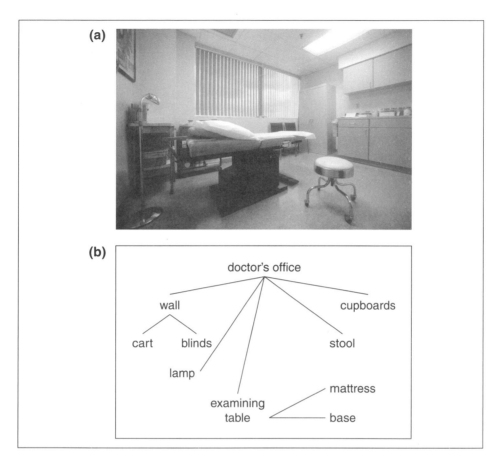

FIGURE 8.8   (a) A photograph of a common scene. (b) A possible *structural description* of the photograph.

VISUAL LEARNING

Priming

Among the simplest tools vision researchers use for studying the consequences of visual experience are experiments on visual *priming*. Priming refers to the fact that once a stimulus has been presented to the eyes, the visual system will respond differently to that stimulus thereafter. Consider newborn infants, who do not orient to a new sight or sound in the same way the second time it is presented. Or consider adult human study participants, whose response in detecting the sudden appearance of a light or tone is delayed or facilitated by a prior occurrence of that event. Priming can even be observed in single neurons by using animal electrophysiology and human brain imaging. Here, the neural response to any event changes significantly in subsequent presentations of that event to the same complex of neurons.

Simple familiarity with a visual object—meaning that the object has been seen but is not associated with any positive or negative consequences—usually results at a neural level in a reduced response to that object on repeated presentations. Neuroscientists say the neural response has been *attenuated* or *habituated* by the prior presentation of the object. The primary consequence of an attenuated response to familiar objects is a heightened response to novel objects. We can think of this as a way for the visual system to keep track of changes in the visual environment. Changes that represent new objects are deserving of closer inspection than those that occur to familiar objects, on the grounds that it is important to evaluate the danger of new objects before completing ongoing tasks involving familiar objects. In this sense, response attenuation for familiar objects represents an evolutionarily early warning system that probably has a high degree of survival value.

When the visually sensitive regions of the brain are compared for the degree to which they show response attenuation to familiar objects, an interesting pattern emerges. There is no region in the brain in which familiar objects produce a larger amount of neural activation than that produced by novel objects. The response to novel objects is invariably greater. This means that all regions are influenced by the familiarity-novelty continuum. However, in some regions the degree of response attenuation is much greater than in others. Roughly speaking, response attenuation for familiar objects increases as one moves up within the anatomical cortical hierarchy from area V1 to the far reaches of the temporal lobe. At the level of area V1, the novelty bias is weakest. It is strongest at the top of the ventral, or "what," pathway in the temporal lobe; it is also very strong at the top of the dorsal, or "where," pathway in the parietal lobe.

The simplest interpretation of this pattern is that learning has its strongest effects at the top of the anatomical hierarchies, where objects and locations are represented in the form that appears to be linked most closely to the way we experience those objects and locations. We should not think, however, that these experiences don't rely on activity in area V1; instead, the memory for these visual experiences is likely stored through neural activity in those regions. At the time we experience familiar objects, re-entrant neural activity will be required to link up these neurons involved in the memory of the object with those neurons responding to the current sensory input from our eyes.

Mere exposure: Emotional rewards of familiarity

Seeing objects repeatedly not only influences our memory and subsequent perception of them, but it also affects the extent to which we "like," or are attracted to, them. In fact, it is fair to say that mere exposure promotes a positive emotional response. Numerous studies have shown that being repeatedly exposed to the same emotionally neutral object, and for no apparent reason, leads participants to choose that object over others in subsequent tests of simple preference. The other "less-liked" objects are not inherently less desirable, as is evident when different groups of participants prefer different subsets of objects, depending on which objects they have seen with the greatest frequency in the recent past.

A recent study by Robert Zajonc and his colleagues (Monahan, Murphy, & Zajonc, 2000) illustrates the power of the mere exposure effect. These researchers selected participants who were not familiar with written Chinese, divided them into two groups, and showed both groups a series of randomly chosen characters, each for a very brief flash. The only difference was that one group saw 25 different characters whereas the other saw 5, each presented five times in random order. When participants filled out a post-study questionnaire that included items regarding their mood, those who had seen 25 novel characters were in a less positive mood than those who had seen only 5, but in repeated presentations. Apparently, mere repetition can elicit a more positive emotional state. But is this positive state linked to the specific characters that each group saw?

This question was addressed in another study by the same researchers. They again compared two groups of participants treated in the same way as in the first study, but this time the groups subsequently rated three kinds of visual items for their emotional appeal: the Chinese characters shown in the initial study phase, novel Chinese characters somewhat similar to those shown in the study phase, and random polygons. The group who received the repeated presentations of 5 characters rated them as more appealing than did the group who saw characters only once. They also rated the somewhat similar but never seen previously characters as more appealing than did participants who saw 25 different characters. Even the latter ratings were more positive than those of participants who never saw any Chinese characters in the study phase. The researchers concluded that mere exposure to an object not only increases the viewer's positive emotional state but also links that state to the specific objects that the viewer saw.

We can think of this link between vision and the emotional appeal of an object in terms of a primitive form of associative learning. In fact, it may be no different from Pavlov's dog, which learned to salivate in response to a ringing bell (a conditioned response) in addition to its natural tendency to salivate in response to food. The ringing bell (the unconditioned stimulus) was paired repeatedly with the presentation of food (the conditioned stimulus), which on its own was able to evoke the salivation response (the unconditioned response). This pairing eventually formed a learned association in the dog's brain between the unconditioned stimulus and the unconditioned response: namely, the bell and the salivation response.

What are the unconditioned stimuli and responses in the mere exposure effect in humans? An initial presentation of a novel object may activate an approach tendency (to explore and learn more) and an avoidance pattern of response (to avoid possible danger). These are unconditioned responses in all organisms with sensory systems. If the consequence of an initial, tentative exploration is that there is no danger, then the approach tendency is strengthened. This may be what is involved in the "imprinting" form of learning exhibited by chicks and goslings.

From this perspective, it may be that the absence of danger following the presentation of a stimulus is rewarding in itself. This would make "absence of danger" an unconditioned stimulus, leading to "pleasure of safety" as the unconditioned response. The experience of safety can certainly be rewarding when compared to the alternative: namely, danger. The repeated presentation of the safe object can therefore be thought of as the conditioned stimulus. If this pairing is self-rewarding because of the relative safety it affords, then the reward can be linked to the content of the stimulus (the conditioned stimulus) that generated the reward in the first place.

Added support for this theory comes from an examination of the links between the release of endorphins in the visual portions of the brain (the body's natural opiate-reward system) and the strength of the novelty response. The novelty response grows stronger as we ascend the anatomical visual hierarchy, following the ventral visual pathway from area V1 to the temporal lobe. But the release of endorphins also tends to be stronger as we ascend this hierarchy. Thus there is (1) more neural activity associated with the novelty response, and (2) a correspondingly stronger release of endorphins. These correlations provide a neural basis for the links among scene recognition, familiarity, and the positive emotional responses associated with the repeated presentation of scenes that are neither noxious nor dangerous. Perhaps someday scientists studying the concepts of visual "beauty" and "aesthetics" will be able to anchor their theories in these basic physiological principles.

Adaptive learning

One of the greatest challenges to the human visual system is that objects, people, locations, and events that are most important to survival and well-being cannot be specified ahead of time—at least not in any detail. Before a baby is born, there is no way to prepare its brain to recognize the particular human faces that will become most important to it in later life. There is no way to prepare its brain to recognize the objects and environments with which that baby will interface. Even after birth, things change. Humans move to new locations, make new friends, and gain new relatives. The visual system must be flexible enough, both at birth and throughout life, to adapt to its surroundings so it can see and remember new objects and people and see and understand new environments.

How is this done? We have seen that the visual systems of all humans are alike in many respects. They incorporate a sensitivity to light of various wavelengths and a propensity to analyze the world through the mechanisms of color vision (Chapter 3), edge detection (Chapter 4), object recognition (Chapter 5), temporal coherence (Chapter 6), and spatial orientation (Chapter 7). But all these mechanisms and commonality only get us so far in answering the question. They don't explain, for example, how after spending a few months in a desert environment humans have an improved ability to discriminate among shades of brown, oatmeal, and tan; or how after becoming skilled in a new activity (such as rock climbing, tennis, or playing the piano) humans can discriminate among certain visual events that novices do not see at all. For example, rock climbers can see indentations and outcroppings in rock that will support their body weight. Non-rock-climbers cannot see them even when they are pointed out. Tennis players can see the direction of spin on the ball as it comes over the net, whereas tennis fans see only the ball's speed. Piano players can "hear" written notes on the page before their fingers elicit those notes on the keyboard.

A hint into the workings of such improved discrimination is evident in an important side effect of being an expert in a given visual domain. In addition to "tuning" the person to the visual features and relations that are important for optimal performance, expertise also involves becoming "untuned" to features and relations that are not needed. It is as though there are limits on how many resources the brain can devote to the visual analysis of a given class of objects. Having tuned itself to being expert at one kind of analysis, it has become less sensitive to other visual features and relations that are present but not necessary for the task at hand. This observation is reminiscent of limits of visual attention in the realm of object perception. Attending to one object or location entails withdrawing attention from other objects and locations. However, in the case of expertise, the consequences of visual selection have a long-term effect on the way the visual system approaches new events.

A vivid example of visual tuning and untuning involves a kind of expertise we all share: face recognition. We are all experts at making subtle distinctions among faces, such that members of our own families seem different from one another even when other people can perceive the family resemblance. It is important to realize that the visual differences among members of a single family are not an "objective truth." Many later-born children in large families store in their memory the numerous times in which teachers and other acquaintances have confused them with an older sister or brother.

On a group level, the consequences of expertise in face recognition can be seen in studies of face perception among races. Our ability to identify and remember faces is better when they are similar to our own racial or ethnic group. A typical way to study this effect involves the new-old recognition task discussed earlier. Imagine being shown 32 pictures of faces you have never seen before, at a steady rate of 1 face every 2 seconds. Sixteen faces are members of your own racial or ethnic group and another 16 are members of a different one. This is the "study" session, and the pictures constitute the "old" faces for the upcoming memory test. In the memory test, you are shown another set of 32 pictures of faces. Within each of the two racial or ethnic groups in this set, 8 faces are ones you saw in the study session and 8 are "new" ones you never saw before. Your task is to indicate whether each face in the memory set is "new" or "old." If you are only guessing, you will be able to get no more than 50 percent of your answers correct.

The phrase *cross-race face deficit* refers to the finding that for many people, accuracy in this test is better for faces in their own racial or ethnic group than for others. It is more difficult for people to see and remember the facial differences of groups other than their own. Keep in mind that this finding cannot be based on racial or ethnic differences in overall face similarity. If that were the case, all people would confuse the faces of some groups more than others. Rather, the finding is that faces of members of groups other than one's own are more easily confused.

What do we miss seeing in the faces of people from other groups that leads to the cross-race face deficit? How has our natural expertise in familiar faces led to a decreased sensitivity to unfamiliar kinds of faces? Don't the faces of people from other groups have more or less the same kinds of visual features and variations as our own? If so, why aren't we equally well tuned to them?

These questions are now being studied by vision scientists who follow an approach that relates to the general principles of object recognition we discussed in Chapter 5. One principle is that recognition for the purposes of *basic level* identification involves a different visual task than recognition for the purposes of *subordinate level* or *superordinate level* identification. At the basic level of identification, we distinguish all objects by their functional classes, such as faces, horses, cars, and trees. At the subordinate level, we distinguish among the faces of "Fred," "George," and "Angela" and among trees such as "fir," "cedar," and "spruce." At the superordinate level, we distinguish among higher-order groupings of objects such as "animal," "plant," "artificial," "natural," and so on. Being an expert on a topic involves approaching the objects in that domain at the subordinate level rather than at either the superordinate or the basic level. Vision scientists are exploring whether the cross-race face deficit is an example of this general principle.

If the cross-race face deficit occurs because we see people from other groups as belonging to "that *group*" and we see people from our own group as belonging to "an *individual* I may know," there should be predictable consequences for laboratory tests of face recognition. For example, for tests in which individual identity is important, faces from other groups should be at a disadvantage. We have already seen this in the new-old face recognition task applied to same- and cross-group faces. However, for other tests, such as those in which membership in the "other group" is important, faces from other groups might be at an advantage in the visual analysis.

A study by Dan Levin (2000) supporting this hypothesis used a visual search task, shown in Figure 8.9, in which participants searched either for (1) a face of their own racial group among faces from another group, or (2) a face of another racial group among faces from their own group. Before the testing session, all faces were equated on display qualities of overall luminance and shape distinctiveness. On average, the participants' search was fastest and most accurate when the target was a cross-race face; faces from other racial groups "stand out" when seen among faces of our own group, whereas those of our own group do not stand out in the same way in the company of faces from other groups. Scientists who study visual search call this phenomenon *search asymmetry*. It is an indication that the target stands out because the viewer's visual system marks it as containing an unusual feature. Because the faces in such studies are carefully controlled for differences in average luminance and shape distinctiveness, the unusual feature must be one that is labeled as such by the viewer's visual system.

Other evidence consistent with this interpretation arises from the finding that not all participants show a cross-race effect, either in the new-old recognition task or in the visual search task. This finding is interesting because performance on the two tasks is correlated, with the same participants who show a cross-race *deficit* in recognition also showing a cross-race *advantage* in visual search. Thus the additional visual features they use when they see cross-race faces—features that identify those faces as belonging to the "other" category—can influence participants' vision negatively or positively, depending on the task.

How permanent is the cross-race effect? Several studies have shown that after a few hours of training with faces from another group, the cross-race effect disappears in most participants. This finding is also consistent with the idea that expertise in face recognition among members of your own group does not mean that an entirely different set of facial features is used in the recognition of faces from your own or another group. Instead, over and above the features you have learned to use in recognizing faces, there are additional features—probably at the basic level of object recognition—that you have learned to use whenever you encounter a face from another group. As familiarity with individuals from those groups increases, the cross-race effect seems to disappear. According to the basic versus subordinate level of distinction, increased familiarity removes the basic level of identification from the recognition process you now use to see those individuals. This is consistent with the reports of many people who associate frequently with people of other racial or ethnic groups; they often claim they no longer "see" the skin color or group-specific features of those individuals.

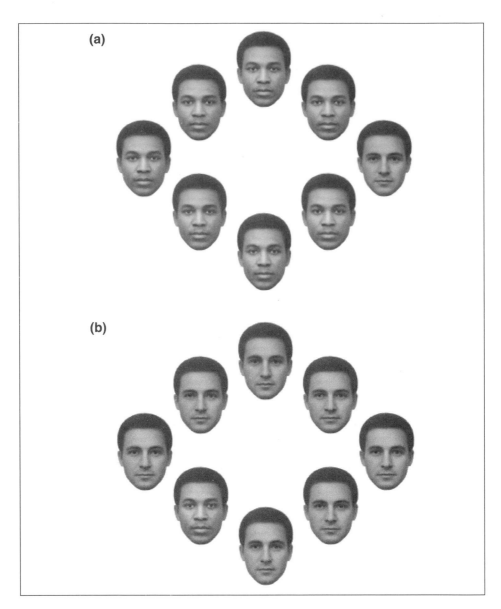

FIGURE 8.9 A sample visual search display from a study in which participants tried to find a target face as quickly as possible. **(a)** Same-race target: The target face was from the same racial group as the participants, whereas the distractor faces were from another racial group. **(b)** Cross-race target: The target face was from a different racial group from the participants, whereas the distractor faces were from the same racial group.

How does expertise change the brain?

Although experts see certain features of objects and relations in visual scenes that non-experts do not, it is not easy to determine the precise ways in which expertise has changed the brain. The traditional approach assumes that the lowest levels of the visual system are the most fixed, permanent, and universal across individuals, whereas the highest levels are the most influenced by experience. In this view, the sensory information that the brain works with in the cortical visual areas is always the same, regardless of training, culture, and experience. The later-developing regions of the brain—such as the frontal and parietal lobes—are responsible for the different perceptions and responses that develop with expertise.

It is not hard to see how such a view might hold sway among vision scientists. It has a comfortable familiarity with the classical approach in the physical sciences, whereby a vast array of higher-order chemical reactions can be explained in terms of the combinations of a small number of basic elements. It also reconciles the rich experience of conscious perception with the seeming inflexibility in the behavior of single neurons when examined by means of electrophysiological techniques. (At least, these neurons seemed relatively inflexible in the reports that followed Hubel and Wiesel's initial discoveries, as we discussed in Chapter 4.) Flexibility in the brain, called *plasticity* by neuroscientists, could also be understood through the metaphor of a hierarchy wherein adaptability increased as one went to the top.

Despite its appeal, this view of the learning brain has not taken firm hold among researchers studying the influence of experience and training on vision. The chief obstacle has been the results from thousands of experiments. Early on, these experiments largely consisted of behavioral measurements, but increasingly they have been joined by studies of electrophysiology in animals and brain imaging in humans. Results have shown that when an individual develops a new visual skill, its consequences can be felt and measured all the way down to the lowest levels of the visual brain.

For example, in numerous studies participants underwent thousands of trials on the most mundane, albeit difficult, visual discriminations. A typical learning phase involved hour upon hour of discriminating between two bars that differed only subtly in orientation, in one region of the vision field, and seen only by a single eye. The main result was that the learning that occurred was narrowly confined to the conditions under which it was acquired. The same discrimination tests on a different pair of orientations, or in a different visual field location, or for the eye that had not received the original training, showed no benefits of the learning. The benefits of training were for a small range of conditions that differed only slightly from conditions used in the learning phase.

Researchers Meerav Ahissar and Shaul Hochstein (Ahissar & Hochstein, 1997) have shown that this finding is in sharp contrast to the effects of training on easy visual discriminations. Participants who have spent time in training to make a general discrimination—say, detecting a large difference in orientation—demonstrate correspondingly general learning effects in tests following the training. Training in the easy tasks generalizes to other easy discriminations of targets and visual locations for which participants were not trained. The easy kind of visual training even helps in subsequent learning of difficult discriminations. The principle is that train-ing on easy tasks benefits a wide range of performance, whereas training on hard tasks has benefits specific to the tasks.

Many of our own experiences in learning skilled tasks corroborate this conclu-sion. For example, learning to play the easy scales on a musical instrument has benefits for playing difficult pieces. Learning to play a single difficult musical piece exclusively, however, provides little benefit for playing other difficult pieces on the same instrument.

Learning influences the single neuron

The recent development of sophisticated electrophysiological techniques has en-abled neuroscientists to measure the visually guided behavior of monkeys while recording the activity of individual neurons in the monkeys' brains. This has en-abled the scientists to answer questions that recently were considered unanswer-able: for instance, *how is the behavior of an individual neuron changed after the participant—in this case, a monkey—has learned a new visual skill?*

In a study by Natasha Sigala and Nikos Logothetis (2002), monkeys were trained to discriminate between two kinds of fish, as shown in Figure 8.10. The drawings of the fish varied on four dimensions of shape—dorsal fin, tail, ventral fin, and mouth shape—but for each monkey tested, a different pair of shape di-mensions was relevant to the discrimination. For example, one monkey had to cat-egorize fish on the basis of dorsal fin and tail and ignore equal but irrelevant variations in ventral fin and mouth. All the monkeys learned to sort the fish until they could do so with almost perfect accuracy.

Once the categories had been learned, single neurons were identified in the in-ferior temporal lobe of each monkey that responded selectively to the drawings. Then the researchers examined more closely the firing patterns of the neurons to determine whether the patterns differed significantly according to the presence of each shape dimension. This analysis isolated certain neurons that had a reliably dif-ferent firing pattern, depending on which features were present. A majority of these neurons were selective for one of the diagnostic visual features the monkey had used to classify the fish and not selective for the non-diagnostic features. Thus the neurons had become part of a larger network that was sensitive to the rele-vance of visual features in the task. Bear in mind that these neurons were not merely responding to the diagnostic features because they were prewired as detec-tors for them. If that were the case, the experiment would have produced these re-sults for only some visual features and in only some monkeys. Rather, the pattern occurred across different monkeys and regardless of which features served as the basis of the object categorization task.

Results such as these indicate that the behavior of neurons in the temporal lobe is shaped by the nature of the visual task. We can no longer think of the receptive

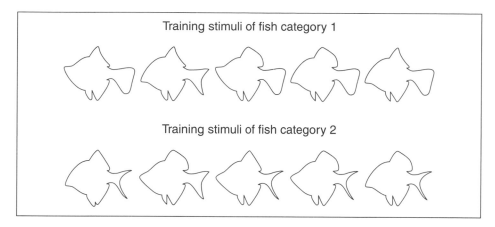

FIGURE 8.10 Fish that vary on several visual dimensions. Monkeys were trained to discriminate these drawings by using different subsets of features.

fields in these neurons as representing fixed templates that are assembled in different ways to recognize objects. A more accurate characterization is that the brain is being changed by the environment and by the tasks it has to perform.

The neural basis of face expertise

Our expertise for recognizing human faces is evident in certain measures of brain function. Of long-standing significance in this regard is a highly specific form of brain damage—occurring at the junction of the occipital and temporal lobes, most often on the right side—that leaves the individual with a profound inability to recognize well-known people on the basis of visual appearance. This condition is *prosopagnosia*. A "pure" prosopagnosic demonstrates object recognition that is accurate in all respects except for the ability to identify an individual on the basis of vision alone; however, the prosopagnosic *is* able to identify the individual on the basis of voice or touch.

In healthy study participants with no brain damage, this region of the cortex shows activity in brain imaging studies that isolate face recognition from other forms of object recognition. This region is close to a cortical landmark called the *fusiform gyrus*, which some scientists have begun to call the *fusiform face area*, or FFA. Its location is shown in Figure 8.11. It is as close as vision scientists have come to identifying a region of the brain devoted to a single function.

This close link between behavior (face recognition) and a neural module (the FFA) has given vision scientists the unique opportunity to ask questions such as *What makes face perception special when compared with other forms of object recognition that are not as closely linked to a specific brain area?* and *Is this region of the brain*

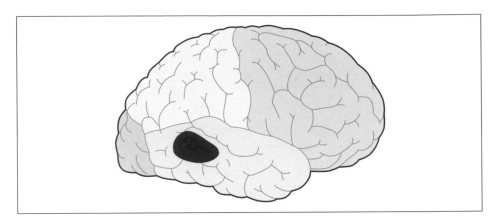

FIGURE 8.11   The fusiform face area, also known as FFA, in humans.

devoted only to face perception, or is it involved in other forms of object recognition for which prolonged training has occurred? Research indicates that face perception is special—not in an innate, "hardwired" sense but in that it involves object perception for a unique combination of visual conditions. First, because the distinctions in shape among faces are subtle, considerable learning and expertise are required. Second, faces must usually be discriminated at a subordinate (i.e., individual people such as "Bob") rather than basic (i.e., faces of people versus other objects such as chairs) level of description. Third, the distinctions among faces involve configurations and spatial relations among features, rather than hard-to-discriminate features. The latter characteristic is often referred to as *holistic perception.*

The important role of expertise in the neural activity of the FFA is evident in studies using non-human faces and non-faces as stimuli. For example, in one study (Haxby et al., 2001) the FFA responded to cat faces, although the response was not as large as for human faces. Damage to the FFA in some individuals reportedly reduces a preexisting familiarity with certain stimuli: (1) pictures of individual mountain peaks (in an experienced mountain climber) and (2) pictures of individual cows in a personal herd (in a dairy farmer with similar brain damage).

The most direct evidence of the importance of expertise in establishing a specific neural response in the FFA comes from studies in which participants become experts, during the course of the experiment, in an artificial class of objects. Michael Tarr and his colleagues (Tarr & Gauthier, 2000) designed a unique collection of never-before-seen objects affectionately known as Greebles. Several are shown in Figure 8.12. Once the objects are learned well enough such that participants can categorize them accurately into "family" or "gender" groupings, the FFA response measured with brain imaging techniques is similar in many ways to the response for the perception of human faces.

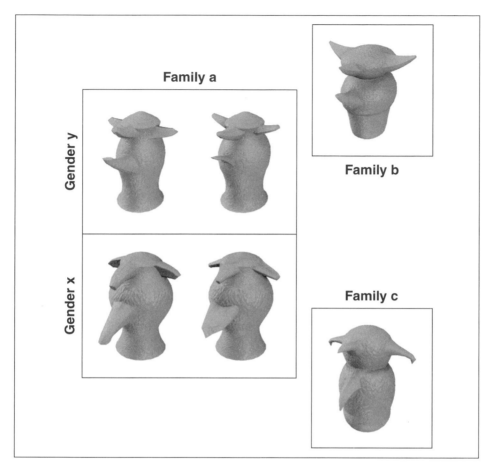

FIGURE 8.12   Artificial objects, called Greebles, that are used in studies of the role of expertise and configurational properties in visual learning. Greebles have features that are used to define families (a, b, c) and genders (x and y).

The behavioral consequences of learning about Greebles are also similar to those for human faces. For instance, face perception is sensitive to a well-known *configurational effect*: Study participants recognize a part of an individual's face (e.g., "Bob's nose") faster when it is shown in the context of Bob's face than when it is shown inside a scrambled or distorted version of his face. An important finding is that the configurational effect does not occur when the same faces are shown upside down or when non-face objects (e.g., houses containing doors and windows) are tested. Yet when Greebles are learned to a high level of accuracy, they produce the same configurational effects as well-known human faces.

Another measure of brain activity that is very sensitive to the perception of faces is an early component of the averaged brain waves derived from event-related potential (ERP) recordings. It appears between 100 and 200 ms after a face is presented to healthy participants who have been asked to discriminate or identify faces, but not when they have been asked to inspect pictures of other ordinary natural and artificial objects. The brain waves of individuals with prosopagnosia also fail to show this component.

A recent study by James Tanaka and colleagues (Tanaka & Curran, 2001) used the ERP signature of face perception to test participants who were longstanding experts of either birds or dogs. Participants had the task of identifying both types of animals in a variety of photographs. Sometimes they had to indicate whether the object was an animal (superordinate categorization); at other times they simply had to indicate whether the animal was a bird or a dog (basic level categorization); and at other times they had to identify the subspecies to the best of their ability (subordinate level categorization). Testing two kinds of expert participants on animals that were both within and outside their realm of expertise ensured that any differences in identification or associated brain activity could not be attributed to peculiarities of the testing materials.

The results showed that each group of experts produced a "face-like" set of ERP signals in response to pictures of the animals with which they were highly familiar. Dog trainers who were very familiar with different breeds of dogs generated ERP signals like those of ordinary individuals inspecting a human face. The same was true for birders categorizing pictures of birds. Yet when the pictures were outside the participants' realm of expertise, the signal was no longer present. Another important feature of the results was that the same signals occurred for a wide variety of questions the participants were asked to answer. This finding indicates that the brain activity being measured was not a function of the kind of recognition task the participant was performing; rather, it is consistent with a change in the brain that occurs because of the participants' expertise. Thus scientists wonder whether the specialty accorded to face perception in the brain is indeed innate or whether it occurs because of the important role faces play in our well-being and survival. We may be experts in face perception not by virtue of our biology, which has a hard time guessing which faces will be important to us, but out of sheer necessity. From the moment we are born, recognizing faces and facial expressions is central to our very survival.

Even imprinting is flexible!

Most of us know what *imprinting* is. We think of it as a form of learning that evolutionarily "simple" animals undertake to tune their visual system during a "critical period" in development so that they can recognize an important caregiver or food provider. This view of imprinting has become popular through the stories in introductory psychology textbooks, most of which refer to the ethologist Konrad Lorenz, who raised ducklings that followed him around a farmyard simply because he was the first living thing they had encountered when emerging from their eggs. More recently, the popular film *Fly Away Home* used the concept of imprinting in its depiction of an eccentric biologist and his daughter, who raised Canadian geese that followed an ultralight aircraft. Because of the biologist's success in imprinting the goslings on the aircraft, he was able to teach them to migrate south for the winter—something the last few generations of Canadian geese had begun neglecting to do.

In this view, imprinting is a highly adaptive form of learning because it permits a newborn to acquire a visual object detector that is appropriate for its survival. With the exception of a few ethologists and one biologist with an ultralight aircraft, the object detector gets tuned to the newborn's mother or some other animal that serves as the mother. In fact, "mother substitution" stories regularly appear in the popular press. Within the last month of this writing, there was a poignant story about a lioness in Africa that had taken to mothering a recently orphaned fawn. As far as the biologists observing both animals could tell, an imprinting process had occurred for both the lioness and the fawn. (In this case it turned out to be much less than adaptive for the fawn, which was killed and eaten after a few days by another lion in the pride.)

The complementary side of this view of imprinting is that once acquired, the visual object detector is applied in a rather rigid way. Baby chicks will come running at the sight of a cardboard cutout that resembles the mother hen. Gull chicks will peck for seeds near a stick decorated with a red dot, simply because their mother has a similar dot on her bill. This is where the conventional discussion of imprinting usually ends: It's a form of learning that not only is highly adaptive to the animal's environment but also, once acquired, produces a "template" that is rigidly and crudely applied to the learned collection of visual features regardless of the context. As such, it is easy to think of imprinting as a form of learning that has "evolutionary" or "survival" value for simple organisms, but not as a form of learning that applies to complex visual systems such as our own.

Vision scientists are beginning to discover that both assumptions are wrong. Simple animals are *not* rigid and context-independent in their application of imprinting, and human visual learning of many kinds *does* resemble imprinting in its early stages. One way to reconcile these new insights is through the proposition that imprinting is a "first step" in many kinds of learning. Perhaps a new object template must be set up in the visual system before that template can be made context- and task-sensitive. Let's begin by considering what we know about the way young animals take context into account in their visual learning.

Peak shifts in learning

A day-old chick will approach a wide variety of conspicuous objects, even pictures on a touch-sensitive screen at one end of the pen. Brightly colored squares, pictures of seeds, and images of candidate mother hens can all be presented on the screen and the behavior of the newborn chicks can be monitored, including pecks at the screen. This provides a convenient way for scientists to study imprinting and learning in young chicks in a way that is both natural (the chicks engage in behavior that they normally would anyway) and systematic (the experimenter controls the pictures, their timing, and their relationship to the chicks' behavior).

Any spontaneous tendency on the part of the chicks to approach or avoid the pictures on the screen is soon magnified by the chicks in a self-regulating way. If the experimenter increases the exposure time for the pictures that initially elicit a small 'approach' tendency from the chicks, then the chicks respond by approaching this picture even more. For pictures that initially elicit a small 'avoid' tendency in the chicks, the opposite occurs. Thus the initial phase of imprinting seems to take care of itself, through the subtle opposing tendencies on the part of the chicks to explore novel objects and to avoid danger.

The spontaneous tendencies are also easy for the experimenter to manipulate. For instance, if one of two pictures is consistently paired with a reward, such as a puff of warm air, and the other is not, then the rewarded picture soon takes on the role of "imprinted" mother. But a chick's learning, and the modification of its visual brain, don't end there. This is evident if the chick is tested on pictures that are systematically different from the ones it learned during the imprinting phase. To understand this, let's assume that the imprinted picture is a blue rectangle (slightly taller than wide) and the foil picture (unrewarded in training and therefore no longer approached by the chick in tests) is a blue square. What will happen when we now test the chick on a series of rectangles, ranging from one that is much taller than the original rectangle to one that is much flatter than the original square? The chick will demonstrate a *peak shift*: Its most preferred picture will be a rectangle that is more extreme than the imprinted one. The chick will essentially prefer a "super" rectangle in the sense that it is an extreme or cartoon version of the original stimulus.

On the basis of the results, some scientists might say that the chick has learned a "concept" in the course of imprinting. In this case the concept seems to be "tallness," which is relational, rather than the absolute template for a specific rectangle one might assume, based on the standard understanding of imprinting. Proof of this concept is evident in additional tests in which a restricted set of rectangles is again presented, this time ranging from the square at one extreme to even flatter rectangles at the other. The chick now prefers the square over the other alternative "mothers." Clearly, the chick's brain has learned the relevant feature dimension for its "mother," which in this case is height, and it tries to find instances of the "mother" in which this feature is most evident. The template is therefore not a particular photograph-like image of the mother, but more likely a "shopping list" of important features. We might even call this a *structural description*.

Flexible imprinting in humans

The ability of humans to form visual templates of new objects, much as a newborn chick forms a template of its mother, is only the tip of the iceberg in visual learning. With even small amounts of experience in recognizing objects, we soon begin to adjust and fine-tune those templates so that we place more importance on the highly diagnostic features of the object and less importance on its incidental features. We also begin to keep track of correlations between certain environmental conditions and the diagnostic importance of certain features of the object. Vision scientists refer to this process of creating structure out of visual experiences as *unitization*. The term refers to the effective units in our visual experience that we treat "as one."

For many well-known objects, it is easy to establish the visual units that form the basis of our perception. The parts of a bicycle, for example, are its frame, wheels, handlebars, and seat. Each unit could be decomposed further, depending on our purpose in analyzing the bicycle. However, one of the practical problems in research on visual unitization is the possibility of preexisting units, gained through evolution or personal experience, that can be used to perform a task. To get around this problem, some scientists have designed artificial stimulus sets in which the units that are relevant to the task could not preexist in the set of visual templates formed by the participants.

Figure 8.13 shows a variety of artificial objects that consist of a semicircular lower curve bounding a jagged upper edge made up of five distinct and replaceable short segments. There are a total of ten possible segments that can occupy each of the five locations in an object; thus if sampling occurs without replacement, there could be a total of 30,240 ($10 \times 9 \times 8 \times 8 \times 6$) different objects in this artificial world.

In a study by Robert Goldstone (2000), participants saw these objects on a computer screen, one at a time, and tried to categorize them as quickly as possible into one of two groups. The rule for one of these tasks is shown in Figure 8.13, where object ABCDE belongs in Category 1 and the other five objects belong in Category 2. Note that participants could not see the letters shown in the figure. To be accurate in this task, all five segments had to be inspected. If even one of them was missed, it might mean that an object from Category 2 would be mistakenly assigned to Category 1. The results showed steady and significant improvements in the speed of decision making over several hundred training trials.

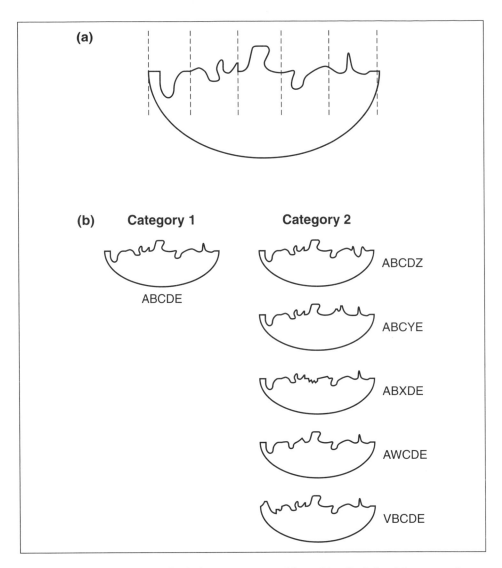

FIGURE 8.13 (a) An artificial object consisting of five arbitrarily defined "segments," where each segment is the jagged edge shown between the dotted reference lines. There are ten possible parts in all, and each part has been assigned a label: A, B, C, D, E, V, W, X, Y, Z. (b) Objects can be assigned to categories. In this example, only one object (ABCDE) is assigned to Category 1, and the others are assigned to Category 2. Each object in Category 2 differs by only one segment from the object in Category 1. This means that in order to correctly classify ABCDE, each of its segments must be identified as appearing in its correct location.

But what had the participants learned? An important clue came from comparing this task with a similar one in which only *one* segment, rather than all five, was relevant to distinguishing between Categories 1 and 2. In this task, there were no improvements in decision-making speed over the same number of training trials. This suggests that participants in the first task were forming visual templates that included two or more segments as a connected, higher-order "part" of the object in Category 1.

To test this hypothesis, researchers used the same five segments to define Category 1, but this time the segments could appear in random order within the object. Thus DEBAC and EACDB were now also members of Category 1. The results again showed no improvement in accuracy with training, consistent with the theory that participants in the original task had learned to see higher-order "parts" in the object in Category 1. In this task, consistent and predictive parts could never be formed because all five segments might appear in any order.

Allowing two diagnostic segments of the object to be interspersed with a randomly chosen nondiagnostic segment also did not lead to improvements in accuracy over time. Apparently, the template formed through learning could not accept interchangeable "parts" intervening among the critical parts.

Finally, in experiments in which the number of contiguous diagnostic segments systematically varied from one to five (as in the first task), the size of the improvement over time in decision-making speed increased as a direct function of the number of diagnostic segments required to make the decision. Not only was the training effect greater for objects with more critical segments, but the time over which the improvements occurred was also greater.

One important lesson from these experiments on visual unitization is that the process of forming visual templates is very different from that of developing photographic film. Although it takes no longer to process and develop a photo of a crowd than a photo of an individual, it does take longer for the visual brain to construct templates of objects that are complex (i.e., that have a large number of diagnostic features) than templates of simple objects. Once they have been constructed, the two kinds of templates may be applied to the visual world equally quickly, but that end result hides all the mental work that went into the construction of the template in the first place.

In another series of experiments by Robert Goldstone (2003), designed to probe the inner workings of visual learning, participants were trained to sort sixteen faces into two categories. These faces, shown in Figure 8.14, were designed by creating digital composites, or morphs, of two or more faces. Each face appeared on a computer screen, one at a time, and participants had to decide if it was a member of one group or another. For example, in a training task, participants learned to sort the faces into two groups according to the category boundary denoted by the solid line in Figure 8.14. After they could do this with a high level of accuracy, they switched to a second task involving a different boundary. The boundaries differed only in that the face category was shifted by either 90 degrees or 45 degrees, as shown in Figure 8.14 by the dashed lines.

The participants who switched to the category boundary differing by 90 degrees had a much easier time learning the new rule than those who switched to a

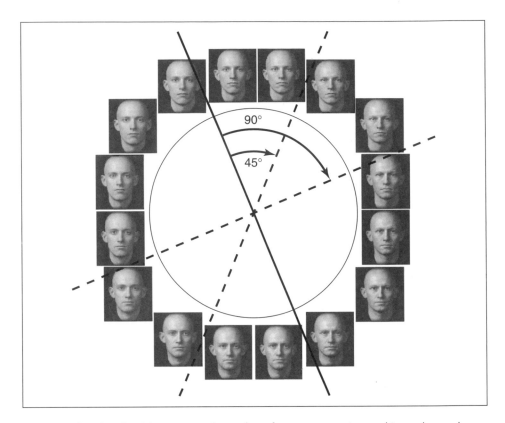

FIGURE 8.14   Participants were shown these faces, one at a time and in random order, and had to sort them into two groups of eight. In a training task, participants sorted the faces according to the category boundary represented by the solid line. In a second task, they sorted the same face according to the category boundary represented by either of the dashed lines. Transferring to a decision rule that differed from the original by 90 degrees was easier than transferring to one that differed by only 45 degrees.

boundary differing by only 45 degrees. This is surprising for two reasons. First, simply using the original decision rule should have given a higher level of initial accuracy in the second task when the category boundary was shifted by only 45 degrees. Six of the eight faces in each of the old categories would still be correctly identified. In contrast, only four of the eight faces would retain their category membership when the boundary shifted by 90 degrees. Simply predicting performance transfer according to the number of faces that had to be reassigned to different categories leads to a predicted result opposite to the one that occurred.

Second, category boundaries differing by 90 degrees in this set of faces are completely incompatible in terms of the dimensions being used to sort faces into categories. If we call the diagnostic visual dimension in the first task "A," whatever it is, and we call the task-irrelevant visual dimension "B," whatever it is, then a 90-degree shift in the decision rule means that A becomes irrelevant and B becomes diagnostic. This should produce maximum confusion if learning involves focusing attention on certain visual dimensions and ignoring others. Learning about a 45-degree shift in the category boundary, on the other hand, should produce less confusion because partial continuity remains between the previously attended and unattended dimensions.

Vision scientists interpret these results to mean that visual learning involves more than simply attending to the visual features relevant for a given task; rather, it involves analyzing the relations among objects. Having performed this analysis, participants not only are able to attend to relevant features for a given task but also are able to transfer the analysis to a new task. The templates learned in the formation of a new visual category contain information about the dimensional structure of the objects in that category in addition to information about how these dimensions should be attended to in a given situation. Vision scientists describe this form of attention as *weighting* visual dimensions appropriately for the task at hand.

PROBLEM SOLVING BY VISUAL SIMULATION

A puzzling consequence of damage to a visual area in the brain is that the effects extend well beyond seeing and recognizing objects and events. For instance, people who have an agnosia for certain classes of objects (e.g., faces, artificial objects, animals) because of damage to a specific brain region often also report difficulty forming mental images of those objects they can no longer see or recognize. This is not surprising, given that imagination and vision largely make use of the same neural equipment. More interesting is that these people also experience difficulty in solving what appear to be simple "conceptual" problems involving objects for which they are blind.

For example, if a person who has difficulty recognizing common fruits is asked *Is an orange smaller than a cantaloupe?* he may have difficulty answering even though he has no trouble indicating verbally that he understands what an orange and a cantaloupe are and what their distinctive features are. He will also likely have no trouble responding to other questions of factual knowledge that are of equal difficulty for healthy people, such as *Does the U.S. government function with a two- or three-party system?* The specific impairment in the ability to see and form mental images of certain objects has restricted the agnosic's ability to answer simple factual questions about those objects. It is as if the inability to visualize certain objects has a direct influence on his ability to think about those objects in the most basic of ways. In many cases, conceptual knowledge may be grounded in the stored visual information about the objects we "know."

This theory was recently studied by Lawrence Barsalou and colleagues (Barsalou, Solomon, & Wu, 1999). They tested typical college students by asking them to generate words describing properties of a verbal concept under one of three conditions. The concept of "lawn" is an example of a stimulus word in the experiment. One group of participants was instructed to form vivid mental images of "lawn" before trying to generate any descriptive words. We can call this the *mental imagery* group. A second group was asked to describe the characteristics that are typically true of the concept of "lawn." Because these participants received neither explicit "imagery" nor "conceptual" instructions, we can call them the *neutral* group. A third group was asked to say all the words and ideas that came immediately to mind when they first heard the word "lawn." We can call them the *word association* group.

The main prediction was that when participants in the neutral group first heard "lawn" they would immediately begin mentally picturing a lawn on the basis of previous visual experience. They would actually be imagining a specific lawn, in a particular setting, viewed from a certain perspective. As participants consulted their mental image they would first notice global features (e.g., overall size) and surface features (e.g., color, texture) of the scene, and then more detailed features (e.g., individual blade shape) and contextual properties (e.g., surrounding and background objects). If the prediction was correct, then participants in the neutral group would give responses very similar to those of participants in the mental imagery group, who were explicitly instructed to imagine specific scenes involving "lawn." Their responses would also differ quite a lot from those of participants in the word association group, who were instructed to retrieve words (i.e., concepts) associated with "lawn."

The verbal responses of all three participant groups were carefully analyzed, using procedures in which the experimenters did not know the originating group membership of the words being coded. For example, with "lawn" as the concept, the response *plant* was coded as a taxonomic category, *blades* as an entity property, *you play on it* as a situational property, and *makes me feel good* as an introspective property. Within these broad categories, each property was further assigned to one of thirty-seven pre-designated categories. For example, *plant* was coded as a superordinate category, *blades* as an external component of an entity, *you play on it* as a situational action, and *makes me feel good* as an evaluative introspection. These analyses showed that the neutral group responded very much like the mental imagery group (whose reports largely referred to visually accessible features) and very differently from the word association group (whose reports featured a greater mix of conceptual knowledge). Thus the neutral group apparently formed images spontaneously in order to perform their task.

This interpretation was supported by results derived from another condition. Whereas some participants in each group were asked to respond to the concept of "lawn," another set of participants in each group received "rolled-up lawn" as the stimulus. The prediction was that if participants' ability to reveal conceptual knowledge were influenced by the visual characteristics of their imagination, then "rolled-up lawn" would elicit different responses from "lawn," specifically because under each stimulus different characteristics of "lawn" are made visible and others are selectively hidden. The test results confirmed this prediction. Participants in the neutral and mental imagery groups mentioned features such as *dirt* and *roots* more frequently and *green* and *blades* less frequently. Control concepts such as "snake" and "rolled-up snake," which do not differ as greatly in their visual characteristics, also revealed correspondingly fewer differences in elicited responses.

In general, Barsalou's team found that subtle changes in the modifiers used with a stimulus word had significant consequences on the kinds of thoughts elicited by participants. For example, the stimulus "comfortable car" elicited perceptual properties related to the interior, whereas "shiny car" elicited properties on the exterior. The modifying words seem to serve as cues to the mental simulations we construct, based on our past experiences with related concepts.

We even use these past experiences in creative ways to build mental images of objects or events we have never experienced. For example, if the stimulus word is "glass car," our responses will be consistent with a mental image that assumes the appearance of a see-through automobile—something it is unlikely we have actually seen. Yet our response would be based on visual experiences we actually have had. When an existing mental image is not available for a phrase composed of familiar words, we can nevertheless productively construct a suitable mental image from our existing visual memories.

Research on ideas or concepts, measured by verbal responses, shows that our experience of the world through vision governs our thoughts about those ideas or concepts. Physical transformations of objects are mimicked in our imagination such that actual physical shifts in objects' orientation, position, and size have analogous consequences when we simply imagine these shifts taking place. The time required to mentally rotate objects in three dimensions is directly related to the time required to physically manipulate those objects. In the world of conceptual knowledge and problem solving, a related principle seems to be that the cognitive effort involved in solving a problem can be related to the physical effort involved in undergoing the corresponding transformations in the real world. This is why describing the imaginary interior of a "convertible car that you are standing beside" is so much easier than describing the imaginary interior of a "car with tinted windows that you are viewing at a distance." At a conceptual level, there is no reason why the interior of a car with tinted windows should be any harder to describe. We can only conclude that much of our thinking relies on our internal eye.

LIMITS OF THE IMAGINATION

The philosopher Thomas Hobbes wrote in 1651, "There is no conception in man's mind which hath not at first, totally or in parts, been begotten by the organs of sense." The biologist Charles Darwin wrote in 1874, "The imagination is one of the highest prerogatives of man. By this faculty he unites former images and ideas, independently of the will, and thus creates brilliant and novel results."

In this chapter we have seen that our imagination owes much to our visual system. The close relationship between vision and thought gives us insights into both the limitations and the strengths of our imaginative abilities. On the one hand, we have seen that our ability to remember, learn, and imagine is often closely tied to recent visual experiences we have had. On the other hand, we have also seen that our visual imagination sometimes helps us think in ways that go far beyond what we have already seen. This ability of our visual system to "go beyond" its own experiences will be surprising to us if we have persisted in thinking of our visual system as a passive and faithful recorder of reality. However, if we have taken the lessons of this book seriously and have come to understand that every aspect of our visual system is designed to "go beyond" the physical stimulus presented to the eye, then this creative aspect of our imagination is less surprising. In fact, our visual imaginative abilities can be properly understood as yet another facet of the general tendency to construct visual reality in such a way as to improve our adaptation to our environment.

FURTHER READING

Behrmann, M. (2000). The mind's eye mapped onto the brain's matter. *Current Directions in Psychological Science, 9*, 50–54.

Gauthier, I., Tarr, M. J., Anderson, A. W., Skudlarski, P., & Gore, J. C. (1999). Activation of the middle fusiform "face area" increases with expertise in recognizing novel objects. *Nature Neuroscience, 2*, 568–573.

Rouw, R., Kosslyn, S. M., & Hamel, R. (1997). Detecting high-level and low-level properties in visual images and visual percepts. *Cognition, 63*, 209–226.

Sarris, V. (1994). Contextual effects in animal psychophysics: Comparative perception. *Behavioral and Brain Sciences, 17*, 763–764.

Solomon, K. O., & Barsalou, L. W. (2001). Representing properties locally. *Cognitive Psychology, 43*, 129–169.

Tootell, R. B. H., Hadjikhani, N. K., Mendola, J. D., Marrett, S., & Dale, A. M. (1998). From retinotopy to recognition: fMRI in human visual cortex. *Trends in Cognitive Sciences, 2*, 174–183.

Zajonc, R. B. (2001). Mere exposure: A gateway to the subliminal. *Current Directions in Psychological Science, 10*, 224–228.

9 CONSCIOUSNESS

- Why can't we see our eyes move when we look at ourselves in the mirror?
- How is it possible to act on the basis of visual information without ever seeing it?
- Can subliminal advertising really influence what people buy?
- Do we really see the "forest" before the "trees"?
- How do our expectations change what we see?
- Is it possible to study the contents of private experience in a scientific way?

POINTING THE WAY

Try to imagine a laboratory version of a task you perform many times each day. The task involves using your arm and finger to point to a target somewhere in your visual field. You do this when you point out an interesting object for someone else to look at, when you press an elevator button, and when you move your hand to make contact with the ball in many sports. In a modern laboratory equipped to study visually guided action sequences of this kind, one version of this task has been simplified so that only two visual signals are involved and movement of your arm can be measured along a single direction.

Now imagine that you are the participant in an experiment of this kind. The session begins with you sitting in a chair, looking down at a table on which a computer mouse rests comfortably in your right hand. The computer will record each movement of the mouse. You are wearing special goggles that monitor where your eyes are looking at all times. The onset of a small light at the center of the table is your signal to bring the mouse to the "home" position under the light. Once your hand has found the central position, only a second or so will pass before a second light appears suddenly to your left on the table. Your job now is to move the mouse to the location of the new light as quickly as possible. Figure 9.1 illustrates these conditions.

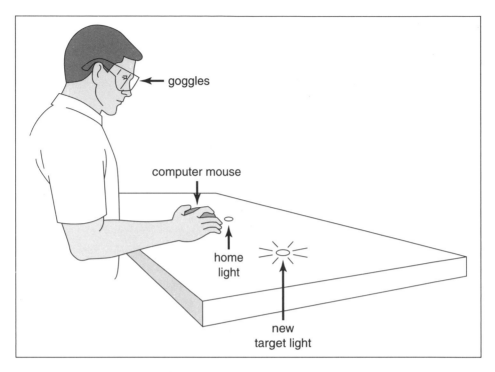

FIGURE 9.1   A typical laboratory set-up for studying visually guided action.

As you perform repetitions of this task, you may begin to daydream and be startled by the experimenter's voice informing you that you have successfully completed fifty movements and that the session is over. As you can tell from imagining the scene, this task would require very little effort on your part and each movement would take less than a second to perform. Nonetheless, it is a complex task for your brain and muscles to perform, and researchers are only beginning to understand the sophisticated brain processes used to orchestrate it. The task also turns out to be a very effective way to separately study some of those visual processes of which you are consciously aware and those of which you are not conscious at all.

Let's first consider what is known about visually guided action from careful measurements of the movement sequences in this task. The first action that occurs in response to the light shining on the table is not a movement of the hand, as you might suspect, but a rapid movement of the eye in the general direction of the light. This occurs because the eye weighs much less than the arm, so its muscles can initiate a movement faster than the arm's stronger but larger muscles. The first eye movement (also known as a *saccade* because it involves a rapid jump in space; see Chapter 5) is quickly followed by a second saccade that brings the target light into focus at the center of your eyes. The second saccade is often called a *corrective saccade* because it hones in on the precise location of the target light. Its primary purpose is to bring the high-resolution center of the eye, the fovea (Chapter 2), in line with the target light, thereby enabling the arm to be guided precisely to the target location.

Figure 9.2 shows a typical graph of the arm movement, where the speed of movement is plotted over time from the onset of the target light. Plotting speed makes most of the movement measures that researchers are interested in readily visible in a single graph. We can see how long it takes to initiate the movement by noting when the speed first registers as a positive value; we can see how long the entire movement lasts by noting when the speed returns to zero. By noting when the rising curve begins to descend, we can compare the amount of movement time spent in the acceleration and deceleration portions of the curve. Finally, we can interpret any deviations from smooth changes in speed as interruptions in the smooth execution of the movement. These are *movement corrections.*

Researchers Mel Goodale and his colleagues (Goodale, Pélisson, & Prablanc, 1986) were making these kinds of measurements one day when they decided to fool the study participant. Their purpose was to test a theory that the visual information used to guide the arm was not the same as that used to inform the participant of what he had seen. (This may sound preposterous right now, but please suspend judgment until you hear the outcome of the experiment.) On some trials, instead of simply turning the light on and leaving it on as a target for the participant's arm, the researchers flashed the light briefly and then turned on another light in a nearby location, about 10 percent farther away from home than the initial target location. An important factor is that they timed the offset of the initial target light and the onset of the final target light to coincide with the execution of the first saccade in the eye movement sequence. This meant that the target jump occurred during *saccadic suppression,* the sharp reduction in vision that occurs during each saccade. You can experience the effects of saccadic suppression for yourself by following the instructions in Box 9.1.

In the visually guided action experiment in which the target was sometimes displaced, participants did not notice the target jump. This was predicted from experiments on the saccadic suppression effect many years earlier. The result that surprised the researchers was that participants' arm movements took the target jump into account even though the participants were unaware that a jump had occurred. A velocity plot like the one in Figure 9.2 revealed that arm movements to the displaced target took longer to complete and had more deviations than arm movements to a stationary target in the same final target location. Thus the arm had taken the new visual information into account. In this sense, saccadic suppression applies to our conscious awareness of visual targets but not to the visual guidance of action toward those targets.

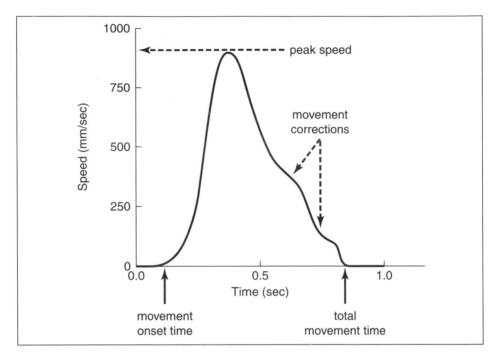

FIGURE 9.2   A graph of the relationship between the speed of arm movement and the time that has elapsed from the onset of a new target in a visually guided action task.

In this chapter, we will consider many experiments that distinguish between vision that leads to conscious experiences and vision that influences behavior in the absence of awareness by the participant. The experiment described above is typical of these in many ways. For example, the participants were young healthy adults with no known neurological impairments. Also, the methods involved making systematic changes to an image presented to the participants and then measuring the influence in at least two ways: (1) measuring the contents of the participants' experience, or their ability to make a direct report of what they saw (e.g., the target jump)—this is a measure of conscious awareness; and (2) measuring changes in behavior that participants may or may not have been aware of (e.g., the velocity profile of the arm movement)—this is a measure of action. Any differences in the way that image changes influence the two measures are evidence for a dissociation or disconnect between conscious awareness and action. On another level, the previously discussed experiment is also typical in that its results do not always lead to clear conclusions. In fact, experiments like this often generate more questions than answers.

BOX 9.1

The unconscious effects of saccadic suppression

For this demonstration you will need a handheld mirror and a friend. Begin by looking at one of your own eyes in the mirror. Now, as quickly as you can, shift your gaze to look at your other eye. Do this several times so that you are well practiced in making eye movements of this size. Did you see your eyes move at any time? Most likely you did not. If you are not sure, try the next step in the demonstration. It will show you what the same eye movements look like when you can see them clearly.

Have your friend face you as she looks alternately at one of her own eyes in the mirror and then the other. Watch her eyes closely by looking at them from above the edge of the mirror. You will notice that your friend's eye movements are very easy to see. There is nothing subtle about them. Yet you cannot see the same eye movements in the mirror when you are the one making them.

This is the phenomenon of *saccadic suppression*, a blindness to small changes in object position that may occur while you are making a saccade (Chapter 5). Normally, you are safe in assuming that the world does not undergo changes specifically timed to coincide with your eye movements. As such, saccadic suppression poses no great risk to you. Moreover, it has great benefits because otherwise changes in the position of objects on the retina, from one eye movement to the next, would result in a considerable smearing of the retinal image through the mechanisms of visible persistence (Chapter 6). The design of your visual system favors the information loss that accompanies saccadic suppression, rather than the faithful recording of actual—but counterproductive—image smearing.

Another kind of eye movement that you *can* see for yourself is *smooth pursuit movement*. Look at one of your eyes in the mirror again, and rotate your head slowly back and forth. Now, move the mirror slowly back and forth while you fixate on one of your eyes. In both cases you will have no trouble seeing your eyes rotate in their sockets, an action that serves to keep a moving visual target centered on the retina. It just so happens in this demonstration that the moving visual target is one of your own eyes seen in a mirror. But the same principles apply to the eyes tracking any moving object. For instance, you can watch your friend's eyes smoothly pursuing a target by having her watch your finger as you slowly move it around in front of her.

The dual purpose of smooth pursuit is (1) to keep an image of a moving object stationary on the retina, and (2) to keep an image of a still object stationary on the retina while the eyes, head, and body are in motion. There is no need for a suppressive mechanism involving smooth pursuit movements because their main purpose is to keep an object stationary on the retina while the eyes or the object are in motion.

There are many ways in which the previous experiment is not typical of research in vision for conscious and unconscious perception. For example, many of the most important experiments in this area have involved individuals with specific forms of brain damage, not healthy college students. Moreover, other important research has involved animals trained to perform certain tasks at the same time that direct recordings of their brain activity were being made.

By considering these various types of experimental methods and participants, in this chapter we will explore current knowledge about vision that leads to conscious experiences and how it differs from vision that influences action but not awareness.

WHAT'S AT STAKE IN THE SCIENCE OF VISUAL CONSCIOUSNESS?

In this chapter we will review concepts such as *vision*, *awareness*, and *unconscious influence* in order to ground our discussion on some common understandings. Then we will consider evidence that vision involves much more than what is accessible to us through personal experience. The evidence will come from studies of individuals with neurological conditions, electrophysiology in animals, and healthy young adults performing visually guided tasks. In discussing this work, we will confront a range of theoretical positions concerning how conscious and unconscious visual processes may be linked. (I will not try to defend any of these views very strongly for a simple reason: Of all the topics covered in this book, the study of consciousness is the least mature. Theoretical positions on this topic will likely change in the next few years more rapidly than positions on most of the other topics addressed in this book.) Along the way, we will consider some of the implications of the division between conscious and unconscious vision for issues that arise in everyday life, including training for skilled performance, ethics in action, and the effectiveness of subliminal advertising.

Vision

At the beginning of this book I went to some lengths to make the case that vision is not what we often think it is. Vision is not a passive process of faithfully recording the pattern of light that falls upon our eyes. It is instead a very active construction project involving the eye and many parts of the brain working together. We have seen many times in this book that previous experiences, along with the current goals and expectations of the observer, play as important a role in vision as the pattern of light that initiates the process.

In terms of the purpose of vision, I argued that it was not enough to claim—as some philosophers have—that its main goal is to enable organisms to sense the world from a distance. This was certainly a nice consequence of vision, but from a biological perspective it evolved as a solution to much more fundamental problems: avoiding predation while simultaneously acquiring food and attracting mates. From the perspective of these criteria, human vision favored the speedy response over the richly detailed and long-lasting neural representation. Actions, it turned out, were more important to survival than detailed, photograph-like mental representations. Furthermore, the main way of implementing change in a visual system in response to changing environmental conditions was—to use a construction metaphor—"renovating" rather than building from scratch. Multiple visual systems, serving fundamentally different purposes, are deeply interwoven in the human brain.

In all the previous discussion I sidestepped an important question concerning vision. Now, in this chapter, we must face it head-on: *Should we use the term* vision *to include all the ways in which the analysis of light by the eye and brain influence our behavior? Or should we reserve the term for only those processes involving light that influence our awareness?* One strong argument for the first, more encompassing definition is that it contributes in a seamless way to the study of vision across species, among humans, and even across biological and artificial visual systems. All can be studied by using the empty-box approach (Chapter 2), which addresses the relations between light patterns "going in" and behavior "coming out."

But there are equally strong arguments for the second, more strict definition. For example, human brains—and likely those of other biologically related creatures—expend a great deal of energy providing their hosts with a sense of self and of an external world (other, or non-self). Philosophers and other writers have studied this function of the brain for thousands of years. Indeed, it was out of this tradition of study of the mind and the self that the modern study of perception originated. Historically, vision was of direct interest as a topic of study because it was understood to be a sensory system that not only provided information about the world at a distance but also created an experience of the world and the self in it at the same time. This experience component has often been regarded as an important dividing line between humans and other species. Many scholars have argued that the conscious experiences of humans are qualitatively different from those of other animals.

In modern vision science, the issue of how to define vision with respect to conscious experience is best resolved by allowing for the possibility of both kinds of vision, not by taking sides with either of the two positions. Opting for one side exclusively leaves the modern scientist with too narrow a scope. For example, choosing to study only the relations between light and behavior comes dangerously close to the position (which has sometimes been taken) that the study of visual experience is peripheral and of little consequence to an understanding of vision. This position begins with a narrow perspective, that of methodological behaviorism, and rules out all topic matter that does not lend itself easily to this analysis. However, choosing to restrict vision to the narrow topic of human visual experiences ignores important consequences of visual processing, even for humans, such as unconscious but visually guided actions and even the possible unwanted effects of subliminal advertising.

Modern vision scientists tend to use the term *vision* both when they are describing visually guided actions of which the observer is unaware and when they are considering experiences influenced by light that are the private and exclusive domain of the observer. Scientists use different additional language for the two cases, often reserving the word *perception* for vision that results in a conscious experience and the phrase *vision for action* when they don't mean to imply that any conscious experience necessarily accompanies the visual influence on behavior. But not only the language must distinguish these possibilities. With increasing frequency, modern vision scientists are measuring visual influence in a variety of ways so that the distinction, if it exists, is as apparent in the data as it is in the realm of possibility. But I don't want to make this sound easier than it actually is. There is much work left to be done in this regard.

Awareness

What is involved in the conscious experience of a visual event? One of the most difficult aspects of this question is that it involves data to which only one person has direct access: the person having the experience. Although we may believe that we are having the same experience as someone else undergoing the same events, or that we can feel what it must be like to "be in someone else's shoes," the problem is that this is in fact privileged information. It is privileged in the sense that there is no known way to verify whether two experiences are indeed the same. The technical term for this kind of knowledge is *first-person data*. The terms *subjective experience*, *phenomenology*, and *introspection* are used interchangeably in this regard.

This kind of knowledge stands in sharp contrast to the kind scientists are more familiar with, which in this context is called *third-person data*. The general methods of science have been carefully developed so that they pass the test of being objective, meaning that a scientific experiment can, in theory, be carried out by another scientist, somewhere else, following the same procedures. An *established finding* is one in which the results come out in more or less the same way when the reported procedures are repeated. The caveat *in principle* is added to convey the assumption that the other scientist has access to the same materials, apparatus, participant population, and techniques of analysis that the original scientist had in conducting the experiment. This may not always be the case, but it is a practical limitation, not a basic or theoretical one.

In terms of the question of visual awareness, the person having the visual experience is the first person, whereas the scientist conducting the experiment and all the other readers of the scientist's summary of first-person reports are the third persons.

It is important to note that no matter what is claimed in a written report of a study of conscious experience, the data being reported are always third-person data: They are presented to the reader on the basis of what the participant having the experience reported by voice or some other action. They are never directly first-person data—not unless we are the one having the experience. In that case, as far as everyone else is concerned, our own reports must be treated as third-person data.

This fundamental dilemma in the study of awareness has bedeviled philosophers for many years and continues to be a persistent obstacle in the scientific study of consciousness. Some philosophers have even claimed that it is an intractable problem, one that can never be solved, thereby making a true science of consciousness an impossible dream. Others refer to it with considerable respect as a hard problem, one that can be solved in principle but that is a long way off from that goal because of our present understanding of the brain. The same philosophers contrast this hard problem with what they perceive as the relatively easy problem of finding correlations between patterns of neural activity and third-person data concerning subjective experiences.

As a practical matter, most vision scientists interested in the study of consciousness are not too concerned about the ultimate question of whether first-person data can ever be subjected to proper scientific treatment. They are more concerned with the so-called easy problem—which to them is difficult enough—of finding out which neural states correspond to third-person accounts of subjective experiences and of finding order in the third-person accounts themselves. For anyone entering this field of study today, many lifetimes of work remain to be done.

Unconscious influence

About twenty years ago, two companion papers by Anthony Marcel (1983a, 1983b) appeared in the journal *Cognitive Psychology* that had a profound influence on the modern study of conscious and unconscious vision. The experiments described in these papers that attracted the most attention, both from researchers and from the general public, involved participants making a speeded decision as to whether a series of letters spelled a word (e.g., *doctor*, *bread*) or not (e.g., *tocdor*, *dreab*). This task was performed immediately after seeing a briefly flashed display in which another word was presented and followed by a random pattern mask. The duration of the briefly flashed and masked words, called *primes*, were adjusted for each participant so that when they had to guess whether a word or only a blank had been presented as a prime, accuracy was only a little above the chance level of guessing at 50 percent. The durations ranged from 30 to 80 milliseconds. The critical factor in the experiment was whether the briefly flashed prime words were related in meaning to the subsequent word for which the participants had to make a word-nonword decision. For example, the prime word *nurse* followed by the target word *doctor* was an example of two words closely related in meaning. In contrast, the prime word *bread* followed by the target word *doctor* was an example of an unrelated pair of words. The prime word *bread* followed by the target stimulus *tocdor* was an example of a non-word control trial.

The results showed that when the prime word was meaningfully related to the target word, participants were able to identify the target word more rapidly than when the prime word was unrelated in meaning. The existence of such a semantic priming effect was not surprising, since reading a word was expected to be influenced by other words that have been read recently. The controversial claim of the study was that the priming effect occurred for words that were never consciously experienced by the participants because they were presented at durations for which participants could only guess whether a word had ever been presented. Here was a seemingly rigorous demonstration of visual perception, in the form of word reading, unaccompanied by the usual conscious experience of having read the prime words responsible for the effect.

Many researchers criticized these results on the grounds that it was not clear from the methods whether in fact on some trials participants had seen the prime words briefly—in the usual way that one thinks of "seeing," complete with the conscious experience of the words. Others wondered whether participants might have forgotten "seeing" the words as rapidly as they had appeared, with the pattern mask playing an important role in this kind of "forgetting."

The critics who eventually had the greatest impact on the interpretation of unconscious word priming experiments pointed out that in terms of conscious experiences, visual awareness is not an all-or-nothing event. Whereas some briefly flashed words might be experienced clearly, others might be experienced in a more vague sense. That is, a given participant might be sure that the word began with certain letters, or he might only see that the last letter consisted of straight lines. He might even have the experience of thinking of a certain word without really seeing the word at all. In any case, the possibility existed that prime words might be experienced in part, incompletely, or differently from target words, so these critics set out to determine the visual threshold of the prime words by using more than one procedure.

Philip Merikle and his colleagues (Merikle, Joordens, & Stolz, 1995) approached this problem by trying to come up with the strictest possible test of visual perception. They presented one of four prime words on each trial (the color terms *orange*, *blue*, *green*, and *yellow*) and asked participants to make a forced-choice guess as to which word had been presented. The researchers adjusted the duration of these words' presentation until accuracy reached the chance level of 25 percent. They then presented the prime words immediately prior to color patches that participants had to name as rapidly as possible. Priming in this case was expected to lead to faster color naming when the prime word and color patch were congruent (e.g., both *orange*) than when they were incongruent (e.g., prime word = *orange*, color patch = *blue*). However, priming had no effects under these conditions, so the researchers concluded that unconscious priming did not occur when a strict objective threshold of awareness was first established.

When the same researchers used a less strict measure of perception, which they referred to as the *subjective threshold of awareness*, they found evidence of unconscious priming. In this condition they randomly mixed an equal number of prime displays containing a color word with prime displays that were blank, and then they asked participants to report seeing a word or not. When the researchers next used durations of the prime words that led to accuracy levels of chance guessing, evidence of priming occurred once again, with congruent color words and patches resulting in faster color naming than incongruent words and patches.

Merikle and his colleagues interpreted the difference between the two results as evidence against true unconscious reading of the prime words. Instead, they argued, there are many facets to visual awareness, and participants implicitly adopt criteria for what constitutes "awareness" that may vary widely for different tasks. For example, if participants are asked to report on whether or not they have seen a printed word, they seem to adopt the strict standard of having to have a high degree of confidence in the word's identity before saying "yes." This allows for the possibility of perceptual influences from words that they experienced but saw less clearly than the implicitly adopted criterion for "seeing."

However, when participants have to guess which one of four words was presented and must choose one answer even if they are unsure, they use all the available information they have experienced, including hunches and feelings that are not particularly visual in content. Once all these experiences have been removed from the situation by reducing performance on the guessing task to chance levels, there is no longer any visual information remaining to be used in the word priming effect. The words are no longer being read. By this definition, then, there is no perception of printed words without awareness.

Although you might think that this sort of evidence settled the case of unconscious perception once and for all, you can rest assured it did not. The main reason this issue is far from settled is that there is no agreement on what kind of third-party data constitutes the correct index of first-person experience. According to Marcel, the author of the original unconscious priming study, a direct report based on the participant's personally set criterion for awareness is an adequate measure of "awareness." In contrast, critics such as Merikle who distinguish between objective and subjective thresholds for awareness are unwilling to trust the participant in setting this criterion. They want to evaluate the participant's "awareness" by using the more stringent criterion of whether the prime word provides any visual information that can be used to influence guessing. However, in adopting this more stringent criterion, they move farther away from the first-person data. This measure of awareness is no longer tied to the participant's report of his own experience. It is based instead on his actions. But what if these actions occur without any accompanying awareness of the visual information guiding them? Is it possible that this approach has ruled out the very possibility of measuring perception without awareness?

I will not try to resolve this ongoing debate. At this point in the scientific study of consciousness, it is more important to understand the difficult issues involved. If nothing else, such an understanding will prevent us from having an unquestioned acceptance of the claims being made in other studies on the relations between action and consciousness—or, for that matter, in studies on neural activity associated with visual awareness. In each study we will encounter, you should ask careful questions about the assumed links between the first-person experiences of the participants—whether human or animal—and the third-person data being presented as an index of those experiences.

DISSOCIATING VISION FOR PERCEPTION AND AWARENESS
Neurological conditions

Some of the most compelling examples of perception without awareness are cited in studies of people who have suffered a form of brain injury.

The split brain: Rethinking consciousness

Beginning in the 1940s, one of the treatments of last resort for a particular kind of epilepsy was the surgical sectioning (cutting) of the corpus callosum, the bundle of nerve fibers that connect the left and right cerebral hemispheres. Epilepsy is a syndrome that involves periods of chaotic electrical activity in the brain, called *seizures*. When seizures begin in one region of the brain, they sometimes spread to the corresponding location in the other hemisphere via the nerve fibers in the corpus callosum. This tends to initiate a cascading sequence of increasingly chaotic activity. Left unchecked, this activity leads to cell death and brain damage. Sectioning the corpus callosum is a treatment that reduces the damage that would otherwise occur in epileptics. It is considered a treatment of last resort because several drugs are quite effective in reducing seizure activity. When these fail or become less effective, in many cases the surgical sectioning of the corpus callosum is a treatment option of great benefit. People who undergo this treatment are called *split-brain patients*.

Perhaps the most remarkable feature of split-brain patients is the surprisingly small effect of the surgery on reports of their conscious experiences. Patients who have undergone the surgery do not report experiencing the world any differently from before. Most of them are overjoyed at the reduction in seizure activity that

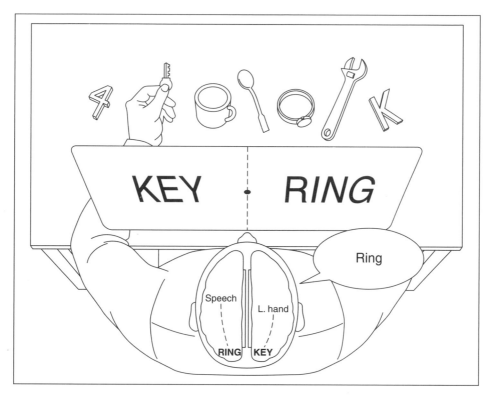

FIGURE 9.3 A typical testing situation for research with split-brain patients. Visual images (in this case, words) are flashed briefly to either the left or the right side of the fixation marker, and the hand on the same side as the image is used to make a response to that image.

enables them to have more productive lives. Furthermore, friends and relatives do not notice any drastic change in either their behavior or their reports of how the world appears to them.

However, careful testing in the laboratory reveals interesting disconnections between these individuals' vision for consciousness and their vision for action. For example, in a typical experiment, split-brain patients are shown words or images in a series of brief flashes. The images may be presented to either side of the fixation marker, as illustrated in Figure 9.3. The images appear for a period that is too short to initiate an eye movement, usually 200 ms or less, so that the experimenter can be sure that each picture is shown to only one side of the fovea in each eye.

As discussed in Chapter 2, this means that an image in the right visual field is ultimately projected to the parts of the eyes that send signals to the left hemisphere of the cortex, and a picture in the left visual field is relayed to the right hemisphere. If the hands are used to make responses in the experiment, there is also a convenient mapping between visual field and side of response because the control of action is *contralateral* (meaning "on opposite sides") in the same way that visual processing is. The same hemisphere that receives a visual image (from the contralateral visual field) is responsible for guiding the hand on that side of space. All in all, this makes visual experimentation with split-brain patients very easy. They can respond to images on one side of space with the arm or finger on the same side.

The results obtained in this kind of study, however, are not nearly as straightforward as the procedure itself—and this is what makes them so fascinating. For example, a split-brain patient might be presented with an image of a cup on the right. If she is asked to name the object, she will say "cup"; if she is asked to reach under a screen with her right hand to pick out a corresponding object using only her sense of touch, she will correctly choose a cup from an assortment of objects. However, if she is next shown an image of a spoon on the left side, she will likely say she sees "nothing" when asked to name the image. Yet when asked to reach under the screen with her left hand to guess the object that is shown, she will likely examine all the objects and then correctly hold up the spoon. Moreover, when asked what object she is now holding in her left hand, she may give an inappropriate response, such as "pencil."

Here is a clear dissociation between vision for conscious report and vision for action in the right hemisphere of the split-brain patient. What does it imply about the conscious experiences of the right hemisphere? If our answer relies on the patient's ability to describe her experiences in words, we will conclude that the right hemisphere is not visually conscious. This is because the patient seems unable to report seeing objects flashed in the left visual field. Even when asked to name an object being held by the left hand, but not seen, the patient is unable to identify the object correctly.

Yet this conclusion might not be fair because only the left hemisphere may be capable of producing coherent speech. Moreover, the "talking" left hemisphere also has a tendency to dominate in matters where each hemisphere has had different sensory inputs. The left hemisphere interprets and rationalizes the larger experience, even to the point of coming up with plausible stories for the actions of the right hemisphere. Perhaps the right hemisphere is having perfectly normal conscious experiences but is unable to get the speech-producing left hemisphere to talk about them. Such an experience of being conscious while at the same time being trapped inside of an uncommunicative hemisphere may be one of the deficits that result from the sectioning of the corpus callosum.

In that case, it would seem reasonable to find a nonlinguistic measure of the right hemisphere's experiences. The action system might be exactly that kind of measure. If we accept the actions of the right hemisphere as an indication of what was seen, then we will conclude from this experiment that the right hemisphere is conscious of the picture of the spoon because it is able to guide the hand to the correct object.

But just as we saw in our discussion of what counts as a measure of awareness, it is a logical possibility that these actions may occur without any accompanying awareness of the visual information guiding them. The right hemisphere might indeed be a *zombie* in the sense that it can initiate behavior similar to that of someone with consciousness, but without the experiences that occur in someone with visual consciousness. Or it may indeed be a fully conscious hemisphere but be unable to communicate with the outside world because of a lack of language. This is precisely the kind of conundrum that makes the scientific study of consciousness so difficult.

Some researchers who work extensively with split-brain patients think there are important individual differences in this regard. They point out that in only a very small number of split-brain patients is the right hemisphere able to comprehend linguistic material. An interesting finding is that only these patients are also able to perform simple nonlinguisitc perceptual matching tasks, such as indicating whether two shapes are the same or different, with objects shown simultaneously to both hemispheres. Some researchers thus conclude that a right hemisphere without language capacity is considerably less sophisticated in cognitive ability than a nonhuman animal such as a chimpanzee.

This view is at odds with the commonsense belief that for the average split-brain patient the right hemisphere has experiences similar to those of the left hemisphere, with the exception that the patient is unable to communicate these experiences in words. Instead, it argues for a close link between linguistic capability and consciousness. According to this view, patients in whom the right hemisphere is unable to comprehend speech may have a qualitatively different form of visual experience, or none at all. The right hemisphere may indeed be a zombie— and a not very bright one at that. At the same time, critics of this position argue against linking linguistic communication and consciousness so closely. However, the burden of proof now falls on them to demonstrate that nonlinguistic actions are appropriate third-person measures of first-person experiences.

Blindsight: Acting without seeing

In Chapter 2 we encountered Dan, a young man who had undergone the surgical removal of area V1 in his right hemisphere as treatment for noncancerous tissue growth. Although this left him unable to report the presence of objects in his left visual field, Dan was still able to point to these objects, grasp them appropriately, and even guess their identity correctly when given a small number of response options. This indicates that area V1 is both centrally important to the construction of visual experiences and at the same time not critical in the control of visually guided reaching. Other brain areas must be involved in the support of that function.

The distinction between vision for perception and vision for action has been studied most extensively (Milner & Goodale, 1995) in a patient known as DF, who suffered brain damage because of a lack of oxygen (anoxia) to the visual areas immediately adjacent to areas V1, V2, and V3. Although she had profound difficulties in reporting the size, shape, and orientation of simple objects, her hand and arm movements toward the very same objects were unimpaired. For example, when she was asked to indicate the size of the blocks seen from a distance by using her thumb and forefinger to indicate the dimensions, her movements bore no relationship to the size of the blocks. Her verbal reports of the blocks' dimensions were no more discriminating. Yet when asked to reach out and pick up the blocks, her thumb and fingers moved to match the width of the blocks and her reaching distance was appropriate.

A similar dissociation was apparent in DF's judgments of orientation. When asked to indicate the angle at which a postcard would have to be held in order to be placed into a slot, she was unable to do so either by using words or by indicating the correct position when holding the card. However, when asked to place the card into the slot as if to mail it, she did this without error—or at least at the same level of accuracy as healthy individuals serving as controls in the study.

Ataxia and Balint's syndrome: Seeing but being unable to act

Individuals who have suffered damage to the posterior parietal cortex often show neglect of objects in a certain region of space, especially if the damage is to the right hemisphere (Chapter 2). Occasionally damage to certain regions in the posterior parietal cortex results in patients still being able to recognize the identity and meaning of objects but having great difficulty reaching appropriately for those objects. This condition is *optic ataxia*. Not only do these patients have trouble reaching for the objects, but they also display impaired grasp size in accordance with the objects' size. They are only able to pick up a given object after making many fine adjustments to their grasp, a process that is not evident in the grasping performance of healthy individuals.

An important point for our present discussion is that the same patients have no difficulty using other senses to control their reaching and grasping. They can effortlessly locate a spot on one arm with a finger from the other if the spot has been identified by touch. These patients also have no difficulty verbally describing the relative locations of objects and their approximate sizes. Therefore, their reaching and grasping problem has nothing to do with their voluntary action system or their visual system in isolation. Rather, the problem involves the combination of those systems in visually controlled action.

This contrast of neuropsychological disorders that do damage to seeing (as in patient DF) and acting (as in patients with optic ataxia) selectively reveals in a functional way the two kinds of vision mentioned earlier in this chapter: vision for perception and vision for action. One influential theoretical framework that guides much modern research proposes that the two forms of vision have different evolutionary histories and should be considered as separate visual systems serving different functions, in much the same way that cones and rods are the dividing point for two interleaved visual systems. Whereas the latter case involves retinal receptor systems for dim and bright light, the former involves systems for action and perception. This framework, called the *dual visual system theory*, is chiefly promoted by the neuropsychologist David Milner and the neuroscientist Mel Goodale (Milner & Goodale, 1995).

The action system, which consists of the dorsal stream in the human cortex (Chapter 2), is considered the older system, the one we share in many respects with all other animals that use vision to guide action. This system has rapid input, generates rapid eye movements to locations of possible interest, and has direct links to the brain regions that initiate action through the muscles. Notice that in order to grasp something or to avoid stepping on something, it is not essential to know precisely what it is or what it is used for. Its color, surface texture, and name are usually irrelevant to how large our grasp must be in order to hold it, pick it up, or step around it. This action system also does not seem to require visual awareness in order to operate smoothly.

The perception system, which is based in the ventral stream in the human cortex (Chapter 2), is considered to be the more recent system. It may have been added to the larger brains of humans and other mammals to coincide with the much more complex thought processes that such a brain afforded. Its specialty is fine-grained categorization using the dimensions of color, texture, form, and meaning. Most important for purposes of this chapter, it constructs a sense of conscious experience. It is the system we use when we actually attend to the contents of our experience, when we reflect on the way things look. As such, it performs computations that permit us to see the approximate size of the object regardless of its distance from us. It permits us to see the surface color of an object regardless of the peculiarities of current lighting conditions. In short, this is the system for perception after the visual constancies (such as size constancy, color constancy, and position constancy) have been determined.

Acting without seeing

It is sometimes difficult to gauge the extent to which dissociations between visual awareness and action in individuals with brain damage actually apply or generalize to the visual system's functioning under healthy conditions. Perhaps the dissociations we have been talking about are indeed artifacts of brain damage; perhaps visual awareness is disconnected from other aspects of visual functioning only under these unusual conditions. However, studies involving healthy participants also lead to this conclusion.

In order to better understand this, let's return to the kinds of experiments described at the beginning of this chapter. Exactly what kind of visual information can be used in an unconscious way? How is this visual information different from the kind that is available to our experience?

Masked word priming

Earlier in this chapter when we were discussing the difficulty of measuring visual awareness, we introduced the possibility of visual influences on word reading that could occur without any subjective awareness on the part of a study participant that an influencing word or picture—the prime—had been presented. The procedure used to induce these effects is masked priming. As shown in Figure 9.4, it typically involves the brief presentation of a prime word or picture followed by an unrelated word or picture—the mask. This is followed by a visible word or picture—the target—to which the participant must respond. The experimenter is interested in the influence of the unseen prime word or picture on the response to the visible target. Any influence, whether to improve or to impair performance on the visible target, indicates that the unconscious processing of the prime is related to the processing of the visible target. These relations can be studied by systematically testing the types of primes that do and do not have an influence on any given task.

One of the most successful methods for separating the influence of conscious and unconscious processes on masked priming involves a task in which participants try their best *not* to use some visual information they have been shown. Philip Merikle and his colleagues (Joordens & Merikle, 1993) call this an *exclusion task*. In a typical study participants carry out a word-stem completion task: They must find an English word that begins with a certain three letters. For example, when presented with the letters *bot*, they might reply with *bottle*, *bottom*, *botany*, and so on. This is not a difficult task for native speakers of English.

Because the exclusion task is a masked priming procedure, the items in the word-stem completion portion are preceded by a brief presentation of a prime word and a mask. Any influence of the prime word on the completion of the word stem can be taken as evidence of priming. But is this influence a *conscious* one?

The twist in the procedure that helps to isolate conscious and unconscious influences is the critical instruction to the participant to "complete the word stem with any word other than the one that was shown in the prime display." A security check that participants are performing the task is built right into the procedure: It involves presenting the primes over a range of exposure durations. When the prime appears for one-half second or more, participants report they can see the

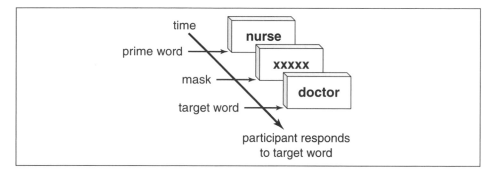

FIGURE 9.4   The typical events in a masked priming experiment.

word clearly. As a result, they complete the word-stem task with words that do not include the prime. Any participants who are unwilling or unable to perform this basic part of the task are excluded from further consideration.

An important control condition is the likelihood of participants choosing the prime word to complete the stem when it has not been shown. There is, of course, some probability that participants will use certain prime words spontaneously to complete the word-stem, so perception of the prime must be calibrated against this baseline likelihood of responding with it in the absence of any visual input.

The critical conditions in the study are those in which the prime word is presented briefly and then masked. Under these conditions, participants tend to select an ending to the word-stem that makes it the same as the prime with a higher frequency than (1) in the baseline condition, where there is no visual input, or (2) in the long prime exposure condition, where the prime word is visible to participants and thus is almost never selected. The increase in prime word selection in the brief exposure condition over the baseline condition is then taken as a measure of unconscious word reading.

Studies of the exclusion task indicate that the degree of unconscious influence obtained from a mask priming procedure is directly related to the degree to which attention is focused on the location of the prime. Namely, increasing the focus of attention on a single prime location results in a much smaller measure of unconscious reading and a much larger degree of visual awareness. Similar results obtain for participants' degree of motivation to guess what the briefly presented prime might have been. Increasing participants' motivation to see the prime—for example, by paying them money for correct answers—also results in a smaller measure of unconscious influence and greater visual awareness. These findings are consistent with many people's intuitions that our visual awareness is richer and more detailed when we focus single-mindedly on a task and when our motivation levels are moderately heightened. However, when we are distracted, visual processing may proceed in much the same way for some well-learned tasks such as word reading, but the results of these processes may never reach our visual awareness.

Maintaining a stable visual world

As we saw at the beginning of this chapter when we introduced the ideas of unconscious corrections in saccadic suppression and arm movements, many of the most powerful examples of unconscious visual processing in healthy human observers are evident in the action system. And one of the most important functions of the action system, in terms of eye movements, is the maintenance of a stable visual world. Our unconscious corrections relate to our visual awareness in the same way that modern image stabilization technology relates to a pleasing video recording.

Let's try an experiment taken from a study by Heiner Deubel and colleagues (Deubel, Schneider, & Bridgeman, 1996). Imagine sitting in a chair with your eyes aimed at a solitary X in the center of a computer screen. You are wearing a pair of special eyeglasses that are able to tell the computer where your eyes are aimed at any moment. The experimenter says that when you are ready, you may press a key to begin. This will cause the X you are looking at to disappear while another X appears on the screen in an unpredictable location. Your job will be to move your eyes as quickly as possible to the new X. The computer will measure the movement of your eye to the new location.

However, just as in the visually guided action experiment described earlier, the experiment has been designed to fool you on some trials. On many trials, the X that is the focus of your eye movement disappears just as you begin your eye movement and then it reappears slightly to one side or the other of its original location near the time your eye lands. We can call this spatial displacement the *target jump*. The visual experience that is measured is your report of whether you were able to detect the jump.

Researchers can tell that target jumps of this kind are processed by the parts of the brain that govern eye movements because the record of participants' eye movements shows a quick corrective saccade to the final location of the target when it has jumped. However, the parts of the visual system that govern participants' experienced sense of object position are apparently unaware of these processes because participants rarely detect a jump that is 10 percent or less of the total saccade distance. Instead, the typical experience is of a perfectly stable target X.

Yet there is one way to make the target jump very obvious in the participants' experience: by turning off the target X on the screen shortly before the jump occurs. In other words, the experiment is identical to the previous one, with the exception of a brief period during which the target X disappears from the screen. Now, the participants easily detect even small jumps. In fact, these jumps are even more noticeable than similar-size jumps made by targets right at fixation. What has happened? How could maintaining continuous visibility of the target make it difficult to detect the jump, whereas removing some of this information from view makes the target jump visible in the participants' experience?

This finding points to two important features of visual processing that help us understand the differences between visual information that is used for action and visual information that forms the contents of conscious experience. We mentioned the first feature in Chapter 5 when we discussed scene perception and change blindness. The design of the conscious visual system seems to depend on the assumption that the world around us is, for the most part, standing still. We can call this the *stable world assumption*. One reason the conscious visual centers need to make this assumption is that visual signals to our eyes are almost constantly undergoing some form of motion. The motion arises from the body, head, and eye movements of everyday life, as well as from the various objects and surfaces that are moving against the larger stationary background in our visual environment. The interpretation of all these motions requires an anchor, or reference point. The visual system uses the objects of fixation as those anchors. As a consequence, small displacements to these objects during the saccade go unnoticed in our experience so that we can evaluate the motion of other objects relative to the anchor.

At the same time, the eyes need to maintain fixation on certain objects, especially if they are to be used as reference points for evaluating the positions and movements of other objects. To maintain fixation under conditions of head, eye, and object movement, the eyes' guidance system must therefore be exquisitely sensitive to small changes in head and object position. But there is no need to send all the information involved in those computations to the parts of the brain responsible for our conscious experience of the seen world. It is much easier for that system to simply assume that objects will not move during the brief 10 ms or so that it takes to execute a saccadic eye movement. That is putting the regularities in our visual environment to good use. It saves brainpower for more important things.

The second important feature of visual processing is revealed by the finding that erasing the target shortly before the eyes land on it permits the participant to see small jumps in the target position that occurred during the saccade. This finding points to the importance of reentrant processes in determining the contents of our conscious experience. The fact that jumps are seen in briefly erased targets indicates that all the information needed to experience the jumps is potentially available to the conscious visual system. But the key word is *potentially*. The continued presence of the displaced target on the screen seems to mask the jump in the same way that a second shape presented after a first shape masks the visibility of the first shape (Chapter 6). In both cases, the visual system apparently updates its understanding of the shape by incorporating the most recent visual information. Earlier information—such as the original target shape in masking or the original spatial position in the eye movement study—is abandoned.

How does this abandonment occur? In both cases, the visual system's hypotheses about the identity and spatial position of an object that are generated in higher-level brain regions are likely being compared with the ongoing sensory activity in lower-level regions. Briefly erasing the target in the jump detection task and removing the second shape in the masking task permit the initial hypothesis entertained by the higher-level regions to be confirmed in the fading trace of the neural activity generated by the target. However, leaving the displaced target and the masking shape in view increases the likelihood that the visual system will abandon the initial hypothesis in favor of one that matches the ongoing sensory input.

In a sense, one can say that "the eyes have it" in terms of resolving perceptual conflicts between ongoing sensory activity and ongoing activity initiated by higher visual centers. This bias is probably very beneficial because it enables us to experience new visual scenes that violate our well-learned expectations. However, in some unusual viewing conditions—such as visual masking and target displacement experiments—this bias leads to an illusion of target position that can be studied in the laboratory. Recall that in pathological conditions such as retinitis pigmentosa (Chapter 2), the absence of normal sensory input results in hallucinations that are based on unconstrained hypothesis-generating abilities of our higher visual centers.

This interpretation of the insensitivity of conscious vision to a target's actual position was recently put to a stronger test by Deubel and colleagues (Deubel, Bridgeman, & Schneider, 1998). These researchers simply included one more object in the eye movement experiment. If you were a participant in this experiment, you would be told that when you are looking at the central X and have been given the ready signal, two new objects will appear on the screen in an unpredictable location. One object will be an X just like the one you are looking at now. This is the one to which you should move your eyes as quickly as possible. The other object will be an O that appears a little above the new X. It is of no consequence to your primary task, which is to fixate on the new X. However, following the eye movement made to the new X on each trial, you are asked to indicate whether you saw either the new X or the O move from its original location.

Unknown to you, the observer, the experiment has been designed so that two conditions have been varied, generating a total of four different movement scenarios. Either the target X or the non-target O undergoes a small jump during the time you are moving your eyes to the new target location. Also, either the target X or the non-target O is erased briefly from the screen shortly before the jump in one of the objects occurs. The question now is, *Under which of these four conditions will perception accurately reveal whether a displacement of the object has occurred?*

The answer is predictable from our discussion leading up to this experiment, but it is also disturbing to our deeply held beliefs that seeing is perceiving. The object that is erased shortly before the jump in any of the objects is almost always seen as the object that jumped. This means, for example, that observers see a stationary O appear to move and a jumping target X appear to stand still in displays on which the stationary O is erased shortly after the eye movement has begun. Similarly, when the target X actually stands still and the O jumps, the X is seen to jump on trials in which it is erased briefly. These results highlight both the extent to which the conscious visual system assumes that continuously visible objects are stationary and the extent to which the ongoing sensory input dominates our perceptual experience.

Illusions of perception and action

An important consequence of the dual visual system theory is that ventral stream processing is aimed at forming representations of objects and scenes that are object-based. Thus the goals of vision within this system are to identify objects, to localize them in space relative to other objects, and to categorize their meaning properly with respect to other objects. This enables us to form long-lasting memories of visual events—memories we can use to reconstruct visual events from the past and to simulate visual scenarios that have never occurred.

As we saw in Chapter 5, in order to accomplish these goals our perception must be based on the intrinsic attributes of objects, such as their relative size, three-dimensional shape, and surface reflectance properties. What this means for the situational properties (aspects of the image that vary with scene lighting and observer viewpoint) is that these variables must be ignored and sometimes even discounted. The result is that our conscious experience of objects obeys the constancies (Chapter 5): Objects are seen as being the same size, shape, and color under a wide variety of viewing conditions.

In contrast to these goals, the main aim of dorsal stream processing is to facilitate interactions between ourselves and the objects in our world. Actions must be based on the immediately present conditions of surrounding objects, including their distance from us, their size relative to us, and their orientation with respect to us. These kinds of representations are called *viewer-centered* rather than *object-centered*: In order to reach, grasp, and pick up an object, we must use vision to calculate the object's size relative to our hand. Its size relative to other surrounding objects is of much less importance. Because of the constantly changing conditions that arise with changes in our position and the position of moving objects, visual calculations of immediate conditions must take precedence over memory for past conditions. Because immediate action is at stake, precision of action and speed of response take precedence over visual awareness and long-term memories of object properties.

An easy way to test these ideas is to see whether visually guided actions and object perception are subject in the same way to visual illusions based on object constancies. A simple example comes from studies of the role of context in the perception of object size. Look at the circles in Figure 9.5. The same-size disc

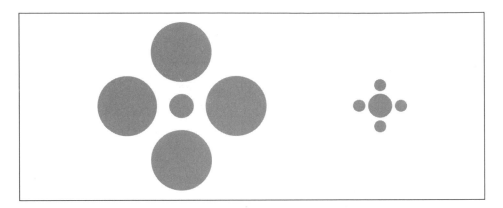

FIGURE 9.5   The center circles in these two displays do not appear to be the same size. This is a contrast illusion involving object size. Objects surrounded by larger objects appear smaller than same-size objects surrounded by smaller objects. Although this illusion is stable for perceptual judgments of size, the system guiding the hand's actual grasp of the center discs is not as susceptible to the illusion.

appears on each side of the figure, surrounded on the left by larger circles and on the right by smaller circles. The differences in context result in an illusion that vision researchers have measured many times over the past one hundred years. It is an illusion of contrast because the direction of difference in apparent size between the target and the context is exaggerated. The disc surrounded by larger circles appears to be smaller than the one surrounded by smaller circles.

Over the past ten years, several researchers have measured the apparent size of the target discs in a different way. Instead of having participants make perceptual judgments, they have asked them to reach out and pick up actual discs (small chips of the same size) that are surrounded by different-size discs. Attached to the participants' hands are lightweight sensors, on the thumb and forefinger, that signal the actual position of these digits in three-dimensional space as the movement is being made. When grasp sizes are examined, they show a significantly reduced and sometimes negligible difference between the two conditions. This is consistent with the dual visual system theory, which claims that visually guided action is based on the properties of objects with respect to the viewer, rather than on the perceived properties of the objects relative to one another. Once again, the hand and the mind's eye seem to be guided by different information.

Results showing a similar dissociation between action and perception have been reported for judgments of the slope of a hill in a real-world setting (Bhalla & Proffitt, 1999). Anyone who has ever had to run up a steep hill after already being tired from a long run will appreciate these findings. First, when faced with making an estimate of the steepness of a hill viewed head-on, conscious perceptual estimates

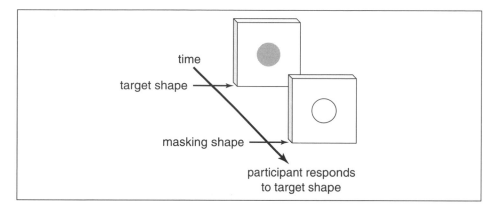

FIGURE 9.6 Typical visual images and the sequence of events used to study metacontrast masking.

of slant exaggerate the steepness. Second, if one is tired when making the judgment, the steepness is exaggerated even more, consistent with the extra effort that will be required to run up the hill in that tired condition. However, in either situation, if the hill's steepness is assessed by the movements one makes with the legs and feet, then no exaggeration (no illusion) is recorded. Human action seems calibrated to the actual properties of the visual stimulus, whereas perceptual judgments take into account such subjective factors as the amount of extra effort required to make the motor movements in comparison to similar movements on a flat surface.

Masked visually guided action

We discussed standing wave masking in Chapter 6, where we learned that it is a very effective way to make a visible target become invisible. A simplified version of this form of masking is *metacontrast masking*. It can be accomplished by flashing a target shape briefly—say, a round disc flashed for 50 ms—followed by a masking shape that closely surrounds the target shape. The spatial relations among the shapes and the sequence of events are illustrated in Figure 9.6, where the masking shape resembles a donut.

When the donut shape is presented 50 to 100 ms after the target disc, it becomes very difficult to see the disc. In fact, when the timing between the onset of the disc and the onset of the donut is adjusted for individual participants, they report the target shape as completely invisible.

One of the interesting features of metacontrast masking, and one that puzzled researchers as long as forty years ago, was that certain perceptual decisions about the target disc were unaffected by the masking donut. For example, if participants were instructed to press a key as soon as they detected the onset of the disc, their speeded responses were not influenced by the subsequent presentation of the donut. This result seemed odd because it implied that some part of the visual brain could respond to the disc even though there was apparently no visual awareness of the disc itself.

In recent years, researchers have followed up and extended this finding to include more complicated actions, such as pressing one of the two keys or pointing to a specific location on the screen. The intriguing result is that masked targets can influence the motor responses even though the target shape exerting the influence cannot be detected above chance levels when using an objective measure of the threshold. Remember that this is the most stringent measure of conscious perception.

In one study by Hartmut Leuthold and colleagues (Leuthold & Kopp, 1998), participants had to indicate the location of a target shape; the exposure duration of the target was reduced until accuracy in this task was at a chance level. At the same exposure durations, the participants' motor response to the location of a distinctive shape in the masking display was influenced by the location of the unseen target shape. In another study using similar procedures (Klotz & Neumann, 1999), the masked shape exerted an influence on a manual response to the shape of the mask. In yet another study (Schmidt 2002), the color of the unseen target had a strong influence on an action made in response to the color of the mask.

All these findings are powerful demonstrations of visually guided action in healthy individuals that does not seem to rely on visual awareness of the object guiding the behavior. It is interesting to compare these findings of unconscious visual influences on action with findings from studies of unconscious word reading. Recall that in those studies, evidence of unconscious priming effects on reading seemed to disappear when an objective measure of the threshold of awareness was used. That is, word priming was possible at prime exposure durations for which participants were unable to discern whether a word had been presented (the subjective threshold), but not when participants were forced to guess which of four alternative words had been presented (the objective threshold). Then unconscious reading seemed to evaporate.

The studies we have just considered do not fall victim to the same fate. In fact, studies of masked targets that influence actions of the hand show that these actions can be influenced unconsciously even when the threshold of awareness is assessed by using the strictest procedure involving forced choices among a small set of alternatives. A reasonable interpretation is that the dorsal stream visual processes that guide the eye and hand are less likely to result in conscious experiences than are the ventral stream processes that are required for reading words.

Another interesting implication of these studies of unconscious action relates to our experience of free will. In what sense do we choose our own actions if studies such as these illustrate that some of our actions are initiated without our awareness? This is an important question, one that we can't possibly do justice to in this chapter. For now, let's keep in mind that the actions being influenced were the ones the participant did intend to make all along. The unconscious influence that was measured simply enabled the actions to begin more rapidly or to occur in a slightly different location than would have occurred otherwise. There are no reports in the scientific literature of unseen images being shown to healthy participants that resulted in complex actions that surprised the participants.

Acting on threats and negative emotions

Certain visual images that lead to the most rapid unconscious actions are those of facial expressions depicting fear or anger and those that contain information threatening to our survival. I haven't included examples of such pictures because they are emotionally upsetting. If you simply imagine some gory and frightening images, you will be on the right track. In studies using backward masking of briefly presented pictures of this kind, participants had negative emotional reactions to emotionally neutral pictures when they were presented immediately after the masked presentations of emotionally disturbing images. The negative emotional reactions can be measured by having participants give ratings of attractiveness to the neutral pictures that follow the masked negative images and by recording physiological responses—such as heart rate and galvanic skin response—to the unseen images.

Research based on animal models and on neuropsychological patients points to a lower brain structure called the *amygdala* as being critical in the evaluation of visual images for negative emotions such as fear. Animals and patients with damage to the amygdala do not react to threatening visual images in the same way as healthy individuals. One of the leading theories in this area by Joseph LeDoux (1996) proposes that the rapid processing of images by the amygdala can result in very rapid actions designed to move an individual away from the source of danger. This theory assumes the existence of visual pathways that go from the eyes to the amygdala, through the thalamus, without first entering the visual cortex. Moreover, the projections from the amygdala to the visual centers in the cortex are much stronger than the projections from the cortex to the amygdala, suggesting that the amygdala acts more as an early warning system for the conscious visual centers than as a center whose processes are guided by visual awareness. Figure 9.7 shows the position of the amygdala with respect to several other brain structures.

The visual fear circuit is therefore believed to operate completely outside of visual awareness in humans, although the results of its analysis can travel to the conscious ventral stream. Important to our discussion of action and awareness, this means that we can take rapid actions to avoid danger without having to wait

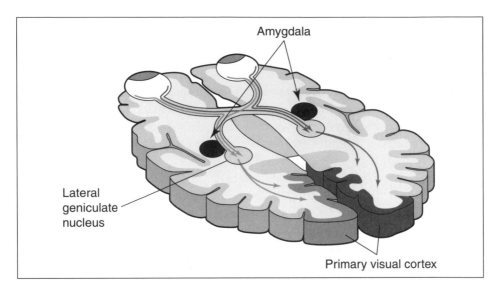

FIGURE 9.7   A schematic picture of the visual pathways from the eyes to the primary visual cortex. The visual fear circuit involves the direct connection from the eyes to thalamus to the amygdale (shown as small black ovals near the lateral geniculate nucleus of the thalamus).

for the relatively slow conscious visual processes to be complete. But it is important to remember that such rapid actions depend on a cursory analysis of the visual image. Thus the system can be fooled, although this error is conveniently on the side of caution.

A simple laboratory illustration of unconscious visually guided action in response to emotionally negative images involves the reflexive orienting effect that occurs in response to the sudden appearance of a new object in the visual field (Chapter 5). However, rather than using emotionally neutral objects such as squares and discs, these studies use images of actors depicting facial expressions ranging from negative (fear, anger) to neutral (calm) and positive (happy). Brendan Bradley and his colleagues (Bradley, Mogg, & Millar, 2000) presented pairs of these images to participants in a brief flash, one on either side of fixation, followed by a pattern mask. The pattern mask made it difficult, if not impossible, to identify the emotional expression of the face in a direct test. The participants' main task was to detect the onset of a neutral stimulus (a disc) that appeared randomly on either side of fixation following the presentation of faces and mask.

The important finding is that the target generates a more rapid response when it appears in the location of a face depicting a negative emotion than when the same target follows a face depicting neutral or positive emotions. This suggests that the negative face activates an automatic orienting response to its location, presumably in order to warn the participant of possible danger. Under normal circumstances, such a reflex would lead to a more detailed evaluation of the stimulus under conditions of full visual awareness. In the experiment, this process has been short-circuited by the presence of the backward mask.

Findings such as these, showing that emotionally charged stimuli are processed outside of visual awareness, force us to rethink our everyday association of emotions with conscious states. How something "feels" to us is often what we mean when we speak of emotions on a daily basis. Yet these results reveal that the emotional value of a visual image can be evaluated well before any corresponding feeling wells up inside us. This suggests that we need to distinguish between questions of awareness and questions of processing in this area, just as we do in all aspects of vision. In the same way that we have learned that our visual experience of "red" is not the same thing as our ability to respond to the redness of an apple, so is our experience of fear not the same thing as our ability to respond appropriately to the objects that produce our experience of fear. The actions we may initiate on the basis of "fearful" stimuli can occur before we have any experience of fear.

Skill and the zombie within

Researchers who study skilled human performance have noted for a long time that increases in skill are accompanied by a decrease in awareness of the perceptual elements and component actions that make up the skill. One of the areas of visual-motor skill that many people have in common involves driving an automobile. How many times have you driven to a well-known location, such as your place of work or your home, and been surprised to realize later that your conscious memory holds almost no record of the drive? Think of all the highly sophisticated decisions and actions that you made along the way. How few of them were you aware of at the time you made them? Most of us take driving skills so for granted, once we have learned them, that we forget how many hours of hard work and concentration it took to develop these skills. This seems to be the case for many visual-motor skills, including sight-reading while playing a musical instrument, touch-typing, and playing any number of sports.

Once we are proficient in a visual-motor skill, we often let something inside us take over control of the skill as though we are on "autopilot." This does not mean that we are any less conscious of the visual world in our immediate surroundings. Rather, it seems to mean that we are free to be conscious of different aspects of the environment from those we needed to be aware of when we were learning the skill. In particular, a skilled performer no longer needs to be aware of the execution of components of the skill. She can instead be more aware of the larger goals, of which the skill components themselves are sub-goals that she executes automatically. In driving, for example, we can attend to the task of navigating in an unfamiliar environment while the tasks of applying the appropriate amount of pedal, steering, and visual checking before making lane changes take care of themselves. In tennis, we can be primarily aware of where we intend to place the ball with the next swing of the racket rather than being primarily aware that we need to prepare the racket for each stroke of the ball by transferring our weight to the appropriate foot and executing a back swing.

Some researchers refer to the development of automaticity in a skill as the training of the *zombie within*. The term *zombie* is appropriate because it refers to a person who has all the usual characteristics of other human beings, with the important exception that the zombie lacks any consciousness and subjective experiences. The zombie responds efficiently to visual events according to the way he or she has been trained but is otherwise unable to act or make decisions. To do so would require a zombie trainer—the conscious mind. But, of course, these are only convenient and incomplete metaphors. In truth, no amount of training results in a performance that is impossible to influence or override by conscious processes.

Indeed, one of the ways that athletes in competition often try to gain advantage over one another is through ploys designed to have the conscious minds of their opponents override the zombie within. They know that if the well-trained zombie can be gotten "off his game" through intervention on the part of the conscious mind, his athletic performance will suffer. From general strategies such as these flow tactics such as time-outs in basketball, called by the opposite team's coach just before a member of the other team attempts a game-winning free throw. The minute or two that the free thrower spends thinking about that critical shot can have devastating consequences on his execution of the shot. The zombie, who can sink more than nine of ten free throws on any given day in practice, is now influenced by the intervention of the self-reflective self. This is the same self that can calculate the personal shame and simulate the experience of missing the shot before it even occurs. But it takes the extra minutes of the time-out to do so.

This conceptualization of the "normal" divided mind—one, a highly trained zombie ready for the rapid performance of certain skilled actions; the other, a more deliberate and self-reflective philosopher—is consistent with the dual visual system conceptualization of vision for action and perception proposed by Milner and Goodale (1995).

Subliminal advertising

What do the effects of masked word priming and other examples of perception without awareness imply for subliminal advertising? This marketing technique has a long and controversial history in both the advertising world and the scientific community. Much of the controversy stems from the fact that the concept of successful subliminal advertising depends on a series of separate assumptions. Often, proponents of one position present arguments in favor of a certain assumption while critics present opposing evidence—but against a different assumption.

Let's try to understand the concept of subliminal advertising by first considering each of the assumptions that would need to be true for such advertising to be effective. I should note at the outset that there are at least two senses in which subliminal advertising could be considered "effective." A relatively weak sense of its effectiveness would be demonstrated by improved sales for a product as compared with sales levels under no advertising at all. A stronger sense of its effectiveness would be demonstrated by improved sales as compared with sales levels under conventional advertising. I will list the assumptions for *visual* subliminal advertising, but similar assumptions exist for *auditory* as well.

1. *Subliminal perception is possible.* The concept of subliminal advertising assumes that vision can influence a viewer's thoughts, feelings, or actions even though the stimulus responsible for them is never part of the viewer's awareness. This is the least controversial assumption. In this book I have presented many examples of actions and thoughts that are influenced by visual stimuli outside of awareness.

2. *The advertising must be subliminal.* It's one thing to demonstrate subliminal perception in the lab. It's quite another to demonstrate that a specific advertising tool is subliminal when shown to the consuming public. Indeed, this is practically impossible to do. For example, suppose that a subliminal technique was lab tested and that most individuals (say, 90 or 95 percent) were unable to make accurate reports of the material that was presented even though it influenced their actions. This would generally be seen as an adequate demonstration of subliminal perception. Now, suppose that following the introduction of this advertisement to the consuming public, sales increased by a small percentage—which is often all that is required to obtain a good return on the money spent on advertising. Did the increase in sales occur because of the subliminal advertising? Or did it occur because a small percentage of people actually saw the material and bought the product? This is one case where proving the existence of a concept in a lab does not necessarily prove that the same concept was at work in the everyday world.

3. *Subliminal perception must open the pocket book.* That is, the thoughts, feelings, or actions generated by subliminal perception must ultimately result in consumer behavior. This assumption is much more difficult to defend, as to date no studies have shown that a given advertisement is both subliminal and successful in influencing consumers to buy. There have been individual studies of subliminal perception and individual studies showing that advertising makes a difference to consumer behavior, but no studies

documenting that specifically subliminal ads improve sales. We must also note that the kinds of actions shown to be influenced by subliminal images are generally those that the subject had already planned to initiate anyway. The unseen image may have speeded up the reaction, or intensified it, or even inhibited it; in no case was an action initiated that was not already part of the repertoire of behaviors that the observer intended to make.

4. *Subliminal perception is a stronger influence on behavior than perception with awareness.* Although this assumption is not required, strictly speaking, for subliminal advertising to be effective in the weak sense, it is the one that generates the most controversy. Critics of the use of subliminal advertising see this assumption as an infringement on the generally accepted societal right of freedom to choose. Advocates of subliminal advertising, however, see this as the main reason one should consider it. After all, why bother with the technical difficulties of implementing subliminal advertising if it works no better than conventional advertising? Unfortunately for both camps, there is no evidence from laboratory studies that the thoughts and actions generated by subliminal stimuli are any different from those generated by words and images. If anything, the subliminal effects are more difficult to demonstrate, shorter lived, and more variable.

These four assumptions about subliminal advertising help to make it clear that subliminal perception and effective subliminal advertising are really not the same. Although subliminal perception may enable us to make accurate guesses regarding the characteristics of stimuli that are hard to see, so far there is no evidence that it will influence us to, say, drink Coca-Cola or eat Ritz Crackers.

THE CONTENTS OF VISUAL CONSCIOUSNESS

If you are reading about the scientific study of consciousness for the first time, it is easy to get the impression that researchers of consciousness are more interested in the unconscious workings of the brain than in the products of those processes that the brain makes available to our awareness. In much of what we have covered so far in this chapter, the emphasis has been on behavior that is influenced by processes outside the scope of our awareness. There are many reasons for this apparent imbalance, including the difficulties we talked about earlier of dealing with first-person data. Another reason relates to the counter-intuitive—and fascinating—nature of experiments that probe the unconscious. It is impossible to predict the results of those experiments merely by thinking about our own experiences. This gives the research an intrinsic appeal that is difficult to deny.

At the same time, we must keep in mind that much of the research in visual perception addressed in this book is about the contents of consciousness in one way or another, even though it may not have been framed in those terms when we first encountered it. This is because vision researchers have learned to write in the careful phrases of behavioral scientists. Although they realize their data often constitute a summary of human observers' perceptual reports, they usually do not go out of their way to signal this to the reader. It is simply part of assumed knowledge in the vision research community. For example, this community does not need reminding that the standard tasks of target identification or visual discrimination are third-person measures of the contents of visual awareness. However, if you are a newcomer to this field, it is important to remind yourself of this from time to time.

In this section, I want to shift the emphasis back to vision that results in conscious awareness. To do this, we will explore a few recent findings in vision research that are exerting a powerful influence on the way scientists now understand the link between visual processes and visual awareness.

Reverse hierarchy theory: Seeing forests before trees

A longstanding puzzle in vision research concerns the kind of information that viewers first are able to identify when they encounter a new scene. Human observers seem to be aware of the general content of the scene well ahead of being aware of specific details. This initially seems contrary to knowledge about the progression of visual processes, which in the feedforward sweep go from simple feature analyses to complex object categorization.

One of the ways this puzzle has been studied involves flashing naturalistic scenes very briefly and having viewers answer questions about the scenes' content. To the surprise of the early researchers in this area, including Irving Biederman (1981), quite a rich and complex impression of a scene can be obtained from a picture that is flashed for as brief a time as 100 ms, or $\frac{1}{10}$th of a second. The richness is not in detail but in overall meaning, or gist. As discussed in Chapter 5, reported details are accurate only for a small portion of the scene, usually the one object or small region to which the viewer could attend in the brief flash. Instead, viewers report a very accurate impression of the gist of the scene. This impression enables them to say, for example, whether the scene depicts a seashore or an office interior. They also have a very good idea of the overall spatial layout of objects in the scene, such as where the larger objects and surfaces are in relation to one another. Finally, viewers have quite accurate impressions of the emotional content, such as whether the people depicted were "angry" or whether the scene was "happy."

Another kind of experiment that addresses the same issue uses artificial displays that have visual structure at more than one level, as shown in Figure 9.8. These compound displays, introduced by David Navon (1977) enabled researchers to make the detail at one level of visual structure—say, the small individual letters—completely independent of the details contained in the other level—say, the large composite letters. Participants' task is to detect the presence of a given target

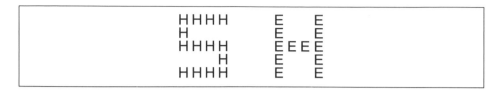

FIGURE 9.8   Displays of composite visual letters that are used to study the level of detail in a pattern that is available to a viewer's awareness first. In these artificial stimuli, viewers cannot predict the type of organization at one level (e.g., the small, individual letters) from the type of organization at another level (e.g., the large, composite letters).

letter—say, an H—as rapidly as possible. Many studies have reported the same finding: Participants detect a target at the global level (the large, composite letters) more rapidly than the same target when it appears at the local level (the small, individual letters). Moreover, this finding occurs (1) even though the target letters appear many times at the local level, and (2) for letter sizes over a large range. Human observers seem tuned to see the "forest" before the "trees."

Artists have sometimes explored the same principle of vision. Figure 9.9 (see color appendix) shows one of the more famous pictures of this kind. The painting is not only hierarchical in structure but also perceptually bistable, or ambiguous. That is, if you see the man's face in the large bust at the center of the painting, then you will not be able to see the group of people that form his eyes. However, if you can see the group of people, then the bust vanishes from your visual awareness. As predicted from the experimental results we have just reviewed, most viewers see the man's face before seeing the group of people.

What is paradoxical about this? Why shouldn't the visual brain be geared to providing the viewer with awareness of the gist, the layout, and the emotional content of a scene before providing him or her with viewer awareness of the finer details? The paradox occurs because these findings suggest that the objects of our immediate visual awareness are at the extreme end of the feedforward chain of neural events that occur in response to a new scene. Throughout this book we have seen that the neural processes of vision are organized in a hierarchical fashion, with the neurons in the earliest stages of cortical processing registering very simple visual features (motion direction or edge orientation) within a very small window (the receptive field), and neurons at successive stages of processing being tuned to increasingly complex visual properties and also being sensitive to these properties over increasingly large receptive fields. This is the anatomical cortical hierarchy we described in Chapter 2.

The fact that we as observers are aware of the "forest" before the "trees" in a scene has prompted some vision researchers, including Shaul Hochstein and

Merav Ahissar (2002), to say that in terms of visual awareness, the cortical hierarchy is reversed. With a minimum of time and effort, we can become aware of the products of the most sophisticated neural processes, including the gist, the layout, and the emotional value of a scene. With a little more time and effort, it is possible to become aware of the specific objects in a scene; and with the greatest effort and investment in time, we can become aware of the specific scene details at individual points and edges. If this overview of visual awareness is correct, then it helps to confirm that visual awareness is intimately related to the reentrant, or feedback, sweep of processing. The initial processing in vision, of which we are largely unaware, proceeds in the feedforward direction up the cortical hierarchy. Visual awareness and the ability to learn an explicit perceptual skill proceed in a direction that follows the reentrant brain connections from higher to lower visual centers. "Paying attention" seems to be inversely related to the detail level at which attention is required, with attention to fine detail requiring the greatest time and effort.

Missing the unexpected: Inattentional blindness

What aspects of the visual world are we aware of when an unexpected visual event occurs? We have seen many times in this book that vision acts in the pursuit of two goals that are often at odds: (1) to track an object through space and time so that we can maintain consistent behavior with respect to it, and at the same time (2) to be ready to evaluate new and unexpected events with respect to their relevance to us. Using an example from our evolutionary past, we would not be well served by a visual system that enabled us to hunt some game so effectively that we would be unaware that we ourselves were being stalked by another animal. In the modern world, we would not be well served by a visual system that enabled us, while driving in traffic, to be aware of a green traffic light to the exclusion of any awareness of a small child wandering into the intersection.

What rules govern our visual awareness when a new visual event interrupts an ongoing visual task? Arien Mack and Irv Rock (1998) studied this question during the 1990s by using a heroic experimental procedure known as the *inattentional blindness technique*. In these studies, participants saw a series of displays involving a difficult visual discrimination, as shown in Figure 9.10. For several displays presented in sequence, participants had to judge whether a vertical or horizontal target line appeared to be longer. The brief presentation of the two lines was followed by the prolonged display of a visually "noisy" mask designed to prevent participants from consulting any visible persistence that might remain from the brief flash of the two lines.

The line length discrimination task was in fact a cover for the real purpose of the experiment, which was to see whether participants would be aware of an unexpected new visual item. The new item was presented along with the two target lines

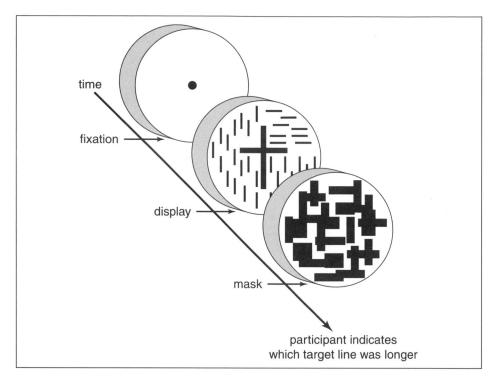

FIGURE 9.10   Display used to study inattentional blindness for unexpected events in the visual periphery. The surprise feature of this display that most participants failed to see was that the texture in one of the four quadrants of the display was different from the texture in the other three quadrants.

on the fourth trial in the sequence. Immediately following the display, participants were asked whether they had noticed anything about the display other than the two target lines. Of course, to measure the impact of these displays in the complete absence of any expectations, only one display could be presented to each participant. This is what made the procedure truly heroic: Hundreds of participants had to be tested in this way in order to determine the reliability of results for any given test object. The researchers could use subsequent test displays shown to the same participants to compare visual awareness for objects when something in addition to the two lines was expected, but they could study visual awareness under the conditions of complete surprise only from a single display for each participant.

The main finding from this procedure came as a shock to the vision research community: A large variety of visual events presented in this way go undetected by the vast majority of observers. For example, if the target lines appeared against a distinctive background texture in each of the three lead-in displays, and then in the fourth display one of the four background quadrants had a distinctively different texture, more than 75 percent of participants failed to notice the difference. This was surprising because the same visual texture differences caused "pop-out" in visual search and texture segmentation studies (Chapter 5). Those results had always been interpreted as demonstrating the automatic and "pre-attentive" nature of texture segmentation.

When smaller distinctive shapes served as the unexpected visual events in the fourth display, many more participants detected them and were able to report some of their attributes correctly. For example, only 25 percent of participants missed a small diamond shape such as the one shown in Figure 9.11. Of the participants who reported seeing this shape, most were also able to correctly indicate its color and location, whether it flickered, and whether there were one or two such shapes. However, it is interesting that most participants who noticed the shape were unable to correctly report whether it was a circle, a square, or a diamond. This suggests that the unexpected appearance of a distinctive object in the visual field can enter our awareness—at least under some conditions—but unless we have more time to attend to the object, we will see only some of its attributes.

Let's not forget the relatively large minority of participants (25 percent or so) who missed the distinctive shapes when they were not expecting to see them. What were these participants doing? Results from a small change in the procedure, as shown in Figure 9.11, gave an important clue. When the two target lines appeared at one of several locations surrounding fixation and the unexpected object appeared directly at fixation in the fourth display, visual awareness of the unexpected object did not increase. Instead, now 80 percent of participants denied seeing anything at all! Moreover, they could not guess what the object might have looked like, and they could not even select the correct object in a forced-choice recognition test.

These findings suggest that visual awareness is not simply a "gate" that opens up conscious access to some visual processes, but that an equally important aspect of awareness is the deliberate repression of information from spatial locations to which we are not attending. When the target lines were centered at fixation, participants were prepared to judge line lengths extending into the visual periphery, so new visual events in those regions were expected. Because they couldn't be prepared to move their attention away from all of those regions, they were able to detect most of the unexpected small objects. However, when the lines to be judged appeared in one of several locations around the fixation point, participants could be certain that the lines would not occur right at that point. When the surprise objects appearing right at fixation violated this expectation, most of them went unnoticed.

Some studies of inattentional blindness have examined the extent to which visual awareness is restricted to other features of the task at hand besides spatial location. For example, Daniel Simons and his colleagues (Simons & Chabris, 1999)

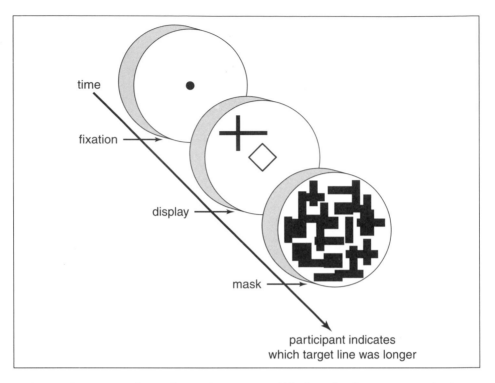

FIGURE 9.11 Display used to study inattentional blindness for objects presented at fixation. The surprise feature of this display that some participants failed to see was the diamond pattern presented at fixation following three previous displays without it.

wondered whether a man in a gorilla suit—who usually would be quite visually distinctive—would go unnoticed in a small crowd of people if he was unexpected and not related to the visual task at hand. In short, the expected answer was "yes!" Participants in the "gorilla" study had the task of watching a videotape of a team of three people dressed in a single color (e.g., white) pass around a basketball while another team of three people (e.g., dressed in black) tried to intercept the ball. The participants' primary task was to count the number of successful passes made by the team with the ball during a short viewing period. While this was going on, a man in a gorilla suit entered the scene and marched through the area of the ball game. He paused briefly at the center of the screen, thumped his chest a few times with both fists, and then walked out of view of the camera.

More than 50 percent of participants were completely unaware of the man in the gorilla suit; they were indeed surprised when they watched the tape a second time with instructions to look for him. More important, their failure of awareness varied according to whether they were monitoring the white-suited or the black-suited team. Fully 58 percent of participants monitoring the black-suited team de-tected the man in the gorilla suit, but only 27 percent of participants who were monitoring the white-suited team did so. Apparently, visual awareness of the unex-pected is determined not only by the spatial factors of the task at hand but also by the color factors of the primary task.

These laboratory results are relevant to many everyday situations where safety is important. One example from the literature on automobile safety comes to mind be-cause it seems to match the "gorilla" study directly. One of the most common traffic accidents involving cars and motorcycles includes a car turning left at an intersection directly in the path of a motorcycle entering the intersection at the same time. Dri-vers of the car consistently report not seeing the motorcycle before it was too late to avoid the collision, at the same time that they report paying full attention to the road and the traffic conditions. The car drivers usually infer from these aspects of their awareness that the motorcycle must have been exceeding the speed limit to a consid-erable extent. How could they have missed seeing the motorcycle otherwise? The answer seems to be—as in the "gorilla" study—that car drivers do not expect to see motorcycles in the same way that they expect to see cars entering intersections. The research of Peter Hancock and colleagues (Hancock, Wulf, & Thorn, 1990) sup-ports this answer. These researchers examined driving habits separately for car drivers who were either familiar or unfamiliar with motorcycles. Drivers with a high degree of familiarity with motorcycles were less likely to turn into the path of an oncoming motorcycle, both when their traffic accident histories were examined and when their behavior was tested in a driving simulator. Thus visual awareness depends on our ex-pectations, in both the real world and the laboratory.

Awareness in single cells

Something surprising happens when each of our eyes sees a different image. Rather than seeing both images, or even seeing one image as a transparency over the other image, the brain chooses to provide only one of the images to our expe-rience at a time. Somewhere in the brain, an all-or-nothing choice takes place to bring the contents of one image to consciousness instead of the other. But this choice is not final. If we continue to view the same two images over a few minutes, they alternate in our awareness. After we see one image for only a few seconds, the scene suddenly switches to the other image; after we view that one for a time, we again see the original image. This phenomenon is called *binocular rivalry*. The term refers to the spontaneous competition that occurs whenever each of our eyes sees a different image. This is a competition over the control of visual awareness, not over the control of visual input, since both eyes are looking directly at per-fectly good images and neurons corresponding to each image are equally active in the earliest stages of visual processing.

BOX 9.2

Binocular rivalry

The simplest way to experience binocular rivalry is to first learn to fuse disparate images in the two eyes. The images in Figure 9.12a will help you do this.

Hold your book level with the horizon, and look at the two images in Figure 9.12a with your eyes slightly crossed. When they are crossed, you will see three outline squares and three lower dots instead of only two. The middle square and dot are an illusion; they are the fused image that your brain constructs from the different image in each eye. You will be able to tell how much to cross your eyes by looking to see whether the middle square and lower dot are centered with respect to the two squares and dots on either side. When they are centered and your eyes are relaxed in this new position, what do you see in the center position? If you have properly fused the different images in each eye, you will see a triangle floating in front of a disc, which in turn is floating in front of the largest square in the background. You have achieved *stereofusion*.

Now try the same exercise with the two images in Figure 9.12b. You should be able to cross your eyes so that you see a central square and its lower dot in the same way that you did in Figure 9.12a. But what do you see inside the central square now? Because the two images you are trying to fuse are so different, your visual system settles on seeing one of the images at a time. Do your best to hold the image of the fused square and dot for as long as you can so that you get a sense of the reversals in appearance that occur spontaneously. For a while you will see the image of one face. Then you will see the other face. The two images will alternate back and forth if you are able to hold your crossed eyes steady for a minute or so.

It is difficult to create the ideal conditions for binocular rivalry outside of the vision laboratory, but it is worth trying because the exercise will give you insight into the phenomenon even if the final result is not completely satisfying to you. Box 9.2 and Figure 9.12 offers some tips for creating binocular rivalry without special equipment.

In the vision laboratory, researchers can induce binocular rivalry in one of two straightforward ways. An *optical solution* involves a pair of wedge-shaped displacing prisms, one in front of each eye, so that although the eyes are aligned as if to receive input from the same place in space, they are actually receiving input from two adjacent locations. This is shown in Figure 9.13. Now two different images can be placed in the two locations. When the observer looks through the prisms, he sees only one image at a time.

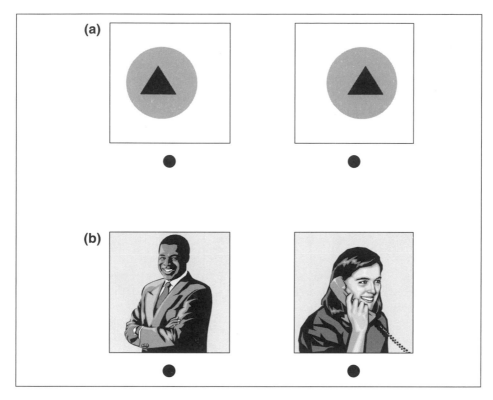

FIGURE 9.12 **(a)** A pair of simple images that can be used to practice stereofusion using the cross-eye technique. The only difference in the two images concern the relative lateral positions of the triangle and the disc, allowing them to appear at different depths when the viewer's eyes are crossed. **(b)** A pair of images that can be used to experience binocular rivalry. The interiors of the two squares are so different that the brain can see only one at a time.

An *electronic solution* that induces the same experience—but that is considerably more expensive—involves a pair of glasses equipped to show a different digital image to each eye. If the participant closes one eye while wearing these glasses, he sees only a single image. If he keeps both eyes open, each eye receives a different image and binocular rivalry ensues.

Binocular rivalry is an ideal phenomenon with which to study visual awareness in an animal, using electrophysiological techniques that can probe the brain directly, because the task does not require much in the way of behavior on the part of the animal. It merely needs to learn to indicate what is currently on view as far as it is concerned. Furthermore, the perception that guides its behavior is such an all-or-nothing event that the interpretation of the data is straightforward. For example, a monkey can be easily trained to press a key on the right whenever a particular face

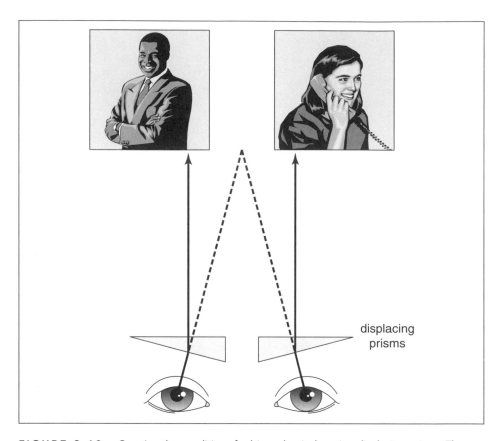

FIGURE 9.13　Creating the conditions for binocular rivalry using displacing prisms. The eyes converge as though fixating on the same point, as indicated by the dashed lines. However, the displacing prisms bend the light so that in fact each eye sees an entirely different image, as indicated at the end of the arrows. In the viewer's experience, the images will alternate because the brain can see only one at a time.

appears on a computer screen. The monkey learns this by earning a slice of banana as a reward for pressing the correct key. Similarly, it can earn another banana slice whenever it sees a starburst pattern and reliably presses a key on the left.

When the monkey has learned to make the two responses consistently, it is fitted with a device that records activity from specific neurons in carefully chosen brain sites. This enables the experimenter to find neurons that respond to only one of the pictures—say, the face. Next, the monkey is shown a binocular rivalry display that presents the face to one eye and the starburst to the other eye. Now, the monkey's responses become an index of which picture is seen at any point in time.

Adding a simple twist to this procedure provides an important check on the reliability of the assumptions. In humans viewing a binocular rivalry display, when one of the images is abruptly switched to another image, the new image wins the competition for perception—at least for a short time—before perceptual alternations begin again between the two images on view. If monkeys trained in this procedure experience the same surprise image switch, they behave completely as expected: Their key presses indicate that they also see the new surprise images. Having established this background, we are now ready to see how neurons in different regions of the monkey's brain correlate with the images it sees.

Recordings from single neurons in cortical areas V1, V2, V4, and MT (the middle temporal area) show little correlation between the monkey's responses and the activity level of those neurons that previously responded to images of a face. However, recordings from the superior temporal sulcus (STS) and inferotemporal (IT) cortex show a very different correlation. Here, over 90 percent of the neurons are active when the monkey indicates with key presses that it sees a face. This result is consistent with Milner and Goodale's (1995) dual visual system theory, which claims that only ventral stream processes make their results available for awareness.

Many researchers have been tempted to think of binocular rivalry as a competition for consciousness between the signals coming from the two eyes. However, there is now very good evidence that binocular rivalry is a competition between high-level and central representations involving different objects or scenes. These neural representations are very likely in the temporal cortex, where neurons receive input from both eyes, and almost certainly not in the earliest representations of area V1, where input from each eye is still separate. If this is the case, then the term *binocular rivalry* is a misnomer. The rivalry is instead between high-level perceptual hypotheses that are at odds with one another. These kinds of rivalries occur for many images that require only monocular viewing, as shown in Figure 9.14.

In one very clever experiment demonstrating this point (Logothetis, Leopold, & Sheinberg, 1996), researchers presented each eye with a pattern of stripes that differed in orientation. One pattern consisted of stripes on a positive diagonal; the other pattern was on a negative diagonal, as illustrated in Figure 9.15. At random intervals, the two patterns would switch between the two eyes. The question was whether the perception of one set of stripes and the other would follow the input to the eyes, where patterns changed under the experimenter's control; or whether the perceptions would alternate under the internal control of the brain, in which case the same set of stripes would continue to be seen even though its input alternated randomly between the eyes.

The results showed that the perceptions of the two sets of stripes alternated in exactly the same way, with one orientation being seen for a period followed by the other orientation. This occurred regardless of whether a given set of stripes always appeared for the same eye or whether its presentation alternated between the eyes. The contents of visual awareness are therefore best understood as a "conclusion"

FIGURE 9.14   Examples of multistable or ambiguous visual images.

that the brain reaches with regard to the visual input. Multistable viewing conditions—which exist in binocular rivalry displays and ambiguous pictures—demonstrate that this conclusion does not rest on visual input alone. We have made this point many times in this book. Vision is an active process of construction, a point that is equally true when we speak of the contents of visual awareness.

UNUSUAL FORMS OF VISUAL CONSCIOUSNESS: SYNESTHESIA

One of the most fruitful ways to study visual awareness is to compare the reports and behavior of people who claim to have different conscious experiences in response to the same visual events. We saw in Chapter 3 that this was a very effective way to understand color vision. By comparing the color perceptions of individuals with three cone types and those with only two, and more recently of individuals with four cone types, we can better understand the basis of color vision. Differences in these individuals' genetic makeup has been useful in helping to establish the evolutionary history of color vision in humans.

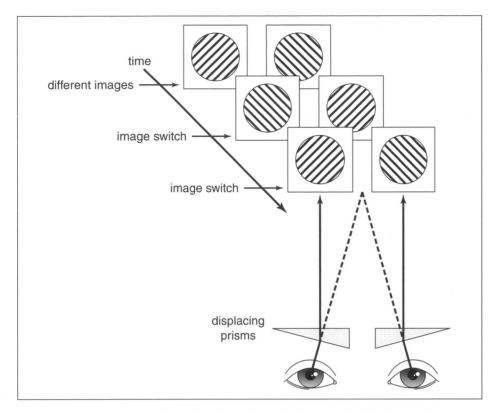

FIGURE 9.15   Displays for studying binocular rivalry that periodically alternate between eyes. The displacing prisms bend the light for each eye so that each sees a different image.

The same approach works in trying to understand the basis of visual awareness in domains other than color vision, such as the visual experiences of people known as synesthetes. In its broadest definition, a *synesthete* is someone who experiences ordinary sensory events in extraordinary ways. Estimates of the incidence of synesthesia in the general population are about one in two thousand. As an example of the typical report associated with synesthesia, some individuals say that whenever they are shown a printed letter or a digit, they involuntarily see a specific color in association with the printed character. Some report that the color appears as a thin veil floating above the printed character; others report that the character itself takes on a colored tinge. However, in both cases the mapping of reported colors to specific characters is consistent and stable over time. For example, a synesthete who reports seeing the digit 7 as yellow and 3 as red will report the same digit-color mappings every time he or she is asked over a long period. The synesthete will also claim to have no choice in the matter; these experiences have occurred for as long as he or she can remember. Synesthetes are often surprised to learn that other people don't have the same experiences.

One aspect of synesthesia that makes it a convenient "natural experiment" for the study of consciousness is that it offers the possibility of testable consequences of otherwise private visual experiences. Consider, for example, many synesthetes' claim that black printed digits appear to them to have specific hues. Critics who might otherwise scoff at these reports as being fantasies of an overly rich imagination can put their doubts to a direct test. After all, the experience of seeing colored digits should have testable consequences on visual tasks in which the apparent color of a digit would otherwise have a behavioral effect.

Researchers tested several self-reporting synesthetes in exactly this kind of experiment (Smilek et al., 2001). The basic task was a color naming task in which participants tried to name, as rapidly as possible, the color of the ink in which a digit was printed. For ordinary participants (non-synesthetes), the particular colors matched to particular digits had no influence on the task. Color naming was quite fast (between 500 and 600 milliseconds) in all cases because there was no intrinsic relation between the printed digits and their colors. However, for synesthetes, the digit-color mapping made a great deal of difference. When digits appeared in the colors normally seen by synesthetes, color naming was as fast as it was for the comparison participants. In contrast, when digits appeared printed in colors that were incongruent for a given synesthete, color-naming times slowed by 200 to 300 milliseconds. The baseline speed at which color naming was accomplished by synesthetes, along with the magnitude of the naming interference measured for incongruently colored digits, indicated that the colors "seen" by synesthetes had influences that were as automatic and involuntary as those that occurred when ordinary participants were asked to name the ink color of a given word.

One of the important clues to the neural basis of the synesthetic experience is that it does not require the sensory experience of a digit in order to induce the experience of color. For example, in the case of synesthetes who see printed black digits in color, simply thinking about the digit can evoke the experience of color. Since there is no feedforward signal to initiate the usual digit-color experience, the visual experience must be driven by conceptual input—in other words, these experiences can be generated entirely by the reentrant sweeps of neural processing. As we have seen many times in this book, a fundamental sensory experience—in this case, color perception—can be triggered in the complete absence of a corresponding sensory event.

The claim that this is a tangible visual experience, as opposed to a memory of past experience, has also been tested with the color-naming task: Participants named actual color patches following the presentation of a simple arithmetic problem. For example, for a synesthete who claims to see the digit 7 in yellow, researchers would present a yellow color patch for naming immediately following presentation of the problems $3 + 4 = ?$ and $5 + 1 = ?$ Because the answer to the first problem is color congruent with the synesthetic experience of the digit 7 and the answer to the second problem is not, seeing the yellow color patch following the first problem should speed color naming. This is exactly what Philip Merikle and his colleagues documented when testing a digit-color synesthete, with the incongruent problems slowing color-naming responses by over 200 ms (Dixon et al., 2000).

PROBING THE CONSCIOUS MIND ON-LINE

One approach to the study of visual awareness in the everyday world that was pioneered by Russell Hurlbert (Hurlbert & Heavey, 2001) and is gaining in popularity is *descriptive experience sampling*. In this procedure, participants go about their daily activities in the usual way except that they carry a personal beeper that the experimenter has programmed to go off at random intervals throughout the day. When the beeper goes off, the participant immediately jots down in a notebook the characteristics of that particular moment; then, within a 24-hour period, he or she undergoes an in-depth and highly structured interview aimed at probing the question *What was the content of your inner experience at the moment the beep went off?* The structured interview is designed to equip the participant with a greater range of verbal tools for communicating what he or she is experiencing at any point in time, although it is very careful not to guide the participant to a particular description of any given moment. For example, if the participant reported to be reading when the beeper went off, the questions would be aimed at what the participant was thinking about and what visual images were being experienced.

This method of exploring the contents of consciousness takes at face value participants' verbal reports of their inner experiences. Although many researchers are uncomfortable taking such verbal reports as indicative of awareness, they cannot deny that the reports have the benefit of being generated directly by the observer in question. As such, they are "close" to the intended subject matter, even if that subject matter has been filtered through the categories of natural language. The method has also been shown to be reliable over time for a given individual. One of the interesting findings that emerged from this work is that there are considerable differences among individuals in the extent to which visual images dominate their thoughts. Some participants report almost no inner speech and a preponderance of visual images, whereas others report frequent inner speech and almost no visual images. Future research will likely search for correlations between the observers' reported subjective states and the brain areas that are active during the activities that generate these reports.

Preliminary research in this area has examined the patterns of brain activity that accompany *transcendent moments* or *peak experiences*. One interesting finding is that when an individual such as a Buddhist monk is meditating and experiencing sensations that he describes as "calm, unity, and transcendence," the event is asso-ciated with increased activity in the frontal lobes and decreased activity in the pari-etal lobes. The increased activity in the frontal lobes is consistent with the concentrated effort required to achieve and maintain the deeply meditative state, which would be expected to involve the executive functions of the frontal lobes. The corresponding decrease in activity of the parietal lobes is also consistent, since this brain region is usually involved when the spatial positions of objects are im-portant in a cognitive task. The accounts of transcendence that refer to "out of body" experiences and a loss of distinction between "self" and "other" are there-fore consistent with reduced activity in the brain regions important for represent-ing spatial frames of reference.

LIVING IN THE ZONE

When top-level athletes describe their most satisfying personal moments in sport, they tend to mention a cluster of subjective features. These include a feeling of total concentration and involvement in the activity, calm mastery and control over the situation, unity of the mind's intentions and the body's actions, and fulfillment and exhilaration over having achieved such a high level of performance. This constellation of reports is so consistent that researchers have documented it independently numer-ous times over a vast range of sports, from racecar driving to gymnastics. Some re-searchers have even written how-to books to help non-athletes achieve a similar state of awareness in mundane tasks such as driving to work and taking a test. In the ath-letic world, attaining this state of consciousness is often referred to as "being in the zone," "having the flow," or sometimes merely "being unconscious."

This state is of interest to vision scientists for several reasons. First, it is a first-person experience that we all seem to understand and are able to discuss with oth-ers without being able to confirm that we are really talking about the same thing. A skeptic of the science of consciousness might argue that in doing so we are using the slipperiness of natural language to fool ourselves about the similarity of these experiences. Yet the fact that communication about it is possible and reliable sug-gests an underlying core experience that many people share.

To appreciate this, contrast everyday talk of the "zone" experience with imag-ined talk of another subjective experience that only few individuals share but that we all could fake if we wanted to: digit-color synesthetic experience. Imagine that a friend told you she saw ordinary printed black digits in distinctive colors, and you, wanting to play along, claimed you saw the same thing. It wouldn't take long for communication to break down as you fabricated reports of experiences and your friend probed them for similarity with her own. Of course, your faked reports would fare even less well if you were a participant in an experiment on the auto-matic effects of digit-color synesthesia. Shared experiences of awareness like "being in the zone" give hope to scientists looking for reliable phenomena in the study of consciousness.

Second, "being in the zone" is the self-reported relationship between a diminished awareness of the elements of skilled performance and a heightened awareness of the larger context in which the performance takes place. Some people refer to it as being at once physically relaxed and mentally alert. This is consistent with one of the necessary preconditions for achieving the "zone" experience: mastery of the basic skills of the sport. Without these skills becoming automatic, too much of our awareness is occupied with their action elements. There is little room left in our awareness for experiencing the moment. Research shows that if novices attempt to experience the moment, their sports skills suffer almost immediately. Even—or perhaps especially—in the domain of consciousness, there are severe limitations on the number of events that we can attend to with success. Thus, for example, we can choose to spend the day working on our golf game or enjoying the outdoors and conversations with our friends. Unfortunately, without first making a considerably larger investment in the acquisition of better golf skills, we are unable to do both at the same time.

VISUAL CONSCIOUSNESS AND VISION SCIENCE

The focus in this chapter, on the distinction between vision that results in conscious experience versus visual processes that are inaccessible to our awareness, has helped make it clear why a science of vision is necessary. If our visual experiences provided us with a transparent window to the reality around us and to our own visual functioning, then it would be perfectly reasonable to study vision from the comfort of our armchairs. What we experience when "seeing" would in fact be all there would be to study. "Seeing" would be "believing," and "what we see" would in fact be "what we get."

In contrast to this naïve view of vision, what we have learned in this chapter is that much of vision operates beneath the radar screen of our awareness. We point, grasp, and duck for objects well before we experience the visual attributes of those objects that are guiding our behavior. We are able to acquire the meaning of a word or a naturalistic scene without being aware of many of the particular features of the image that gave rise to our experience. We fail to be aware of many of the objects that appear in our field of view when we are not expecting them to occur. At the same time, these "unseen" objects have measurable influences on our behavior, and they "color" our experiences of the objects we are aware of. Clearly, our personal experience is an unreliable guide to the many analyses of light undertaken by our eye and brain.

Having acknowledged the importance of studying vision in all its forms, we must next acknowledge that vision science has a long way to go in providing a complete understanding of how its various forms might work individually, and an even longer way to go in providing an understanding of how unconscious and conscious vision might work together in the healthy brain. It sometimes appears that scientific progress is being made more rapidly on those aspects of visual functioning that never become conscious than on the difficult problems surrounding our conscious experience of what we see. However, that should not deter us from pressing on to the ultimate challenge of trying to understand both the visual analyses conducted by the brain and the brain's ability to provide us with rich visual experiences.

FURTHER READING

Chalmers, D. J. (1996). *The conscious mind: In search of a fundamental theory*. New York: Oxford University Press.

Creem, S. H., & Proffitt, D. R. (1998). Two memories for geographical slant: Separation and interdependence of action and awareness. *Psychonomic Bulletin & Review, 5,* 22–36.

Csikszentmihalyi, M. (1991). *Flow: The psychology of optimal experience*. New York: HarperCollins.

Goodale, M. A., & Milner, D. A. (2004). *Sight unseen*. New York: Oxford University Press.

Logothetis, N., & Schall, J. (1989). Neuronal correlates of subjective visual perception. *Science, 245,* 761–763.

Proffitt, D. R., Stefanucci, J., Banton, T., & Epstein, W. (2003). The role of effort in perceiving distance. *Psychological Science, 14,* 106–112.

Springer, S. P., & Deutsch, G. (1985). *Left brain, right brain*. New York: Freeman.

CREDITS

Art

Figure 1.2: Shepard, R. N. (1990). <u>Mind Sights</u>. New York: WH Freeman.

Figure 2.12: Reprinted from *Trends in Neuroscience*, Vol. 23, V. A. F. Lamme and P. R. Roelfsema, "The Distinct Modes of Vision offered by Feedforward and Recurrent Processing," pp. 71–579. © 2000, with permission from Elsevier.

Figure 3.1: ©1995 Edward H. Adelson. Used by permission of the author. For more information, see: http://www-bcs.mit.edu/people/adelson/checkershadow_illusion.htm

Figure 4.16: Fiorani, M. Jr., Rosa, MGP, Gattass, R., and Rocha-Miranda, C. E. (1992). "Dynamic surrounds of receptive fields in primate striate cortex: A physiological basis for perceptual completion?" *Proceedings of the National Academy of Sciences* 89, pp. 8547–8551.

Figure 4.26: Originally published by C. M. Mooney (1957). *Canadian Journal of Psychology*, 11, p. 219. Reprinted with kind permission of Dr. Sandy Wiseman, University of Toronto, Canada.

Figure 5.15: Hoffman, D. D. (1998). <u>Visual intelligence</u>. New York: W.W. Norton.

Figure 5.24: Albert, M. K. (2001). "Surface perception and the generic view principle." *Trends in Cognitive Science* 5, pp. 197–203.

Figure 5.25: Biederman, I. (1987). "Recognition-by-components: A theory of human image understanding." *Psychological Review*, 94, 115–147.

Figure 5.26: Biederman, I. (1987). "Recognition-by-components: A theory of human image understanding." *Psychological Review*, 94, 115–147.

Figure 6.8: Sheth, B. R., Nijhawan, R., & Shimojo, S. (2000). "Changing objects lead briefly flashed ones." *Nature Neuroscience*, 3, 489–495.

Figure 6.13: Scholl, B. J., & Tremoulet, P. D. (2000). "Perceptual causality and animacy." *Trends in Cognitive Science*, 1, 56–61.

Figure 6.14: Scholl, B. J., & Tremoulet, P. D. (2000). "Perceptual causality and animacy." *Trends in Cognitive Science*, 1, 56–61.

Figure 7.2: Bressan, P., Garlaschelli, L., & Barracano, M. (2003). "Anti-gravity hills are visual illusions." *Psychological Science* 14, pp. 441–449. Reprinted by permission of Blackwell Publishing Ltd.

Figures 7.5a and 7.5b: Shimamura, A. P., & Prinzmetal, W. (1999). "The Mystery Spot illusion and its relation to other visual illusions." *Psychological Science* 10, pp. 501–507. Reprinted by permission of Blackwell Publishing Ltd.

Figure 8.10: Sigala, N., & Logothetis, N. K. (2002). "Visual categorization shapes feature selectivity in the primate temporal cortex." *Nature*, 415, pp. 318–320.

Photos

Figure 2.1f: Dr. Krish Singh et al., Wellcome Laboratory for MEG Studies, Ashton University, U.K.

Figure 3.21: B. Pinna et al., 2001.

Figure 3.22: J. Tanaka et al., 2001.

Figure 4.5: Special thanks to Jason Gold for the band-pass filtered manipulations.

Figure 4.25: CNAC/MNAM/Dist. Reunion des Musees Nationaux/Art Resource, NY

Figure 5.18: P. Mamassian et al., 2001.

Figure 7.1: Photo courtesy of www.photochris.com. Reprinted with permission of Dr. Paola Bressan.

Figure 7.3: Photo courtesy of Dr. Art Shimamura, University of California, Berkeley.

Figure 7.7: Ian Howard Photo, York University.

Figure 8.9: D. T. Levin, 2000.

Figure 8.12: M. J. Tarr & I. Gauthier, 2000.

Figure 8.13: R. L. Goldstone, University of Indiana, Bloomington.

Figure 8.14: R. L. Goldstone, University of Indiana, Bloomington.

Figure 9.9: *Slave Market with the Disappearing Bust of Voltaire*, 1940. Oil on canvas, 18¼ × 25⅜ inches. Collection of The Salvador Dali Museum, St. Petersburg, Florida. © 2004 Gala-Salvador Dali Foundation, Figueres (Artist Rights Society [ARS] New York. © 2004 Salvador Dali Museum, Inc.

akinetopsia (motion blindness) a form of blindness to motion, caused by brain damage or disease

Alberti's window (da Vinci's window) the intersection of the rays of light from a scene as they pass through a two-dimensional plane in front of the viewer

amacrine cells cells in the retina of the eye that transmit signals laterally among ganglion cells

ambiguous figure (bistable figure) an image with two or more perceptual interpretations that tend to alternate with one another

amygdala a midbrain structure involved in the evaluation of the emotional content of visual images

anatomical visual hierarchy the arrangement of the visually sensitive regions of the cortex according to their anatomical distance (number of synapses or steps) from area V1

animation the illusion of motion that occurs when a sequence of still drawings is viewed in rapid succession

anomaloscope a tool used by ophthalmologists to detect color anomalies such as dichromacy in humans

anoxia a sustained lack of oxygen to the brain

anti-gravity hills (magnetic hills) locations on earth where "downhill" and "uphill" seem reversed, so that a ball appears to roll uphill

apperceptive agnosic an individual who does not recognize objects or shapes even though he or she can discriminate color, luminance, and motion in detail

area V1 (primary visual area) the first cortical location to which neural signals are sent from the eye, lying at the back of the brain

area V4 (cortical color center) a region in the cortex of monkeys that is sensitive to color (cortical color center is the corresponding region in humans)

area V5 a cortical region involved in the analysis of motion; also called the medial temporal cortex (MT)

arrow-junction a relationship among three edges in which one of the angles is greater than 180 degrees

associative agnosic an individual who does not recognize objects even though he or she can see, describe, and draw their shapes

attached shadow a portion of an object that receives less light because it is blocked by another portion of the same object

attention any process by which some information is selected at the expense or neglect of other information

attentional blink a period of reduced sensitivity to visual targets when viewing a rapid sequence of images following the detection of a first instance of the target class

attentional capture an involuntary tendency for visual attention to be attracted to the location of new information in a scene

axons the long extensions of neurons that transmit signals to other neurons

backward masking a reduction in the visibility of a stimulus caused by the presentation of another stimulus later in time

basic level the general class of an object (e.g., "chair," "person," "tree") as opposed to a specific member of the class (e.g., "armchair," "George," "cedar")

behavioral experiment an activity in which data are collected from one or more study participants in the form of responses to a carefully designed stimulus; also called a psychophysical test

behaviorism a philosophical movement of the 1920s and 1930s claiming that the science of perception is restricted to measuring actions that can be observed

binding coordinated activity among a group of neurons

binocular disparity (disparity) the horizontal displacement that occurs when each eye views a scene from a slightly different viewpoint

binocular rivalry the perception of only one image when each eye is presented with a different image

bipolar cells cells in the retina of the eye that receive their input from the cone and rod receptors

blobs small islands of color-sensitive cortical neurons in area V1

brightness the perceived intensity of a light source

broadband light light in which all visible wavelengths are represented

calcarine fissure an anatomical landmark on the cortex, separating representations of the upper and lower visual field

candela a measure of light emitted from a solitary candle shining directly onto a surface that is 1 square meter in area, at a distance of 1 meter; approximately $\frac{1}{1000}$ watt

canonicality the viewing perspective that permits an object to be identified most rapidly

cast shadow a region of a surface that is blocked from receiving direct light by another object

category detection the ability to detect an instance of a general class of possible scenes (e.g., a beach scene)

chance level of guessing the probability of guessing the answer to a question correctly when one has no information

change blindness the failure to notice a change in a scene during a brief interruption in viewing because of an eye movement, an eye blink, a shift in viewpoint, or a flickering image

color antagonistic (color opponent) relating to a neuron that is excitatory for one color (e.g., red) and inhibitory for the complementary color (e.g., green)

color averaging color mixing that occurs when each area of color occupies a relatively small region of space

color constancy the phenomenon of the intrinsic color of a surface being visible regardless of the color of the ambient light

color contrast the phenomenon of a color appearing more vivid when it is placed beside its complementary color

color gamut the full range of colors that are possible with a given technology (e.g., color television) or medium (e.g., set of paints)

color opponent (color antagonistic) relating to a neuron that is excitatory for one color (e.g., red) and inhibitory for the complementary color (e.g., green)

color spindle (color solid) a three-dimensional representation of colors based on the perceptual qualities of hue, brightness, and saturation

complex cells edge-detecting neurons in area V1 that are specific for orientation but not location

compound stimulus an object with two levels of visual structure in which the elements of the structure at one level are independent of the elements of the structure at the other level (e.g., a "face" formed from vegetables arranged in the appropriate configuration)

computational vision an approach to studying vision that emphasizes the analysis of light and images through the selection of appropriate computations; related to artificial intelligence, biological cybernetics, robotics, and machine vision

computer-assisted tomography (CAT) scans images of the brain's structure in live individuals based on tissue density

concavity a feature of a surface that is indented with respect to the viewer

cones (cone receptors) cells in the retina of the eye that are responsive to light under typical daylight conditions

configurational effect the phenomenon of a part of an object (e.g., "Bob's nose") being recognizable when it is shown in the correct context (e.g., "Bob's face") rather than when it is shown in a scrambled or distorted context

congenital achromatopsia a genetic condition associated with the underdevelopment or absence of cone receptors in the eye

conservative response strategy guessing "no difference" in a discrimination task when one has not seen any difference

contingent attentional capture the tendency for one's attention to be directed to features of a stimulus for which one has been prepared

contralateral meaning "on opposite sides," usually referring to visual fields with respect to cerebral hemispheres (e.g, the left visual field is contralateral to the right hemisphere)

contrast the magnitude of a change in luminance; calculated by taking the difference in luminance at an edge and dividing that difference by the sum of the luminances on each side of the edge

convexity a feature of a surface that bulges out with respect to the viewer

corrective saccade a second saccade that hones in on the target position after an initial saccade has been made to the general area of a target

cortex the convoluted gray matter forming the outer surface of the brain

cortical blindness a form of blindness caused by brain damage or brain disease, not by eye damage or eye disease

cortical color center (area V4) a region of the cortex of humans that is sensitive to color (area V4 is the corresponding region in monkeys)

cortical magnification factor the degree to which cortical neurons representing the central part of the eye register finer detail than the neurons representing the peripheral visual field

counting slow and effortful visual enumeration of a large number of items

covert spatial orienting the movement of attention (i.e., the mind's eye) to a location in an image or scene while gaze (i.e., the physical eye) is stationary

critical flicker fusion the lowest rate of flicker that a viewer is able to see as a steady source of light

cue (depth cue) a clue to three-dimensionality (i.e., depth) that can be conveyed via a single image or eye

cyclopean eye the illusion that visual direction is determined from the center of the viewer's head

da Vinci's window (Alberti's window) the intersection of the rays of light from a scene as they pass through a two-dimensional plane in front of the viewer

degrees a measure of the size of a visual stimulus; degrees of visual angle describe a segment of an imaginary circle (360 degrees) surrounding the viewer

depolarizing (firing) the discrete activity of a neuron in response to a signal from another neuron

depth cue (cue) a clue to three-dimensionality (i.e., depth) that can be conveyed via a single image or eye

detection sensing the presence (as opposed to the absence) of a visual stimulus

deuteranope an individual whose color vision lacks medium-wavelength (i.e., green) receptors

dichromacy (dichromat) color vision based on two types of wavelength receptors; a common form of colorblindness in humans

discrimination the sensing of a difference between two or more visual stimuli

disparity (binocular disparity) the horizontal displacement that occurs when each eye views a scene from a slightly different viewpoint

dominant eye the eye a viewer uses to sight and align targets

dorsal stream a region of the cortex lying along the back of the brain

dual visual system theory a theory according to which the ventral stream is responsible for conscious vision and the dorsal stream is responsible for the on-line control of visually guided action

electrophysiological recording a recording of the small amounts of electrical activity in the cells of the brain

empty box approach the study of a phenomenon without knowing the inner workings of a structure that is responsible for the phenomenon

end-stopped cells edge-detecting neurons in area V1 that are specific for orientation, location, and length

event-related potential (ERP) recordings recordings of the averaged neural activity in the brain that can be detected through the scalp in response to a stimulus

excitatory referring to a cell that becomes more active (fires more vigorously) in response to a stimulus

exemplar a specific object from a general class of objects

extinction a mild form of hemispatial neglect in which an object can be seen on either side of the visual field unless there is another object on the other side of the visual field

feature migration an illusion in which the features in one image are seen as appearing in another image that appears immediately after it

feedback processing the phenomenon in which neural signals progress backward, or "down," in the anatomical visual hierarchy

feedforward processing the phenomenon in which neural signals progress forward, or "up," in the anatomical visual hierarchy

figure a shape that has perceptual "ownership" of an edge

firing (depolarizing) the discrete activity of a neuron in response to a signal from another neuron

first-order edge an edge defined by an abrupt change in the luminance or hue of a surface

first-person data the experiences of a study participant in a behavioral experiment or psychophysical test

fixation the brief period between eye movements when the eyes are stationary, gazing at a single location

flash-lag effect an illusion in which the perceived location of a brief flash of light lags behind the perceived location of a moving object

floater a spot that is seen as moving against a blue sky but that actually originates from debris within the fluid of the eye

focus of expansion the center of an optical flow pattern where there is no motion

foreshortening (texture compression) the systematic decrease in the vertical spacing of texture elements with increasing distance in an image or picture

Fourier analysis a mathematical process by which an image is transformed into a set of simple sinusoidal (i.e., sine wave) gratings

functional magnetic resonance imaging (fMRI) a process that provides images of the brain's function in live individuals, based on changes in blood flow related to neural activity

fusiform face area (FFA) a cortical region involved in the perception and recognition of faces

fusiform gyrus a cortical landmark (*gyrus* means "valley") in the temporal cortex near the location of the fusiform face area (FFA)

ganglion cells neurons in the eye that transmit signals about light to the brain

generic viewpoint the assumption that a relationship between two or more edges will be maintained from a variety of viewpoints

gist the meaningful context in which visual objects are seen

grand illusion of complete perception the experience of seeing a wide-angled field of view that is rich in color and detail

gratings a visual pattern that has regular changes in contrast along one dimension

gravitational upright the direction pointing away from the force of gravity

ground a shape whose visible boundaries are defined by the "accident" of one object occluding another

height in the plane (proximity to the horizon) a clue to three-dimensionality (i.e., depth) given by the tendency for objects close to the horizon to be associated with greater distance from the viewer

hemispatial neglect (unilateral neglect) a failure to notice visual objects and events in one-half of the visual field

hertz (Hz) units of measurement for cycles or alternations per second

hierarchy of visual processing the increased sophistication of response and increased size of the receptive field that accompany each step in the visual neural streams

holistic perception perception that depends on the configurations and spatial relations among features rather than on the presence versus absence of the features themselves

horizon the edge separating the ground from the sky in an image or picture

horizontal cells cells in the retina of the eye that transmit signals laterally among bipolar cells

horizontal processing the phenomenon in which neurons communicate with other neurons at the same level in the anatomical visual hierarchy

hues color categories that correspond to differences in wavelength

hue-saturation-brightness (HSB) referring to the three dimensions of the color spindle; also a name for the color space represented by the spindle

hypercolumns modules of cortical neurons in area V1 that are able to analyze edges of all orientation as seen by either eye for a specific region of the retina; approximately 0.5 to 1 mm square and 2 mm deep

ill-posed problem a problem in which complete specification of the factors leads to many possible solutions

illusion a discrepancy between physical reality and perception of that reality

image a two-dimensional representation of the projection of light from a three-dimensional scene

imprinting a form of learning during a developmentally critical period in which certain features are associated with food and nurture

inattentional blindness technique an experimental procedure for studying the perception of unexpected visual stimuli while participants are engaged in an effortful visual discrimination task

inhibitory referring to a cell that becomes less active (reduces its firing rate) in response to a stimulus

intrinsic color the way a surface reflects light over a broadband spectrum of wavelengths

inverse tangent a mathematical function needed to calculate the size of a visual stimulus in degrees of visual angle

isomorphic involving point-to-point correspondence

lateral geniculate nucleus (LGN) a midbrain structure in the visual system that relays neural signals from the eye to the brain; the main neural pathway from the eye to the brain in humans

layout the spatial arrangement of objects in a scene

lens a transparent medium that bends light; the human eye has a lens at the front to help focus light on the retina at the back of the eye

liberal response strategy guessing "there is a difference" in a discrimination task when one has not seen any difference

light the portion of the electromagnetic spectrum that is visible to humans

lightness the perceived amount of light reflected by a surface

magnetic hills (anti-gravity hills) locations on earth where "downhill" and "uphill" seem reversed, so that a ball appears to roll uphill

magnetic resonance imaging (MRI) high-resolution images of the brain's structure in live individuals based on tissue density

magno neurons relatively large cells in the visual stream that transmit signals regarding crude shape and movement

magno-encephalography (MEG) recordings recordings of magnetic field differences in the brain that can be detected through the scalp in response to a stimulus

medial temporal (MT) cortex a cortical region involved in the analysis of motion; also called V5

metamers color mixtures that are not distinguishable from each other or from spectral colors

microelectrode a tiny glass tube filled with saltwater and used to record electrical activity from a neuron

migraine equivalent the experience of a pre-migraine aura in the absence of a later migraine headache

minutes of arc a subdivision of the measure of visual size in degrees; 1 degree = 60 minutes of arc

monocular relating to one-eyed vision

moon illusion the illusion that the horizon moon appears to be larger than the zenith moon

Mooney face an image of a human portrait that has been thresholded

motion parallax the clues to three-dimensionality (i.e., depth) given by the changing images that occur as the viewer moves

mystery spot locations on earth where objects appear to change in size as they move around and pendulums appear to hang obliquely

nanometer (nm) one billionth of a meter; the human eye is sensitive to electromagnetic radiation in the range of 360 to 780 nm

neural oscillation (oscillation) a wave of neural activity that increases and decreases in cycles, often repeating between twenty and sixty times a second

neural synchrony patterns of neural activity in two or more neurons that are similar in temporal microstructure

new-old recognition the ability to discriminate a stimulus that has never been seen before (i.e., new) from one that has been seen before (i.e., old)

novelty bias the tendency to be alerted to the presence of new information in a scene

object constancy (object invariance) the intrinsic visual properties of an object—such as its size, color, and shape—regardless of viewing conditions

object invariance (object constancy) the intrinsic visual properties of an object—such as its size, color, and shape—regardless of viewing conditions

object perception seeing the visual properties of an object

object recognition knowing the meaning of a visual object

object-centered referring to a representation in which objects and object-relations are registered with respect to the objects rather than the viewer

occlusion a clue to three-dimensionality (i.e., depth) from the partial view of objects that are more distant or hiding behind objects nearer to the viewer

off-center ganglion a ganglion cell with a receptive field defined by an inhibitory center and an excitatory surround

on-center ganglion a ganglion cell with a receptive field defined by an excitatory center and an inhibitory surround

optic chiasma the place where half the optic nerve fibers cross from one side of the brain to the other, so that signals from each side of the retina are sent to corresponding locations in the brain

optic disc a region at the back of each eye, slightly toward the nose, that is completely insensitive to light because it is filled with nerves and blood vessels exiting the eye

optic nerve the bundle of ganglion cell axons that exit the eye at the optic disc

optical flow the pattern of relative retinal motion that occurs whenever the eye moves toward a surface or a surface moves toward the eye

optokinetic tremors small eye movements that are constantly being made when viewing a scene

oscillation (neural oscillation) a wave of neural activity that increases and decreases in cycles, often repeating between twenty and sixty times a second

overt spatial orienting the movement of gaze (i.e., the eye) to a location in an image or scene

parvo neurons relatively small cells in the visual stream that transmit signals regarding spatial detail and color

peak experience (transcendent moment) the coordinated experience of emotional calm and an understanding of how all things fit together

peak shift the tendency for an exaggerated version of a learned stimulus to be the most preferred by the learner

perspective the phenomenon of equal distances in a scene becoming increasingly smaller in an image or picture as distance is increased

photometer a device for measuring the number of photons projecting onto a region of space

photon catch the number of photons that make contact with the light-sensitive receptors in the eye

photopic relating to vision under relatively high-intensity conditions (e.g., office lighting, daylight), when the cone receptors are active

pictorial depth the clues to three-dimensionality (i.e., depth) that can be conveyed via a single image or eye

pictorial size constancy the phenomenon of seeing objects in pictures as being appropriately sized regardless of their apparent distance from the viewer

plasticity a characteristic of the brain that enables changes to occur because of learning and experience

point source a source of light that is infinitely small, in theory

Ponzo illusion an illusion of two equal lines appearing to be of unequal length when placed in the context of converging lines

positron emission tomography (PET) scans images of the brain's function in live individuals, using radioactive tracers carried in the blood

primary visual area (area V1) the first cortical location to which neural signals are sent from the eye, lying at the back of the brain

priming a changed response to a stimulus based on a previous experience with an identical or closely related stimulus

problem of object invariance the problem of how objects that are very different in image size, image shape, and image color nevertheless appear to be the same size and shape in the physical world

prosopagnosia an inability to visually recognize well-known individuals despite being able to recognize common objects and to recognize the same individuals by means of hearing and touch

protanope an individual whose color vision lacks long-wavelength (i.e., red) receptors

proximity to the horizon (height in the plane) a clue to three-dimensionality (i.e., depth) given by the tendency for objects close to the horizon to be associated with greater distance from the viewer

psychic blindness a form of blindness caused by brain damage or brain disease, not by eye damage or eye disease

psychophysical function the measured relationship between probability of visual detection and the intensity of a stimulus

psychophysical test an activity in which data are collected from one or more study participants in the form of responses to a carefully designed stimulus; also called a behavioral experiment

receptive field the preference of a visual neuron for particular visual properties in a particular location of the retina

rectilinearity edges in an image or scene that meet at right angles

red-green-blue (RGB) referring to the three dimensions of the color gamut of a television or computer monitor

response bias the tendency to respond with "no difference" or "there is a difference" when one has not seen any difference

retina the light-sensitive layer of cells at the back of the eye

reverse engineering the process of trying to determine how a device works by taking it apart and examining its components

rods (rod receptors) cells in the retina of the eye that are only responsive to light under dim lighting conditions

saccade an eye movement from one location in a scene to another location

saccadic suppression the reduced visibility that occurs during a saccade

saturation the purity of hue in a color

scene the world of three-dimensional objects and surfaces that reflect and absorb light

scene boundary extension the tendency, when drawing from memory, to provide more detail about the background than was actually present

scene perception the larger spatial context in which individual objects are seen

schematic memory memory for an image that is rich in gist (i.e., meaning) but not in details (i.e., specific features)

scotopic relating to vision under dim lighting conditions (e.g., low lighting, twilight), when the rod receptors are active

search asymmetry a change in the results of a visual search experiment that comes from reversing the roles of target and distractor

second-order edge an edge defined by an abrupt change in the texture, motion, or depth of a surface

shade a three-dimensional volume in a scene that receives less light than other regions because an object blocks light from shining directly into it

shadow the two-dimensional shape in an image or picture that is the visible evidence of shade in a scene

simple cells edge-detecting neurons in area V1 that are specific for orientation and location

size constancy the phenomenon of an object's size being perceived regardless of viewing distance

smooth pursuit eye movement the ability to move one's eyes so as to maintain fixation on a moving object (or on a stationary object while the viewer is moving)

space constant the smallest spatial difference that can be discriminated by the eye

spatial frequency the average rate of change in luminance over one of the spatial dimensions of an image

spatial structure the geometry of a scene, including the location and orientation of all objects and surfaces in that scene

spectral colors colors corresponding to the wavelengths in the light spectrum

speed of sight the time from the onset of a visual event to the experience of that event by an observer

standing wave masking a cycling visual display of two images of equal duration in which one image is seen while the other is invisible

step (synapse) the connection between individual neurons

stereofusion the perception of a scene in depth, based on the fusion of features in each eye that have binocular disparity

stereofusion region the narrow band of depth in which disparate images in the two eyes are resolved as objects that are at different distances from the viewer

structural description a hierarchical description of the spatial and semantic (i.e., meaningful) relations among objects in a scene

structure from motion the clues to an object's volume that are given by the changing images of the moving object

subitizing the rapid and automatic visual enumeration of a small number of items

subjective edges edges that can be seen but that are not physically present in an image; also known as virtual edges and illusory edges

subordinate level the specific members in a class (e.g., "Fred," "George," and "Angela" are members of the class "people"; "fir," "cedar," and "spruce" are members of the class "trees")

superior colliculus (SC) a midbrain structure in the visual system that relays neural signals from the eye to the brain, involved in movement perception and eye movements

superordinate level a higher-order category than the basic level, one encompassing two or more basic-level categories (e.g., "inanimate" includes "chairs" and "cups")

synapse (step) the connection between individual neurons

synchronized change change to features in a visual display that occur at the same time

task-set bias the tendency to see what one is expecting to see

temporal integration the ability to fuse two images presented at different points in time through visible persistence

temporal resolution the ability of the visual system to resolve events over time; also called temporal acuity

temporal visual hierarchy the arrangement of the visually sensitive regions of the cortex according to when they first receive information about a stimulus

tetrachromacy (tetrachromat) color vision based on four types of wavelength receptors; a suspected rare form of color vision in humans

texture compression (foreshortening) the systematic decrease in the vertical spacing of texture elements with increasing distance in an image or picture

texture gradient the systematic decrease in the size and spacing of texture elements with increasing distance in an image or picture

texture perspective the systematic decrease in the horizontal spacing of texture elements with increasing distance in an image or picture

third-person data the responses made by a study participant in a behavioral experiment or psychophysical test

threshold a stimulus intensity that permits an observer to detect the stimulus 50 percent of the time

threshold measure an average or summary of a series of thresholds measured in an experiment

thresholding transforming an image so that all the luminance values below some cutoff point are converted to black and all the luminance values above the same cutoff point are converted to white

time constant the smallest temporal difference that can be discriminated by the eye

T-junction a relationship among three edges in which one angle is exactly 180 degrees

topographic relating to a point-to-point mapping from one image to another

transcendent moment (peak experience) the coordinated experience of emotional calm and an understanding of how all things fit together

transcranial magnetic stimulation (TMS) a brief and powerful magnetic discharge, delivered through the scalp, that disrupts normal neural activity in a specific region of the brain for a very brief time

trichromacy (trichromat) color vision based on three types of wavelength receptors; typical color vision in humans

tritanope an individual whose color vision lacks short-wavelength (i.e., blue) receptors

unbiased response strategy guessing randomly in a discrimination task when one has not seen any difference

unilateral neglect (hemispatial neglect) a failure to notice visual objects and events in one-half of the visual field

unitization the process by which visual experience is structured so that the viewer sees individual objects

vanishing point a location in an image or picture where the distances among surfaces are no longer perceptible

ventral stream a region of the cortex lying along the side of the brain

viewer-centered referring to a representation in which objects and object-relations are registered with respect to the viewer rather than to the objects themselves

visible persistence the visual experience associated with neural activity that continues after a stimulus has disappeared from view

visual agnosia a form of blindness caused by brain damage or brain disease, not by eye damage or eye disease

visual angle a measure of the size of a visual stimulus; degrees of visual angle describe a segment of an imaginary circle (360 degrees) surrounding the viewer

visual enumeration the task of determining how many items of a given kind are in a scene, including rapid subitizing for small numbers and slower counting for large numbers

wavelength profile a summary of the relative amount of light reflected by each of the wavelengths

well-formed problem a problem in which complete specification of the factors leads to only one solution

Y-junction a relationship among three edges in which all angles are greater than 90 degrees and none is greater than 180 degrees

zombie a hypothetical individual with all the usual characteristics of humans except that he or she lacks consciousness, or subjective experience

REFERENCES

Ahissar, M., & Hochstein, S. (1997). Task difficulty and the specificity of perceptual learning. *Nature, 387,* 401–406.

Alais, D., Blake, R., & Lee, S.-H. (1998). Features that vary together over time group together over space. *Nature Neuroscience, 1,* 160–164.

Allen, S. W., & Brooks, L. R. (1991). Specializing the operation of an explicit rule. *Journal of Experimental Psychology: General, 120,* 3–19.

Bach-y-Rita, P., Tyler, M. E., & Kaczmarek, K. A. (2003). Seeing with the brain. *International Journal of Human Computer Interactions, 15,* 285–295.

Barnard, P. J., Scott, S., Taylor, J., May, J., & Knightly, W. (2004). Paying attention to meaning. *Psychological Science, 15,* 179–186.

Barsalou, L. W., Simmons, W. K., Barbey, A. K., & Wilson, C. D. (2003). Grounding conceptual knowledge in modality-specific systems. *Trends in Cognitive Sciences, 7,* 84–91.

Barsalou, L. W., Solomon, K. O., & Wu L. L. (1999). Perceptual simulation in conceptual tasks. In M. K. Hiraga, C. Sinha, & S. Wilcox (Eds.), *Cultural, typological, and psychological perspectives in cognitive linguistics: The proceedings of the 4th conference of the International Cognitive Linguistics Association, Vol. 3* (pp. 209–228). Amsterdam: John Benjamins.

Bhalla, M., & Proffitt, D. R. (1999). Visual-motor recalibration in geographical slant perception. *Journal of Experimental Psychology: Human Perception & Performance, 25,* 1076–1096.

Biederman, I. (1981). On the semantics of a glance at a scene. In M. Kubovy & J. R. Pomerantz (Eds.), *Perceptual organization* (pp. 213–253). Hillsdale, NJ: Erlbaum.

Bisiach, E., & Luzzatti, C. (1978). Unilateral neglect of representational space. *Cortex, 14,* 129–133.

Bradley, B. P., Mogg, K., & Millar, N. H. (2000). Covert and overt orienting of attention to emotional faces in anxiety. *Cognition and Emotion, 14,* 789–808.

Bressan, P., Garlaschelli, L., & Barracano, M. (2003). Antigravity hills are visual illusions. *Psychological Science, 14,* 441–449.

Bridgeman, B. (in press). Influence of visually-induced expectation on perceived motor effort: A visual-proprioceptive interaction at the Santa Cruz Mystery Spot. *Psychonomic Bulletin and Review.*

Brockmole, J. R., Irwin, D. E., & Wang, R. F. (2002). Temporal integration of visual images and visual percepts. *Journal of Experimental Psychology: Human Perception and Performance, 28,* 315–334.

Brooks, R. A. (2002). *Flesh and machines: how robots will change us.* Pantheon Books.

Casati, R. (2004). *Shadows: Unlocking their secrets, from Plato to our time*. New York: Vintage.

Chun, M. M., & Jiang, Y. (1998). Contextual cueing: Implicit learning and memory of visual context guides spatial attention. *Cognitive Psychology, 36,* 28–71.

Crawford, L. E., & Cacioppo, J. T. (2002). Learning where to look for danger: Integrating affective and spatial information. *Psychological Science, 13,* 449–453.

Darwin, C. (1874). *The descent of man and selection in relation to sex* (2nd ed., reprinted 1990). London: The Folio Society.

Deubel, H., Bridgeman, B., & Schneider, W. X. (1998). Immediate post-saccadic information mediates space constancy. *Vision Research, 38,* 3147–3159.

Deubel, H., Schneider, W. X., & Bridgeman, B. (1996). Post-saccadic target blanking prevents saccadic suppression of image displacement. *Vision Research, 36,* 985–996.

Di Lollo, V. (1980). Temporal integration in visual memory. *Journal of Experimental Psychology: General, 109,* 75–97.

Dixon, M. J., Smilek, D., Cudahy, C., & Merikle, P. M. (2000, July 27). Five plus two equals yellow. *Nature, 406,* 365.

Eagleman, D. M., & Sejnowski, T. J. (2000, November). Latency difference versus postdiction: Response to Patel et al. *Science, 290,* 1051.

Egeth, H. E., & Yantis, S. (1997). Visual attention: Control, representation, and time course. *Annual Review of Psychology, 48,* 269–297.

Fiorani, M., Jr., Rosa, M. G. P., Gattass, R., & Rocha-Miranda, C. E. (1992). Dynamic surrounds of receptive fields in primate striate cortex: A physiological basis for perceptual completion? *Proceedings of the National Academy of Sciences, 89,* 8547–8551.

Folk, C. L., & Remington, R. W. (1998). Selectivity in attentional capture by featural singletons: Evidence for two forms of attentional capture. *Journal of Experimental Psychology: Human Perception and Performance, 24,* 847–858.

Gibson, J. J. (1966). *The senses considered as perceptual systems*. Boston: Houghton Mifflin.

Gibson, J. J., Olum, P., & Rosenblatt, F. (1955). Parallax and perspective during aircraft landings. *American Journal of Psychology, 68,* 372–385.

Gold, J., Bennett, P. J., & Sekuler, A. B. (1999). Identification of band-pass filtered letters and faces by human and ideal observers. *Vision Research, 39,* 3537–3560.

Goldstone, R. L. (2000). Unitization during category learning. *Journal of Experimental Psychology: Human Perception and Performance, 26,* 86–112.

Goldstone, R. L. (2003). Learning to perceive while perceiving to learn. In R. Kimchi, M. Behrmann, & C. Olson (Eds.), *Perceptual organization in vision: Behavioral and neural perspectives* (pp. 233–278). Mahwah, NJ: Erlbaum.

Goodale, M. A., Pélisson, D., & Prablanc, C. (1986). Large adjustments in visually guided reaching do not depend on vision of the hand or perception of target displacement. *Nature, 320,* 748–750.

Gregory, R. (1966). *Eye and brain: The psychology of seeing*. London: Weidenfeld & Nicolson.

Hancock, P., Wulf, G., & Thom, D. (1990). Driver workload during differing driving maneuvers. *Accident Analysis and Prevention, 22,* 281–290.

Haxby, J. V., Gobbini, M. I., Furey, M. L., Ishai, A., Schouten, J. L., & Pietrini, P. (2001). Distributed and overlapping representations of faces and objects in ventral temporal cortex. *Science, 293,* 2425–2430.

Henderson, J. M., & Hollingworth, A. (2002). Eye movements, visual memory, and scene representation. In M. A. Peterson & G. Rhodes (Eds.), *Analytic and holistic processes in the perception of faces, objects, and scenes.* New York: JAI/Ablex.

Hochberg, J. E., & Brooks, V. (1962). Pictorial recognition as an unlearned ability: A study of one child's performance. *American Journal of Psychology, 75,* 624–628.

Hochstein, S., & Ahissar, M. (2002). View from the top: Hierarchies and reverse hierarchies in the visual system. *Neuron, 36,* 791–804.

Hollingworth, A., & Henderson, J. M. (2003). Testing a conceptual locus for the inconsistent object change detection advantage in real-world scenes. *Memory & Cognition, 31,* 930–940.

Howard, I. P., & Childerson, L. (1994). The contribution of motion, the visual frame, and visual polarity to sensations of body tilt. *Perception, 23,* 753–762.

Howard, I. P., & Hu, G. (2001). Visually induced reorientation illusions. *Perception, 30,* 583–600.

Hurlburt, R. T., & Heavey, C. L. (2001). Telling what we know: Describing inner experience. *Trends in Cognitive Sciences, 5,* 400–403.

Intraub, H. (1997). The representation of visual scenes. *Trends in Cognitive Science, 1,* 217–222.

Jameson, K. A., Highnote, S. M., & Wasserman, L. M. (2001). Richer color experiences in observers with multiple photopigment opsin genes. *Psychonomic Bulletin & Review, 8,* 244–261.

Joordens, S., & Merikle, P. M. (1993). Independence or redundancy? Two models of conscious and unconscious influences. *Journal of Experimental Psychology: General, 122,* 462–467.

Klotz, W., & Neumann, O. (1999). Motor activation without conscious discrimination in metacontrast masking. *Journal of Experimental Psychology: Human Perception and Performance, 24,* 976–992.

Kosslyn, S. M., & Rabin, C. (1999). The representation of left-right orientation: A dissociation between imagery and perceptual recognition. *Visual Cognition, 6,* 497–508.

Kosslyn, S. M., Alpert, N. M., Thompson, W. L., Maljkovic, V., Weise, S. B., Chabris, C. F., Hamilton, S. E., Rauch, S. L., & Buonanno, F. S. (1993). Visual mental imagery activates topographically organized visual cortex: PET investigations. *Journal of Cognitive Neuroscience, 5,* 263–287.

LeDoux, J. (1996). *The emotional brain: The mysterious underpinnings of emotional life.* New York: Simon & Schuster.

Leuthold, H., & Kopp, B. (1998). Mechanisms of priming by masked stimuli: Inferences from event-related potentials. *Psychological Science, 9,* 263–269.

Levin, D. T. (2000). Race as a visual feature: Using visual search and perceptual discrimination tasks to understand face categories and the cross-race recognition deficit. *Journal of*

Experimental Psychology: General, 129, 559–574.

Liu, C. H., Collin, C. A., Rainville, S. J. M., & Chaudhuri, A. (2000). The effects of spatial frequency overlap on face recognition. *Journal of Experimental Psychology: Human Perception and Performance, 26,* 956–979.

Logothetis, N. K., Leopold, D. A., & Sheinberg, D. L. (1996). What is rivaling during binocular rivalry? *Nature, 380,* 621–624.

Mack, A., & Rock, I. (1998). *Inattentional blindness.* Cambridge, MA: MIT Press.

Marcel, A. J. (1983a). Conscious and unconscious perception: An approach to the relations between phenomenal experience and perceptual processes. *Cognitive Psychology, 15,* 238–300.

Marcel, A. J. (1983b). Conscious and unconscious perception: Experiments on visual masking and recognition. *Cognitive Psychology, 15,* 197–237.

Marshall, J. C., & Halligan, P. W. (1988). Blindsight and insight in visuospatial neglect. *Nature, 336,* 766–767.

Merikle, P. M., Joordens, S., & Stolz, J. A. (1995). Measuring the relative magnitude of unconscious influences. *Consciousness and Cognition, 4,* 422–439.

Mills, S. L., & Massey, S. C. (1999). AII amacrine cells limit scotopic acuity in central macaque retina: An analysis with calretinin labeling, confocal microscopy and intracellular dye injection. *Journal of Comparative Neurology, 411,* 19–34.

Milner, A. D., & Goodale, M. A. (1995). *The visual brain in action.* Oxford, England: Oxford University Press.

Monahan, J. L., Murphy, S. T., & Zajonc, R. B. (2000). Subliminal mere exposure: Specific, general and diffuse

effects. *Psychological Science, 11,* 462–467.

Mooney, C. M. (1957). Age in the development of closure ability in children. *Canadian Journal of Psychology, 11,* 219–226.

Moore, C. M., Yantis, S., & Vaughan, B. (1998). Object-based visual selection: Evidence from perceptual completion. *Psychological Science, 9,* 104–110.

Nasanen, R. (1999). Spatial frequency bandwidth used in the recognition of facial images. *Vision Research, 39,* 3824–3833.

Navon, D. (1977). Forest before trees: The precedence of global features in visual perception. *Cognitive Psychology, 9,* 353–383.

Neitz, J., Carroll, J., & Neitz, M. (2001, January). Color vision: Almost reason enough for having eye. *Optics & Photonics News,* 26–33.

Palmer, S. E., Rosch, E., & Chase, P. (1981). Canonical perspective and the perception of objects. In J. Long & A. Baddeley (Eds.), *Attention and performance IX* (pp. 135–151). Hillsdale, NJ: Erlbaum.

Peli, E., Lee, E., Trempe, C. L., & Buzney, S. (1994). Image enhancement for the visually impaired: The effects of enhancement on face recognition. *Journal of the Optical Society of America A, 11,* 1929–1939.

Pinna, B., Brelstaff, G., & Spillmann, L. (2001). Surface color from boundaries: A new "watercolor" illusion. *Vision Research, 41,* 2669–2676.

Poeppel, E. (1997). A hierarchical model of temporal perception. *Trends in Cognitive Science, 1,* 56–61.

Potter, M. C. (1976). Short-term conceptual memory for pictures.

Journal of Experimental Psychology: Human Learning and Memory, 2, 509–522.

Potter, M. C., O'Connor, D. H., & Oliva, A. (2002). Remembering rooms but not viewpoints. *Journal of Vision, 2,* 516.

Previc, F. H. (1994). The relationship between eye dominance and head tilt in humans. *Neuropsychologia, 32,* 1297–1303.

Rensink, R. A., O'Regan, J. K., & Clark, J. J. (1997). To see or not to see: The need for attention to perceive changes in scenes. *Psychological Science, 8,* 368–373.

Rodriguez, E., George, N., Lachaux, J. P., Martinerie, J., Renault, B., & Varela, F. J. (1999, February). Perception's shadow: Long-distance synchronization of human brain activity. *Nature, 397,* 430–433.

Sacks, O. (1987). *The man who mistook his wife for a hat.* New York: Summit.

Sanocki, T. (2003). Representation and perception of spatial layout. *Cognitive Psychology, 47,* 43–86.

Schmidt, T. (2002). The finger in flight: Real-time motor control by visually masked color stimuli. *Psychological Science, 13,* 112–118.

Scholl, B. J., & Nakayama, K. (2002). Causal capture: Contextual effects on the perception of collision events. *Psychological Science, 13,* 493–498.

Shepard, R. N. (1967). Recognition memory for words, sentences and pictures. *Journal of Verbal Learning and Behavior, 6,* 156–163.

Shepard, R. N., & Metzler, J. (1971). Mental rotation of three-dimensional objects. *Science, 171,* 701–703.

Sheth, B. R., Nijhawan, R., & Shimojo, S. (2000, May). Changing objects lead briefly flashed ones. *Nature Neuroscience, 3,* 489–495.

Shimamura, A. P., & Prinzmetal, W. (1999). The Mystery Spot illusion and its relation to other visual illusions. *Psychological Science, 10,* 501–507.

Sigala, N., & Logothetis, N. K. (2002, January). Visual categorization shapes feature selectivity in the primate temporal cortex. *Nature, 415,* 318–320.

Sillito, A. M., Jones, H. E., Gerstein, G. L., & West, D. C. (1994, June). Feature-linked synchronization of thalamic relay cell firing induced by feedback from the visual-cortex. *Nature, 369,* 479–482.

Simons, D. J., & Chabris, C. F. (1999). Gorillas in our midst: Sustained inattentional blindness for dynamic events. *Perception, 28,* 1059–1074.

Simons, D. J., & Levin, D. T. (1998). Failure to detect changes to people during a real-world interaction. *Psychonomic Bulletin and Review, 5,* 644–649.

Smilek, D., Dixon, M. J., Cudahy, C., & Merikle, P. M. (2001). Synaesthetic photisms influence visual perception. *Journal of Cognitive Neuroscience, 13,* 930–936.

Standing, L. (1973). Learning 10,000 pictures. *Quarterly Journal of Experimental Psychology, 25,* 207–222.

Standing, L., Conezio, J., & Haber, R. N. (1970). Perception and memory for pictures: Single trial learning of 2,560 visual stimuli. *Psychonomic Science, 19,* 73–74.

Tanaka, J., Weiskopf, D., & Williams, P. (2001). The role of color in high-level vision. *Trends in Cognitive Science, 5,* 211–215.

Tanaka, J. W., & Curran, T. (2001). A neural basis for expert object recognition. *Psychological Science, 12,* 43–47.

Tarr, M. J., & Gauthier, I. (2000). FFA: A Flexible Fusiform Area for subordinate-level visual processing automatized by expertise. *Nature Neuroscience, 3,* 764–769.

Vitz, P. C., & Glimcher, A. B. (1984). *Modern art and modern science.* New York: Praeger.

Vogel, E. K., & Luck, S. J. (1997, November 20). The capacity of visual working memory for features and conjunctions. *Nature, 390,* 279–281.

Vogel, E. K., Woodman, G. F., & Luck, S. J. (2001). Storage of features, conjunctions, and objects in visual working memory. *Journal of Experimental Psychology: Human Perception and Performance, 27,* 92–114.

Weichselgartner, E., & Sperling, G. (1987). Dynamics of automatic and controlled visual attention. *Science, 238,* 778–780.

Zajonc, R. B. (2001). Mere exposure: A gateway to the subliminal. *Current Directions in Psychological Science, 10,* 224–228.

Zeki, S., Aglioti, S., McKeefry, D., & Berlucchi, G. (1999, November). The neurological basis of conscious color perception in a blind patient. *Proceedings of the National Academy of Science, 96,* 14124–14129.

Note: Italicized page numbers indicate figures. A- numbers indicate the appendix of color figures. G- numbers indicate the Glossary.

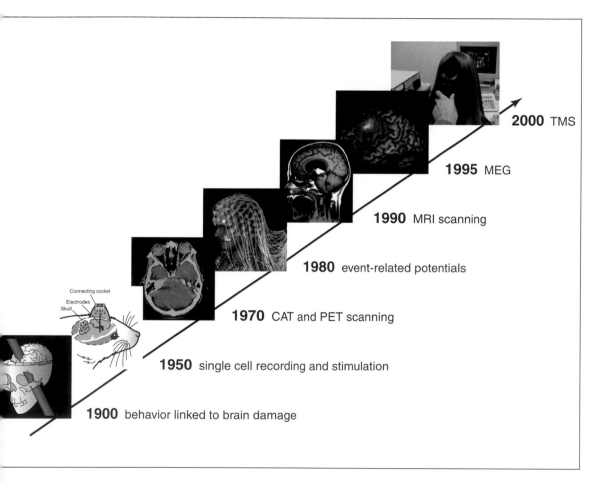

FIGURE 2.1 Important benchmarks from the twentieth century showing the evolution in methods for understanding the structure and function of the human brain.

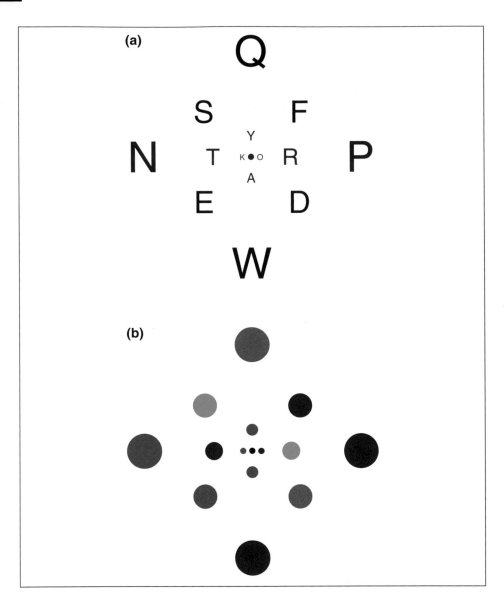

FIGURE 2.6 The cortical magnification factor. **(a)** The letters in this diagram are scaled in size so that when you fix your gaze on the black dot at the center, each letter is approximately equally readable. **(b)** The color patches are scaled in size so that they are also about equally visible when you fix your gaze on the central black dot.

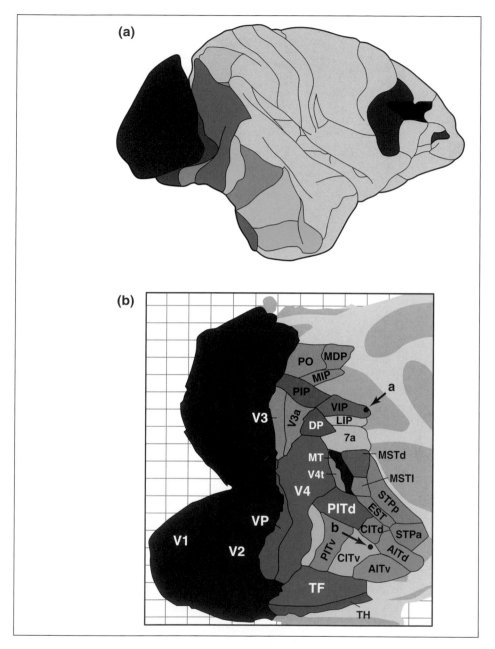

FIGURE 2.7 An overview of the locations of the visually sensitive regions of the monkey's cerebral cortex, shown **(a)** in anatomical arrangement on the cortical surface, and **(b)** as an imaginary smoothed cortical surface. Visually sensitive regions are shown in color, along with abbreviations that are known to physiologists. Other regions are shown in gray.

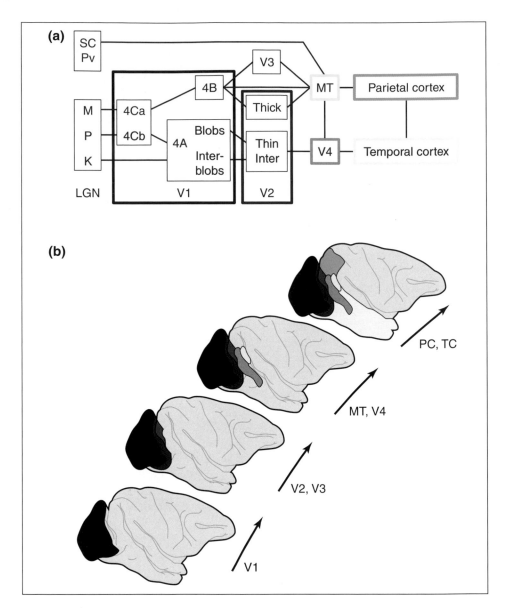

FIGURE 2.9 The anatomical hierarchy in the visually sensitive regions of the cerebral cortex in the monkey. **(a)** Schematic diagram showing connections. **(b)** Corresponding regions on the cortical surface. The labels for each region (abbreviations) are well known to physiologists but need not concern us yet.

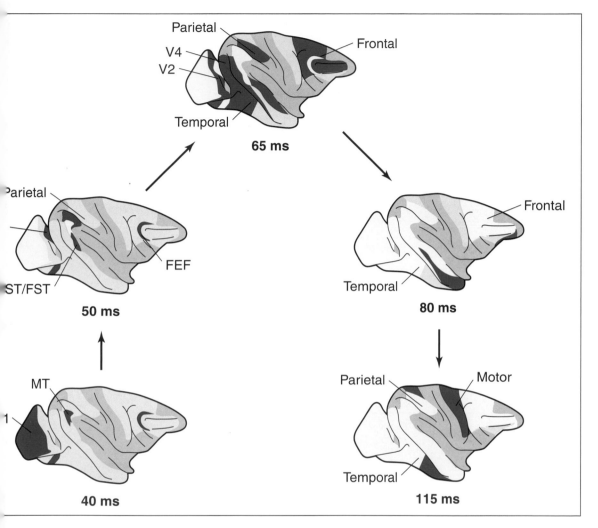

FIGURE 2.11 A diagram of the temporal order of visual information in visually sensitive regions of the monkey cortex. Newly active regions at each time period are indicated in red. Milliseconds is abbreviated as ms. The labels (abbreviations) for brain regions, again, are well known to physiologists.

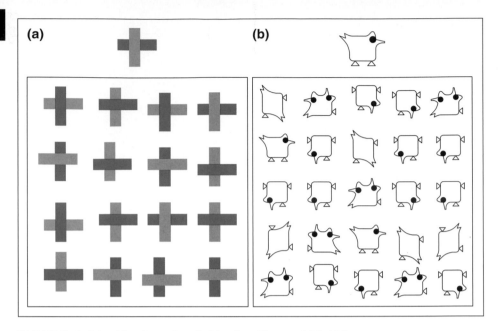

FIGURE 2.16   Visual search task: (a) colored bars and (b) chickens.

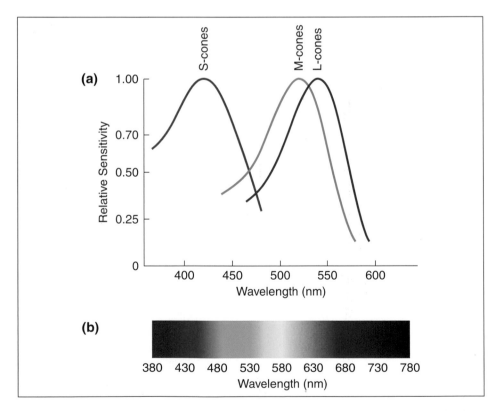

FIGURE 3.3   (a) The relative sensitivity of cones to light of different wavelengths. (b) The colors of the rainbow as perceived by an individual with three types of cones.

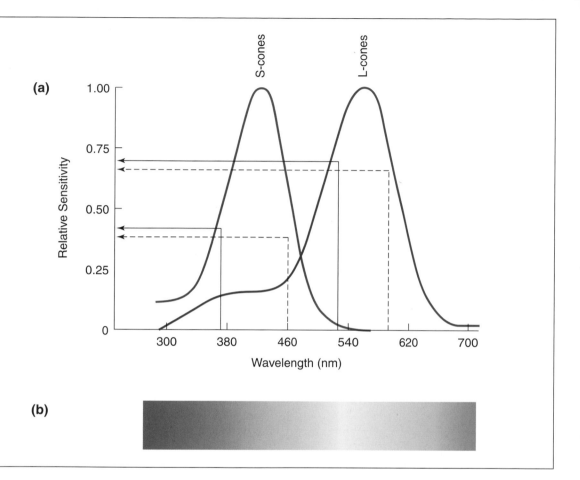

FIGURE 3.4 The relative sensitivity of S- and L-cones to wavelength. **(a)** The consequences of two different light mixtures. One mixture (solid lines) consists of equal amounts of 530 nanometer and 375 nanometer light. The second mixture (dashed lines) consists of equal amounts of 600 nanometer and 460 nanometer light. Although these stimuli are physically very different, they both lead to equivalent patterns of activity in the S- and L-cones. **(b)** The colors of the rainbow as perceived by an individual with only two types of cones.

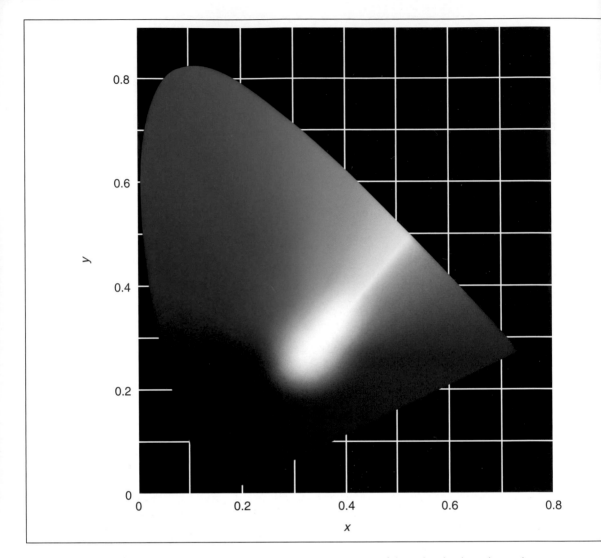

FIGURE 3.14 The CIE color space, which is a variant of the color disc based on a three-color primary system. It is the standard space used in color vision research. The space is a two-dimensional slice through the three-dimensional color solid of which it is understood to be a part. Slices higher in the plane correspond to brighter colors, and slices lower in the plane correspond to darker colors.

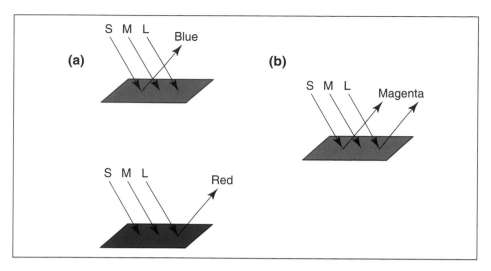

FIGURE 3.15 **(a)** The relative amount of light reflected from two painted surfaces, one blue and the other red. The length of the arrows indicates the relative amount of light reflected for different wavelengths along the visible spectrum. The blue surface reflects short wavelength light, and the red surface reflects long wavelength light. **(b)** Mixing the paint from the two surfaces results in a new pigment that reflects the combination of these component wavelengths, but now in reduced amounts of each. Mixtures of blue and red turn out as a relatively dark magenta or purple.

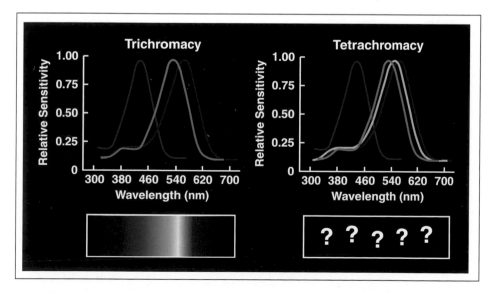

FIGURE 3.16 The postulated wavelength sensitivity functions for the four cone types of tetrachromats, as compared with those of trichromats.

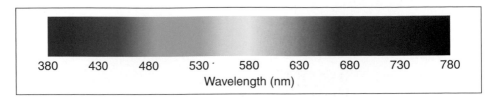

FIGURE 3.17   How many distinct bands of color can you see?

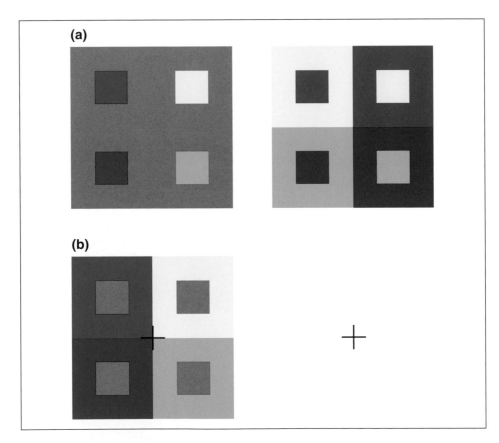

FIGURE 3.18   Color contrast. **(a)** Colors appear less vivid against a neutral gray background than against a background of complementary colors. **(b)** Staring at the black cross for 20 to 30 seconds and then switching your gaze to the black cross on the empty background will create a negative afterimage, meaning that the regions that were blue will now be yellow, and so on. The gray patches themselves will take on the color that was previously the surround.

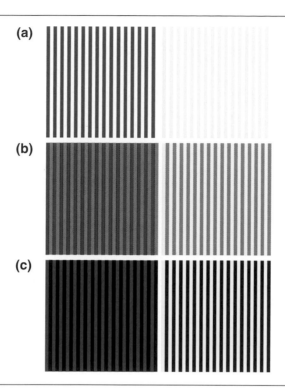

FIGURE 3.19 Color averaging. The blue and yellow paints used in these three panels of stripes are identical. The only aspect that varies is the color of the intervening stripes, which are **(a)** white, **(b)** gray, and **(c)** black. The intervening "neutral" stripes have an *averaging* effect on the colored stripes that can be seen in two ways. First, the blue and yellow stripes appear more saturated against a darker background; second, the contrast in brightness between blue and yellow increases with this apparent increase in color saturation.

FIGURE 3.20 Examples of neon color illusions.

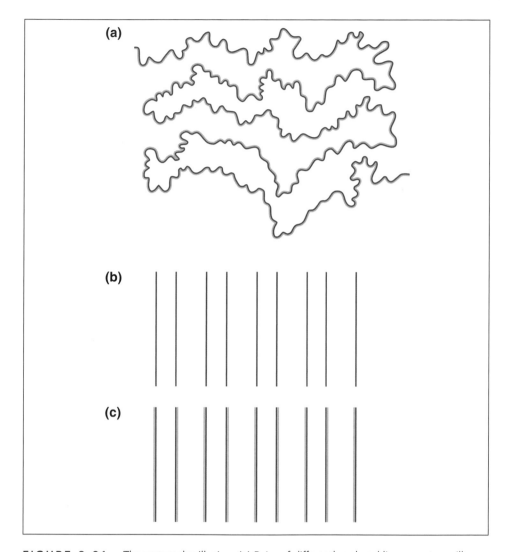

FIGURE 3.21 The watercolor illusion. **(a)** Pairs of differently colored lines create an illusion in which regions enclosed by the lighter color appear to be tinted in the same color even though no actual color is present in the region. **(b)** When lines are all the same color, spatial proximity determines grouping. Observers see this as a series of narrow regions (the figures) separated by wider regions (the backgrounds). **(c)** When lines are bicolored, the region between lighter colors is seen as the figures even though the spatial proximity between lines favors the grouping in (b).

FIGURE 3.22 Typical, atypical, and gray-level pictures of a natural scene.

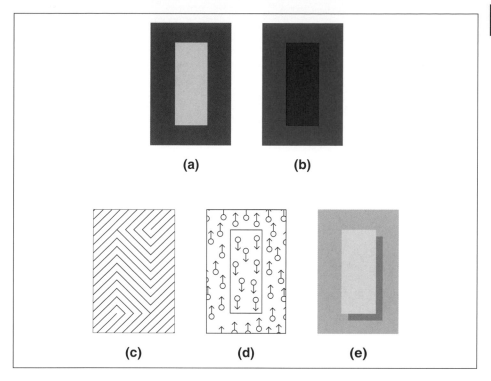

FIGURE 4.1 First-order edges based on spatial differences in **(a)** luminance and **(b)** color. Second-order edges based on spatial differences **(c)** texture, **(d)** motion direction, and **(e)** three-dimensional depth.

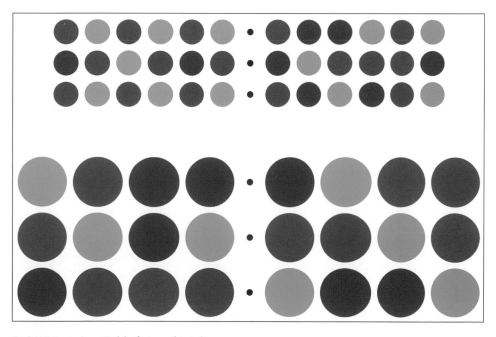

FIGURE 4.9 Field of view: **(b)** Colors.

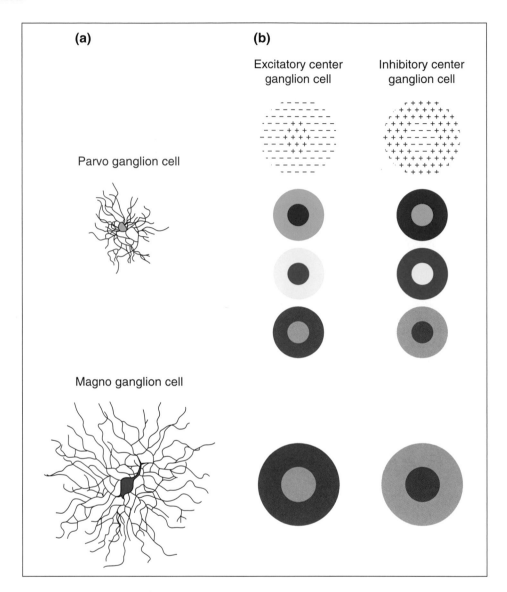

(a)

(b)

Excitatory center
ganglion cell

Inhibitory center
ganglion cell

Parvo ganglion cell

Magno ganglion cell

FIGURE 4.10   A wide variety of receptive fields are found among ganglion cells. Two dimensions help to organize this variety: **(a)** the physical size of the neuron (*parvo*, meaning small, and *magno*, meaning large), and **(b)** whether the central area of the cell's receptive field is excitatory (plus signs) or inhibitory (minus signs) to stimulation. Additional subtypes can be found among the parvo cells because some are organized to respond to contrasting colors (red-green and blue-yellow), whereas others are organized to respond to differences in luminance (black-white). Magno ganglion cells are organized primarily to signal differences in luminance, although some can signal color differences without preserving the direction of those differences.

FIGURE 5.1 When you look at a scene or photograph, your eyes make a series of fixations (circles) on different locations. Each fixation lasts only a few hundred milliseconds. Where your fixations are located depends on the kind of information you are trying to gain.

FIGURE 5.2 Pairs of pictures used in the flicker method for studying change blindness. Observers view a screen in which the two frames of a picture pair are flashed in alternation, separated by a blank interval of 80 ms or more. There is a large change in the picture at one particular location from one frame to the next—one that is quite evident when no blank interval occurs between frames. However, this local change in the scene is lost among all the other changes that occur when the entire picture disappears and reappears. Under these conditions, the observer cannot detect the change until the changing object becomes the focus of his or her attention.

FIGURE 5.3   First, cover Figure 5.4 with a piece of paper. Then select one of these cards to remember. In the trick that follows, the card you select will vanish even though you have kept its identity a secret.

FIGURE 5.4   Your secret card has vanished!

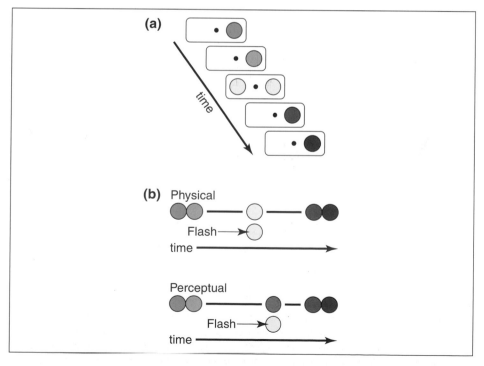

FIGURE 6.8   Displays in a color-comparison task involving a disc changing gradually in color and a briefly flashed disc. **(b)** Participants do not see the two discs as being identical in color, as they really are, but see the gradually changing disc as being more 'red' than the flashed disc.

FIGURE 7.1 Photograph of an anti-gravity hill in Magnetic Hill, New Brunswick, Canada: the nearest stretch of road seems to run downhill, although cars and balls will actually roll toward the camera.

FIGURE 9.9 Slave Market with the Disappearing Bust of Voltaire (1940) by Salvador Dali.